PRINCIPLES AND TYPES OF SPEECH COMMUNICATION

Ninth Edition

PRINCIPLES AND TYPES OF SPEECH COMMUNICATION

Ninth Edition

Douglas Ehninger

Bruce E. Gronbeck   *The University of Iowa*

Ray E. McKerrow   *University of Maine at Orono*

Alan H. Monroe

Scott, Foresman and Company

Glenview, Illinois

Dallas, Tex.   Oakland, N.J.   Palo Alto, Cal.   Tucker, Ga.   London, England

All illustrations in this book are by
Carol Naughton and Associates

Photo credits are on page 433 and are an extension of this copyright page.

An Instructor's Manual to accompany *Principles and Types of Speech Communication*, Ninth Edition, is available. It may be obtained through a Scott, Foresman representative or by writing to Speech Communication Editor, College Division, Scott, Foresman and Co., 1900 East Lake Avenue, Glenview, Illinois 60025.

Library of Congress Cataloging in Publication Data

Main entry under title:

Principles and types of speech communication.

    Previous ed.: Douglas Ehninger, Alan H. Monroe,
Bruce E. Gronbeck. 8th ed. cl978.
    Includes bibliographies and index.
    1. Public speaking.   I. Ehninger, Douglas.
II. Ehninger, Douglas.   Principles and types of
speech communication.
PN4121.P72   1981   808.5'1   81-13574
ISBN 0-673-15538-2   AACR2

1 2 3 4 5 6 7 -KPF-86 85 84 83 82 81

Preface

The Ninth Edition of *Principles and Types of Speech Communication* continues the process of revision and revitalization of the basic concepts, principles, and practices which have marked this book for nearly half a century. It incorporates the latest social-scientific and analytical research findings in the field of human communication and public speaking, and presents new material on argumentative speaking and communication analysis and criticism. However, the Ninth Edition affirms this continuing awareness of recent developments in the field of speech communication while never losing sight of the original vision of Alan H. Monroe, whose pedagogical genius has inspired teachers of public speaking since 1935. The resulting blend of the new with the traditional, we believe, is a highly practical and informed public communication textbook, concise in presentation, well-balanced in content, compact in aspect.

Among the extensively redeveloped chapters are those on the Speechmaking Process, Listening, Audience Analysis, the Motivated Sequence, Beginnings and Endings, Language, Speeches to Inform, Speeches to Persuade and Actuate, Argumentation and Reasoning, and Speech Evaluation and Rhetorical Criticism. Every chapter from beginning to end has been revised and updated in terms of scholarly references, examples, and vocabulary. In addition, we have kept and expanded a series of ideas and concepts which received favorable comment from users of the Eighth Edition: the treatment of motivational appeals; the development of types of supporting materials; the illustrative program for organizational patterns; the three-step treatment of outlining; the grouping of modes of communication—language, nonverbal behaviors, paralinguistic vocal cues, and visual aids—in a single section; speeches to entertain in the "special occasions" chapter; types of speeches before groups; and brief but useful treatments of interviewing and group discussion.

Uniquely characteristic of this new edition is the increased attention paid to an emerging concept in communication theory, the idea of "communication rules." Care is taken throughout to identify and discuss people's expectations for communicators, that is, the "rules" or standards against which you will be measured whenever you ascend the platform to deliver a speech. Also increased throughout is the amount of specific advice on "how-to-do-it." Thus, while the Ninth Edition's commitment to theory and research is stronger than ever, there is simultaneously a redoubled effort to keep the book preeminently practical.

Further enriching the pedagogical thrust of the text itself are the study materials, reworked by Professor Judy Jones of the University of Illinois, which round out each of the book's twenty-one chapters. The "Chapter Report" and "Problems and Probes" are designed to stimulate and extend learning *outside* the classroom; the "Oral Activities" are aimed at guiding and making more effective the work done *in* the classroom; and the "Suggestions for Further Reading" are intended to broaden an understanding of the speech communication process and to encourage pursuit of topics of particular interest. Additional suggested speaking and study assignments, lists of supplementary books and films, instructional procedures, speech-evaluation forms, and sample test questions for each chapter are available in the instructor's manual, *A Guide to Using Principles and Types of Speech Communication, Ninth Edition*, authored by Linda Moore of the University of Akron. This manual may be obtained from the publisher on request.

To reflect the contemporary character of the text, increase the ease with which it may be read, and heighten its visual appeal, the book has been completely redesigned typographically. Abundant and originally conceived drawings, diagrams, and charts illustrate key concepts and processes and help ensure comprehension and retention. The photographs have been selected to depict important facets of public speaking, and on occasion, to extend crucial concepts.

Overall, as coauthors, we have sought to carry forward the basic philosophy, ideas, and aspirations for effectiveness in oral communication which characterized the life and work of the book's original author, Alan H. Monroe (1903-1975), and its second author, Douglas W. Ehninger (1913-1979). Credit goes to Professor Monroe for the book's primary thrust and organizational pattern, and to Professor Ehninger for its seriousness of tone, its breadth of vision, and its cultural sensitivities. We trust that the Ninth Edition continues to reflect the profound influence of both of these pioneers in the fields of communication and rhetorical studies.

We have been greatly aided and encouraged in the preparation of this revision by the critical insights and sound advice of a number of speech communication scholars and fellow educators. Among these are: Winifred Brownell, University of Rhode Island; Ethel Glenn, University of North Carolina—Greensboro; William Kushner, Glassboro State College;

Douglas Losee, Humboldt State University; Howard H. Martin, University of Michigan; Ronald J. Matlon, University of Arizona; Eric William Skopec, Syracuse University; Aileen Sundstrom, Henry Ford Community College; and L. Keith Williamson, Wichita State University.

We are indebted also to the following people who provided feedback on the Eighth Edition: M. Eric Beaven, Steven M. Buck, Anthony Buckley, Elton S. Carter, Dianne L. Cherry, Faye Clark, Wanda S. Cook, Mary Louise Cornwell, Bobbie Dietrich, Edwin J. Hollatz, David Jamison, Susan Kasle, Bradford L. Kinney, James A. Knear, Bruce B. Manchester, J. Mazza, Karen McCallum, Joyce C. Parks, Peggy S. Pate, Richard G. Rea, R. D. Richey, Charles I. Romero, Stan Schmidt, Alice Rich Schwarz, D. T. Shannon, Mary Louise Shannon, Geraldine J. Smith, Fleur W. Steinhardt, James E. Vincent, and Denise Vrchota.

And, finally, we wish to thank Scott, Foresman and Company for the extensive resources and talents it invested in this project. The overall shape of the Ninth Edition has been guided by Speech Editors JoAnn Johnson and Barbara Muller. The word-by-word preparation and polishing of the text has been in the able hands of Anita Portugal who also guided the material through production. We are grateful for Scott, Foresman's expertise in and commitment to speech communication.

Public speaking is a skill, a science, and an art. In one often too short term or year, students are given a chance to learn to talk publicly with more confidence, more knowledge, more skill, and more effect than they had before. If this is achieved, they will contribute their own small but important part toward making the world a more informed, a more humane place to live and work. If they do, our intentions in preparing this revision will have been richly fulfilled.

Bruce E. Gronbeck
Ray E. McKerrow

Contents

PART TWO

PUBLIC SPEAKING: PREPARATION AND ADAPTATION TO THE AUDIENCE   *60*

PART FOUR

PUBLIC SPEAKING: TYPES AND OCCASIONS 284

SAMPLE SPEECHES FOR STUDY AND ANALYSIS

FIGURES, DIAGRAMS, AND CHARTS

PRINCIPLES AND TYPES OF SPEECH COMMUNICATION

Ninth Edition

PART ONE

PUBLIC SPEAKING

A Communication Process

1

The Public Speaker and the Speechmaking Process

The activity that we call public address or public speaking or speech communication represents an aggregate of interpersonal and verbal skills that integrate and ultimately forward the interests of a society. The prefix *com-* (from the Latin *cum* meaning "with") and *munus* (referring to a service performed for the culture) are combined in our word *communication*—the idea of sharing experience publicly for the common good. Communicating publicly, therefore, is an activity that pervades the lives of most adults. Most people are called on frequently to present an oral message of some length and complexity to a sizable number of listeners. You will make many speeches in your social life; your job may require oral presentations to colleagues and customers; and you may well feel compelled to speak in public gatherings.

Speechmaking in Society

The Social Realm

We probably talk most often in our everyday social situations. Parents of young children discuss the closing of the local elementary school and the attendant problems. Luncheons with friends produce animated discussions of senior citizen housing, comparison shopping, and the upcoming local election. Members of special interest groups and church committees listen to reports in order to set up next year's projects and meeting dates. And, neighbors chat about rezoning the block and afterschool child-care services.

Much of the "speechmaking" in your social life occurs in relatively informal ways. Nevertheless, the rudiments of public speaking are all present: introductions, bodies, and conclusions; central ideas or propositions along with supporting materials; the use of voice, face, gestures, and body for transmitting the messages from one person to others. Some of these social occasions will demand all the speaking skills you possess.

The Work Realm

The world of work, for most people, is primarily a world of communication. Written memos, position papers and reports, job descriptions and procedural instructions, letters to clients and responses to complaints, and promotional materials cross most desks in America daily. The channels of oral communication also bear major loads—committee discussions, employment and appraisal interviews, instructions from supervisors to their subordinates, inquiries for information and advice, luncheons and conferences with clients and colleagues. Indeed, the study *College Education and Employment* found that, beyond a person's entry-level job, specialized college training becomes less important for success than do general skills in interpersonal relations, oral and written communication, and business know-how.[1] And, in reference to oral communication skills specifically, another study—*College Education on the Job*—found that speaking with others in a clear and forceful fashion is important for almost all occupations of college graduates, and crucial for administrators, managers, sales personnel, allied health workers, educators, social workers, and counselors.[2] It is little wonder, therefore, that graduates of liberal arts programs as well as business schools, engineering colleges, and other professional programs list oral communication training as a determining factor in work-related success.[3]

The environment in which you will find yourself from nine to five, therefore, depends on public "speeches." These speeches are somewhat more formal than the ones you offer to friends, family, and neighbors. That is because (a) your purpose or task is often more specific than it is in social interaction, and (b) your audience's expectations are usually very concrete in most work situations. You and your neighbors, for example, may have an informal discussion about the state of the economy, but as a mid-level supervisor in a business you will have to discuss much more specific indicators of economic growth or decline. This occurs because your business is interested only in one portion of the economy and because your colleagues are accustomed to hearing reports that follow a fairly traditional form. Thus, work-related speeches tend to be more formalized, narrower, and more focused than those you give in social settings.

The Public Realm

The most formalized speechmaking tends to occur in the public realm—in political gatherings, lecture settings, ceremonial occasions, or religious groups. We tend to think of the speakers for these occasions as "complete public speakers," that is, as persons who present speeches *to* and *for* an audience. Both "to" and "for" are important notions, because we expect public speechmakers to offer us some "thing"—an idea, opinion, or course of action which solves a problem or informs us in some area in which we are ignorant; they should bring something important "to" us. We also expect them to do something "for" us. Politicians are called "public servants" because they are acting on our behalf when they negotiate agreements, debate budgets, and propose legislation; competent lecturers are expected not only to inform but often also to entertain us; ceremonial orators help us to celebrate an occasion or event or person by leading that celebration or commemoration; and preachers are guiding us, as a community of believers, in religious ceremonies.

The effective public communicator must have something to say and know how to say it within the customs and traditions governing the event or setting. Presidents, lecturers, orators, and preachers carry weighty messages to their audiences, and are expected to "sound like" presidents, lecturers, orators, and preachers.[4] Their speeches must be both substantively compelling and emotionally moving.

The points we have been driving at are these: (1) Although your idea of a "speech" may be such that you cannot see yourself giving one, the facts are that you have talked and will talk publicly a good deal. Even in a day of mass media and computerized written communications, giving speeches remains a vital part of everyone's lives in social, work, and public arenas. (2) While you may think of "speeches" as highly structured and formal productions, they actually tend to vary a good deal in terms of their seriousness, breadth, and complexity. Few of us will make our living as public servants and orators of renown, but all of us will address more public audiences than we perhaps realize. (3) Finally, even though speech settings and purposes may vary considerably, the event we call "making a speech" tends to be characterized by a limited set of core elements or skills. It is to those basic elements that we now shall turn our attention.

The Basic Elements of Speechmaking

In spite of the variations in speechmaking which occur from realm to realm, setting to setting, and even speaker to speaker, there nevertheless exists a fundamental process of oral communication. That is, in every speech we will find a series of elements or aspects which interact with each other; a "speech" is not a thing, it is a communicative event. Because the event involves more than one person, each with unique needs and interests, and because a speech extends through time and space, it is useful to examine each element separately, and then to put them together in an overview of the entire process. Because all of the elements interact dynamically—with each element in some significant way affecting all other elements—we may term the whole process a *speech transaction*. We will begin, however, by examining the individual elements: the speaker, the message, the listeners, the channels, and the communicative situation.

The Speaker

Insofar as the speaker is concerned, all speech transactions are conditioned by four factors: (1) *communicative purpose;* (2) *knowledge of subject and communication skills;* (3) *attitudes toward self, listeners, and subject;* and (4) *degree of credibility.*

Speaker's Purpose

Every speaker seeks to achieve some purpose or satisfy some desire. Except in the rarest of circumstances, you do not speak to others out of accident or whimsy. You speak to achieve some goal. Your purpose may be as simple as the wish to appear sociable, or, at the other extreme, as complex as the desire to alter cherished values or to advocate dangerous courses of public action. You may wish to provide entertainment, call attention to a problem, test an idea, refute an assertion, ward off a threat, establish or maintain status, or gain any number of other ends. The important point is this: Public speaking is a *purposive activity;* that purpose, in large measure, controls what you say and even how you say it.

Speaker's Knowledge

In every speaking situation the speaker's knowledge of the subject and mastery of communication skills determine important characteristics of the message and the effectiveness with which it is transmitted.

Speaker's knowledge of the subject • Occasionally, we all like to listen to certain speakers because they possess impressive personalities or because they are witty or entertaining; sometimes, we do not especially care what the speaker says. Usually, however, audiences demand something—something worth thinking about or doing. If speakers have but surface knowledge of the subject matter, listeners normally will feel cheated and hence the communication process will be short-circuited. A speaker's knowledge of the subject, in other words, in some ways controls audience response. It also controls the actual shape of the speech— what is emphasized, what is used as supporting material, and how everything is organized into a coherent message. A person's base of knowledge comes partially from experience, partially from additional research; from that knowledge speakers select and systematically present a portion of a topic area relevant to the audience's needs and expectations.

Speaker's mastery of communication skills • In order to succeed in the world of oral communicaton, one must acquire, refine, and integrate a series of fundamental skills. We will see as we work our way through this book that the term "communication skills" encompasses a wide variety of abilities—setting communicative goals, finding and assembling relevant information, organizing messages in coherent and compelling ways, illustrating them visually when necessary, and delivering them in a manner which clarifies and emphasizes key no-

tions. You already possess many of the requisite skills; through practice, instruction, reading, and observation of other speakers, you will improve your command of the others.

Speaker's Attitudes

In every speaking situation the speaker's attitudes toward self, listeners, and subject significantly affect what is said and how it is said.

Speaker's attitude toward self • All of us carry about with us a picture of ourselves as persons—a self-conception or image of the kinds of individuals we are and of how others perceive us.[5] That image is highly complex; it is derived from numerous experiences in numerous settings; it controls our self-evaluations and the ways we interact with others.

This self-image influences how we are likely to behave in a given speaking situation. If we have a low estimate of our abilities or are unsure of our opinions or knowledge, we tend to advance ideas hesitatingly. Our voice becomes weak and unsteady, our body stiffens, and our eyes watch the floor rather than audience members. If we have great self-confidence, we may move in the other direction—adopting an overbearing manner, disregarding the need for facts and logical demonstrations, riding roughshod over the feelings and needs of listeners.

Ideally, we must have enough self-confidence to believe firmly in our ability to communicate something worthwhile to others, and yet enough sensitivity to their intelligence, needs, and integrity to keep the audience foremost in mind while speaking.

Speaker's attitude toward listeners • Equally important in communicative transactions are your attitudes toward those listeners. Each time we speak, we do so from a certain status or role position—as parent or child, instructor or student, boss or employee. These role positions, in turn, affect our power relationships with audiences, determining whether we are superiors, inferiors, or equals. And third, those power relationships often affect the actual ways we talk to others publicly.

If we perceive someone as intellectually inferior, we tend to use simple vocabulary, clear structure, and concrete ideas; if someone seems politically inferior, we may talk condescendingly, self-confidently, assured of our own status. Or, if we view our auditors as superior to ourselves, we are likely to talk in a deferential or highly qualified manner, protecting our "selves" and sometimes even distrusting our own thoughts. It becomes important, therefore, for speakers to think seriously about their own perceptions of their relationships to listeners, and to adjust their speaking styles and even speech content based on their attitudes toward those listeners.

Speaker's attitude toward subject • Finally, our behavior as speakers inevitably is influenced to a greater or lesser degree by how we feel about the subject we are discussing. Do you really believe what you are saying? Do you find your subject matter interesting or boring? Is it crucial that your auditors know about it? Is it relevant to someone's needs? Your answers to these questions are reflected in how you use your voice and body, in the intensity of the language you use while communicating your ideas, and even in your actual selection of ideas.

In summary, as a speaker you convey—verbally and nonverbally—how you feel about yourself, your audience, and your subject matter, and you make many verbal and nonverbal decisions while preparing and delivering a speech based on those attitudes. Often, of course, you do not consciously think about your attitudes toward self, others, and subject. You should keep them in mind, however, because they affect your communication style and the impressions which others form of you and what you are saying.

Speaker's Credibility

In every speaking situation the speaker's success in winning agreement, inspiring confidence, or promoting ideas and action is significantly affected by the listeners' estimate of his or her credibility. The term "credibility"—and its relatives, "image" or

The professor's impressive academic qualifications, his dignified bearing, and his confident, authoritative manner add up to high credibility.

"ethos"—refer to the degree to which an audience finds a speaker to be a trustworthy, competent, sincere, attractive, and dynamic human being. Social scientific research has repeatedly demonstrated that to the extent that speakers are able to heighten an audience's estimate of these qualities, they will significantly increase the impact of a message. Although we do not have room to review all of the conclusions reached by researchers, the following generalizations are representative of ways in which the factors of credibility work in communicative interactions: *(a)* References to yourself and your own experience—provided they are not boasting or excessive—tend to increase your perceived trustworthiness and competence, and references to others (authorities) tend to increase your perceived trustworthiness and dynamism. *(b)* Using highly credible authorities increases your perceived fairness. *(c)* If you can demonstrate that you and your audience share common beliefs, attitudes, and values, your credibility will increase. *(d)* Well-organized speeches are more credible than poorly organized speeches. *(e)* The more sincere you appear to be, the better your chances of changing your listeners' attitudes.[6]

An audience's perception of the speaker's credibility, in other words, is affected by a broad range of communicative behaviors and in turn can decisively affect the degree to which the speaker is accepted and successful. Your ability to project yourself as a competent, trustworthy, sincere, attractive, and dynamic person may well determine the fate of your message. The message and the messenger are usually inseparable in the minds of listeners.

The Message

In all speech communication transactions, the message which the speaker transmits is made up of the same three variables: content, structure, and style.

Content

That the messages we transmit to our listeners have a content—are about something we want them to be aware of—is obvious. What is less obvious, however, are the many different sorts of content which comprise a message. There are, of course, "ideas"—assertions about the state of the world, facts and figures, analogies and examples, generalizations as well as more specific statements. But the content of a speech also includes your feelings about those ideas, interpretations of ideas you wish your audience to accept, courses of action you want the listeners to pursue, desires you are attempting to arouse in them. Many different kinds of "meanings" make up the content of a speech.

Structure

Any message we transmit is of necessity structured or organized in some way, simply because we say some things first, others, second, and still others, third, fourth, and so on. Even if you seem to ramble on, auditors will seek structure, will look for a pattern which makes the message seem coherent. It becomes incumbent upon a speaker, therefore, to provide a structure or pattern in order to guide the audience's attempt to find coherence. That structure may be as simple as numbering the points one will make ("First, I will discuss . . . , next I will . . . and finally, I will . . ."), or as complex as a full outline with subpoints and subpoints within those. One way you control the clarity and force of your message, therefore, is by providing a recognizable pattern for it.

Style

The third variable in every spoken message is style. Just as we must select and arrange the ideas we wish to convey to audiences, so also must we select words, arrange them in sentences, and decide how to reveal our own self-image to that group of hearers. Selecting and arranging words as well as revealing ourselves to be certain sorts of persons are matters of "style." Given the innumerable word-selection choices, the great varieties of sentence structures, and even the many sorts of self-images (or "personae") available to the speaker, a good many styles are possible. Styles can be "personal" or "impersonal," "literal" or "ironic," "plain" or "elevated," even "philosophical" or "poetic"; such labels refer to particular combinations of vocabulary, sentence syntax (arrangement), and images of the speaker. What we call style, therefore, really has nothing to do with "prettiness" or "stylishness"; rather, it includes those aspects of language use that convey impressions of speakers, details of the world, and emotional overtones.[7]

The Listeners

In all forms of speech, the listeners—like the speaker—have goals or purposes in mind. Moreover, the way a message is received and responded to varies according to the listener's (1) knowledge of and interest in the subject; (2) level of listening skill; and (3) attitude toward self, speaker, and the ideas presented.

Listeners' Purpose

Listeners always have one or more purposes they want to fulfill. Listeners, no less than speakers, enter into the speech transaction in search of rewards. They may wish to be entertained or informed, advised or guided. These purposes form their expectations—expectations, as we shall see, which control to whom, how, and why they listen. Speakers who violate those expectations—turning an informative talk, say, into a political harangue—risk ineffectiveness or even failure.

Listeners' Knowledge of Subject and Command of Listening Skills

In speech transactions, the listeners' knowledge of and interest in the subject affect significantly how the message will be received and responded to. Speakers often are told to address listeners "where they are." "Where they are" is determined by two factors—their knowledge of the topic, and their personal interest in it. A knowledgeable audience is bored by an elementary speech, whereas one with little knowledge is confused by a technical description. Disinterested listeners may even go so far as to walk out on a speaker who has not made the topic relevant to their interests. An important aspect of what we shall be calling audience analysis, therefore, is a matter of (1) gauging listeners' prior knowledge so as to achieve an appropriate level of intellectual or ideational sophistication in the speech, and (2) finding ways to make the message relevant to the beliefs, desires, and motivational springs of the auditors.

Speakers also must try to estimate the listening skills possessed by their auditors. With relatively homogeneous audiences, this may be easy to do. For example, we would expect a group of six-year-olds to have short attention spans, little ability to follow complex chains of reasoning, and a strong need to "see" ideas via visual aids and graphic descriptions; in contrast, we would expect graduate students to be able to sustain attention for long periods of time, to follow multi-stepped logical progressions, and to grasp abstract concepts with relative ease. In other situations, however, it is difficult to predict the auditors' degree of listening sophistication. The speaker then must constantly survey the listeners, looking for signs of understanding or puzzlement, acceptance or rejection. Those signs or cues are termed *feedback*—reactions "fed back" to speakers during the process of communication. "Reading feedback" is often the speaker's only way of determining a listener's skills of comprehension.

The knowledge and interest of these board members keenly affect their listening attitudes at a public hearing on state educational policies.

Listeners' Attitudes

In every speech encounter, the listeners' attitudes toward themselves, the speaker, and the subject significantly affect how they interpret and respond to the message. Just as the speaker's communicative behavior is influenced by his or her attitude toward self, subject, and listener, so do these same factors affect the listeners' responses. Listeners with low self-esteem tend to be swayed more easily than those whose self-image is stronger. Listeners whose own opinions seem to be confirmed by the views of the speaker are also susceptible to great influence. Moreover, as a rule people seek out speakers whose positions on issues they already agree with, and they retain longer and more vividly ideas which they strongly approve.[8] In other words, listeners' attitudes—which comprise another extremely important area for audience analysis—can be used (or, conversely, must be overcome) by speakers who wish to maximize their communicative effectiveness.

The Channels

All speech communication is conditioned to a greater or lesser extent by the channels through which the message is transmitted. The transaction between speakers and listeners occurs through several channels. The *verbal channel* carries the words, the culture's agreed-upon symbols for ideas. The *visual channel* transmits the gestures, facial expressions, bodily movements, and posture of the speaker; these tend to clarify, reinforce, or add emotional reactions to the words. At times the visual channel may be supplemented with a *pictorial channel*—so-called "visual aids," such as diagrams, charts, graphs, pictures, objects, and the like. The *aural channel*—also termed the paralinguistic medium—carries the tones of voice, variations in pitch and loudness, and other vocal modulations produced by the speaker's stream of sounds; like the visual channel, the aural channel heightens some meanings and adds others. Because these four channels are heard and seen by listeners simultaneously, the "message" is really a combination of several messages flowing through all of these pathways. Successful speakers learn to control or shape the messages flowing through all four channels.

The Communicative Situation

All speech communication is affected by the physical setting and social context in which it occurs.

Physical Setting

The physical setting in which speech occurs affects to a considerable extent listeners' expectancies as well as their readiness to respond. Persons waiting in the quiet solemnity of a cathedral for the service to begin have quite different expectations than do theatergoers gathered to witness the opening of a new Broadway play. Listeners at an open-air political rally expect a different sort of message from those gathered to hear a scholarly lecture on political theory presented in a college classroom.

The furniture and decor of the physical space also make a difference. Comfortable chairs and soft-hued drapes tend to put discussion groups at ease and to promote a more productive exchange. The executive who talks to an employee from behind a large desk set in the middle of an impressively furnished office with the title "President" on the door gains a natural advantage not only because of a superior position but also because of the physical setting.

Social Context

Even more important than physical setting in determining how a message will be received is the social context in which it is presented. A "social context" is a particular combination of persons, purposes, and places interacting communicatively: *Persons* are distinguished from each other by such factors as age, occupation, power, degree of intimacy, knowledge. These factors in part determine how one "properly" communicates with others. You are expected to speak deferentially to your elders, your boss, a political leader with "clout," a stranger whose reactions you cannot immediately predict, or a learned sage. The degree to which people are superior to, equal with, or inferior to each other in part determines each one's communicative style. Certain *purposes* or goals are more or less appropriately communicated in different contexts as well. Thus, a memorial service is not a time for attacking a political opponent, although a "meet the candidates" night is. In some contexts it is considered unreasonable to threaten someone before you have tried to find reasonable compromises. Some *places* are more conducive to certain kinds of communicative exchanges than others. Public officials are often more easily influenced in their offices than in public forums, where they tend to be more defensive; sensitive parents scold their children in private rather than in the middle of a party.

Another way of saying all this is to observe that societies are governed by customs, traditions, or what we now are calling *communication rules*. A "communication rule" is a guide to communicative behavior; it specifies, more or less precisely, what can be said to whom and in what circumstances. Some communication rules are very explicit—e.g., "Children should be seen and not heard." Others are seldom stated out loud: Sooner or later we all learn to address superiors by their titles and last names and inferiors by their first names, even though probably no one has told us to do so. Some rules apply to many different situations, as does the rule "Be polite in greeting and saying goodbye to others," whereas other rules—such as those we call the rules of parliamentary procedure—operate only in special situations. While communication rules are guides to communicating, they can, of course, be broken. Occasionally, rule breaking is inconsequential; sometimes, it determines success or failure; and always, rule breaking involves a certain level of risk. Those who frequently uttered obscenities at mass meetings during the '60s, for example, risked rejection by their listeners, or at least some of them; the use of obscenities to indicate strength of commitment and degree of rejection attracts some auditors and repels others. Rule-breakers may succeed in some circumstances, and lose in some.[9]

In summary, the social context in which we speak determines an audience's judgment of *appropriateness* and *competency*. We learn to communicate appropriately and competently by learning and, usually, following the communication rules that govern our society. You have spent your lifetime learning those rules; we will cite many of the more explicit ones that govern public speaking throughout this book.

Interaction of the Elements in Public Communication Processes

All speech communication, thus, entails a complex pattern of interaction among the five primary elements: speaker, message, listeners, channels, and situations. A public speech can be considered an *interaction* of these elements because:

- A change in one element usually produces changes in all others. So, for example, if a speaker's attitude toward the listeners is optimistic and enthusiastic, that attitude may be reciprocated by audience members who get caught up in the excitement. On the other hand, if a speaker adopts a highly formal style in building a message, the audience is likely to react with solemnity and seriousness.

- No single element controls the entire process. It is a mistake, we think, to consider a speech as a "thing" or even a speaker as the controlling mechanism. Undoubtedly, because "you" the speaker construct the message— with your ideas, feelings, and communicative capabilities—speeches are more or less extensions of that "you." But that message is modified by the way you use communicative channels, by audience expectations and listening skills, and even by the setting in which you present it. All five elements endlessly affect each other as a speech unfolds through time and space.

It also is useful to think about a speech as a *transaction*. Inherent in the notion of "transaction" is the idea of selective exchange:

- I prepare a speech to "give" to you, and you in turn give me your attention and even your reactions (called feedback).

- From among all of the things I *could* say about some subject, I *actually* select only a few, and tailor them to your interests, wants, and desires, as well as to limitations of time and space. You, in turn, from among all of the reactions you could have to my speech, select a few things to say about me, and about what I have said.

- As I assert my right to speak to fellow human beings, you assert your right to listen or not, to react as you see fit.

THE SPEECH COMMUNICATION TRANSACTION

Speaker

Influenced by past conditioning, present situation, communicative purpose, level of knowledge, speaking skill, attitudes toward self, subject, and listener

Message

Has content, structure, and style

Channel

Limits or shapes messages to one or more

Listener

Influenced by conditioning, purpose, situation, and attitudes toward self, subject, and speaker

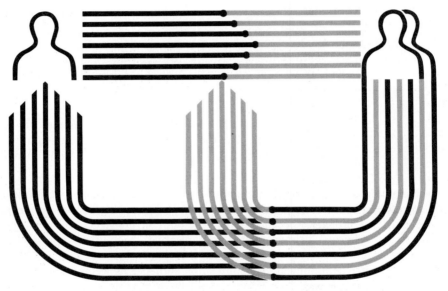

Feedback

Causes speaker to alter his or her verbal or nonverbal behavior

Feedback

Causes speaker to modify message

Response

Feedback to the speaker in the form of visual or verbal signals

Even though, therefore, we tend to think about speeches as "one way" communication, actually the influences flow in two directions—from speaker to listener and from listener to speaker. The notion of selective transaction is crucial in understanding the speech-making process, for speakers and audiences modify each other's behaviors and thoughts. *Indeed, one of oral communication's primary advantages over other modes of communication—written and electronic—is that it is a transaction, a face-to-face process of mutual give-and-take.* It is a uniquely human mode of information sharing and decision making.

The Skills and Competencies Needed for Successful Speechmaking

Because public speaking is an interactive process whereby people transact various kinds of information exchange and decision making, one must possess or acquire certain skills to make that process work. Six basic qualities, in particular, merit attention in this brief overview: (1) *integrity,* (2) *knowledge,* (3) *sensitivity to listener needs,* (4) *sensitivity to speaking situations,* (5) *oral skills,* and (6) *self-confidence and control.*

Integrity

We suggested earlier that trustworthiness is an important dimension of one's credibility or *ethos.* The need for creating a sense of one's trustworthiness or integrity, indeed, cannot be overemphasized. Especially in a day of electronic advertising and mass mailings—when every pressure group, cause, and special interest can worm its way into the public mind, often with conflicting analyses and recommendations for action—integrity becomes all important. How do people sort out good from bad analyses, prudent from imprudent recommendations?

Ultimately, most of us make our decisions—especially in areas where we have little firsthand experience—by deciding whom we should trust. If you have a reputation for moral rectitude, for careful support of your ideas, for fairness in treating opponents, and for a deep-felt commitment to the betterment of your peers, your effectiveness as a speaker will increase markedly. Liars and cheats occasionally win a battle, but they seldom win the war. Your reputation for reliability and high motives is perhaps your single, most powerful means of exerting influence as a speaker.[10]

Knowledge

When Daniel Webster was aked how he was able to prepare his famous reply to Senator Robert Y. Hayne on such short notice, he said that the ideas had come to him like thunderbolts which he needed only to reach out and seize, white hot, as they went smoking by. This store of thunderbolts was no accident. Over many years Webster's constant study of law, literature, politics, and human nature had filled his mind with an abundant supply of facts, illustrations, and arguments at his instant command. Successful public communicators in all ages have had a similar arsenal upon which to draw.

If you would broaden your knowledge and enhance your understanding of the world and the ideas and values of people within it, you, too, must read widely and observe carefully. The background you already have, when carefully considered and supplemented by additional study, will provide sufficient material for your practice speeches. Selecting and organizing that material will help you marshal and clarify your thinking. Indeed, you will do well to begin in just this way—by talking about things that are vivid parts of your own personal experience. As you grow in skill and confidence, you will want to reach beyond im-

One way to pursue your interest and expand your knowledge of a speech topic is to use the resources of a good library.

mediate and familiar topics. You may wish to investigate and speak about ideas and developments relevant to your personal future—your job, your chosen career, or profession. Be careful also to acquire knowledge and develop interests *outside* your work, however. To become a well-rounded and interesting speaker, you must know about more than a single subject. Keep abreast of current happenings in your world, your country, your community by reading at least one daily newspaper, listening frequently to news broadcasts, and watching well-documented telecasts.

Expertise, as we noted when discussing credibility, is a prime requisite for anyone wishing to have verbal impact on others. As you acquire skills in research and analysis, you will employ your knowledge more and more successfully when speaking.

Sensitivity to Listener Needs

Sometimes we talk publicly simply to hear ourselves talk; occasionally we talk for purely *expressive* reasons. Usually, however, we speak for *instrumental* reasons—to give others information or ideas, to influence their thoughts or actions. The most successful public speakers are "other-directed," concerned with meeting their listeners' needs and solving their problems through oral communication.

To be an other-directed public communicator, you must be particularly sensitive to the desires, needs, and queries of your listeners. Generally, this means you must regard your auditors as intelligent, feeling creatures—as people "worth" taking into account as you prepare and deliver speeches. More specifically, this also means that you have to be willing to engage in audience analysis. Large portions of this textbook will be devoted to increasing your skills in audience analysis, concentrating upon such questions as:

- What aspects of my listeners' backgrounds will affect how they react to me and my messages?

- What hopes, fears, and other motives have brought them to this speech, and how can I go about fulfilling those hopes, alleviating those fears, and reacting to the other motivations I sense?

- How can I gain and hold their attention throughout my speech, to be sure that they do not miss important ideas or consequential actions?

- How can I best organize my speech to make my ideas clear to them? What sort of language should I use to make them comfortable and to make my message clear and forceful? With what sorts of delivery patterns will they be most satisfied? What kinds of supporting materials will seem sensible to them?

These and other more specific questions confront any speaker who seeks sincerely to respond to listener needs. It is impossible, of course, to analyze the specific needs of each listener, but, as we will suggest later, there are certain generalizations you can arrive at in preparing to speak. Sometimes you will miscalculate—misconstrue the temperament and desires of this or that audience. Such is the life of the public speaker. But often, through the skillful sifting of audience data at your disposal, you can isolate the salient needs of auditors. When you do, your listeners will appreciate your efforts and reward you by judging you to be a competent speaker. Other-directedness represents a competency you cannot afford to ignore.

Sensitivity to Speaking Situations

As we suggested earlier, the physical setting and the social context surrounding a speech exert undeniable pressures on speakers (and their listeners). They create both a *set of expectations* and a *readiness to act* in certain ways.[11] Those expectations are often termed, as we suggested, the "customs" or the "rules" governing some group or setting, and readiness to act is usually discussed as "mind set" or "crowd mentality." Successful speakers are adept at analyzing both conditions. That is, you must be willing to probe the customs or rules possessed by groups. Before you speak to a Rotary Club, for example, you should know what the members "want" from speakers, where you will fit into the program, how formal you are expected to be, to what degree they normally allow speakers to advocate courses of action or to defend causes. Before talking to a church or city council, you should find out how long people are allowed to speak in defending an idea, what level of emotional intensity is normal, what kinds of evidence (personal experience? statistical documentation?) are expected. Furthermore, you certainly will want to find out something about the homogeneity or diversity of the group members, the physical arrangements, and the like, so as to isolate the usual "mind sets" or "response patterns" associated with particular situations: Can you expect to be interrupted while you speak? Is this a group whose members are used to responding immediately, or do they sleep on any decision point before they make it? Are the room and physical arrangements conducive to long speeches, to slide presentations, to freewheeling question-and-answer sessions?

Skills in situational analysis, thus, usually demand that you ask several questions of organization leaders or previous speakers before you step into the situation yourself. If you do not, you are likely to be surprised when you violate some rule—and you are likely to be a good deal less effective. The competent speakers you have seen were all sensitive to speaking situations and their demands. We will give you a good deal more advice on situational analysis, therefore, through the rest of this book.

Oral Skills

Fluency, poise, control of the voice, and coordinated movements of the body mark the skillful public speaker. Combined with qualities of integrity, knowledge, and self-confidence, such skills can significantly increase your effectiveness by enabling you to communicate your ideas forcefully and attractively.

Skill in speaking is gained principally through practice. Practice, however, proceeds best when based on a knowledge of sound principles and carried on under the direction of a competent instructor. Moreover, care must be exercised that in practicing you do not develop distracting habits or acquire an unnatural or artificial manner of delivery. Good public speaking is animated, but it is also natural and conversational. It commands attention not through the use of tricks and techniques, but because of the speaker's earnest desire to communicate. Indeed, many successful public speakers seem merely to be conversing with their audiences. In the chapters that follow we shall extend our consideration of these and other communicative skills and suggest how you may develop, refine, and implement their use in practical speaking situations. Also, at the end of the chapters in this textbook we have provided some "Oral Activities" designed to encourage and guide your practice in mastering these necessary skills.

In sum, we suggest you think of learning to control the oral media of communication—voice, body, gestures—as one of your primary tasks on your road to competency. Just as spelling, punctuation, grammatical rules, word choice, and syntactical patterns represent a series of relatively mechanical skills you must possess in order to communicate effectively via a written mode, so, too, do oral skills demand your attention if you are to succeed in an aural mode.

Self-Confidence and Control

Sixth, the competent speaker has an appropriate measure of self-confidence and self-control. So central are self-confidence and control to effective public speaking that, in a sense, much of what we say in this book is aimed toward developing or strengthening this essential quality. The quality is attained primarily by over-coming a series of fears felt by most Americans.[12]

Three terms refer to three distinct aspects of fear of public speaking: The term *stage fright* usually refers to the physiological manifestations of nervous-ness—clammy hands, a shaking body, dry mouth, cracking voice. By *speech anxiety* we normally mean the psychological blocs we can encounter—forgetting what we were going to say, the fear of failure, the feeling of personal inadequacy. The idea of *communication apprehension* often refers to social pressures a person can feel. So, while you may well find it easy to talk with friends, you may be absolutely terrified at talking with strangers, or while you might not mind speak-ing at a rally, you might find a more formal setting with a podium and seated audience intimidating.[13]

In talking about roadblocks in the way of self-confidence, therefore, we are discussing an extremely complex physiological-psychological-social phenomenon, one which is universally felt. Contrary to what many believe, literally everybody feels such fear, even the most practiced orators. Achieving self-confidence, thus, is a matter of controlling, not eliminating fears. Any "program" for controlling these fears, furthermore, must recognize that speech fright or communication apprehension is normally a matter of both *state* and *trait;* that is, part of your fear is associated with particular settings or occasions, but other apsects of ner-vousness are rooted in your personality itself. Your attack on these fears, there-fore, must involve analysis of both yourself and the others who comprise a speak-ing occasion. Although there is no foolproof program for learning self-confidence and control (save, perhaps, deep psychological counseling, often called "system-atic desensitization"),[14] there are some steps you can take to achieve that sense of control:

1. *Realize that tension and nervousness are normal and even, in part, beneficial to speakers.* This normality means you will have to live with fear, so you might as well resign yourself and get on with controlling it. Also remember that a state of tension often provides a speaker with energy and alertness. As your adrenalin pours into your bloodstream, it acts as a physical charge, increasing bodily movement and psychological acuity—qualities of body and mind you need while speaking.

2. *Know, too, that tension is physiologically reduced by the act of speaking.* As you talk and discover that your audience will in fact accept some of the things you are saying, your nervousness tends to dissipate. Physiologically, your body is using up the excess adrenalin it generated, and psychologically, your ego is getting some positive reinforcement. The very act of talking aloud thus reduces fear.

3. *Talk about topics that interest you.* Speech anxiety arises in part because of self-centeredness; sometimes you are more concerned with (and interested in) yourself than in your topic. One strategy to reduce that anxiety, therefore, is to select topics which in and of themselves excite you, make you want to talk. This tends to make you more topic-centered than self-centered, and there is a corre-sponding reduction in anxiety.

4. *Talk about subjects on which you have considerable expertise.* Confidence in your knowledge, as was suggested earlier, not only increases your perceived credibility but it also helps you control your nervousness. Subject mastery is closely akin to self-mastery. Furthermore, when you are confident of what you are talking about, you are less likely to fear the audience which, you can convince yourself, knows less about the subject than you do.

5. *Analyze the audience and the situation carefully.* The better you think you know who is in the audience and what is expected of you in a particular situation, the less there is to fear. Speech anxiety, after all, is partly fear of the unknown; the more you know, the less there is to fear. And, the more you know about audience and situation, the easier it is for you psychologically to focus on them instead of yourself.

6. *Speak in public as often as you can.* Sheer repetition will not eliminate your fears, but it certainly will make them more controllable. Repeated experiences with audiences of different sizes and types will reduce your apprehension, strengthen your self-assurance, and increase your poise. So, while you are still a student, force yourself to talk up in class discussions, informal bull sessions, and meetings of organizations to which you belong. Outside of school, find time to talk with people of all ages; attend public meetings occasionally and make a few comments. You need not go looking for highly formal speaking occasions; but seize any opportunity for even informal disclosure, and every experience will increase some part of your skill and control.

There are, in summary, few easy ways to self-confidence and personal control in public speaking situations. For most of us, gaining self-confidence is in part a matter of psyching ourselves up, and in part a matter of sheer practice. The knot in your stomach will probably always be there, but it need not twist you permanently out of shape. As your analytical abilities increase—as you become a conscious analyzer of situations, speech purposes, topics, message-constructing skills, and audiences—so will your self-confidence and hence your self-control. Your attention and energy will turn to your subject and your audience as your fears recede. You then will possess the requisite control to succeed.

The Focus of This Book

As you may have gathered from the topics we have considered in this chapter, we are concerned with identifying and improving the sorts of public speaking skills you will need in your social, work, and public lives. Public speaking is a matter of vital concern in this society, and you must be good at it for your own satisfaction and for the betterment of others.

The material presented in this textbook reflects a series of assumptions concerning how you best can prepare for an active and effective life of speaking:

- *General principles.* One way to improve your skills is to understand some general principles of public communication and how it functions. These principles are derived from collective experience which ranges from classical Greece and Rome up to contemporary times, as well as from social-scientific research into communication processes. If you better understand the principles, we believe, you will more easily grasp ideas of what to do and why to do it.

- *Rhetorical choices.* Most of the chapters will contain lists of techniques, categories of analysis, aspects of audiences, forms of organization, and the like. Speaking publicly, after all, is a matter of making choices concerning what to say to whom and how. Once you know some of your options, we believe that you will be more confident in what you are trying to do each time you address others.

- *Guided practice.* A third approach to personal improvement, of course, is personal practice. Such practice can take several forms—in-class or out-of-class exercises (see the chapter-end materials for samples), in-class speeches, out-of-class speeches, "practice" speeches in other classes. The practice of rhetorical choice making and public address form the core activities of this book.

- *Analysis of others' speeches.* A speech communication class is a full laboratory. In a class of, say, twenty students, you may be given anywhere from three to eight or more chances to speak to the class during a term. That means you will listen to anywhere from fifty-seven to well over a hundred other speeches. Listening critically to others provides you with valuable observational opportunities. You get a chance to see what works and what does not work, as different speakers try out various approaches to informing and persuading their audiences. And beyond your public speaking classroom is the rest of the world—itself an even bigger laboratory. Train yourself to analyze every speech you hear, wondering why this speech worked and that speech fell flat. Slowly but systematically you can build up a reservoir of rhetorical principles, one much deeper than a single book can offer.

We are urging, therefore, a multifaceted approach to public speaking skills. Part of that schedule involves study, part of it, practice, and part of it, analysis and reaction. It represents hard work on a job which will continue the rest of your life. It is now time to get on with the task.

REFERENCE NOTES

[1]N. L. Ochsner and Lewis C. Solmon, *College Education and Employment—The Recent Graduates* (Bethlehem, PA: The College Placement Foundation, 1979). See also Carol A. Carmichael, "Most College Grads Satisfied with Jobs," *Chicago Tribune,* September 16, 1979.

[2]Ann Stouffer Bisconti and Lewis C. Solmon, *College Education on the Job—The Graduates' Viewpoint* (Bethlehem, PA: The College Placement Council Foundation, 1976), p. 43.

[3]Carol H. Pazandak, "Followup Survey of 1973 Graduates, College of Liberal Arts," Minneapolis: College of Liberal Arts, University of Minnesota, 1977 (multilith); Jack Landgrebe

and Howard Baumgartel, "Results of the Graduation Requirement Questionnaire for College of Liberal Arts and Sciences Alumni," Lawrence: College of Liberal Arts and Sciences, University of Kansas (typescript); "Instruction in Communication at Colorado State University," Fort Collins: College of Engineering, Colorado State University, July 1979 (multilith); Edward Foster et al., "A Market Study for the College of Business Administration, University of Minnesota, Twin Cities," Minneapolis: College of Business Administration, University of Minnesota, November 1978 (multilith). These and other studies are reported in Samuel L. Becker and Leah R. V. Ekdom, "That Forgotten Basic Skill: Oral Communication," *Association for Communication Administration Bulletin*, #34 (October 1981).

[4]L. S. Harms, "Listener Judgments of Status Cues in Speech," *Quarterly Journal of Speech*, 47 (April 1961), 164–168; Robert Hopper and Frederick Williams, "Speech Characteristics and Employability," *Speech Monographs*, 40 (November 1973), 296–302; James D. Moe, "Listener Judgments of Status Cues in Speech: A Replication and Extension," *Speech Monographs*, 39 (November 1972), 144–47; Susan Milmoe et al., "The Doctor's Voice: Postdictor of Successful Referral of Alcoholic Patients," *Journal of Abnormal Psychology*, 72 (1968), 78–84.

[5]For a discussion of interrelationships between self-concept and communication, see Gordon I. Zimmerman, James L. Owen, and David R. Seibert, *Speech Communication; A Contemporary Introduction*, 2nd ed. (St. Paul: West Pub. Co., 1977), esp. pp. 32–43; and Gail E. Myers and Michele Tolela Myers, *The Dynamics of Human Communication; A Laboratory Approach*, 3rd ed. (New York: McGraw-Hill Book Co., 1980), Chap. 3, "Self-Concept: Who Am I?" pp. 47–72.

[6]These and other generalizations relative to source credibility are most usefully summarized in Stephen W. Littlejohn, "A Bibliography of Studies Related to Variables of Source Credibility," *Bibliographic Annual in Speech Communication: 1971*, ed. Ned A. Shearer (Falls Church, VA: Speech Communication Assoc., 1972), pp. 1–40; cf. Ronald L. Applebaum et al., *Fundamental Concepts in Human Communication* (San Francisco: Canfield Press, 1973), pp. 123–46.

[7]For a useful discussion of communication stylistic choices, see Gary Cronkhite, *Public Speaking and Critical Listening* (Menlo Park: The Benjamin-Cummings Pub. Co., Inc., 1978), esp. pp. 255–72.

[8]See the personality analysis of receivers in Michael Burgoon, *Approaching Speech Communication* (New York: Holt, Rinehart & Winston, Inc., 1974), pp. 64–69.

[9]Much research on physical setting and social context is summarized in Mark L. Knapp, *Essentials of Nonverbal Communication* (New York: Holt, Rinehart & Winston, 1980), Chap. 4, "The Effects of Territory and Personal Space," pp. 75–96. The determinative aspects of social expectations in human communication generally are discussed in such books as John J. Gumperz and Dell Hymes, eds., *Directions in Sociolinguistics; The Ethnography of Communication* (New York: Holt, Rinehart & Winston, 1972) and Peter Collett, ed., *Social Rules and Social Behavior* (Totowa, NJ: Rowman and Littlefield, 1977). And, more specifically, the current state of our knowledge about "rules" and their importance in communication is documented in Susan B. Shimanoff, *Communication Rules; Theory and Research*, Sage Library of Social Research, No. 97 (Beverly Hills: Sage Pub., 1980).

[10]A fuller discussion of the role that personal integrity plays in successful public communication may be found in Otis M. Walter, *Speaking to Inform and Persuade* (New York: The Macmillan Co., 1966), Chap. 8, "The *Ethos* of the Speaker."

[11]The importance of context in determining interpretations of messages is treated well in Irving Biederman, "Perceiving Real-World Scenes," *Science*, 177 (July 7, 1972), 177–80. A book that makes expectations and their effect upon communicative reactions central is Bruce E. Gronbeck, *The Articulate Person; A Guide to Everyday Public Speaking* (Glenview, IL: Scott, Foresman and Co., 1979).

[12]"What Are Americans Afraid Of?" *The Bruskin Report*, 13, #53; "Surveys Reveal Students' Concern Over Jobs, Public-Speaking Anxiety," *Pitt News*, May 1978, p. 4.

[13]Other terms—e.g., "shyness," "reticence," and "audience sensitivity"—have been used in the research on these topics. For a review of the terms and concepts, see James C. McCroskey,

"Oral Communication Apprehension: A Summary of Recent Theory and Research," *Human Communication Research*, 4 (Fall 1977), 78–96.

[14]Programs in systematic desensitization were launched in various parts of the country following the publication of James C. McCroskey, "The Implementation of a Large Scale Program of Systematic Desensitization for Communication Apprehension," *Speech Teacher*, 21 (November 1972), 255–64. Other "programs" have been tried as well: R. J. Fenton et al., "The Use of EMG Biofeedback Assisted Relaxation Training to Reduce Communication Apprehension," paper presented to the Western Speech Communication Association convention, Seattle, 1975; Kim Giffin and K. Bradley, "An Exploratory Study of Group Counseling for Speech Anxiety," Research Monograph 12, Lawrence, KS: Communication Research Center, University of Kansas, 1967; G. M. Phillips, "Rhetoritherapy versus the Medical Model: Dealing with Reticence," *Speech Monographs*, 35 (March 1968), 34–43.

For research discussing a public speaking course's effect on communication apprehension, see Kim Giffin and Gustav Friedrich, "The Development of a Baseline for Studies of Speech Anxiety," Research Report 20, Lawrence, KS: Communication Research Center, University of Kansas, 1968; William D. Brooks and S. M. Platz, "The Effects of Speech Training Upon Self-Concept as a Communicator," *Speech Teacher*, 17 (January 1968), 44–49; R. E. Barnes, "Interpersonal Communication Approaches to Reducing Speech Anxiety," paper presented to the Central States Speech Association convention, Chicago, 1976.

PROBLEMS AND PROBES

CHAPTER REPORT   Assemble a series of different models of human communication; Chapter 2 of Mortensen's book ("Suggestions for Further Reading"), Chapter 3 of Werner J. Severin and James W. Tankard, Jr.'s *Communication Theories; Origins Methods Uses* (Hastings House, 1979), and other books your instructor might suggest are good places to look. As you compare different models, ask yourself such questions as: What elements of the communication process receive primary emphasis in each model? What elements are included in some models, but not in others? What is each model particularly good for (understanding individual differences between people? conceptualizing the varied goals of communication? isolating points at which communication can break down? stressing the two-way nature of communication? other?)? Having answered such questions, write an essay on the topic, "Communication Model-Building."

1.   In a notebook set aside for the purpose, start a Personal Speech Journal. The contents will be seen by only you and your instructor, who may call for the journal at intervals during the term. In your first journal entry, write about yourself in relation to the six basic qualities needed for successful speechmaking. Consider your integrity. (If you haven't engaged in an exercise like this before, it should be fascinating and a source of enlightment for you.) In what areas do you feel you have most knowledge? In what areas would you wish to research to gain more knowledge? Look around your classroom at your classmates who will be your listeners this term. What do you know about their needs? What do you know about the speaking situation you are about to face? What do you still need to learn? What oral skills do you already possess and what others do you wish to gain? And, finally, consider your own self-confidence and control in light of the task before you.

2.   Identify and describe three speech transactions in which you personally participated during the past week. In at least two of these encounters, you should have

been the speaker initiating the interaction. Formulate answers to the following questions:

 a. In which of the three situations—person-to-person, small group, or public communication—did each of these three transactions take place?

 b. What channel or channels did you use?

 c. What was your communicative purpose in each case?

 d. To what extent do you feel you accomplished your communicative purpose in each transaction? Why?

 e. What was the extent of your message-preparation in each of the three instances? If preparation was more mandatory and/or more extensive for one situation than for others, explain why this was so.

 f. Show how, in one of these transactions, the physical setting probably influenced what happened. In another, explain how the social context tended to affect the outcome.

3. Select at least two speech transactions which you observed, but in which you did not yourself participate. Evaluate these transactions, showing *(a)* how the speaker's knowledge (or lack of knowledge) of the subject affected the accomplishment of his or her purpose, and *(b)* how the speaker's skill (or lack of skill) in vocal and bodily communication influenced the transaction.

 ORAL ACTIVITIES

1. To the extent that the physical facilities of the classroom permit, your instructor will arrange for members of the class to seat themselves in a large circle or in smaller groups around two or three separate tables. Informality should be the key-note in this particular activity. After the instructor has completed a brief self-introduction, each class member will provide a self-introduction based generally on the following pattern:

 My name is _____

 My major (or my major interest) is _____

 I am enrolled in this college/university because _____

 _____

 In addition to a grade credit, what I hope to get from this course in speech communication is _____

2. Working in pairs, present pertinent biographical information about yourself to another member of the class. This person, in turn, will prepare a short speech introducing you to the group. You, of course, will do likewise for the student with whom you are paired. When these speeches have been completed, draw up a composite picture of the audience to whom you will be speaking during the remainder of the term.

3. Prepare a two- to three-minute presentation on the topic, "A speech I shall always remember." In specifying why you consider a particular address notable, focus on one or more of the factors in the speech communication process discussed in this chapter.

4. Participate actively in a general class consideration of the subject "Things That I Like (Dislike) in a Speaker." As you and the other members of the class mention your likes and dislikes, your instructor may want to list them in two columns on a chalkboard. At the conclusion of this oral consideration, help your instructor summarize by formulating a composite picture or list of those speaker traits or qualities to which the majority of the class members would respond favorably and those traits or qualities to which the majority would respond unfavorably. Finally, if you (as a class—collectively) find many traits or qualities which you cannot classify in some absolute manner, ask yourself why. Are there variables within situations, contexts, or our perceptions of "proper" social roles that make absolute categorization impossible? What are some of these variables?

 SUGGESTIONS FOR FURTHER READING

Kenneth E. Andersen, *Persuasion: Theory and Practice,* 2nd ed. (Boston: Allyn and Bacon, Inc., 1978), Chapter 1.

Lloyd Bitzer, "The Rhetorical Situation," *Philosophy and Rhetoric,* 1 (Fall 1968), 1–14.

C. David Mortensen, *Communication: The Study of Human Interaction* (New York: McGraw-Hill Book Company, 1972), Chapter 2, "Communication Models."

Susan B. Shimanoff, *Communication Rules: Theory and Research,* Sage Library of Social Research, No. 97 (Beverly Hills: SAGE Publications, Inc., 1980).

Gordon I. Zimmerman, James L. Owen, and David R. Seibert, *Speech Communication: A Contemporary Introduction,* 2nd ed. (St. Paul: West Publishing Company, 1980), Chapter 1.

2

Listening: Speaker-Audience Interaction

As you go through an average day, you will find yourself in the role of *listener* an estimated *forty percent* of your communicative time.[1] As a listener, you bear some of the responsibility for the effective transmission of an idea. Knowing how to listen and what to listen for will help ensure that you uphold your part in the communication interaction. Without good listening there can be no feedback; without feedback, speakers do not have the opportunity to prevent potential misunderstandings by revising their explanations on the spot. In your role as speaker, knowing what contributes to and what impedes effective listening will help you adapt messages to your listeners' needs. As we noted in Chapter 1, communication is a *two-way* transaction. What we have to say in this chapter about the process and skills of listening applies equally to your roles as both speaker and listener—since you cannot communicate fully without assuming the obligations of both roles.

The Listening Process

Lyman K. Steil, President of the International Listening Association, describes listening as "more than merely *hearing* what someone else is saying. There are three other important components: *Interpretation* of what's said, which leads to understanding or misunderstanding; *evaluation*, which involves weighing the information and deciding how to use it, and finally, *responding*, based on what was heard, understood and evaluated."[2]

The initial phase of this complex process is *hearing*, a physiological event whereby sound waves are transformed into auditory nerve impulses. The response to these impulses can be *involuntary* or *voluntary*. For example, you react instantly upon hearing the unmistakable sound of a snake's rattles. Your response is involuntary; the sound is interpreted, evaluated, and responded to without going through a long, complicated chain of reasoning. With other, less-riveting stimuli, however, responses are likely to be voluntary. Depending on your interests, you may turn your attention to the lyrics of a new song being played on the radio or to a speech advocating a ban on nuclear power. These choices require conscious, continual effort on your part.

Voluntarily choosing to listen requires greater attention to the process of interpreting a message than is the case when stimuli provoke an involuntary response. Such stimuli, furthermore, are not composed exclusively of words and sentences. A rasping voice, a vigorous gesture, tenseness of the facial muscles, a body stiff and slightly bent forward—all these indicators are processed by your mind to produce the possible message: "This speaker is talking about Subject X and is very serious in his accusations." Thus, although listening is principally an aural event, it can involve almost all of your senses. It is, in short, *the whole interpretive process whereby you make sense out of communicative stimuli*. Evaluation and response based on words alone may miss the actual or intended meaning of the message being conveyed by the speaker. As this interpretive process is put into play, two questions emerge: What happens when we choose to listen? And, why do we listen closely at one time, but only listen intermittently at another time?

Choosing to Listen

An involuntary response occurs when sound forces itself on you and demands your attention; voluntary listening, on the other hand, may be approached with varying degrees of interest and effort. At times, you may listen with full discrimination. That is, you fully concentrate your sensory equipment upon as many of the auditory, visual, olfactory, and even tactile stimuli as you can in order to understand what a speaker is saying. Listening with full discrimination, however, is very tiring. No matter how much you may wish to hang on someone's every word and gesture, you usually find that you cannot do so. Your body tires, and your mind demands rest. At other times, you listen without discrimination. You simply let the stimuli emanating from the speaker's utterances and movements "wash over" you without making any serious attempt to sort through every word, syllable, and gesture and translate them into messages. You probably often listen to music in this way. In fact, many people work while music is playing in the background. They are aware that the music is present, but as they become engrossed in their work, only occasionally do they think about or fully listen to what is playing. There are times, too, when we find ourselves listening to a verbal message without discriminating sharply among ideas or subpoints. Our subsequent evaluation and response to the message heard in this manner may be faulty—as inaccurate as that to messages we interpret solely on the basis of the words presented to us.

Most of the time, however, you listen with partial discrimination. That is, you normally tune in and out of messages. You often have little choice because your physiological hearing equipment is not perfectly efficient. Scientists estimate that the human organism, unless it is in a state of hypnotic trance, must break concentration or focus every two to five seconds.[3] Hearing, therefore, is intermittent and partial—and so, consequently, is listening.

Sources of Communication Breakdown

The temptation to listen to something else—to other sounds in the room or other thoughts floating around in your mind—is almost overwhelming. What Wayne Minnick has termed your *internal and external perceptual fields* come into play each time you try to listen, as other stimuli (external) and other thoughts (internal) compete with the speaker and message to draw your attention.[4] These perceptual fields and the roles they play are suggested in "The Perceptual Fields of the Listener," page 31.

Because your own stream of thought and other stimuli near you interrupt your concentration, you are likely to miss portions of a speech. Communication may break down when you pass over a speaker's key example or quotation, a summary of steps you are being asked to take, or an important transition. Communication also may break down, however, when your own beliefs, attitudes, or personal values get in the way of listening. Some listeners tend to *debate* with a speaker every step of the way. Some tune out of a message when it appears some *difficult* material such as statistics or complex analyses of problems will be presented. Others will react negatively to a trite or corny introduction and prematurely dismiss a subject as *uninteresting*. A few will become overly critical of the speaker's *delivery and physical appearance*, letting relatively minor negative impressions obscure the necessity of evaluating the intrinsic merits of the whole message. Many listen only for *isolated facts* such as memorable examples or financial benefits instead of seeing how such materials are tied to propositions and "the big picture." And, for some, their own *basic convictions or prejudices or stereotypes* make it impossible for them to evaluate the speaker's ideas fairly and openly. They may interpret and evelute the speaker's words solely in terms of their own biases, and not in terms of the speaker's probable intent.

The sources of communication breakdown are numerous. They may be rooted in physiological processes (hearing), in basic psychological tendencies (perception), and in personal idiosyncrasies (listening habits). We do not mean to imply, of course, that when you listen you must simply disengage your mental processes, uncritically accepting everything you are told. On the contrary, you must work hard to listen well. By hearing as much as you can and by forming accurate mental pictures of what is being said, you can better understand, evaluate, and respond to messages. Thus, you give the speaker a fair hearing and create an appropriate atmosphere for the continued exchange of ideas.

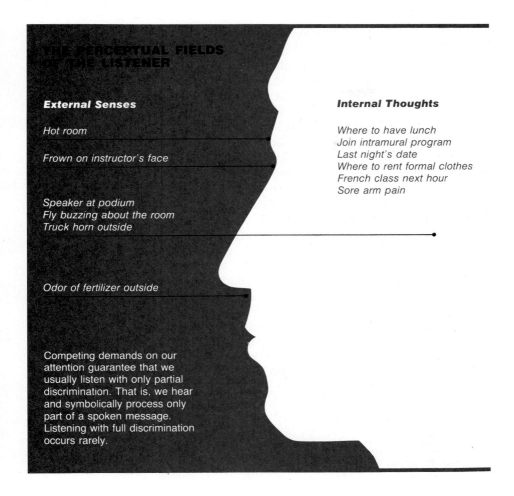

THE PERCEPTUAL FIELDS OF THE LISTENER

External Senses

Hot room

Frown on instructor's face

Speaker at podium
Fly buzzing about the room
Truck horn outside

Odor of fertilizer outside

Competing demands on our attention guarantee that we usually listen with only partial discrimination. That is, we hear and symbolically process only part of a spoken message. Listening with full discrimination occurs rarely.

Internal Thoughts

Where to have lunch
Join intramural program
Last night's date
Where to rent formal clothes
French class next hour
Sore arm pain

Listening Skills

Although listening involves a number of skills that many people perform poorly or only intermittently, it can be improved through application of the techniques of good listening. Good listening is not purposeless, passive, or indifferent. Whether your goal is to *enjoy* what the speaker is saying or the way in which she is saying it, to *understand* the message, or to *evaluate* the proposal being advocated, good listening requires a positive attitude.[5] *People listen well because they want to, not because they have to.* Because listening for comprehension and for evaluation are more complex tasks than listening for enjoyment, let us consider some guidelines for these activities.

Listening for Comprehension

Speakers often do not present ideas in their most completely developed form. Assuming that their listeners can "fill in" or complete the missing data from their own knowledge and experience, speakers adapt their messages to the information already known to the audience. This tendency on the part of listeners is of immense value to speakers: information already known to the audience need not be elaborated on in detail. This leaves the speaker free to present other data to strengthen the position being advocated or further clarify the explanation being proffered. The same tendency to complete the speaker's point, however, may be a source of communication breakdown. Just as the idea can be extended in an appropriate direction by audience knowledge or beliefs, so can the same idea be completed in irrelevant ways. (The figure on page 33 illustrates the potential value of and difficulty associated with the motivation to complete ideas).

Developing good listening habits by practicing the following guidelines will help ensure your accurate perception and reception of messages:

1. *Know why you are listening* • Why do you want to hear this message, or this particular speaker? Unless you have a clearly defined purpose at the beginning, it will be difficult to listen for information that is important to you.[6] It will be virtually impossible to derive any meaningful content from the speech that is pertinent to your interests. Your reason for listening to a speaker may be personal or it may be dictated by extrinsic factors (e.g., the material will be covered on the next exam, or you have been asked to gather data and report to an employer or civic group).[7] In either case, knowing why you are listening will help you determine what to listen for.

2. *Identify the speaker's major or leading ideas, and concentrate closely on each as it is presented* • Unless you carefully identify each major idea as it is stated, and separate it from its developmental material, you may fail to grasp the speaker's dominant thesis. Don't listen for "just the facts," but constantly focus on the major ideas to which those facts are closely connected.

3. *Identify the dominant structure or arrangement of the major points* • Determine whether the speaker is organizing ideas chronologically, in terms of causes and effects, or is perhaps following a problem-solution pattern.* Not only will identification of the overall structure help you remember the speech, but it also will help you understand the direction and nature of the mental path through which the speaker wishes to lead you. Pattern recognition helps you to recall specific information and to determine the speaker's emphasis on particular ideas. When you listen to a speech, constantly look backward and think forward from the basic pattern you have discerned to make sure you understand where the speaker has been and where he or she may be going.

4. *Examine critically the details used to develop and support the major ideas* • Supporting materials—statistics, illustrations, comparisons—help both to prove central theses and also clarify major ideas. Look closely, therefore, at how the supporting data are being used. Does the speaker's use of a specific

---

*For a full discussion of such alternate patterns of speech organization, see Chapter 9.

THE PROCESS OF MESSAGE COMPLETION

Person A, listening to the message, completes it by filling in the missing pieces in one way; and Person B, listening to the same message, completes it in quite another way. Neither has received the *actual* message, but at least Person B has picked up the gist, thanks to an acquired habit of listening to the key ideas and of resolving problems of incompleteness in ways consistent with the speaker's intent.

"Today, I want to talk... seriously... about this country... Journalism *(journalism? My gosh! I have an examination next hour in Journalism!)...* about political candidates around the country, states in counties and cities, telling us *...political lies...about good issues and bad issues,* rhetorically clever moves *...sophomores (is tonight the sophomore dance? should I ask her?)* than candidates who stand for taxes, social security, jobs, inflation, and morals."

"Today I want to talk with you about a serious problem facing this country: the problem of political journalism. I am disturbed that the journalists who follow political candidates around the country, around the states, around the countries, and around the cities spend more time telling us what the various candidates' statements mean *politically* (was it a good or a bad issue, a rhetorically clever move or a sophomoric tactic, good for your party or good for the opposition?) than what the candidates stand for in terms of taxes, social legislation, jobs, inflation, and public morality."

"Today I want to talk... about a serious problem —political journalism. I am disturbed that journalists...follow political candidates around the country... telling us what...the various candidates mean *politically (what does that mean?)*...than what their stands are on taxes ...legislation for the party of opposition *(what does that mean?),* inflation, publicity, morality."

[Message for Person A: Some candidates tell us lies about anything, while others promise more taxes, inflation, and stuff. Obviously, there are no good politicians.]

[Message for Person B: Political journalists twist what politicians are saying so that we don't really know what they are standing for. I still am not sure what is being said here, but...]

instance to illustrate an abstract notion significantly clarify the idea? Does the speaker's statistical analysis of current trends actually support the principal thesis? Or are the numbers thrown in merely to impress you? Is the quoted testimony of the authorities relevant to the problem and useful in comprehending it? By asking yourself such questions, you can appreciably increase your understanding of the idea and its place within the speech as a whole.

5. Relate the speaker's major ideas to your own beliefs, attitudes, values, and behaviors • Having identified why you are listening and focused on the major ideas, dominant structure, and details of the speech, you are now in a position to relate the information to your own experience. What is presented that you can identify with? What beliefs or values do you bring to the occasion that help to "round out" the message? On a more general level, does the speech satisfy your goal or rationale for listening? In asking this question, you are searching for a mental pigeonhole in which to store this communicative experience.

Listening for Evaluation

Evaluative listening is the most sophisticated kind of listening you can engage in. As with listening for comprehension, the process demands that you absorb, sift through, and relate data to your own experience and knowledge. But evaluative listening also demands that you pay close attention to several facets of the speech

This student, engaged in evaluative listening, must first discern the content of the message before she can make a judgment as to its worth and relevance.

situation in order to reach a critical judgment that is a justifiable assessment of the value of the message. In cumulative fashion, your attention moves from discerning the content of the message to appraising its worthiness as a basis for belief or action. Your accuracy and precision in making such judgments will be aided by the following guidelines:

1. Decide why you want to evaluate the speech • How you evaluate a speech, a speaker, or an occasion demands the same sense of purpose that listening for comprehension requires. Are you interested in the worth of the ideas? in the strength of the arguments offered? Do you wish to verify whether the speaker, purported to have certain qualities or abilities, demonstrates them when addressing an audience? Or is it the occasion itself that calls for evaluation? Suppose, for example, you are interested in deciding (evaluating) for yourself whether the congressional seniority system is good or bad. You attend a public gathering likely to produce defenders and denigrators of the system, whose ideas you can listen to and evaluate. You might go to another meeting primarily to judge the personality and possible persuasiveness of a particular speaker, say, a colorful Common Cause lobbyist dedicated to denouncing deficiencies and inefficiences of the system. Or, you might decide to witness firsthand an occasion in which congressional seniority is operative—a hearing before the Senate Administrative Practices Committee. Evaluation of communication events thus can involve a variety of purposes.

2. Determine the speaker's general and specific purpose • Does the speaker seek to entertain you, to present information and increase your understanding, to reinforce your existing beliefs and attitudes, to change your opinions, or to move you to overt action? To what degree is this purpose appropriate to this speaker, this audience, and this occasion? Does this speaker have a hidden agenda,* or at least an important personal gain which might be realized in this speech if this audience reacts as desired? Does this audience expect certain ideas or issues to be presented; and, if so, did those expectations guide the construction of this speech?

3. Assess the clarity of the message being presented • Has this speaker employed proper vocal emphasis and gestures, enough repetition and restatement, illustrations relevant to your experience, analogies that ensure clarification, needed definitions and explanations, an appropriate organizational pattern, carefully built transitions and summaries, visual or aural aids, and concrete language? Has this speaker used enough of these modes, materials, patterns, and devices and in the proper proportion so that the message you receive inside your head seems sufficiently similar to the message shaped and transmitted from inside the speaker's head?

4. Be sensitive to the speaker's attitude toward you as a listener • Are there vocal, physical, or verbal signs that this speaker is thinking more of himself or herself than of the central idea and the audience? What are these signs?

---

*A hidden agenda is a covert purpose, covered or protected by an announced or overt purpose. The telephoner who tells you you are on a quiz program when he or she actually is trying to sell you a merchandising coupon book has a hidden agenda.

Do you sense that this speaker is treating you and the rest of the audience with condescension? fear? contempt? love? respect?

5. *Judge the credibility of the speaker* • To what degree and in what ways do you find this speaker competent, trustworthy, sincere, expert, educated, informed, honest, friendly? Do the central ideas, organization of thoughts, choice of language, voice, gestures, and physical stance tend to strengthen or weaken your impression of his or her credibility?

6. *Test the soundness or reasonableness of the speaker's ideas* • Are the central ideas, the supporting materials, the reasoning, and the language in which these are phrased appropriate to the audience, the occasion, and the speaker? Are the proposals feasible, despite such potentially limiting factors as finances, time, or manpower? Moreover, are there unspoken assumptions, stereotypes, or values which, if brought into the open, would cause you to reflect negatively on the idea or message? In searching for clues to the underlying beliefs and values, listen for such giveaway phrases as "All upright Americans know . . . ." "Unquestionably . . . ." "Our forefathers . . . ." "What could be more natural than . . . ?"

7. *Compare the verbal and nonverbal messages* • Is this speaker's body saying something different from the words? (Often, a speaker will talk confidently, but physically show fear or lack of confidence; or the words will say "This is the truth," but an expression or vocal inflection will say "I am stretching the truth.") Do you tend to believe the words or the body? When nonverbal behaviors differ from verbal messages, listeners tend to accept the nonverbal indicators as more reliable clues to the speaker's intent.[8] More positively, does this speaker use a good delivery—strong voice, well-timed gestures, an active body, and a communicative face—to reinforce key points in the verbal message?

8. *Determine the effect of the message on your beliefs and actions* • Assuming that this speaker's message has found in you a receptive heart and mind, what adjustments will you have to make? Will you have to change your mind about the speaker? Will you have to adjust certain beliefs, intensify or redirect certain attitudes, view your values in somewhat different ways, replace certain planks in your philosophy of life, and alter some of your behaviors accordingly? Are you strong enough to make these adjustments, whatever they are, without trauma or discomfort? In short, what are you going to do with and about this speech? In what specific ways will the speaker's message affect how you think, feel, and act?

These eight activities represent the major obligations imposed on anyone who would listen well and judge fairly. Added to the tasks necessary for comprehension, they suggest the complexity of the communicative undertaking. We all can listen with relatively little critical awareness—and we often do—but to apply the above guidelines successfully requires constant effort. As you seek to comprehend and to evaluate the speeches you will hear in the communication classroom, you will be able to apply the guidelines suggested in this chapter. Honing your skills in this way will allow you to develop a competency that is central to the effective transaction of ideas.

Listening from the Speaker's Perspective

Speakers looking out at a sea of faces may find themselves invigorated by the enthusiastic reactions of the listeners. They also may discover that some audience members look downright bored: some are reading while others are gazing out the window, writing notes to persons nearby, or engaging in any one of a hundred other actions that suggest inattention or disagreement. Many speakers find it encouraging to look at those listeners who appear to be alert and interested in the speech. However, the speaker who observes that many audience members appear inattentive, or that the inattention occurs with frequency during the speech, should be receptive to these communicative cues. Observing audience feedback is an important task in accentuating positive responses and minimizing the negative or indifferent ones.

THE AUDIENCE PROVIDES BOTH DIRECT AND INDIRECT FEEDBACK TO THE SPEAKER

Speaker   **Channel/Message**   **Listener/Audience**

Direct Feedback

Indirect Feedback
approve / disapprove   *regulate / control*

Reacting to Feedback

Because speaker-audience interaction is basically a two-way process, its success ultimately depends not only on the communicative cues that speakers send to listeners, but also on the responses listeners return to the speaker. These responses we have termed "feedback." *Feedback is the listener's verbal and/or nonverbal response to messages received from the speaker.* We may usefully think of feedback as occurring in two forms—direct and indirect.

Direct feedback • Direct feedback is the overt expression of reactions offered by listeners. For example, an audience which applauds or boos the speaker during the course of the speech—as frequently happens at inaugural addresses, political rallies, or keynote speeches—is providing direct feedback. Listeners who ask questions after a speech is concluded likewise are "telling" a speaker what they thought of the discourse. Other direct feedback may be offered less immediately, even well after the speech is over. Thus, a politician can measure speechmaking success by counting votes on election night; a sales representative, by discovering how many orders for a particular product were placed after a sales pitch is made; a teacher, by student reactions recorded on a class evaluation form or by how many students sign up during the next term for a particular course. These, too, are forms of direct feedback, and are at least gross measures of communicative success or failure. Direct feedback, whether immediate or delayed, is one of the speaker's surest gauges of communicative competence.

Indirect feedback • Indirect feedback, on the other hand, represents more covert or subtle expressions of reaction. Indirect feedback includes the signals listeners send back to speakers principally via visual channels, as when they scratch their heads, shift uncomfortably in their seats, and the like. Such actions and movements can be "read" by speakers and can affect the progress of their speeches. Indirect feedback generally serves speakers in two ways. It helps them to *regulate* the subsequent portions of the message, and to assess audience *approval* of the message.

Regulation • Some of these nonverbal messages returned by the audience, whether consciously sent or not, essentially tell speakers what to do while they are speaking. A quizzical frown may send the message, "I don't understand what that means, so could you say it again?" The observant speaker picks up that message and rephrases the idea. An auditor who, in a resigned manner, nods in bored agreement may be saying, "Yes, yes, I know all that—get on with it!" The good speaker, upon seeing such reactions, moves ahead quickly, may even say, "Is that all clear?" and, in the face of more nods, advances to the next point. Listeners who cup their ears are saying "Speak up," and sensitive communicators will do so. In all of these cases, listeners are attempting to regulate or control the course of the communication transaction and are trying to get speakers to alter some aspect of their behavior.

Approval • Other cues flowing from an audience are covert expressions of approval or disapproval. If several listeners frown, speakers may well infer that

The members of this audience are showing positive feedback indicating their approval of the speaker by their overt reactions of applause and facial expressions.

their ideas are not being accepted. If an eyebrow is raised quizzically or a nose is wrinkled in distaste, the speaker may guess that someone wants to say, "Are you *sure* about that?" In contrast, positive actions—nods of assent, broad smiles, auditors leaning forward in anticipation, and the like—show listener approval.

As a listener you often have little control over the signals you send to a speaker. You seldom say to yourself, "Now I am going to express puzzlement/ glee/disapproval/ecstasy." Many of your indirect feedback mechanisms, especially, are unconscious; they are your body's manifestations of your internal reactions; many occur outside of your mental awareness. Other forms of feedback, however, are directly controlled. You make conscious decisions on whether to vote, to ask a question after a speech, or to buy a product. And, for that matter, you may even deliberately frown or smile or look out the window, especially if you have noticed that a speaker looks in your direction fairly often.

Feedback—regardless of the form in which it is provided or the means by which it is expressed—is essential to complete communication. To the extent that you acquaint yourself with the principles and practical applications of feedback, you will both improve the efficiency of your behavior as a listener and enhance the sensitivity of your appeal as a speaker.

Interacting with Listeners

The notion of joint responsibility for the success of oral communication brings us back to this book's principal concern—the speaker's role in public, oral communication. That role significantly affects the public speaker's attitudes toward, responsibilities toward, and relationships with the listeners. Conceivably, you could draw one of two conclusions from the foregoing pages: either (1) speakers can say anything they please because few people in the audience are listening well; or (2) speakers can do much to control and guide listeners' reception of their messages. Actually, both conclusions carry considerable merit. Your messages seldom, if ever, will get through to an audience in all of their completeness and complexity. The psychological processes of listening make it probable that you will be heard in fits and starts, a few words here, some partial thoughts there. But this does not mean that you can say anything you wish, for in spite of all of the listening problems we have identified, an audience can grasp an amazing amount of material. And, more important, you as a speaker can aid that audience in its efforts to appreciate, learn from, and evaluate your messages.

Indeed, a principal purpose of the chapters that follow in this book is to help you make the kinds of communication decisions which promote accurate, productive listening.

Evaluating Classroom Speeches

An important contribution which this course can make in providing you with real-life experience is the opportunity to practice listening. Critical listening skills can be developed in several ways in this classroom as well as in others. You can (1) practice critiquing the speeches of other students, taking part in post-speech discussions; (2) listen critically to discussions, lectures, oral presentations, and student-teacher exchanges in your other classes, identifying effective and ineffective communicative techniques employed by a variety of people in different contexts; (3) make an effort to hear speakers outside of class, in the community, observing carefully their successes and failures and analyzing why they meet with certain reactions; and (4) read the sample speeches in this book, taking them apart systematically to isolate the cues that might have facilitated comprehension and positive evaluation.

While you undoubtedly will become a more informed listener after you have studied this book and engaged in a series of classroom speaking assignments, you nevertheless can start now to become a more proficient listener. First, you can use the Speech Evaluation Form on pages 41–42 as a checklist of listening concerns. Depending upon the particular assignment, the nature of the audience, and the demands of the occasion, some of the checkpoints on the form will be more significant and applicable than others. Use the form, for now, as a general guide, and then later, concentrate upon those aspects of it relevant to a specific speech assignment.

And second, participate regularly in post-speech evaluations, even of early classroom speaking assignments. Do not hesitate to provide direct feedback to your classmates, pointing out what was good, what worked and what didn't seem to work so well, what was clear and what remained cloudy. Good, constructive classroom criticism is both positive and negative—but always supportive. Such oral commentary accomplishes two goals: it provides a beginning speaker with much-needed reaction, and it forces you, the listener, to verbalize your thoughts and recognize explicitly your standards and expectations. In this way, both you and the speaker gain: the speaker acquires a sense of the range of reactions being generated in an audience, and you gain a better sense of your own mind.

Listening, then, is a two-way street, a joint responsibility of speaker and auditor. Only when both parties are sensitive to its points of breakdown and to techniques which can enhance it will oral communication result in a successful transaction. Much of what we will have to say in later chapters will impinge directly upon this process.

Listening Checklist

I. COMPREHENSION
    A. What do I want to obtain from listening to this speaker? Why am I here?
    B. What are the speaker's major ideas?
    C. What pattern of organization (if one can be discerned) is being utilized?
    D. What supporting materials should I retain for later use?
    E. How does this speech relate to my own values, experience, knowledge?

II. EVALUATION
    A. Why is evaluation of this speech important to me?
    B. What is the speaker's purpose?
        1. General
        2. Specific
    C. Is the message conveyed so I can understand it?
    D. How does the speaker feel about me as a listener?
    E. How credible is the speaker?
    F. Is there congruence or contradiction between verbal and nonverbal messages? If contradictory signals are present, what is the "real" message?
    G. How does the message affect my beliefs? How should I act as a result of accepting or rejecting it?

Speech Evaluation Form

The Speaker

_____ poised

_____ positive self-image?

_____ apparently sincere?

_____ apparently concerned about the topic?

_____ apparently concerned about the audience?

_____ apparently well prepared?

_____ voice conversational?

_____ delivery speed controlled?

_____ body alert and nondistracting?

_____ gestures used effectively?

_____ face expressive?

_____ language clear (unambiguous, concrete)?

_____ language forcible (vivid, intense)?

The Message

_____ suitable topic?

_____ clear general purpose?

_____ sharply focused specific purpose?

_____ well-phrased central idea or proposition?

_____ adequately supported (enough, varied, trustworthy sources)?

_____ supporting materials tailored to the audience?

_____ introduced adequately?

_____ concluded effectively?

_____ major subdivisions clear, balanced?

_____ use of notes and podium unobtrusive?

Transmission

_____ voice varied for emphasis?

The Audience

_____ all listeners addressed?

_____ their presence recognized and complimented?

_____ their attitudes toward subject and speaker taken into account?

The Speech as a Whole

Audience's expectations met?

_____

Short-range effects of the speech?

_____

Long-range effects?

_____

Possible improvements?

_____

REFERENCE NOTES

[1]See studies reviewed in Larry L. Barker, _Listening Behavior_ (Englewood Cliffs, NJ: Prentice-Hall, 1971), pp. 3–4; Thomas G. Devine, "Listening: What Do We Know After Fifty Years of Research and Theorizing," _Journal of Reading_, 21 (January 1978), 296–304.

[2]"Secrets of Being a Better Listener," Interview with Lyman K. Steil, _U.S. News and World Report_, May 26, 1980, p. 65.

[3]From "Time Perception" by Herbert Woodrow from _Handbook of Experimental Psychology_, ed. S. S. Stevens. Copyright © 1951 John Wiley & Sons, Inc. Reprinted by permission of John Wiley & Sons, Inc.

[4]Adapted from Wayne C. Minnick: _The Art of Persuasion_, pp. 38–41. Copyright © 1957 Houghton Mifflin Company. Used by permission.

[5]For a further analysis of types of listening, see Andrew R. Wolvin and Carolyn Gwynn Coakley, _Listening Instruction_ (Annandale, VA: Speech Communication Association, TRIP Series, 1980). Their discussion covers appreciative, discriminative, comprehensive, therapeutic, and critical listening activities. Since our focus is on more specific public communication behaviors, we have narrowed our concerns to only three of their categories. Also see Adele Patterson, "Listening as a Learning Skill," _Media and Methods_, 15 (January 1979), 18–20, 80.

[6]Richard Heun and Linda Heun, *Public Speaking: A New Speech Book* (St. Paul, MN: West, 1979), Chapter 3, "Listening to Public Speeches."

[7]Charles R. Petrie, Jr. and Susan D. Carrell, "The Relationship of Motivation, Listening Capability, Initial Information, and Verbal Organizational Ability to Lecture Comprehension and Retention," *Communication Monographs*, 43 (August 1976), 187–94. For other studies of listening skills, see Steven C. Rhodes and Kenneth D. Fransden, "Some Effects of Instruction in Feedback Utilization on the Fluency of College Students' Speech," *Speech Monographs*, 42 (March 1975), 83–89; and Robert W. Norton and Loyd S. Pettegrew, "Attentiveness as a Style of Communication: A Structural Analysis," *Communication Monographs*, 46 (March 1979), 13–26.

[8]Mark L. Knapp, *Nonverbal Communication in Human Interaction*, 2nd ed. (New York: Holt, Rinehart & Winston, 1978), Chapter 6, "The Effects of Physical Behavior on Human Communication."

 PROBLEMS AND PROBES

CHAPTER REPORT   Using the Suggestions for Further Reading at the end of this chapter, and reference sources such as the *Reader's Guide to Periodical Literature,* find out as much as you can about the importance of listening in one of the three realms—work, social, public—discussed in Chapter 1. Summarize your findings in a 500–750 word essay or in a brief speech for in-class presentation.

1.   Lyman Steil suggests that listening is "at the heart of our success" as communicators, whether it be in family life, in business, in society, or in school work. Consider the importance of this statement: it means that the *listener* shares the burden of successful communication. How well do you fulfill this obligation? On a scale of 1–100, rate your listening abilities as a student, son/daughter, friend, employee, and so forth. Then ask your teacher, parent, friend, and employer to rate you as a listener. Check their perceptions with your own.

2.   Think of a course in which you are currently enrolled and having trouble. How are you as a listener in that classroom? Where do you normally sit during class? Do you face any physical barriers to communication? How well can you hear your instructor? Is your seat in the best possible place in the room with the least amount of distractions? Do you sit too close to the door? Are you distracted by conversations or hall movement during classtime? Do you sit near a window? Are you often tempted to look outside? Think about your classmates. Does someone sit near you who captures your attention? What changes could you make to become a better listener in that classroom? Realize that *you* can control your listening environment.

3.   What, to your mind, is the importance of physical setting in good listening? How do you react to noises, uncomfortable temperatures in a room, seating which makes a view of the speaker difficult? Does the arrangement of chairs (rows in auditoriums, circles of chairs in classrooms, across-the-desk seating for conferences) affect your listening habits? Do you listen in one manner when seated in front of a lecturer, in another when talking to a friend at a crowded party? Make some useful generalizations regarding the ways in which the speech situation affects the ease or efficiency with which you listen.

 **ORAL ACTIVITIES**

1. Prepare a two- to three-minute oral statement in response to one of the following topics:
    a. Is there anything wrong with tuning out a boring speaker?
    b. "Nature has given to man one tongue, but two ears that we may hear from others twice as much as we speak." —*Epictetus,* circa 300 B.C.
    c. Can faking attention be harmful?

2. Consider the following question: Can speakers objectively evaluate their own efforts? After a performance assignment, test your self-evaluative skills by completing the Speech Evaluation Form on pages 41–42. When the instructor returns a written critique (and those of any classmates who might also have evaluated the performance), compare these with your responses. Try to account for any differences between your self-evaluation and the evaluations of others.

3. Conduct an experiment to "test" how speakers respond to feedback. Ask some students in a class other than this one to give the instructor positive feedback in response to certain movements that you specify—writing on the board, walking in front of the lectern, reading passages from a book. How does the feedback seem to affect the instructor's behavior? Report your findings in a brief presentation to your speech class.

4. Present a one-minute set of oral instructions for some activity with which the class is not likely to be familiar. Class members should not take notes during presentations, but after each presentation they should try to list the instructions on a notecard. Collect the cards and compare the written versions to the instructions you presented. How do you account for any discrepancies? What could you as a speaker have done to aid your listeners?

5. Challenge your own listening skills. Did you hear what you thought you heard? Approach your instructor after class and say, "I thought I heard you say . . .," or "You listed three main points. Were they . . .?" You will be amazed at how much better you listen if you plan to ask questions about what you heard and you may be pleasantly surprised by your instructor's response. Discuss this activity with other classmates.

 SUGGESTIONS FOR FURTHER READING

Larry L. Barker, *Listening Behavior* (Englewood Cliffs, NJ: Prentice-Hall, Inc., 1971).

Baxter Geeting and Corinne Geeting, *Huh? How to Win Through Assertive Listening* (Sacramento, CA: Communications Design, Inc., 1976).

Linda Costigan Lederman, *New Dimensions: An Introduction to Human Communication* (Dubuque, IA: Wm. C. Brown Company, Publishers, 1977), Chapters 10 and 11, "The Receiver: As Listener" and "The Receiver: Listener Plus."

J. Michael Sproule, *Communication Today* (Glenview, IL: Scott, Foresman and Company, 1981), Chapter 3, "Listening: The Roles Receivers Play."

Andrew R. Wolvin and Carolyn Gwynn Coakley, *Listening Instruction* (Annandale, VA: Speech Communication Association, TRIP Series, 1980).

3

Planning and Preparing the Basic Speech

Let us now turn from our overviews of public communication, the competent public speaker, and listening, and direct our attention more specifically to a preview of the speechmaking process. We use the term *preview* to indicate that the ideas and procedures we are about to outline will be developed at greater length. Our purpose here is to introduce you to the presentational methods—the different ways you can present your speech—and to the essential steps in the preparation of public speeches. This chapter will allow you to visualize the whole procedure, and will provide a foundation for the chapters in Part Two.

Presentational Methods of Speaking

In the strictest sense, the presentational methods of public speechmaking are an aspect of delivery—the eighth and final step in the process. However, because the method of speaking you choose significantly affects many of the other choices you must make in all of the other seven steps, it requires first and immediate attention. In choosing a method of presenting a speech you have four options. That is, you may present a speech in (1) impromptu, (2) memorized, (3) manuscript, or (4) extemporaneous format.

An *impromptu speech* is one delivered on the spur of the moment with no specific preparation. Hence, you must rely entirely on your existing knowledge and speaking skills. The impromptu method is useful in an emergency, but should be restricted to situations which cannot be anticipated. Too often the "moment" arrives without the "spur." Whenever possible, therefore—even if you only think you *might* be called upon to speak—it is better to plan ahead than risk the rambling, incoherent, fumbling presentation which the impromptu method so often produces.

THE PRESENTATIONAL METHODS OF SPEAKING

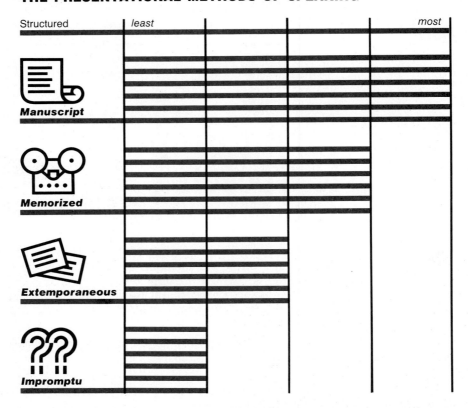

Structured   *least*   *most*

Manuscript

Memorized

Extemporaneous

Impromptu

A *memorized speech* is planned, structured, written out word for word, and then committed to memory. Except in rare instances, avoid this method. When speaking memorized words, you will unavoidably concentrate on them rather than on *ideas*, thus producing a stilted, inflexible speech. If you forget a word or a phrase, you are in danger of losing the entire thread of your thought. Your delivery tends to become excessively formal and oratorical, and you are likely to hurry your words. Even worse, perhaps, the memorized speech makes it impossible for you to adapt to your audience's reaction or feedback.

The *speech read from manuscript*, like the memorized speech, is also written out word for word, and the speaker *reads it aloud* to an audience. When extremely careful wording is required—as in the President's messages to Congress, for example, where a slip of the tongue could upset domestic politics or undermine foreign policies, or in the presentation of scientific reports where exact and concise exposition is required—the manuscript method is appropriate, even necessary. Many radio and television speeches also are read because of the strict time limits imposed by broadcasting schedules. Viewed as a specialized method useful in certain situations, the ability to read effectively a speech from manuscript is important. But you should not resort to it when it is neither useful nor necessary, because its use—like that of the memorized speech—inevitably diminishes the freshness, spontaneity, and adaptability vital to meaningful oral communication.

The *extemporaneous speech,* like the memorized and the read-from-manuscript speech, is carefully planned, systematically structured, and outlined in detail. There, however, the similarity ends. Rather than writing out the speech word for word, the extemporaneous speaker—following a carefully prepared plan or outline—orally "pre-phrases" the speech several times and, if possible, practices it orally in private prior to presentation. With this method, you memorize only the structure or the major-idea sequence. Then, working from this sequence or outline, you practice phrasing the speech, feeling free to express yourself somewhat differently each time you talk it through. You use the outline only to fix the order of the main ideas in your mind, and you practice various wordings to develop the flexibility of expression which may be necessary when you eventually deliver the speech.

If you use the extemporaneous method carelessly or without adequate preparation, the result may resemble the impromptu speech—which unfortunately sometimes leads to a confusion of these two terms. If you use the extemporaneous method properly, however, you can produce a speech nearly as polished as one that is read aloud from manuscript, and is certainly more vigorous, spontaneous, and flexible. For this reason, the extemporaneous method of presentation is superior to both the memorized method and the manuscript method in most public speaking situations. Without sacrificing solidity of content or cogency of organization, it makes possible easy adaptation to feedback from your audience. The extemporaneous speech may, within reasonable limits, be shortened or lengthened; ideas not understood when first stated may be repeated; and examples and other illustrative materials may be altered as the need arises. The speeches you present in class will usually be extemporaneous. Quite aside from this, however, strive to make it your preferred and most frequently used format. The ensuing discussion of the speechmaking process is based primarily on the extemporaneous speech.

The Essential Steps in Speech Preparation

Preparing almost any speech for public presentation involves several steps which occur in essentially three phases:

Phase I: Thinking About Your Speech

1. Selecting and narrowing the subject
2. Determining the general purpose, specific purposes, and central idea or thesis

3. Analyzing the audience
4. Analyzing the occasion

Phase II: Assembling Materials and Ideas

5. Gathering the speech material
6. Making an outline

Phase III: Working on Your Presentational Skills

7. Practicing aloud for clarity and fluency

These tasks, you may find, need not be carried out separately and in exactly the sequence suggested. As you gain experience and better understand your own habits, you may be able to dispense with one or more of the steps or develop a way of working better suited to your own idiosyncrasies. For your first speeches, however, we strongly recommend that you perform all seven steps in the order outlined. That way, you will ingrain in yourself important public communication habits—habits which guarantee that you think through all of your choices consciously before speaking in front of others.

Selecting and narrowing the subject • Ordinarily, in the first phase of your preparation you start by drawing together what you already know that might be worth talking about, and tentatively deciding whether any of your ideas might be developed into a speech. Sooner or later, you select a subject that interests you and one you think is likely to interest your listeners. Narrow this subject so that it fits within the limits specified by asking yourself, "How much can I say about *x* in five minutes?" One of the most common faults of beginning speakers is that they tend to select a topic too broad to be treated clearly and forcefully in the time available. The narrower your subject, the more fully you will be able to explain or prove the essential points, and the more interesting you can make your speech by including a variety of illustrative incidents and instances, supportive statistics, or comparisons.

Determining the general purpose, specific purposes, and central idea or thesis • It is not enough to center your speech in a well-defined subject and have at least a general notion of how to narrow it. You must decide what you want it to do to and for your listeners—why you want to talk to a group of people about it. That "why" involves the answering of three sets of interrelated questions: *General Purpose*—Are you seeking to tell them something they do not know and should know? Do you wish to alter the way they feel about some thing or some problem? Are you seeking to get your listeners to do something about some state of affairs? *Specific Purposes*—Given your topic, specifically what do you want them to know, to feel or value, or to do? Specific purposes allow you to set very particularized goals for your speech and to determine the exact responses you want from your auditors. Thus, generally you might want to inform the members of your audience, but more specifically you might wish them to understand the five steps involved in adopting a foreign-born child. *Central Idea or Thesis*—Can you now state your message in a single sentence? For an informative speech, that sentence is called a "central idea." It is a declarative statement which more or less summarizes your speech, as, for example, "There are five basic steps through which one must go to adopt a foreign-born child." In persuasive speeches, that sentence is called a "thesis" or "proposition," because it summarizes the thrust of the argument you are making, as "In a time of expanding world populations, you ought to consider adopting a foreign-born child instead of giving birth yourself."

Answers to these sorts of questions allow you to further narrow your subject and serve as a constant guide to selecting and organizing the ideas and points to include in your speech. Think of each speech you make as an instrument for winning a particular response from your listeners; determining the general purpose, specific purposes, and central ideas or theses permits the identification of that response.

Analyzing the audience • Listeners are the essential targets of all speeches. A good public speech, therefore, not only reflects your interests and desires as a speaker, but also is responsive to the interests, enthusiasms, preferences, and

The gathering shown here is quite informal with an audience composed of college students. What is called for in this situation is an extemporaneous presentation, aimed at the needs and values of educated young adults.

limitations of the audience to whom it is given. As you plan and prepare the speech, continually put yourself in the place of your audience members, asking how *you* would feel about the facts and ideas being presented. To do this successfully, you have to analyze the people who compose the group—their age, sex, social-economic-political status, origins, backgrounds, prejudices, and fears. Try to find out how much they know about your subject, what they probably believe in and value, and what their probable attitudes are toward you and your subject. In your public speaking classroom, this is easy enough to do—simply ask some people around the room. In other circumstances, you might have to become a bit more creative. But, however you do it, audience analysis is perhaps *the* crucial step in speech preparation, for it is the primary determinant of success in speechmaking.

Analyzing the occasion • Similarly, as we noted in Chapter 1, consider the setting and circumstances in which you will be speaking: Are there specific rules or customs that will prevail? How long will I have to talk? What will precede and follow my speech, and how, if at all, should the preceding and following events affect what I say? Will the physical circumstances be amenable to my speaking style or to my modes of presentation? If not, can I have them altered in some way before I talk? Will I have to use a microphone, or can I reach everyone without one? In other words, analyzing the occasion involves both mundane considerations (e.g., physical setting) and more probing questions (e.g., group traditions). Your answers to both kinds of questions are important for your self-confidence; the answers will allow you to feel more comfortable about the circumstances and about expectations others will have when it is time for you to speak.

Gathering the speech material • As you move into the second phase of preparation, you start by assembling the materials needed to build your speech. At some point in the first phase you probably sorted out and assessed your *existing* knowledge of the subject and made some tentative decisions regarding material you can usefully draw from your personal experiences. Usually, however, you will find that this knowledge and material are not sufficient. You will need to gather *additional* information with which to develop, expand, and reinforce your major points. You may gather valuable materials from conversations and interviews, and from newspapers, magazines, books, government documents, and radio or television programs. Regardless of the time and labor involved, do your research thoroughly. Good speeches are packed with examples, illustrations, stories, figures, and quotations you can discover only by careful search.

Making an outline • Early in your preparation, make a preliminary list of the ideas to be included in your speech and tentatively indicate their arrangement. Do not attempt, however, to draw up a complete outline or final speech plan until you have gathered all of the necessary supporting and illustrative materials. Keep the plan or outline flexible, and continue to adjust it as you feel the need to do so. Only when you have assembled ample data of these kinds should you attempt to set down in final order the main points you expect to make, together

ESSENTIAL STEPS IN THE FULL DEVELOPMENT OF A SPEECH

Delivering the Speech

Speech Practice and Oral Delivery

7. Practicing aloud for clarity and fluency

Building the Speech

6. Making an outline

5. Gathering the material

Surveying the Problem

4. Analyzing the occasion

3. Analyzing the audience

2. Determining the specific purpose of the speech

1. Selecting and narrowing the subject

with such subordinate ideas as are necessary to explain or to prove these points fully.

Later we will consider a number of specific patterns for arranging ideas within a speech. We will consider, too, the various forms an outline may take. (If you feel the need at this time to see some sample outlines, turn to Chapter 9, pages 171–176). For now, however, remember two rules: (1) *arrange your ideas in a clear and systematic order,* and (2) *preserve the unity of your speech by making sure that each point is directly related to your specific purpose.*

Practicing aloud for clarity and fluency • The third phase of your preparation consists of one step—practicing the presentation of your speech as you hope to deliver it to an actual audience. You probably will find that the best method is to talk the outline through aloud, following the planned sequence of ideas, facts, and illustrations. Do this until you have learned the sequence thoroughly and until you can express each idea clearly and fluently. Then, putting the outline aside, think the speech through silently, point by point, to make certain that the ideas are fixed in your mind. Next, go through the speech aloud, but this time do not look at the outline at all. On your first oral trial you may inadvertently omit some points and interchange others, but do not let this worry you. Practice until all the ideas are expressed in their predetermined order and until the words flow easily. The more surely you command your material, the more poise and confidence you will have as you stand before the audience, with your notecards or shortened speaking outline in front of you. The self-assurance every speaker desires largely comes from always knowing exactly what to say next.

When you can go through the speech several times without forgetting major points or without hesitating unduly, you may consider your preparation completed. As you practice speaking from your outline, preserve a mental image of your listeners and project your speech as though you were actually talking to them. That image will help you transfer your best speaking habits from rehearsal to the actual speaking event.

Delivering Your First Speeches

Let's assume that you have prepared and practiced your speech, and that in this concluding and climactic step you now stand before your audience, ready and eager to communicate. "How," you ask, "should I deliver my message? What can I do that will help me communicate what I want to say while I am saying

As a public speaking student, you will be called upon to give various types of speeches in front of your class. If you recall the rules for speech delivery, your talks should meet with some degree of success.

it?" Three simple rules should guide the delivery of your early speeches: (1) be yourself; (2) look at your audience; and (3) communicate with your body as well as your voice.

1. *Be yourself.* Act as you would if you were engaged in an animated conversation with a friend. Avoid an excessively rigid, oratorical, or aggressive posture; but don't lean on a lectern or table or a wall. When you speak, you want the minds of your listeners to be focused on the ideas you are expressing, not on your delivery of them. Anything unnatural or unusual—anything that calls attention from matter to manner—is a distraction and should be avoided.

2. *Look at your listeners.* As we continue to emphasize throughout, watch the faces of your listeners for clues to their reactions. Without this feedback, you will be unable to gauge the ongoing effectiveness of your speech—to know whether you are putting your message across or whether you should make some prompt adjustments. Moreover, people tend to mistrust anyone who does not look them in the eye. So, if you fail to do so, they are likely to misjudge you and undervalue your ideas. And, finally, they nearly always listen more attentively if you look at them while you are speaking.

3. *Communicate with your body as well as your voice.* Realize that as a speaker you are being seen as well as heard. Movements of the body, gestures of the arms and head, changes in facial expression and muscle tension—all can help to clarify and reinforce your ideas. Keep your hands at your sides, so that when you feel an impulse to gesture, you can easily do so. Let other movements of your body also respond as your feelings and message dictate. Do not force your actions, but do not hold them back when they seem natural and appropriate to what you are saying. Try earnestly to transmit your ideas to others, and sooner or later you will make bodily responses of some kind, for they are an integral part of the desire to communicate.

In this chapter we have previewed seven steps for preparing speeches and have offered some advice on delivering your initial speeches. This advice, of course, is not foolproof and naturally you will have to adapt it to your own habits and situation. And too, you may not meet with instantaneous success, for it takes time to ingrain solid, usable communication habits and skills. If, however, you begin working on your speeches as soon as you know you are to deliver them—thinking about them, about what to say and how to say it, as well as engaging in research and in outlining procedures—you will have enough success to increase your self-confidence and effectiveness very soon in varying circumstances.

This chapter has stressed one "magical" key to success in speechmaking—the ability to ask and answer important questions *before* you stand up to speak. By asking pivotal questions concerning your subject matter, your purposes, your central idea or thesis, your audience, the occasion, the material that ought to be included in your speech, patterns that allow you to package your ideas effectively, and your own delivery habits, you can solve possible problems before they arise, clarify goals and desired responses, and prepare yourself psychologically and physically for oral communication. *The key to successful speechmaking is the ability to make conscious, strategically sound rhetorical choices.* If you are specifically conscious of *what* you are trying to do and *how* you are doing it, and if you have rationales—reasons—for *why* you are approaching the speech in the ways you are, your chances for effective communication improve immeasurably.

A Sample Student Speech

The following speech by Russell Walker, a student at Murray State University, was prepared to fulfill an assignment in a basic public speaking course.

Mr. Walker chose to discuss "Reality 101" not only because it reflected a topic of current concern—the "back to basics" movement in education—but also because it met other requirements of a good speech: (1) the topic was something which vitally affected him as a person trying to use practically the skills he supposedly had been taught; (2) it was appropriate to an audience of students facing similar problems; and (3) it could be covered adequately in the time allotted. Notice the clear sense of purpose, the careful transitions built in to lead the listeners step by step, and the use of varied supporting materials (statistics, quotations, examples, restatement). The proposition governing this speech is, "The American educational system has failed to emphasize basic learning skills."

● Reality 101*

Russell Walker

Introduction

"Soap and education are not as sudden as a massacre, but in the long run they can be just as deadly."[1] In these words, Samuel Clemens—better known as American philosopher-humorist Mark Twain—expresses his opinion of two American institutions. We can only hope Twain was wrong about the lethal properties of soap. However, evidence is mounting that he may have been right about education. /1

Former President Gerald Ford recently hailed the advent of a "new realism" in American education.[2] Unfortunately, few educators share his optimism, and many accuse the system of strangling real learning. The view of one Midwestern school-board member is typical: "In many schools," she said, "education exists in name only. Even in affluent, highly respected schools, there is a sense of desperation."[3] A four-month study by the Ford Foundation last spring concluded that "schools will continue to drift toward coma, as standards sink lower and lower."[4] Social critic Ivan Illich has even recommended "deschooling" society, saying that contemporary education has no real value.[5] /2

---

*A speech given at Murray State University, spring term, 1978. Reprinted by permission of Mr. Walker and the Interstate Oratorical Association. Text supplied by Professor Robert Valentine.

These charges are supported by the cold hard numbers of students' scores on the Scholastic Aptitude Tests. The SATs, as they are called, are administered each spring to college-bound high-school juniors and seniors across the United States, and are designed to measure both verbal and mathematical skills. Average scores have taken a nosedive, and are now in their twelfth consecutive year of decline.[6] /3

Unfortunately, the effect of the educational crisis is not limited to test scores on a computer printout; it touches the people, the 3.1 million high-school graduates who roll off the academic assembly-line each year. In Washington, D.C., one student graduated as valedictorian of his class, confidently applied to George Washington University, and then failed to make even half the minimum acceptable score on the admissions test. Joseph Ruth, GWU's Dean of Admissions, commented sadly, "My feeling about this kid is that he's been conned. He's been deluded into thinking he's gotten an education."[7] /4

Proposition
A "new realism"? Hardly. In fact, just the opposite—a delusion, a fantasy of education for millions of students. The system has failed, and failed tragically. The course is Reality 101, and American education is flunking out. /5

Specific Purpose
Let us examine the reasons for the failure of our schools, and a way to correct the catastrophe. /6

Body
Searching for the cause of the problem, many educators have seized upon an easy and readily available solution: lack of funds. Consequently, thus far, the nation's only response to the learning crisis has been to throw federal money at it and hope it will go away. In the 1960s and early 1970s approximately $10 billion in government funds were pumped into efforts to bolster education. The results? A Rand Corporation executive summed them up: "unexpected, temporary, uneven, and frustrating."[8] /7

Such simplistic solutions represent a Bayer Aspirin approach to the problem: Take two federal grants and call me in the morning. While more money may let schools do more of what they were already doing, dollars cannot help if the basic approach is wrong. The roots of the educational dilemma lie deep within the philosophy and goals of the system; specifically, in that system's failure to emphasize basic learning skills. /8

Minimum levels of competence in reading, writing, and simple arithmetic computation have a twofold importance. First, basic skills in these areas are essential for coping with the universe, regardless of occupation. Increasingly the information on which we all base life decisions pours down upon us in a deluge of letters and numbers. These are the symbols of an even more complex world, and students must learn to comprehend and use them well. /9

Secondly, a fundamental understanding of reading, writing, and elementary math forms the basis, for all later learning is built on this simple foundation. /10

Yet our schools are not providing many of their students with these basic skills. The U.S. Office of Education reported in 1976 that 11 percent of the 17-year-olds in those schools cannot read and comprehend an average newspaper page.[9] From CalTech to

Harvard, college professors voice the familiar complaint: "Half the incoming freshmen can't write—and the other half can't even read!" True, many high schools now require seniors to pass a "minimum competence exam" before graduation, but most of these require performance at the ninth-grade level for fear of failing large numbers of students who cannot meet twelfth-grade expectations.[10] Meanwhile, colleges are forced to divert funds from academic programs to finance classes in remedial reading; military-training manuals are rewritten for a sixth-grade reading level, and a University of Texas study last summer finds that fully one out of five adult Americans is functionally illiterate.[11] As performance drops, standards are lowered to match in a self-perpetuating cycle of semi-literacy.   /11

The answer, then, to our educational quandary is to give the teaching of basic learning skills our top priority. The emphasis must begin early, with unpopular but effective rote memorization at the elementary level, and extend through secondary classes to maintain and upgrade students' abilities. We must test students frequently on the fundamentals throughout their educational careers, using meaningful, uncompromised standards of performance. Finally, we must institute at once remedial programs to salvage as many students as possible.   /12

Such a solution is supported by the findings of the Educational Council of the States, as reported in the June 1976 issue of *Science News* Magazine. The Council, in studying educational methods and results over the last six years, documented a definite trend away from rote memorization and repeated drill in the fundamentals, concomitant with the sharp drop in student performance. The laudable purpose of innovators has been to spare students repetitive exercises and allow them greater freedom for creative work; however, meaningful creativity can occur only after those standardized essential learning skills are well in hand. Spelling the same word five different ways is not originality, it is ignorance, and the real world beyond the classroom will treat it as such. Realizing this, the Council's final recommendation to schools was simple and direct: "Teach more basics."[12]   /13

Conclusion
This solution—shifting the emphasis and approach of education in the 16,200 school districts across the country—is not an easy one. Neither is the problem it must solve easy. We can do it—we can reform our schools to instill essential skills in our children—we can do it and we must. For only when we do will American education make a passing grade in Reality 101.   /14

Sources
[1]Samuel Clemens, *The Facts Concerning the Recent Resignation* (1867). [2]Fred M. Hechinger, "Murder in Academe: The Demise of Education," *Saturday Review* 3:16 (March 20, 1976). [3]S. N. Wellborn, "U.S. Education: A Drift Toward Coma," *U.S. News* 81:55 (October 18, 1976). [4]*Ibid.* [5]*Ibid.* [6]George F. Will, "D Is for Dodo," *Newsweek* 87:84 (February 9, 1976). [7]J. Egerton, "Back to Basics," *Progressive* 40:22 (September, 1976). [8]Merril Sheils, "Where Money Fouls," *Newsweek* 87:86 (March 29, 1976). [9]Associated Press Wire Story, June 12, 1976. [10]"Making Diplomas Count," *Newsweek* 87:50 (May 24, 1976). [11]Associated Press Wire Story, January 24, 1976. [12]"Rx Education: Back to Basics," *Science News* 109:391 (June 19, 1976).

 PROBLEMS AND PROBES

CHAPTER REPORT Go through a recent issue of *Vital Speeches of the Day,* available in most campus and city libraries. For each speech you find, locate a statement of purpose; if there is none, read through the speech and construct one. Next, (1) decide what the general purpose of the speech is, and (2) guess at what some of the private purposes of each speaker might have been, given the person, the topic, and the audience. Finally, write an essay on the topic, "Strategies for Communicating Your Purposes to an Audience."

1.   Do you consider the organization of a message important? Why? Does organization have anything to do with changing attitudes? When Chief Joseph of the American Nez Perce tribe surrendered to the U.S. Army in 1877, he delivered the following speech. Read his words of long ago and note his organizational pattern. How does it affect your attitudes?

THE SURRENDER SPEECH

Tell General Howard I know his heart. What he told me before, I have it in my heart. I am tired of fighting. Our chiefs are killed; Looking-Glass is dead, Ta-Hool-Hool-Shute is dead. The old men are all dead. It is the young men who say "Yes" or "No." He who led on the young men is dead. It is cold, and we have no blankets; the little children are freezing to death. My people, some of them, have run away to the hills, and have no blankets, no food. No one knows where they are—perhaps freezing to death. I want to have time to look for my children, and see how many of them I can find. Maybe I shall find them among the dead. Hear me, my chiefs! I am tired; my heart is sick and sad. From where the sun now stands I will fight no more forever.

2.   In your personal speech journal, make a new list of five topics that interest you or look back in the journal for topics of interest you have already noted. Determine a suitable general purpose, specific purpose, and central idea or thesis for each topic. In considering purposes and central ideas, decide whether you wish to tell people about something, alter their views on a subject, or get them to act. This will help you to understand the "why" that underlies your wish to address people on each topic.

ORAL ACTIVITIES

1.   Your instructor will prepare slips of paper containing one word that relates to our American concept of values, such as patriotism, money, religion, sincerity, justice, love, truth, and others. Draw out a topic and return the slip of paper. You will be given ten minutes to prepare a three-minute speech which explains your feelings about this concept. Take notes in your personal speech journal on what others say because when the round of speeches is complete, you should have a fairly good summary of your classmates' attitudes towards these values. From time to time, you may wish to look back and review your findings.

2.   Select a periodical you usually do not read and closely examine the articles it contains. Do they give evidence of being well researched and thoughtfully written? From this examination, how reliable would you consider the periodical as a source? What is its potential value to you in preparing speeches for this or other classes?

3.   Following the principles and guidelines set forth in this chapter, prepare and present a three- to four-minute speech to inform. In this speech you will be ex-

pected to analyze and explain a single concept, idea, or event. Primary attention should be given to subject selection, identifying specific purposes, stating the central idea, organization, and audience adaptation. Use the analysis of an audience and occasion on pages 49–50 as a guide for preparing a similar analysis for this presentation.

4. Listed below are groups of three statements about a single topic. Read each statement in the group, and write what you believe to be the central idea of the message. Compare your phrasing of the central ideas with those of members of your task group.

(a) Many prison facilities are inadequate.
(b) Low rates of pay result in frequent job turnovers in prisons.
(c) Prison employees need on-the-job training programs.

(a) There is a serious maldistribution of medical manpower and service.
(b) The present system of delivering medical service is excellent.
(c) Rural areas have a shortage of doctors.

(a) The concept of democratic government appeals to most everyone.
(b) Democratic government deepens the citizens' feeling of responsibility.
(c) Democratic government reflects the will of the majority.

5. Consider the ways you have been treated as an audience member in college-level classes. Compare your experiences with your classmates', and discuss what instructional tactics are most effective. What indications are there that instructors may adjust their approaches according to audience expectations? When are such adjustments likely to be made? In light of this discussion, what advice would you offer to prospective teachers?

6. You and several other members of your class should attend a speech on campus or in the community. As you listen to the speech, try to assess the following elements: *(a)* the speaker's general purpose, probable specific purposes, and central idea or proposition; *(b)* the major ideas of the speech; and *(c)* the speaker's efforts to use factual and authoritative materials gathered with this particular audience in mind. Later, discuss your findings with other members attending the session. Compare your judgments and try to explain any differences of opinion.

7. Your instructor will divide your class into small working groups. Share your five topics of interest for which you have formulated general purposes, specific purposes, and thesis statements from Number 2 of Problems and Probes. Listen carefully to each other's ideas and purposes, and evaluate the work each has done. Work with a spirit of understanding that will interest and motivate one another.

 SUGGESTIONS FOR FURTHER READING

Erwin P. Bettinghaus, *Persuasive Communication,* 3rd ed. (New York: Holt, Rinehart & Winston, 1980), Chapter 2, "Developing Attitudes and Beliefs: Learning and Balance."

Bert E. Bradley, *Fundamentals of Speech Communication: The Credibility of Ideas,* 3rd ed. (Dubuque: William C. Brown Company Publishers, 1981), Chapter 5, "Selecting the Subject and Purposes."

Wayne C. Minnick, *Public Speaking* (Boston: Houghton Mifflin Company, 1979), Chapter 3, "Finding Speech Materials."

Herbert W. Simons, *Persuasion; Understanding, Practice, and Analysis* (Reading, MA: Addison-Wesley Publishing Company, 1976), Chapter 5, "Behavorial Theories of Persuasion."

J. Michael Sproule, *Communication Today* (Glenview, IL: Scott, Foresman and Company, 1981), Chapter 8, "Public Messages: Getting Started on a Speech."

PART TWO

PUBLIC SPEAKING

Preparation and Adaptation to the Audience

4

Choosing Speech Subjects and Purposes

In Chapter 3 we presented an abbreviated survey of the steps involved in preparing a speech. In this chapter we discuss more fully the first two of these steps, namely, selecting a suitable subject and determining the central concerns or purposes of the speech. These two tasks demand that you consider carefully several interrelated questions about yourself and your interests, your audience, and the occasion, because they represent your initial attempts to form a message suitable to all three of those elements in a communication situation. Although you may well adjust your subject matter and your purposes as you proceed through later steps in the speechmaking process, you nevertheless should do some early thinking about these matters as soon as you know you will be addressing an audience.

Selecting the Subject

On many occasions, the subject of your speech will be determined—at least in part—by the group you are invited to address. If you are speaking at a public hearing on a proposed rezoning of your neighborhood, you need not select a topic, for it is already determined by your audience's concerns and interests. Yet, there are many speaking occasions in which you will have to exercise some choice. In a speech classroom, of course, you must do so. If you are asked to deliver a lay sermon in church, you may have to decide, for example, whether to talk about religious duty, false religiosity, or missionary efforts. If you are to speak to a Rotary Club on some aspect of business economics, should you discuss labor relations or computerized accounting or off-season advertising campaigns? When addressing a school-board meeting devoted to "back to basics" education, you may wish to urge the adoption of better elementary textbooks, teacher in-service training, or special reading programs.

When confronted with the task of choosing a subject, observe the following guidelines:

Select a subject about which you already know something and can find out more • Knowledge you already possess can guide your efforts to find a suitable focus, to tailor the discourse to the specific audience you face, to assess areas in which your knowledge is thin, and to know where to locate additional materials you will need for your talk.

Select a subject that is interesting to you • If you are not sincerely interested in what you are talking about, you will find preparation a dull task, and, more important, your message and your presentation will probably reflect your lack of motivation and enthusiasm.

Select a subject that will interest your audience • The more interest your listeners have in the subject, the less you will have to worry about holding their attention when you speak. A subject may be interesting to an audience for one or more of the following reasons:

A. It concerns their health, happiness, prosperity, or security. (Thus, you might talk to a senior citizens group about Medicare.)
B. It offers a solution to a recognized problem. (You might suggest new ways your citizens' action group can raise needed money.)
C. It is new or timely. (You could talk to your local "Friends of the Library" about libraries which are installing videotaping capabilities.)
D. It is a topic surrounded by controversy or conflict of opinion. (Almost any subject can be approached in this way.)

In sum, remember that even though you are assigned a topic, you still have to make sure it is approached in a way that plays off your own strengths and reflects interests you and your audience at least potentially share. If you experience difficulty in selecting such a subject, study the list of subject categories at the end of this chapter.

Narrowing the Topic

If your subject is interesting to you and (potentially) to your audience, your next task will be to narrow it down to a manageable size. This involves three additional considerations:

Narrow your subject so that you can discuss it adequately in the time at your disposal • In a ten-minute speech, you could not cover adequately "The Rise and Fall of Baseball as the Premier American Sport." Instead, you might, for example, describe three or four changes baseball has made in response to television. Fit the "size" of your topic to the time available.

Gauge your subject so that it is neither above nor below the comprehension level of your audience • If, for example, you want to talk about laser

This speaker who is addressing a group of senior citizens seems to have their rapt attention. She is undoubtedly discussing topics of concern to them—for example, social security, Medicare, worthwhile activities, and other matters related to their interests and needs.

technology to an audience of first-year science students, you might choose to describe only its most basic principles; to a group of senior physics majors, however, you probably would move on to explain in technical terms its various applications.

Narrow your subject to meet the specific expectations of your audience • An audience that expects to hear a discussion of gun safety will probably be puzzled if, instead, you lecture on the need for stricter gun-control laws. People attending the inauguration of a president probably would be more than mystified if the president-elect launched a fifteen-minute comic monologue satirizing the whole ceremony. The announced purpose of a meeting, the demands of particular contexts, and other group traditions can affect an audience's expectations of what it is to hear. If you disregard them, you may seriously undermine the impact of your message.

In other words, selecting and narrowing a topic involves sorting through all the things you *could* say in order to find one, two, or three points you can establish, clarify, and support in the time you have available. Perhaps an example can illustrate this idea. Suppose you decide to talk about gardening. Within that subject are countless narrower topics, including:

- the growth of private or hobby gardening over the last decade (facts and figures on clubs, seed sales, the canning industry);
- methods for preserving homegrown vegetables (canning vs. freezing vs. drying vs. cold storage);
- soil enrichment (varieties of natural and artificial fertilizers, the strengths and weaknesses of each);
- factors to consider when selecting vegetables to plant (plot size, family eating habits, amount of time available for tending, cost of supermarket vegetables of each type);

- available strains of any given vegetable (selection of seeds based on geography, climate, soil characteristics, regional pests/bacteria, uses to which the vegetables will be put, germination and hardiness);
- literature on gardening (library books, TV programs, governmental pamphlets, magazines, seed catalogs, fertilizer company brochures);
- varieties of gardening tools (inexpensive hand tools, medium-cost hand-powered tools, more expensive power machinery);
- year-round gardening (window-box gardening, "grow" lights, cold frames, hot frames, greenhouses).

Each of these, in turn, could be further narrowed, depending upon time limits, your own expertise, and the audience's interests and background. So, in a five-minute speech to an audience already quite well versed in gardening (say, the members of a gardening club), you might choose to talk about the backyard greenhouse you built for less than $300. That speech probably would be more effective than one which discussed all types of "year-round" or sheltered gardening.

Selecting and narrowing a topic may seem like a complicated chore, yet if you carefully examine your own thinking, your audience's situation, time limitations, and the contexts in which you are talking, you can often move through this step with reasonable dispatch.

Determining the Purposes

Once you know what you want to talk about, the next question you face is "why?" Why do *you* wish to discuss this subject? Why might an *audience* desire to listen to you? If you cannot readily answer these questions, you probably will prepare for the speech inefficiently, and you are apt to produce an aimless, rambling discourse. You should approach these "whys" in three ways: first, think about *general purposes* (the reasons people generally have when they speak in public); next, consider the *specific purposes* (the concrete goals you wish to achieve in a particular speech); and finally, focus your thoughts on the *central idea* or *proposition* (the statement of the guiding thought you wish to communicate).

General Purposes

In most communication situations, you address your auditors in order to inform, to persuade, or to move them to action. Thus:

GENERAL PURPOSE	AUDIENCE RESPONSE SOUGHT
To inform	Clear understanding or comprehension
To persuade or to actuate	Acceptance of ideas or recommended behaviors

Usually you talk to others publicly because you possess some knowledge of potential relevance and benefit to them; or because you hope to alter their fundamental beliefs about the world, their attitudes toward life, or the actions they have been or ought to be taking. At times, of course, public communicators may have somewhat different general purposes—to entertain an audience, to help celebrate an event, to apologize for or justify some behavior, to pay tribute to a distinguished individual, and the like—but even these purposes can be translated into basically informative or persuasive goals. The entertainer conveys information or views about the world while giving pleasure to others; the celebrant orients listeners to the significance of an event; the apologist tries to make his or her behavior more understandable and acceptable; and the eulogist highlights in an informative and appreciative manner the key achievements of the person being praised. We will discuss some of these more specialized purposes (see Chapter 18, "Speaking on Special Occasions"), but for the most part we will concentrate on informative and persuasive oral discourse.

To inform • When your overall objective is to help the members of your audience understand an idea or comprehend a concept or a process, or when you seek to widen the range of their knowledge, the general purpose of your speech will be to inform. Such is the goal of scientists who report the results of their research to a group of colleagues, of college lecturers, work supervisors, or public figures who address community groups on subjects in which they are acknowledged experts.

To evoke a response of understanding, you must change the level or quality of information possessed by the members of your audience. By providing examples, statistics, illustrations, and other materials of an instructive nature, you seek to expand or alter their reservoir of knowledge. That change alone, however, may not be sufficient to ensure their understanding. For not only must an informative speech provide raw data, but its message and supporting data must be structured and integrated in such a way that listeners will clearly and quickly perceive the import of the whole. For example, an informative speech on how to build a stereo set must include the necessary information, and must present that information in an orderly sequence of steps. Understanding in this instance will depend not only on learning *what* to do, but also on knowing *when* to do it and *why*. Many of your listeners may already be familiar with much of your information and still lack understanding. No one has ever "put it all together" for them; no one has shown them exactly how to proceed step by step in order to achieve the end desired.

In short, to communicate an informative message successfully, you must relate your ideas to the existing knowledge of the audience; you must organize them so they are easy to follow and remember; and you must present enough concrete examples and specific data to raise appreciably the understanding of the persons addressed.

In summary, when your purpose is to clarify a concept or process for your listeners, when you endeavor to explain terms and relationships, or strive in other ways to widen the range of your listeners' knowledge, the objective of your speech will be to inform. *The response you seek from an informative speech is pri-*

THE GENERAL ENDS OF SPEECH

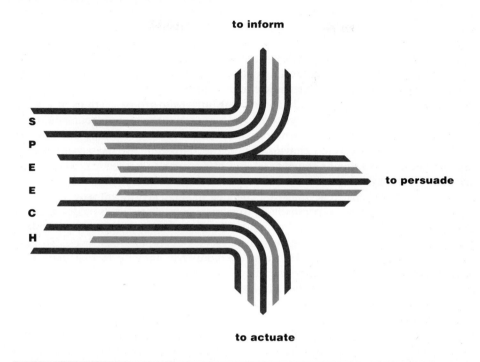

marily conceptual or cognitive—some adjustment in an audience's body of knowledge. Several different types of speeches are usually considered informative; speeches of definition or orientation, demonstrations, oral instructions, reports from committees or task forces, lectures, and so forth, all have information-sharing as their primary thrust. We will further discuss these types of speeches in Chapter 16.

To persuade or to actuate • The purpose of a speech to persuade or to actuate is to influence listener belief or action. While it may be argued that all speeches are in some degree persuasive,[1] there are numerous situations in which speakers have outright persuasion as their primary and most insistent purpose. Promotors and public relations experts attempt to create belief in the superiority of certain products, personages, or institutions; lawyers seek to convince juries; members of the clergy exhort their congregations to lead nobler lives; politicians debate campaign issues and strive to influence voters.

Usually, as a persuasive speaker you will seek only to influence the beliefs and attitudes of your listeners. Sometimes, however, you will want to go a step further and try to move them to *action*. You may want them, for instance, to contribute money, sign a petition, organize a parade, or participate in a demonstration. The distinguishing feature of an actuative speech is that instead of stopping with an appeal to their beliefs or attitudes, you ask your listeners to demonstrate their feelings by *behaving* or *acting* in a specified way.

Whether or not you seek immediate and overt action from the members of your audience, however, you invariably imply that what they believe should influence how they feel. Thus an attorney who wants a jury to believe that a client acted while insane also wants the jurors to feel a certain way about that client, to feel perhaps that the accused is deserving of pity or mercy. Conversely, a speaker who seeks to engender strong feelings about a subject also seeks to intensify listener beliefs and encourage certain kinds of behavior. For instance, in an acceptance speech a presidential candidate not only strives to arouse feelings of loyalty to person and party, but also seeks to reinforce our beliefs about our country's strengths and weaknesses, and to convince us to vote—preferably for him or her—as an act of patriotic behavior. Therefore, although listener acceptance of the speaker's ideas remains the general end of a speech to persuade, the effective speaker will realize that to gain this response from listeners, their beliefs, attitudes, and inclinations to act must be changed in some significant way.

Because the speech to persuade or to actuate characteristically is designed to influence or alter the beliefs and action-tendencies of listeners, you should fill it with well-ordered arguments supported by facts, figures, and examples. To persuade successfully, however, you must do more than provide factual data: you must make your listeners *want* to believe or act as you propose. Therefore, in addition to evidence and arguments, you must also introduce strong motive appeals; you must show how the proposal you advocate is related to your listeners' interests—how it will satisfy certain of their basic drives, wishes, or desires.

The successful speech to persuade or to actuate, therefore, is a psychologically sensitive message. It reorients the auditors' beliefs about the world, or changes their attitudes toward some aspect of it, or moves them to do something about some state of affairs. It demands a systematic, careful assessment, not only of people's knowledge as in the informative speech, but also their psychological springs to action. The next chapters, as well as Chapter 17, will have much to say about constructing rhetorical appeals or strategies for probing audience's beliefs, attitudes, and motivational tendencies.

A *general purpose* for a speech, therefore, is a broad class or type of purpose that specifies a class of responses a speaker desires from an audience. One of these general purposes—to inform, to persuade, to actuate—should always be your major objective. Knowing your general purpose allows you to judge the degree to which your specific purposes and actual speech materials are relevant.

Specific Purposes

A second important way to think about speech purposes is to consider specific purposes, that is, challenges related to a particular topic explored before an actual audience on a specific occasion by a real human being—you. Specific purposes represent actual goals you are attempting to achieve. Though concrete in nature, specific purposes can be extremely wide-ranging. Some of them you may verbalize; for example, you may tell an audience what you want it to understand or do as a result of your speech. Some are private, known only by you; for example, you probably hope to make a good impression on an audience, hope it will approve of and even like you, although you probably would not say that aloud. Usually, a speech has short-term specific purposes, goals you hope to accomplish immediately, and occasionally it even has long-term purposes. So, for example, if you are speaking to the members of a local food cooperative on the virtues of baking their own bread, your short-term purpose might be to get people to go home that night and try out your recipe, while your long-term goal could be to have them change their food-buying and food consuming habits.

Theoretically, therefore, you undoubtedly have any number of private and public, short-term and long-term specific purposes whenever you rise to speak. More practically, however, you will want to reduce that mass of goals to a predominant one. We may define *the* specific purpose of a speech as the *precise response* desired from the audience by the speaker. Formulated into a clear, concise statement, the specific purpose delineates exactly what you want the audience to do, feel, believe, understand, or enjoy.

Suppose, for example, that you are asked to explain to the Campus Democrats how the party's caucus works, in preparation for their actual participation in the county caucuses during an election year. In such a speech, you might have several specific purposes: to demonstrate that caucusing allows for full "grass roots" participation in the electoral process, to review step-by-step the actual procedures for forming "candidate preference groups" the night of the caucus, to explain what happens when a candidate-preference-group is not "viable" according to party rules, and even to show that you yourself are a knowledgeable person and hence a potential leader of the Campus Democrats next time there is an election. The first of these specific purposes is a long-range goal, the next two are short-range goals designed to prepare your listeners for actual participation in the county caucuses, and the fourth is a personal or private purpose. All of these specific goals can be summarized, however, in a statement of *the* specific purpose: "to show members of the Campus Democrats how they can effectively participate in the county presidential caucuses in an election year."

Central Ideas or Propositions

Once you have settled on the specific purpose, you are ready to cast into words a *central idea* or *proposition* (sometimes termed a "thesis statement") which will form the controlling thought of your speech. A central idea is a statement which captures the essence of the information or concept you are trying to communicate to an audience. A proposition, or claim, is a statement which phrases the belief, attitude, or action you wish an audience to adopt. Central ideas, therefore, are characteristic of informative speeches, and propositions form the core of persuasive and actuative discourses. (In Chapter 17, we will discuss the various types of propositions, or claims, in persuasive speeches—claims of fact, claims of value, and claims of policy. See pages 306–308.) The following examples will illustrate the relationships among the topic of a speech, its general purpose, some publicly acknowledged specific purposes, and a central idea or proposition:

Subject: Accident insurance for students
General purpose: To actuate
Specific purposes:

1. to get members of the student council to approve the group insurance policy offered by the ABC Insurance Company.
2. to provide inexpensive accident insurance for students currently without such protection.
3. to demonstrate that the ABC Insurance Company policy is the best one available for the money.
4. to overcome opposition from student council members and to remind the council of its obligations to its constituency.

Proposition: "The student council should approve the purchase of the group accident policy offered by the ABC Insurance Company (because many students do not have access to accident insurance, because it is the duty of the student council to serve its constituency, and because ABC's policy is less expensive than others we have examined)."*

Subject: Cardiopulmonary Resuscitation (CPR)
General purpose: To inform
Specific purposes:

1. to explain the three life-saving steps of CPR.
2. to interest the listeners in signing up for a CPR course.
3. to impress upon listeners their social responsibilities relevant to CPR.

Central idea: "Cardiopulmonary resuscitation—CPR—is a three-step, life-saving technique which anyone can learn for use in emergencies."

Explore carefully your general and your specific purposes before you begin to construct a public message. A sensitivity to general purposes will guide your thinking about speech materials and their structure. A realization of your specific purposes will allow you to understand your own hopes and fears, your potential range of effects on your audience, and the measures by which you may gauge the effects. Considering thoughtfully both general and specific purposes also enables you to define central ideas or propositions—thus capturing in your mind the primary thrust or aim of your speech.

Casting a Title

Finally, even in the early stages of speech preparation, you may wish to phrase a title for your speech. Casting a working title into words allows you to keep clearly in mind the direction and tone of your speech as you prepare it. Later, it

---

*Your proposition statement may or may not include the reasons—the "because" clauses—which justify its acceptance. You may be better able to specify them once you have gone on to the next step, analyzing the audience.

becomes a sort of label for the speech, something announced ahead of time, perhaps, in advertisements or in a chairperson's opening remarks. Hence, the title is a kind of advertising slogan—a catchword, phrase, or brief statement which epitomizes the subject and spirit of the speech in an attractive or provocative form. When Ernest A. Jones, president of McManus, John & Adams, Inc., discussed the effects of advertising techniques in influencing the consumer's buying habits, he titled his speech "The Man with the Split-Level Head." A college student used the title "The Eleventh Commandment" for a speech denouncing our modern-day tendency to condone crime in high places.

What, then, are the requirements of a good title? There are at least three: it should be relevant; it should be provocative; it should be brief. To be *relevant*, a title must be pertinent to the subject or to some part of the speaker's discussion of it. The relevancy of the title "The Eleventh Commandment" was made clear when the speaker pointed out that the commandment "Thou shalt not steal" had been supplemented by a new one, the eleventh, "Thou shalt not get caught." Notice that this title is not a prosaic restatement of the subject, and it is clearly pertinent to the idea the speaker seeks to communicate. Make sure your title does not mislead.

A *provocative* title is one that makes the audience sit up and listen. Sometimes the subject of the speech itself is of such compelling interest that a mere statement of it is provocative enough. In most instances, however, you must find a more vivid or unusual phrasing. At the same time, you must take care not to give away the entire content or message of your speech in the title. Especially if the audience is hostile to your purpose, you must avoid wording your title in a way that makes the purpose too obvious. To entitle a speech for a women's political group "Down with the ERA" is provocative, but unlikely to gain a fair hearing.

Finally, the title of a speech should be *brief and simple*. Imagine the effect of announcing as a title "The Effects on Non-Target Classmates of a Deviant Student's Power and Response to a Teacher-Exerted Technique." Such a title can only be excused when the discussion is a technical one to be presented before a professional audience that has a specialized interest in the subject. In circumstances of that nature, the precise statement of the subject matter may be important. Even so, the title should be as short and simple as possible.

Once you have completed the preparation of your speech, of course, you may adjust your announced title. But, in the meantime, your working title will have kept your mind focused on your purposes and your audience's expected responses.

Selecting Subjects and Purposes: Determining Factors

If you think of public speaking as terminating in specific mental or behavioral responses from others, and if you think about the selection processes we have reviewed in this chapter as helping you specify those responses concretely, you will realize that you have many conscious decisions to make even in these early stages of speech preparation. By way of summary, let us review some of the factors that will determine the actual decisions you must make:

Your private or ultimate aim as a speaker • Your own interests and abilities must be taken into account as you select subjects and purposes. Few of us can talk convincingly about something we have no interest in; few of us dare move into specialized areas where members of the audience are likely to be more expert than we are. Furthermore, at times we must think through carefully how much we are personally willing to risk in front of others. For example, suppose you work for a firm which, you are convinced, is patently sexist in its promotional policies—it seldom promotes women to managerial positions. You find you are given a chance to talk about promotions at an open meeting of the firm: How far

OVERT-COVERT PURPOSE OF SPEECH

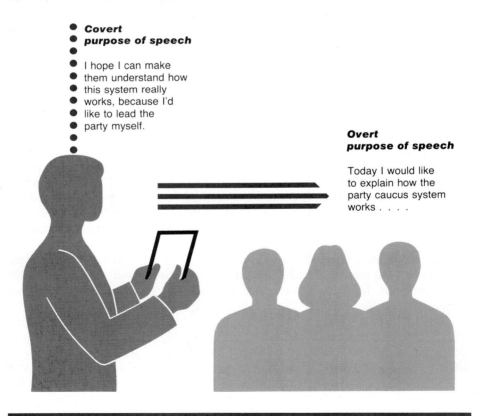

Covert
purpose of speech

I hope I can make them understand how this system really works, because I'd like to lead the party myself.

Overt
purpose of speech

Today I would like to explain how the party caucus system works . . . .

do you go? And what do you say? Your *private aim* may be one of ventilation—getting some ideas and feelings off your chest. Your *ultimate aim*, however, is to get some women—perhaps even yourself—into managerial positions. A harangue on the evils of sexism, replete with threats to report the firm to an equal opportunity agency, might satisfy your private aim, but of course it might well frustrate your ultimate aim by hardening others' resistance to change.[2] Thus, after thinking through the situation, you might decide on a less risky course—say, an informative speech the specific purpose of which is to present a review of numbers of males and females promoted to managerial positions in the firm over the last ten years. You could also point out the number of females presumably ready for promotion within the company and discuss the "head-hunting" agencies which keep records of females interested in managerial positions in firms such as yours. Casting your speech as an "informative" rather than an "actuative" speech urging a strong course of action would allow you to unite your private and ultimate aims.

The authority of the listeners or their capacity to act • For a speaker to demand of a group of students that they "abolish all required courses" would be foolish if the final decision concerning course requirements is in the hands of the faculty. The audience is better advised to take actions within its range of capacities: "Conduct a college-wide survey of student attitudes toward required courses, and present the results of that survey at the next appropriate faculty meeting." As a speaker, limit your specific purposes and propositions to behaviors that are clearly within the domain of your listeners' authority. Asking more will only frustrate them.

The existing attitudes of the listeners • A group of striking workers who believe they are badly underpaid and unfairly treated by their employer probably would be hostile to the suggestion that they return to work under the existing conditions. They might, however, approve submitting the dispute to arbitration by a disinterested person whose fairness and judgment they respect. If you are speaking to an audience whose attitude is hostile to your point of view, you might—by presenting only one speech—convince your listeners that there is something to be said on the other side of the question; but you would probably find it impossible to persuade them to take positive action on it. Your specific purpose, in short, must be adjusted not only to the authority but also to the attitudes of your listeners. Do not ask them for a response you cannot reasonably expect from persons holding their particular feelings or beliefs.

The nature of the speech occasion • To ask people to contribute money to a political campaign fund might be appropriate at a pre-election rally, but to pursue this specific purpose at a memorial service would be decidedly out of place. An athletic awards ceremony is hardly the occasion on which to seek an understanding of how a catalytic converter works. The members of a little theater association would not want to engage in a discussion of finances between the acts

A group of schoolchildren visiting an art museum is listening to a talk on ancient pottery presented by an expert in the field. By gearing the information to a level that the children can easily understand, she is meeting the nature of the speech occasion.

of a play, though they might respond to a brief announcement urging their attendance at a business meeting where the budget will be discussed. Be sure that your specific purpose is adapted to the mood or spirit of the occasion on which you are to speak.

The time limits of the speech • You may be able in a few minutes to induce an audience that opposes your proposal to postpone action until a later time, but you almost certainly will need a much longer time if you hope to change your listeners' feelings and convictions enough to favor your position. Similarly, if your subject is complex, you may be able to inform your hearers, to get them to understand your proposal, in a fifteen-minute speech; but you may need much more time to convince them of its desirability. Do not attempt to get from your audience a response or outcome impossible to attain in the time available.

When you have selected your subject or aspect of your subject and have determined your general and specific purposes on the basis of the five foregoing factors, your speech preparation will be off to a sound start. You will have a central idea or proposition firmly phrased, and hence will be ready to gather your actual materials and to assemble them in ways relevant to yourself, your audience, and the occasion. You will have in hand some yardsticks against which you can measure ideas and materials which come to mind as you research your topic. Finally, you will have increased your self-confidence considerably—you will know better what you are trying to do and how you can go about it. Knowing those "whats" and "hows" will make you feel more secure in your speech preparation skills.

Subject Categories: Aids to Choosing Speech Topics

When you give speeches, especially in your speech class, we suggest that you study the list of subject categories. These categories are not speech subjects; rather, they are *types or classes of material in which speech subjects may be found.* To decide on a suitable subject for a public speech, consider them in terms of your own interests and knowledge, the interests of your audience, and the nature of the occasion on which you are to speak. A list of subject categories and possible topics is on pages 76–77.

REFERENCE NOTES

[1]It can be argued that all speeches are persuasive because, presumably, *any* change in a person's stock of knowledge, beliefs, attitudes, or ways of acting, represents a kind of adjustment of the human mechanism we can term the result of "persuasion," as long as symbols were used to produce the change. See, for example, Kenneth E. Andersen, *Persuasion: Theory and Practice,* 2nd ed. (Boston: Allyn and Bacon, Inc., 1978), Chapter 1, "The Nature of Persuasion." Psychologically, it may be impossible to separate "informative" and "persuasive" messages. Rhetorically, however, that is, in terms of types of speeches, kinds of responses desired, and even kinds of strategies employed, we can separate informative and persuasive speaking. Hence, you will find separate chapters devoted to each later in this book.

[2]Theoretically, this "hardening" process can be explained by any number of psychological models. Within consistency theory (propounded by Percy Tannenbaum and his associates), we would say that any message that is inconsistent or "discrepant" with a person's other beliefs will cause that person to react negatively to it. What is called dissonance theory (offered by Leon Festinger and his colleagues) explains the hardening by arguing that when two perceptions clash explicitly, a person goes into a state of dissonance or "disharmony"; and, because we all prefer to be in a state of consonance or harmony, we must find some way of reducing the psychological pressure. Thus, we discredit the source of the message or the "facts" undergirding it. Similarly, work done by Muzafer Sherif and others at the University of Oklahoma stress individuals' "latitudes of acceptance" and "latitudes of rejection." They have shown that each of us can tolerate rather easily certain amounts of information and certain expressions of attitudes counter to our own—but that we all have limits. Appeals to beliefs or attitudes or actions which represent relatively "small" adjustments—i.e., fall within our latitudes of acceptance—are likely to be successful; but appeals that fall well outside our acceptable limits—within our latitudes of rejection—are likely to make us stronger than ever in our resistance to those ideas or actions. On topics where we have little information or little direct involvement, our latitudes of acceptance are very "wide," but on other topics where we think we know a lot and where we have strong opinions, those latitudes can be very, very, "narrow." Part of your job as an analyst of an audience, therefore, is to gauge the degree of information and commitment of the auditors.

For reviews of these and other psychological explanations of hardening processes, see R. P. Abelson et al., ed., *Theories of Cognitive Consistency: A Sourcebook* (Chicago: Rand McNally, 1968); G. Lindzey and E. Aronson, ed., *The Handbook of Social Psychology,* 2nd ed., Vol. 1 (Reading, MA: Addison-Wesley, 1968), esp. R. B. Zajonc, "Cognitive Theories in Social Psychology," pp. 320–411. For more applicative discussions, see Herbert W. Simons, *Persuasion; Understanding, Practice, and Analysis* (Reading, MA: Addison-Wesley Pub. Co., 1976), Chapter 5, "Behavioral Theories of Persuasion," and Erwin P. Bettinghaus, *Persuasive Communication,* 3rd ed. (New York: Holt, Rinehart and Winston, 1980), esp. pp. 37–49.

SUBJECT CATEGORIES

Aids to Choosing Speech Topics

The beginning speaker often has difficulty in selecting a suitable speech subject. If you find yourself in this situation, we suggest that you study the following list of subject categories. These categories are not speech subjects; rather, they are *types or classes of material in which speech subjects may be found.* To decide upon a suitable subject for a public speech, consider them in terms of your own interests and knowledge, the interests of your audience, and the nature of the occasion on which you are to speak.

Personal Experience

1. Jobs you have held.
2. Places you have been.
3. Military service.
4. The region you come from.
5. Schools you have attended.
6. Friends and enemies.
7. Relatives you like— and dislike.
8. Hobbies and pastimes.

Foreign Affairs

1. Foreign-policy aims.
   – *What they are.*
   – *What they should be.*
2. The implementation of policy aims.
3. Ethics of foreign-policy decisions.
4. History of the foreign policy of the United States (or of some other nation.)
5. Responsibility for our foreign policy.
6. How foreign policy affects domestic policy.
7. War as an instrument of national policy.
8. International peace-keeping machinery.

Domestic Affairs

1. Social problems.
   – *Crime.*
   – *The family: marriage, divorce, adjustments.*
   – *Problems of cities.*
   – *Problems of rural areas.*
   – *Problems of races and ethnic groups.*
   – *Problems of juveniles or the aged.*
   – *Traffic accidents.*
   – *Abortion.*
   – *The drug culture.*
   – *Sex mores.*
   – *Pollution.*
2. Economic problems.
   – *Federal fiscal policy.*
   – *Economically deprived persons and areas.*
   – *Fiscal problems of state and local governments.*
   – *Taxes and tax policies.*
   – *Inflation and price controls.*
   – *International monetary affairs.*
   – *Energy.*
3. Political problems.
   – *Powers and obligations of the federal government.*
   – *Relations between the federal government and the states.*
   – *Problems of state and local governments.*
   – *Parties, campaigns, and nominating procedures.*
   – *The courts Delays in justice. The jury system.*
   – *Congress versus the President.*
   – *Careers in government.*

The Arts

1. Painting music, sculpture.
2. Literature and criticism.
3. Theater, cinema, and dance.
4. Government support of the arts.
5. The artist as a person.
6. History of an art form.
7. Censorship of the arts.
8. Folk arts.

Education

1. Proper aims of education.
2. Recent advances in methods and teaching materials.
3. The federal government and education.
4. Courses and requirements.
5. Grades and grading.
6. Athletics.
7. Extracurricular activities.
8. Meeting the demand for education.
9. Fraternities.
10. Student marriages.
11. Students' role in educational decision making.
12. Parietal rules.
13. Alternatives to college.

Mass Media

1. Radio, television, and film.
2. The press.
3. Use of mass media for propaganda purposes at home or abroad.
4. Censorship of mass media.
   - *To protect public morals.*
   - *For national security.*
5. Advances in media technology.
6. Effects on children.
7. Cable television (CATV).
8. Employment opportunities.

Science

1. Recent advances in a particular branch of science.
2. Science as method.
3. Pure versus applied research.
4. Government support of science.
5. History of science.
6. Science and religion.
7. Careers in science.

Business and Labor

1. Unions.
   - *Regulation of unions.*
   - *"Right-to-work" laws.*
2. Government regulation of business.
3. Ethical standards of business practice.
4. Advertising in the modern world.
5. Training for business.
6. Careers in business.
7. Blue-collar and white-collar status.
8. A guaranteed lifetime income.
9. Portable pensions.

Persistent Concerns

1. "The good life"—what and how.
2. Man and God.
3. Beauty.
4. The ideal society.
5. Life-style—what it is and how to develop it.
6. Parents and children.
7. The tests of truth.
8. Love.
9. Discovering one's self.

PROBLEMS AND PROBES

CHAPTER REPORT   Go through three recent issues of *Vital Speeches of the Day,* and record the titles of the speeches you find. Arrange the titles in three columns, "dull," "incomprehensible," and "provocative." Think about your reasons for assigning each title to one of those columns, and write an essay on the topic, "Strategies for Wording Titles."

1.   This chapter makes clear that for each speech, the speaker must take *occasion* into account. Consider your "classroom occasion"—the room itself, your classmates, and your instructor. How will you decide on your speech topic? You might send around a brief questionnaire asking other students where they stand on several issues that are important to you. Your classmates' answers will give you a composite of their interests. This should help you to decide what your general purpose in speaking might be as well as your specific purpose. (For example, if most of your classmates are already engaged in a daily exercise program, you probably would not want to make a speech to convince them they should begin exercising.)

2.   You and several other members of your class should attend a speech on campus or in the community. As you listen to the speech, try to assess the following elements:

   a. the speaker's general purpose, probable specific purposes, and central idea or proposition;

   b. the major ideas of the speech; and

   c. the speaker's attempts to use factual and authoritative materials gathered with this particular audience in mind. Later, discuss your findings with other members attending the session. Compare your judgments and try to explain any differences of opinion.

3.   If you are having difficulty finding topics that interest you, try a few of these remedies:

   a. Write to the Phil Donahue Show for a copy of available transcripts from recent programs. You may be surprised to find how many timely topics have been aired on television. A copy of Donahue transcripts may be obtained by writing to: Donahue Transcripts, Dept. A, P.O. Box 2111, Cincinnati, Ohio 45201.

   b. Go to the library or a bookstore which offers several different kinds of magazines. Browse through a magazine with which you are not familiar. With what issues does the magazine deal and how do you feel about them? Read the "letters to the editor" section; what kind of issues affect the readers and what is your reaction?

   c. Another way to find topics of interest is to browse through a magazine which espouses a different political viewpoint than you do. For example, if you are politically conservative, leaf through *The Nation;* if you are politically liberal, read *The National Review.* Note your reactions. With what positions expressed by these journals would you like to take exception?

   d. Think of the last time you had a discussion with friends that concerned issues of the day. What was your viewpoint? Was most of what you offered "off the top of your head"? Was it intended to inform, or to persuade? Which topics of conversation most inspire you to offer your opinions?

e. Sit in a crowded restaurant, on a bus, in a bus station, or other places where people might gather for conversation. Take your journal along. Listen to conversations just long enough to get the gist of what is being discussed. Which topics stirred you enough to wish you could join in? Make a note in your journal about which topics most interested you.

4. Using the listening skills that you learned from Chapter 2, listen to a radio news magazine such as National Public Radio's "All Things Considered." (Check your local public radio station for time.) Even if you haven't listened much to news radio, you should find that All Things Considered's way of giving in-depth news reports interesting. Listen to at least one night's news. Take notes during the broadcast. See if you can report to someone else what you heard. In your journal, note your listening problem areas.

ORAL ACTIVITIES

1. Deliver a short impromptu speech on a topic that concerns you. Your instructor will allow a question and comment period from your listeners so that you may see which areas of your topic are of most interest to your audience.

2. Can you think of topics which might be considered as inappropriate subject matter for presentation in this class? Spend a few minutes of class discussion exploring objections to these topics.

3. What topics that interest you are most likely to appeal to your listeners? To be considered controversial by your classmates? List at least five different subjects on which it might be appropriate to give a speech to inform. Do the same for speeches to persuade and to actuate. Meet in small groups with four or five other classmates and share topics. Discuss among yourselves the relevancy and interest level of these subjects. A reporter from each group should report the findings to the entire class. Note in your journal the reactions of your classmates to your list of topics.

SUGGESTIONS FOR FURTHER READING

Bruce E. Gronbeck, *The Articulate Person: A Guide to Everyday Public Speaking* (Glenview, IL: Scott, Foresman and Company, 1979), Chapter 2, "Building the Speech."

Jim D. Hughey and Arlee W. Johnson, *Speech Communication: Foundations and Challenges* (New York: Macmillan Publishing Company, Inc., 1975), Unit 5, "Communicative Purposes."

Robert C. Jeffrey and Owen Peterson, *Speech: A Text With Adapted Readings,* 3rd ed. (New York: Harper & Row, Publishers, 1980), Chapter 3, "The Speaker's Attitude and Purpose."

Brent D. Peterson, Noel D. White, and Eric G. Stephan, *Speak Easy: An Introduction to Public Speaking* (St. Paul: West Publishing Company, 1980), Chapter 3, "Selecting A Topic and Purpose."

Anita Taylor, *Speaking in Public* (Englewood Cliffs, N.J.: Prentice-Hall, Inc., 1979), Chapter 6, "Preparing: The Key to Successful Speeches."

5

Analyzing the Aud
and the Occasion

Effective communication is *audience centered*. As a speak
tive in a communicative transaction when you have s
structive, or persuasive to say. Your speeches will onl
ideas have power if the audience accepts you as someoɪ
your central idea or proposition as a concept worth acce
of course, that you must say only what others already
then intellectual, mental, or behavioral changes would
Rather, you need to find ways to adapt your argument
tions, to fit your perceptions of the world into frames
appreciate. The nature of the audience and the occasion
your selection of the subject matter and specific purpo
the kinds of supporting materials marshalled, the pat
ideas, the language you choose, and the modes of voc
you employ. In this chapter—the third step in the spee
we will examine the factors to be considered as you anaɪ
ence for whom you are designing the speech and the oc
to offer it.

Analyzing the Audience

In an important sense, the concept of *audience* is an im
reality there is no such entity. Each person sitting in an ;
ual; and no matter how people are crowded together
reached electronically by a message, they never lose
while the place of individuality in communication events
attention of late, as a public speaker you are often force
tives of people do have some degree of homogeneity, o

do exist. The concept allows you to think analytically about the collective backgrounds and psychological states of your listeners, and to form useful generalizations about ways audiences probably will behave when confronted with certain messages.

What kinds of generalizations about the backgrounds and personalities of audiences are warranted? Although we do not as yet have definitive answers to this question, thanks to extensive research we do have a considerable body of information concerning audience behavior. When you combine this social-scientific research with common sense, examples from great communicative events of the past, and personal experience, you can improve considerably your abilities to analyze audiences.

The process of analyzing audiences, for most of us, involves the "reading" of two sorts of clues. One set of clues derives from *readily observable* aspects of people—the number of people in the audience, the range of ages represented in the group, their sex, their relative amount of education, groups to which the individuals might belong, and even their cultural or ethnic backgrounds. A second set is comprised of things you can find out about their psychological tendencies. What audience members generally believe in, their attitudes toward particular ideas, people, and events, and the general values they hold dear often are difficult to discover precisely. Nevertheless, these sorts of *psychological inferences* can help you immensely as you construct specific appeals to support central ideas and propositions. Let us examine each set of clues separately, even though they tend to be interdependent in real life.

Composition of the Audience

How can you go about analyzing an audience? You can begin by thinking through everything you already know about it. That thought process, in turn, may be supplemented by talking with the people who are planning the program, with specific members of your audience, and with others who have addressed the group before. In addition, thanks to two generations of social-psychological research, you can begin the process of analysis with certain generalizations in mind. As with all generalizations, however, while they often hold true there are always exceptions, and the generalizations that follow should be thought of as guides to help you examine particular audiences. In essence, they tell you "where" to look, or "what" to consider investigating, as you prepare to probe a group of listeners.[1] We suggest you begin your probing by examining the size, age, sex, education, group memberships, and cultural and ethnic backgrounds which characterize your audience.

Size • In general, the larger the audience, the more heterogeneous or dissimilar its constituent parts, and hence the more diverse its collective beliefs, attitudes, and values. Bearing upon the size factor are these two useful generalizations:

1. *The larger the audience, the more general and comprehensive your appeals may have to be.* If you are offering a list of reasons why an audience should take

The nursing students in this classroom might be considered a "captive audience." The fact that their educational backgrounds are similar makes it easier for the instructor to gear her message to the appropriate level of language and complexity.

action, for larger audiences you must attempt to make those reasons more abstract. For example, the ads in mass-circulation magazines such as *Reader's Digest* have much more general appeal than ads in smaller-circulation magazines such as *Ms.* (women's market), *Popular Mechanics* (men's market), or *Humpty Dumpty* (children's market).

2. *The larger the audience, the more you may need to create sub-audiences.* If, in a given situation, making your appeals general and abstract will weaken their impact, try analyzing your audience in terms of smaller sub-audiences or sub-groups. Proponents of abortion reform, for example, when confronting a large and diverse audience, often direct specific arguments to specific segments of that audience, telling *women* that they have a right to control their own bodies, *religious people* that they have no right to dictate their beliefs to others, *humanitarians* that they ought to relieve the suffering which results from population explosions, and *cost-minded auditors* that abortion reform is cheaper than expansion of social services. A barrage of such different appeals arises from attempts to analyze an audience in terms of sub-groups, each having a strong and readily identifiable vested interest, and each of which may frequently overlap the interest of some other sub-audience.

Age • Ever since Aristotle described the behavioral patterns of young, middle-aged, and old men, there has been a continuing recognition that a person's age affects the way he or she receives messages.[2] Although the age factor in communication has not been fully investigated, enough has been done to suggest a few generalizations useful in analyzing audiences.[3]

1. *People's interests vary with age.* In matters of government, for example, younger people as a group are generally more isolationist than older people. Those in their forties and fifties are especially concerned with taxes, business, and the economy; and older persons are more interested in pensions, medicare, and the availability of social services.

2. *Middle-aged people generally are less self-centered than either younger or older people.* The young, it would seem, are seeking a place in society, and the elderly are watching their group ties deteriorate; hence, both groups are especially susceptible to appeals addressed to the well-being, satisfaction, and security of the self.

3. *People tend to grow more cautious with age.* This tendency is reflected in their buying and living habits, their social and political attitudes, and the degree to which they are open to innovation.

4. *People's social-political activism varies with age.* Across the U.S. population, for example, the least active voters are those in the 18-24 age bracket; the most active, 45-54. The speaker delivering an actuative speech to both young and old simultaneously has an especially difficult task.

5. *Older people are more conservative and pessimistic than younger people.* Generally, according to today's social scientists, older persons seem less willing than the young to believe in humanity's ability to solve the world's problems. This finding reflects an observation Aristotle made over 2000 years ago. "The old," he said, "have lived long, have been often deceived, have made many mistakes of their own; they see that more often than not the affairs of men turn out badly. And so they are positive about nothing; in all things they err by an extreme moderation. They 'think'—they never 'know.' "[4]

Sex • The extent to which a speaker can use gender as a basis for analyzing an audience is difficult to assess. The question of whether intellectual, attitudinal, and behavioral differences between men and women are genetically, biologically, or culturally derived is much discussed these days. As the rise of feminist consciousness in our society suggests, these differences are increasingly attributed to *cultural conditioning.* Therefore, as our cultural attitudes toward male and female roles change—and they have been changing rapidly since the mid-1960s—so must our analysis of gender as an audience factor affecting public speakers and their reception.

A good deal of research through the 1950s and 1960s, for example, documented a series of sex-based generalizations: (1) Women are more persuasible than men; (2) Women seem more susceptible to group pressures than do men; (3) Women have greater humanitarian concern than men; (4) And, in general, social interests of both men and women are governed by the social roles they play. Thus, for example, either the "housewife" or the "househusband" will have the greater interest in children and the home, depending on which of them spends more time in the role of householder.

The development of feminist consciousness in this society, concerted campaigns aimed at undercutting actual and attitudinal sexism, the slow but perceptible progress toward economic and political equality between men and women,

The composition of your audience—their backgrounds, beliefs, attitudes, and values—all are integral aspects in the process of audience analysis.

and the fact that currently one-half of the adult female population of the United States works outside the home—all these social-economic changes have nearly destroyed those four generalizations (except the last one). In their place have come new generalizations: (1) Women, especially (but not exclusively), are highly conscious of *sexist language*—the use of the word "he" when both males and females are being referred to, for example. (Sentences such as "Man has come a long way since he emerged from the caves" are generally taboo.) (2) Likewise, both genders are slowly becoming aware of negative *sex-based stereotyping*—assuming, for example, that women desire marriage more arduously than men do, that women are more emotional than men, that certain occupations are "male" and others are "female." (3) And, we slowly are moving toward an *androgynous society,* one where people are encouraged to possess both kinds of what traditionally have been considered "male" (e.g., tough-mindedness) *and* "female" (e.g., warmth) character traits.[5]

Overall, therefore, it behooves the speaker to find out as much as possible about the individual males and females in a particular audience before accepting either the "traditional" or the "emerging" set of generalizations reviewed here.

Education • As we have suggested, the amount and kind of listeners' education affect how they will react to a message. Specifically:

1. *The greater the education, the less likely the listener is to be affected by outright emotional appeals.* Simply put, well-educated people are more difficult to persuade than less well-educated people.

2. *Well-educated people have more stable, more consistently held beliefs, attitudes, and values than do the less well-educated.* Moreover, when they do change their minds, they are more likely to be influenced by new information. Overall, better-educated people defer more often to verifiable information and arguments rooted in proven factual data, whereas poorly educated persons defer more often to expert judgment and to group pressures.

3. *Educational background affects the listener's (a) desire to keep up with current events; (b) sense of fatalism or pessimism; (c) participation in community affairs; and (d) willingness to express interests, offer opinions, and react from an articulated phi-*

losophy or ideology. Better-educated people usually are more active socially and politically, more often see possible good coming from such activities, and are more willing to talk about their activities than are less well-educated people.

Group membership • Being a member of reference groups, work-related groups, or just plain interest groups influences the way listeners react to public messages. Even though you may feel separated from family or estranged from church, or even though you may think you have outgrown the old high-school gang and neighborhood clique, each of these groups makes unmistakable claims on what you think and how you act. Some of these groups have taught you right from wrong; some, how to resolve puzzling experiences; others, how to greet and get acquainted with strangers, and so on. The influence of experiences you have had with these reference groups, even after you have disassociated yourself from them, lingers on, affecting your behavior in subtle ways.[6] Therefore, when you are analyzing an audience for the purpose of adapting your message effectively, find out first who belongs to which reference group; then try to ascertain what its members do and how they are likely to think and feel about your subject and point of view.

Cultural and ethnic background • Although most of us long ago rejected the notion that races and their sub-groups differ basically, we all recognize that *culturally induced* differences among races, societies, and peoples are facts of social life. To paraphrase Adele Davis, "We are whom we've lived with." Our cultural or ethnic backgrounds not only determine what foods we like and what forms our recreation takes, but, more importantly, what *social rules* we operate by. Because the number of the social rules that affect our thought and behavior is nearly infinite, we cannot begin to list all of those which affect the reception of oral messages. This does not, however, relieve us from our responsibilities as speakers to try to identify and adjust to the social rules—traditions, if you prefer—which may affect our audience.

Given the audience's culture-based backgrounds, are there traditions, expectations, or beliefs that could affect its reception of you and your message? It may be one thing to advocate "mini-parks" in the downtown area of your city to a local Optimist Club and something else to urge that course of action to a meeting of the Chamber of Commerce; Optimist Clubs include people dedicated to civic projects, including beautification and service, whereas Chambers of Commerce tend to represent economically oriented individuals more concerned with economic growth and vitalization than with aesthetics. For a Chamber audience, you probably would have to demonstrate that economic gains could result from spending the money on parks (by attracting more shoppers to the area, for example). Or, if you are a black athlete addressing a predominantly white or predominantly black audience, you might have to adjust the appeals of your speech to the ethnic backgrounds of your audience; old cultural expectations or "images" because of both your race and your avocation might be operating. In other words, thinking about and probing culturally induced social expectations can be crucial as you select ideas and appeals for illustrating or supporting your speech.

Cultural and ethnic background, group affiliation, educational level, sex role, age differential, and audience size—these are the compositional factors that can serve you when you need to know what an audience is like. Recognizing the transitory nature of certain of the generalizations we have made regarding these matters, the tentativeness of others, and the overall caution with which we have advanced them, you will understand that they are intended only as *possible guides* to audience analysis, not an infallible set of rules to be inflexibly applied.

The Audience's Fixed Beliefs and Attitudes

When you turn from such readily observable characteristics of audiences toward more psychologically oriented aspects, your analytical task becomes more complicated. Now you may have to deal with factors of greater complexity and less immediate visibility. One commonly used approach to the task—and the one that we will take—is through listener's beliefs, attitudes, and values.

As soon as children begin to receive impressions of their environment, they start to form opinions and attitudes toward the persons and objects that compose or influence it. These opinions and attitudes may be modified by later experiences; but by the time the infant has grown to adulthood, some of them have become the bases for firmly held beliefs and predictable conduct.

A *belief* may be defined as any proposition or statement which one accepts as true, and which becomes accepted on such bases as evidence, authority, first-hand experience, or faith. An *attitude* can be thought of as a predisposition, based on some set of beliefs, to respond positively or negatively to an idea, person, object, or situation. Thus, statements such as "The Russians are militarily superior to the Americans," "The sun will rise tomorrow," "Henry is six feet tall," and "King George III of England suffered an attack of porphyria in 1788" are beliefs. They are distinguished from other sorts of statements by two characteristics: They are accepted as true, whether they apply to the past, the present, or the future; and they can be supported—or altered—by an appeal to some sort of evidence.* Attitudes, on the other hand, are expressed in such statements as "I prefer raw to cooked carrots," "My dog's better than your dog," "I hate liars," "Killing is immoral," "The Mona Lisa is a beautiful painting," "Stealing is criminal." These statements either articulate a personal preference or

---

*You may notice that we are not using the word "fact" here. That is because in common parlance the word tends to refer only to incontrovertible, specific statements—it refers as much to *your certitude* as it does to your thoughts about the world. So, statements such as "Henry is six feet tall" and "King George III suffered an attack of porphyria in 1788" normally would be called "facts" because they are specific, they represent aspects of the world you can measure or "look up," and because no one probably would dispute them. But, the word "fact" does not apply so well to statements such as "The Russians are militarily superior to the Americans" or "The world is flat," because they are comparatively generalized statements, they are not so easily verified, and they certainly are subject to dispute. Yet, *both* sets of statements, really, are conceptually the same sorts of statements; both include propositions which (a) refer to the world of human affairs, (b) are tested by references to "reality," and (c) are judged to be true or false. Because both sets of statements have so much in common, we will call them both "beliefs" in this book, to avoid confusion.

BELIEFS, ATTITUDES, AND VALUES

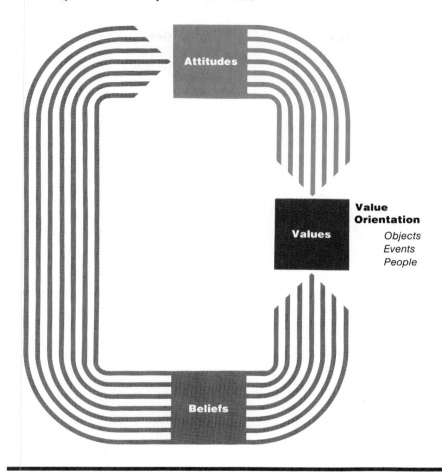

express some sort of social judgment about a class of events, persons, or experiences. They may be characterized by such self-reporting words as 'hate," "like," "prefer," or such judgmental words as "good-bad," "beautiful-ugly," "just-unjust," "right-wrong."[7]

A crucial point to remember about some beliefs and attitudes is that they can be firmly held or *anchored.* If your parents, for example, said over and over through your childhood that "Children should be seen and not heard," and treated you accordingly, you are likely to believe strongly in parental authority, in the importance of not expressing your emotions publicly, and in "good manners" as the basis for all interpersonal relationships. Because you acquired these beliefs and attitudes at a formative period in your life, amidst strong emotional atmospheres, it might be extremely difficult for someone to change your mind on these matters. They are socially anchored, or, as Milton Rokeach would say, "primitive" and hence highly "central" to your self-definition and self-image.[8]

But, by the same token, a speaker could use these beliefs to persuade you. If you have a strong sense of authority, a speaker might convince you to follow the orders from some superior in a firm you were working for; that person, in essence, would be relying on your general respect for authority, a respect you acquired as a youth, hoping you will transfer that respect to a leader in your company, and do your part in the company in the same way you do your part in a family. Fixed beliefs and attitudes, in other words, may be hindrances or they may be powerful springs to compliance and action. We will discuss these matters more in the next chapter, when we consider more specifically motivational appeals to listeners.

Thus, attempting to assess an audience's fixed beliefs and attitudes is an important analytical task, for two reasons: (1) The assessment may help you outline some of the *appeals you can make* within your speech. (2) It allows you to set *realistic expectations* as you plan your talk. Do not try to accomplish too much in a single speech if you know you will run into well-anchored beliefs and attitudes; not all conditions are equally amenable to change through speech communication. In a ten-minute discourse you are not likely to make Republicans out of Democrats, Presbyterians out of Roman Catholics, or libertarians out of authoritarians. But you may well be able to use some of those fixed beliefs and attitudes to produce a moderate amount of change.

The Audience's Values

Because most of us strive for certain sorts of consistency in our lives, it is useful to talk about *values* as general orientations to classes of events, persons, and objects. If, for example, you tend to be a strong advocate of parental authority, you are likely to accept the authority of subject-matter experts, of superiors on the job, of religious leaders, of high-ranking politicians, and the like. If you believe in allowing your children considerable latitude in their lives, you are likely to foster individual initiative on the job or, on an even grander scale, to believe in national self-determination in international relations. These sorts of groupings of beliefs and attitudes we express as generalized values. A *value* may be defined as a relatively abstract conception of the Good or the Desirable as well as the Evil or the Undesirable. Values, because they are "concepts" or "constructs," may be expressed in single words: "honesty," "honor," "efficiency," "humanitarianism," "courage," "prudence," "patriotism," "duty." Or they may be strung together in the form of slogans or mottos: "Liberty, Equality, Fraternity"; "Duty, Honor, Country"; "Law and Order"; "Peace with Honor"; "All Power to the People"; or, a bit more prosaically, "Keep on Truckin'."

Furthermore, we use a variety of labels to characterize what can be termed the *value orientations* of groups within a society. Over the last three decades, for example, Americans have read about the Puritan Ethic, the Establishment, the

Silent Majority, The Counterculture, the Existentialist Stance, Situational Ethics, Freaks, New Politics, the Old Guard, the Button-Down Set, Libbers, Moonies, Rednecks, and Spiro Agnew's infamous Radic-libs.[9]

Value orientations, in other words, represent broad, sweeping concepts (sometimes termed *ideologies*) which members of groups or collectivities apply to basic aspects of life. They can be thought of as clusters or congregations of more specific beliefs and attitudes organized under some general mental category; they are *response tendencies*, that is, concepts which people bring to mind when confronted with certain people, objects, and events. So, for example, in 1975 J. W. Prescott postulated a general value of "bodily pleasure and violence" which he said explained why one group of people whose attitudes he assessed held firmly to the following propositions:

With regard to pain:

1. Harsh physical punishment is good for children who disobey a lot.
2. Capital punishment should be permitted by society.

With regard to sex:

1. Prostitution should be punished by society.
2. Nudity within the family has a harmful influence upon children.
3. Sexual pleasures help build a weak moral character.
4. Abortion is a punishable offense against individuals and society.

With regard to drugs:

1. Alcohol is more satisfying than sex.
2. Drugs are more satisfying than sex.

With regard to politics:

1. Conservatism is better than liberalism.[10]

This study points out that you often cannot simply attack one attitude; because attitudes and beliefs become interlocked with each other, you usually have to deal with the valuative orientation or ideology.

As a communicator whose task it is to understand listeners and to relate harmoniously and productively to them, you need to be highly sensitive to values and value orientations. Unless you recognize the difference that may exist between you and members of your audience and take definite steps to bridge them, you cannot hope to cope effectively with the conflicts and controversies such cultural discrepancies are almost certain to generate. Unless you can discover *common ground* between and among them, you may well be in communicative trouble. Again, our discussion of motivational appeals in Chapter 6 will center on ways to use knowledge you have gained while analyzing an audience's values to construct a potentially effective speech.

The Audience's Attitude Toward the Speaker

The attitude of an audience toward you as a speaker will be based in part upon (a) your known reputation and, in part, upon (b) your behavior during the speech. Regarding your prior reputation, two factors are especially important: (1) the degree of your listeners' *friendliness* toward you, and (2) the degree of their *respect* for you and your knowledge of the subject. The potency of these factors may vary widely. A mother's affection for her small son, for instance, may be very strong; but her respect for her son's judgment may not be. On the other hand, the mother may have the greatest respect for the judgment of a neighbor even though she dislikes her as a person. Respect and friendliness are two different attitudes, but as a speaker you must attempt to take both into account.

As we noted in Chapter 1, when you begin to speak and throughout the entire time you are talking, the audience consciously or subconsciously assesses your credibility from many points of view. Among other things, they ask: (1) Are you a *competent* speaker? Do you give evidence of intelligence and expertise? (2) Are you *admirable?* Do you appear to be a good person? (3) Are you *trustworthy?* Do you seem honest, just, fair, and sincere? (4) Are you *dynamic?* Are you energetic, alert mentally? (5) Are you *courageous?* Do you seem to have strength and firmness? Collectively, these factors point up the need to know your subject thoroughly, to respect your audience, and to deliver your speech with sincerity and vigor.

Currently, as we noted in Chapter 1, much is being written about *communicator style*—a phrase that refers to particular combinations of words used, grammatical sentence structures employed, and "images" or "personae" projected by speakers. An audience's judgment of you can be determined in part by the way it judges your personal style. Opening a speech by saying, "Glad you-all let me come this evening to get down with you," might be adjudged a perfectly suitable introduction for a speech to a class of college sophomores, but it probably would be considered inappropriate—not to mention unintelligible—by a meeting of the Daughters of the American Revolution. The *content* of the greeting, to be sure, would be suitable for any group, but the *style* is likely to produce negative judgments concerning the speaker. You must be sensitive, therefore, to the attitudes an audience forms of you simply by listening to your language choices (or, for example, watching how you stand, use the podium, or dress, as we will see later).[11]

The Audience's Attitude Toward the Subject

Sometimes people are *interested* in a subject; sometimes they are *apathetic* about it. In either case, the orientation of their interests will have considerable impact on their perception of and response to a communication. Some researchers place *prior audience attitude* among the most crucial variables that determine speaking success.[12] If, for instance, the listeners are unfavorably disposed toward the speaker's subject or purpose, they may: (*a*) distort the substance of the message,

(b) psychologically or physically leave the field, (c) discredit the communicator, or (d) use a host of similar defense mechanisms to avoid accurate perception of the speaker's intent and message-content.

An audience may be apathetic or neutral if its members see no connection between the speaker's subject and their own affairs. When your analysis indicates that your listeners will be apathetic, you will need to show them how they are directly concerned with the problem you are discussing; or you will need to arouse their curiosity about some novel aspect of the subject. Use all available means for holding and involving their attention. (See pages 151–156.) Even when the members of your audience are already interested, you cannot neglect entirely the problems of commanding and holding attention; but when your listeners are apathetic, you must make a special effort to retain their interest.

Interest (or the lack of it) is only one aspect of an audience's attitude toward your subject. *Expectancy* is another. For example, as soon as we hear that a speech will be about the Gay Lib movement, many of us begin to form favorable or unfavorable attitudes toward the speaker and the subject. As a general rule, the more the listeners know about your subject or the stronger the beliefs they hold concerning it, the more likely they are to have well-defined expectations. These expectations may be troublesome, for frequently they operate as listening barriers or as filters which distort the meanings that the audience assigns to your message. The introduction of your speech presents a special opportunity to create or to correct these audience expectations. All the time you are talking, however, you should bear in mind the problem of listener expectation, and make adaptations accordingly.

The Audience's Attitude Toward the Speech Purpose

If, with no preliminaries at all, you told the members of your audience the specific purpose of your speech, what would be their reaction or response? This "attitude toward speech purpose" is not the frame of mind you hope your audience will hold at the end of your speech; it is the one that exists *before you begin*. Since audience predisposition is seldom uniform, many different shades of attitude may be represented. It is best, therefore, to determine—by prior analysis— what attitude is *predominant* and to adapt your speech to that view while making allowances for variations in the character or intensity of listener belief.

When the general end of your speech is *to inform*, the attitude of your listeners toward the speech purpose will be governed largely by their attitude toward the subject, that is:

    (a) interested, or   (b) apathetic.

When your general purpose is *to persuade*, the listeners' attitude toward the speech purpose will be governed also by their attitude toward the specific belief or action which is urged; hence, their attitude will be one of the following:

    (a) favorable but not aroused;
    (b) apathetic to the situation;
    (c) interested in the situation but undecided what to do or think about it;

This park ranger is conducting a nature tour of visitors to a National Park. His audience is composed of persons of diverse backgrounds and ages. Therefore the information he presents should be of a general nature and his explanations kept at a general level that all his listeners can understand.

(d) interested in the situation but hostile to the *proposed* attitude, belief, or action; or

(e) hostile to any change from the present state of affairs.[13]

Determining the predominant attitude of your audience toward your subject and purpose should guide you in selecting your arguments and developing the structure and content of your message. If your listeners are apathetic, begin your speech on a point of compelling interest or startling vividness. Show them how your subject affects them. If they are hostile to the proposal, you may wish to introduce it more cautiously, emphasize some basic principle with which you know they agree, and relate your proposal to it. If they are interested but undecided, provide plenty of proof in the form of factual illustrations, testimony, and statistics. If they are favorable but not aroused, try to motivate them by using appeals that touch directly their desires for pleasure, independence, power, creativity, ego-satisfaction, and the like.

No analysis of an audience made prior to a speech is certain to be fully correct, and even if it is, audience attitudes may shift even while you are speaking.[14] Hence, you must watch listeners' reactions closely when your subject is announced and continue to do so throughout your entire speech. The way your hearers sit in their seats, the expressions on their faces, their audible reactions—laughter, applause, shifting about, whispering—all are clues to their attitude toward you, your subject, or your purpose. The conscientious communicator develops a keen awareness of these signs of *feedback* on the part of the audience and adapts his or her remarks accordingly.[15]

Analyzing the Speech Occasion

To this point, we have emphasized the necessity of analyzing the audience for whom your speech is designed. An equally important aspect of your preparation is an analysis of the occasion on which you will be speaking. Indeed, aspects of the two are usually inseparable. In making such an analysis, you should consider carefully a series of key variables: The nature of the occasion, the prevailing rules, the physical conditions, and events preceding or following your speech.

The Nature and Purpose of the Occasion

Is yours a voluntary or a captive audience? A voluntary audience attends a speechmaking event primarily because of interest in the speaker or the subject. A captive audience is required to attend, perhaps at the explicit instruction of the boss or under threat of a failing grade in a course. In general, the more "captive" your audience, the less initial interest they will show and the greater will be their resistance to accepting your information or point of view.

Are people interested in learning more about your subject, in taking some positive action concerning it, or have they perhaps come to heckle or embarrass you? Are your subject and purpose in line with the reason for the meeting, or are you merely seizing the occasion to present some ideas you think important? Are you one in a series of speakers whom the audience has heard over a period of weeks or months? If so, how does your speech subject relate to those subjects which have been previously presented? These are important questions you will need to answer when you are analyzing the nature and purpose of the occasion.

In other words, the nature and purpose of the occasion—as well as the interest level you can sense among those attending it—often dictate a series of general decisions you will make in your approach to the speech transactions. On some occasions, you will deliver a formal address, on others, an informal talk. On some, you will be well advised merely to offer some new information, on others you will be expected to take firm stands on public policies. And there may be occasions when you will discuss only a narrow aspect of some topic because other people are treating other aspects.

The Prevailing Rules or Customs

Will there be a regular order of business or a fixed program into which your speech must fit? Is it the custom of the group to ask questions of the speaker after the address? Do the listeners expect a formal or informal speaking manner? Will you, as the speaker, be expected to extend complimentary remarks, or to express respect for some tradition or concept? Knowing the answers to these questions will help you avoid feeling out of place and will prevent you from arousing antagonism by some inappropriate word or action.

In addition to probing the general customs prevailing in some group, you may need to go a step further by discovering specific "rules" for formulating your messages. If you are delivering a report on some research you have undertaken, you will be expected to review the research of others on your topic before you discuss your own study. A member of the U.S. Senate must always refer to an opponent as "The Honorable Senator from Tennessee" even if he or she is going to disagree violently with that person. The speaker at the Friars' Club of New York is expected to mercilessly but good naturedly excoriate the person who is the object of that evening's "roast." One part of your task of understanding *communication rules*, therefore, is a matter of analyzing with specificity the customs and traditions governing particular audiences in particular places.

The Physical Conditions

Will your speech be given out-of-doors or in an auditorium? Is the weather likely to be hot or cold? Will the audience be sitting or standing; and, if sitting, will the members be crowded together or scattered about? In how large a room will the speech be presented? Will an electronic public-address system be used? Will facilities be provided for the audiovisual reinforcements you will use, or must you bring your own? Will you be seen and heard easily? Are there likely to be disturbances in the form of noise or interruptions from the outside? These and similar environmental factors affect the temper of the audience, their span of attention, and the style of speaking you will have to employ as you make adjustments to the speech environment or situation.

Events Preceding or Following Your Speech

At what time of day or night will your speech be given? Immediately after a heavy meal or a long program, both of which may induce drowsiness and reduce listener interest? Just before the principal address or event of the evening? By whom and in what manner will you be introduced to the audience? What other items are on the program? What are their tone and character? All these things will, of course, influence the interest the audience may have in your speech. In some instances, you will be able to use the other events on the program to increase interest or belief in your own remarks; sometimes they will work against you. In any case, you must always consider the effect which the program as a whole may have on your speech.

In summary, "occasions" represent a constellation of audience expectations governed by the fact that all societies "set apart" certain spaces and certain events for listening to particular kinds of speeches from particular sorts of speakers.[16] That "set-apartness" often takes the form of communication rules—rules you are expected to follow if you are to be judged a "competent" and "appropriate" messenger. As we noted in Chapter 1, you may well feel constrained to violate those rules upon occasion, in order to shake a group out of its complacency and lethargy, in order to feel better about yourself by upbraiding a group to whose standards you have too long conformed. When you are moved to violate norms of tradition, civility, or custom, remember you do so at some risk. You, and you alone, will have to decide whether the risk is worth it. You might be physically removed from the group, as is the child who screams in the middle of a wedding ceremony. Or your boldness might be rewarded, as was Representative Barbara Jordan when, during the 1976 Democratic National Convention in a keynote speech, she castigated rather than complimented the delegates for their false sense of unity and commitment. (See her speech on p. 378.) The risk is yours, and must be taken only after a careful assessment of yourself, your audience, and the occasion.

A Sample Analysis of an Audience and an Occasion

In this chapter we have surveyed what is perhaps a dizzying array of choices you must make as you analyze your audience and occasion. Those choices, however, will sort themselves out if you work systematically, trying to make them one step at a time. Observe how one student analyzed her audience as she prepared a speech on behalf of an intercollegiate athletic program for women. Notice how she used the facts at her disposal to draw a picture of the persons making up her audience, and how she planned to adapt her remarks to their concerns and attitudes:

I. *Title:* FROM SPECTATOR TO PARTICIPANT: ATHLETICS FOR WOMEN.

II. *Subject:* Intercollegiate Athletic Competition for Women Students.

III. *General Purpose:* To actuate.

IV. *Specific Purpose:* To get the Board in Charge of Intercollegiate Athletics to institute a program of intercollegiate sports for women students.

V. *Specific Audience:* The Board in Charge of Intercollegiate Athletics, consisting of the Director of Athletics, the Assistant Director of Athletics, Director of Men's Intramural Sports, Director of Women's Intramural Sports, six coaches of men's varsity sports, five elected faculty members, and five elected student representatives. One intramural director, one faculty member, and one student representative are women.

VI. *Analysis of Occasion:*
   A. *Nature:* Annual meeting of the Board to approve the budget for the coming year.
   B. *Prevailing Rules:* A strict time limit of five minutes for every speech made to the Board, plus any time needed for questions by Board members.
   C. *Precedents and Consequences:* Speech will be given late in the afternoon, after Board has heard many other requests. Board members probably will be tired. After all requests have been heard, the Board will still have to draw up the budget.
   D. *Physical Environment:* Board will meet at tables set up in an auxiliary gymnasium, surrounded by athletic equipment.

VII. *Analysis of Audience:*
  A. *Composition:*
    1. *Size:* Twenty Board members, plus additional spectators.
    2. *Age:* Five members are of college age; fifteen members are between 30 and 55.
    3. *Sex:* Seventeen males, three females.
    4. *Occupation:* Collegiate personnel with special interests and qualifications in athletics.
    5. *Education:* One third were physical education majors in college, most with advanced degrees; one third are undergraduates; one third are Ph.D.'s in arts or sciences.
    6. *Membership in Groups:* All are members of Board as well as of general academic community. The factors influencing both groups can be made salient in the speech.
    7. *Cultural-Ethnic Background:* Two Board members are black (but this not a factor here).
  B. *Knowledge of Subject:* Board members have:
    1. Specialized knowledge of nature of intercollegiate competition in sports.
    2. General knowledge of present women's intramural athletic program.
    3. Probable knowledge of current campus controversy over question of an intercollegiate sports program for women.
  C. *Beliefs, Attitudes, and Values:*
    1. *Political:* Board is undoubtedly aware of general charge of sexism in the athletic program and wishes to avoid politicizing its functions.
    2. *Professional:* Board members believe strongly in values of college athletics generally.
    3. *Economic:* Board undoubtedly is worried about increased cost of intercollegiate athletic program, yet well aware that a portion of its money comes from student fees.
  D. *Attitude Toward Speaker:* Probably suspicious.
  E. *Attitude Toward Subject:* Interest mixed with uneasiness and uncertainty about extent and nature of program to be proposed.
  F. *Attitude Toward Speech Purpose:* Most Board members are probably undecided; a few may be hostile.

VIII. *Proposed Adaptation to Audience and Occasion:*
  A. Introduce speech with thanks for fine intramural program now available to women. Make reference to surrounding facilities and equipment.
  B. Keep language of speech positive, but not so strong as to polarize neutral or undecided listeners.
  C. Stress primarily the values of intercollegiate competition for women. Mention—but with this predominantly male audience, do not overemphasize—the matter of equality between the sexes.
  D. Show a knowledge of the financial problems faced by the Board. Ask only for women's field and track competition for coming year, with more sports to be added later. Demonstrate how maximum participation may be realized at minimum cost.
  E. Be prepared to answer Board's possible questions concerning number of women interested, neighboring schools which could furnish competi-

tion, estimated cost of proposed program, available locker room facilities, equipment, etc.

IX. *Proposition:* "The Board in Charge of Intercollegiate Athletics ought to institute a program of intercollegiate sports for women students because . . ."

At this point, the speaker is ready to think more specifically about the actual content of the speech—particular kinds of material and types of motivational appeals to build into it. We will continue this analysis after reviewing such matters in the next chapter.

REFERENCE NOTES

[1]The following sources enlarge upon our discussion of backgrounds and personalities of audiences: Paul D. Holtzman, *The Psychology of Speakers' Audiences* (Glenview, IL: Scott, Foresman and Co., 1970); Marvin Karlins and Herbert I. Abelson, *Persuasion: How Opinions and Attitudes Are Changed* (New York: Springer Pub. Co., Inc., 1970); Howard H. Martin and C. William Colburn, *Communication and Consensus: An Introduction to Rhetorical Discourse* (San Francisco: Harcourt Brace Jovanovich, 1972); Stephen W. King, *Communication and Social Influence* (Reading, MA: Addison-Wesley Pub. Co., Inc., 1975); C. David Mortensen, *Communication: The Study of Human Interaction* (New York: McGraw-Hill Book Co., 1972); Kenneth E. Andersen, *Persuasion: Theory and Practice*, 2nd ed. (Boston: Allyn and Bacon, Inc., 1978); and the forthcoming Carroll C. Arnold and John Waite Bowers, eds., *Handbook of Rhetorical and Communication Theory* (Boston: Allyn and Bacon, Inc., in press for 1982), esp. the chapter by Gerald Miller, Michael Burgoon, and Judee Burgoon, "The Functions of Communication in Changing Attitudes and Gaining Compliance," which is an excellent research summary.

[2]Aristotle, *Rhetoric*, p. 1389b.

[3]Alfred Hero, "Public Reaction to Government Policy," in John P. Robinson, Jerrold G. Rusk, and Kendra B. Head, *Measures of Political Attitudes* (Ann Arbor: Survey Research Center, Institute of Social Research, 1969); Leonard Broom and Philip Selznick, *Sociology*, 4th ed. (New York: Harper & Row, Publishers, Inc., 1968); James N. Morgan and others, *Productive Americans* (Ann Arbor: Survey Research Center, Institute for Social Research, 1966); Angus Campbell and others, *The American Voter* (New York: John Wiley & Sons, Inc., 1964); A. W. Bowden and others, " 'Halo' Prestige," *Journal of Abnormal and Social Psychology*, 28 (January–March 1934); S. E. Asch, "Studies of Independence and Conformity: A Minority of One Against a Unanimous Majority," *Psychological Monographs*, 70 (1956), No. 9; Janet L. Wolff, *What Makes Women Buy* (New York: McGraw-Hill Book Company, 1958); Theodore M. Newcomb and others, *Social Psychology* (New York: Holt, Rinehart & Winston, Inc., 1965); David Krech and others, *Individual in Society* (New York: McGraw-Hill Book Company, 1962); C. E. Swanson, "Predicting Who Learns Factual Information from the Mass Media," in *Groups, Leadership and Men: Research in Human Relations*, ed. H. Guetzkow (Pittsburgh: Carnegie Institute of Technology Press, 1951); and E. J. Brown, "The Self as Related to Formal Participation in Three Pennsylvania Rural Communities," *Rural Sociology*, 18 (December 1953); all as cited in Howard H. Martin and C. William Colburn, *Communication and Consensus: An Introduction to Rhetorical Discourse* (New York: Harcourt Brace Jovanovich, Inc., 1972), Chapter 4, pp. 74–79.

[4]Aristotle, *Rhetoric*, p. 1389b.

[5]The current amount of research on androgyny being done by psychologists and sociologists prohibits its review here. But, for an introduction to the concept, see. B. Thorne and N. Henley, *Language and Sex: Difference and Dominance* (Rowley, MA: Newbury, 1975).

[6]See Irving L. Janis, *Victims of Groupthink* (Boston: Houghton Mifflin Co., 1972).

[7]These definitions and our general discussion of beliefs and attitudes is based in part on Chapters 2 and 3 of *Beliefs, Attitudes, and Human Affairs,* by Daryl J. Bem.

[8]See Milton M. Rokeach, *Beliefs, Attitudes, and Values: A Theory of Organization and Change* (San Francisco: Jossey-Bass, Inc., 1968), and his *The Nature of Human Values* (New York: Collier-Macmillan, Free Press, 1973). See also Douglas Ehninger and Gerard Hauser, "The Communication of Values," in the forthcoming *Handbook of Rhetorical and Communication Theory* (cited in n. 1).

[9]For discussions of predominant value-orientations in American society, see Robin M. Williams, *American Society: A Sociological Interpretation,* 3rd ed. (New York: Alfred A. Knopf, Inc., 1970), Chapter 11. Williams has analyzed possible shifts in saliency and intensity of his value-orientation categories in his "Changing Value Orientations and Beliefs on the American Scene," in *The Character of Americans: A Book of Readings,* rev. ed., Michael McGiffert, ed. (Homewood, IL: Dorsey Press, 1970), pp. 212–30. The Yankelovich public-opinion survey reported in Otis M. Walter and Robert L. Scott, *Thinking and Speaking: A Guide to Intelligent Oral Communication,* 3rd ed. (New York: The Macmillan Company, 1973), pp. 110–11, indicated that most Americans who were surveyed ascribed to the values of hard work, thrift, strength of character, organized religion, competition, private property, law and order, and compromise as essential for progress. See also Frank E. Armbruster, *The Forgotten Americans: A Survey of the Values, Beliefs and Concerns of the Majority* (New Rochelle, NY: Arlington House, Inc., 1972).

[10]J. W. Prescott, "Body Pleasure and the Origins of Violence," *The Futurist,* 1975, pp. 64–74, as summarized in and modified by Philip G. Zimbardo, Ebbe B. Ebbesen, and Christina Maslach, *Influencing Attitudes and Changing Behavior,* 2nd ed. (Reading, MA: Addison-Wesley Pub. Co., 1977), pp. 51–52.

[11]For an article which summarizes at least some of the research on communication style and development, see Jessie G. Delia and Ruth Anne Clark, "Cognitive Complexity, Social Perception, and The Development of Listener-Adapted Communication in Six-, Eight-, Ten-, and Twelve-Year-Old Boys," *Communication Monographs,* 44 (Nov. 1977), 326–45. Adapting your communication style to others, of course, runs the risk of self-persuasion; you may well change your own mind about ideas as the result of extensive audience adaptation. See Edward M. Bodaken, Timothy G. Plax, Richard N. Piland, and Allen N. Weiner, "Role Enactment as a Socially Relevant Explanation of Self-Persuasion," *Human Communication Research,* 5 (Spring 1979), 203–14.

[12]See, for example, Muzafer Sherif and Carl L. Hovland, *Social Judgment* (New Haven, CT: Yale Univ. Press, 1961).

[13]Traditionally, it has been assumed that audiences hostile to the speaker's proposal or opposed to any change in the existing state of affairs are most difficult to persuade. For qualifications of this point of view, however, see Wayne N. Thompson, *Quantitative Studies in Public Address and Communication* (New York: Random House, Inc., 1967), pp. 38–39.

[14]Such changes during the course of a speech are often dramatic. See Robert D. Brooks and Thomas M. Scheidel, "Speech as Process: A Case Study," *Speech Monographs,* 35 (March 1968), 1–7.

[15]On adapting to feedback, see Paul D. Holtzman (cited in n. 1), pp. 33–36, 117.

[16]The literature on "occasions" is beginning to expand, and promises to be a fruitful area of research. For some samples, see J. C. Faris, " 'Occasions' and 'Non-Occasions,' " in *Rules and Meanings: The Anthropology of Everyday Knowledge,* ed. Mary Douglas (Baltimore: Penguin Books, 1973), pp. 45–59; Edwin Black, "Electing Time," *Quarterly Journal of Speech,* 59 (April 1973), 125–29; Thomas B. Farrell, "Political Conventions as Legitimation Ritual," *Communication Monographs,* 45 (Nov. 1978), 293–305; Bruce E. Gronbeck, "Dramaturgical Theory and Criticism: The State of the Art (or Science?)," *Western Journal of Speech Communication,* 44 (Fall 1980), 315–330. A basic article which should form the heart of all theoretical discussions of occasions is Lloyd Bitzer, "The Rhetorical Situation," *Philosophy and Rhetoric,* 1 (Jan. 1968), 1–14.

PROBLEMS AND PROBES

CHAPTER REPORT The relationships between beliefs/attitudes/values and one's behavior are complex; sometimes, beliefs, attitudes, and values seem to control our behavior, and at other times, our behaviors seem to create within us particular conceptualizations. Read either Leon Festinger's *When Prophecy Fails* or E. H. Schein, I. Schneider, and C. H. Barker's *Coercive Persuasion,* both of which are case studies of beliefs, attitudes, values, and behaviors. Prepare a book report, concentrating upon what they tell you about thought and behavior.

1. Using your journal, study the speaking situation that faces you in your classroom. Begin with an audience analysis. What are the most common elements shared by your class members? In what areas are they most different? Develop a questionnaire that will help you discern less readily observable aspects of your classmates' beliefs, attitudes, and values.

2. Study the occasion of your speaking situation with regard to your classroom. Note the nature and purposes of the occasions on which you will speak. What are the pervading rules and customs you will need to follow? What physical conditions are apparent within the classroom? Try to predict the events that will precede and follow your speech. Make a journal entry of your findings so that you may refer to them during the course of the term.

3. Read or listen to a speech in which the values, beliefs, and attitudes of the listeners are hostile toward the purpose of the speaker. Analyze the speech to ascertain as well as you can how the speaker has endeavored to overcome the hostility or apathy and influence the audience to accept his or her purpose and message.

4. Select a suitable subject and use it to frame a specific purpose for a five-minute speech to persuade *(a)* an audience that is favorable, but not aroused; *(b)* an audience that is interested, but undecided; *(c)* an audience that is apathetic; *(d)* an audience that is hostile toward the proposition or recommendation; and *(e)* an audience that is opposed to any change from the present situation.

5. Immediately (or as soon as possible) after giving a speech, note your audiences' reactions to you *during the course of the speech.* Did they seem attentive? Were there points in your speech where you thought you lost them? Did anyone look bored? What other reactions did you notice?

ORAL ACTIVITIES

1. After your instructor has divided the class into four-person groups, meet with the other members of your group and discuss with them the next round of speeches to be presented: the actual topic you intend to use, your general and specific purpose, development of your idea or proposition, your speech plan or outline, useful kinds of supporting materials. Criticize each other's plans and preparation, offering suggestions for changes and more specific adaptations to this particular classroom audience. After discussing and evaluating the potential of your speech with a portion of your audience, you should be able subsequently to

develop and present a better and more effectively adapted message to the class as a whole.

2.   As a student of speech communication, you can learn something about the principles of audience analysis by observing how such public-opinion pollsters as Dr. George Gallup analyze "the great American audience" to derive the samples on which they base their predictions. Together with several other members of your class (as your instructor may designate), investigate these methods as described in books, magazine articles, and newspaper surveys, and report on them orally, either in individual presentations or in an informal discussion with the class as a whole.

3.   Gather some advertisements (not want ads) and bring them to class. In groups, share your advertisements and see if you can determine the audiences for which they were intended. What needs are the advertisers trying to meet? Are they trying to create needs? What tactics do they use? How effective do you think these tactics are?

 ## SUGGESTIONS FOR FURTHER READING

R. P. Abelson et al., eds., *Theories of Cognitive Consistency: A Sourcebook* (Chicago: Rand McNally, 1968).

Daryl Bem, *Beliefs, Attitudes, and Human Affairs* (Belmont, CA: Brooks/Cole Publishing Co., 1970).

Gary L. Cronkhite, "Perception and Meaning," in *Handbook of Rhetorical and Communication Theory,* ed. Carroll C. Arnold and John Waite Bowers (Boston: Allyn and Bacon, Inc., in press for 1982).

Bruce E. Gronbeck, *The Articulate Person: A Guide to Everyday Public Speaking* (Glenview, IL: Scott, Foresman and Company, 1979), Chapter 10, "Changing Attitudes."

Gerald R. Miller, Michael Burgoon, and Judee Burgoon, "The Functions of Communication in Changing Attitudes and Gaining Compliance," in *Handbook of Rhetorical and Communication Theory,* ed. Carroll C. Arnold and John Waite Bowers (Boston: Allyn and Bacon, Inc., in press for 1982).

6

Determining the Basic Appeals

In the preceding chapter we emphasized the importance of analyzing your audience in order to discover its *social characteristics* and its *cognitive structures*. Who people are, what experiences they have had, and what they believe in all determine how they will respond to your speeches. Equally important, however, in governing these responses are their *motives*—their basic needs or wants or desires. In this chapter we will examine the concept of "motive" as a psychological construct, discuss ways in which speakers can tap people's motivational structures through the use of motivational appeals, and finally, offer you some advice on how (and how not) to use such appeals as you construct speeches.

Motivation and Motive Needs

We may think of a *need* as some desire, want, or uneasiness which individuals sense or think about when considering their own situation. That need may arise from physiological considerations—pain, lack of food, or an uncomfortable room—and it may come about for sociocultural reasons, as when you feel left out of a group or wonder whether your peers judge you to be a "nice" person. If that need is deeply felt, it may impel you to do something about your situation, for example to eat, to adjust the thermostat, to ask to be let into a group. In these situations you have been motivated to act. A *motive need*, then, is a tendency to move or act in a certain direction, an impulse to satisfy a psychological-social want or a biological urge.

A Classification of Motive Needs

The classification of fundamental human needs most often cited today is, probably, the one developed by psychologist Abraham H. Maslow.[1] Maslow presents

MASLOW'S HIERARCHY

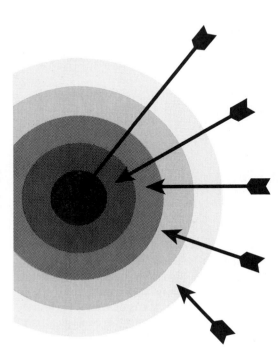

Self-Actualization
Self-fulfillment:
to be what one can be

Esteem Needs
Self-esteem from achievement,
competence, mastery,
confidence, reputation,
recognition, status

Belongingness and Love Needs
Love and affection with family,
friends; acceptance and approval
by social groups

Safety Needs
Security, stability, protection,
structure, orderliness, law,
predictability, freedom from fear
and chaos

Physiological Needs
Food, drink, sleep, sex

the following categories of needs and wants which impel human beings to think, act, and respond as they do:

   1. *Physiological Needs* • for food, drink, air, sleep, sex—the basic bodily "tissue" requirements.

   2. *Safety Needs* • for security, stability, protection from harm or injury; need for structure, orderliness, law, predictability; freedom from fear and chaos.

   3. *Belongingness and Love Needs* • for abiding devotion and warm affection with spouse, children, parents, and close friends; need to feel a part of social groups; need for acceptance and approval.

   4. *Esteem Needs* • for self-esteem based on achievement, mastery, competence, confidence, freedom, independence; desire for esteem of others (reputation, prestige, recognition, status).

   5. *Self-Actualization Needs* • for self-fulfillment, actually to become what you potentially can be; desire to actualize your capabilities; being true to your essential nature; what you *can* be you *must* be.[2]

   These "needs," according to Maslow, function as a *prepotent hierarchy;* that is, lower-level needs must be largely fulfilled before higher-level needs become operative. Persons caught up in the daily struggle to satisfy physiological and safety needs will, for example, have little time and energy left to strive for "esteem" or "self-actualization." Once these basic requirements of living are satisfied, however, higher-level drives take over. We should note, moreover, that as individuals we tend to move upward or downward between one level and another as our life progresses or regresses. Maslow's category of basic human needs and the hierarchical order in which they stand are illustrated in "Maslow's Hierarchy," page 102.

Finally, it should be noted that motives do not always automatically produce certain courses of action. Physiologically, an individual may sense a sharp feeling of pain from not having eaten for two days; yet, because of social-cultural needs or pressures, this person will not gobble down a chocolate cake when presented with one, but will sit politely with fork and napkin. The need for social approval may control the way a person satisfies physiological needs. Nevertheless, the hierarchy of prepotency is useful in conceptualizing human motivation, even if individuals vary in ways they manifest those needs.

Motivational Appeals

Recognizing the power of motive needs to impel human action, you may ask: How can I as a public speaker go about creating, using, and satisfying such needs? How can I translate these basic needs, wants, or desires into verbal acts—into effective public communication? The answer to both of these questions is: with the use of motivational appeals.

A *motivational appeal* is either (1) a *visualization* of some desire and a method for satisfying it, or (2) an *assertion* that some entity, idea, or course of action can be or ought to be linked with an impulse-to-human-action—that is, a motive.

Suppose, for example, that you had been dating a person for some time, and decided one evening that it was time to declare your love. As the evening progressed, you thought about how you were going to talk to your friend. You even created little "movies" in your head—perhaps full pieces of dramatic dialogue—as you rehearsed your speech. Will I be suave, casual, or a stumbling fool? Will I find the words, the looks, the actions to move my beloved? Will the person respond to me with tears or laughter, flippantly or seriously? Here we see the power of visualization. In visualizing various scenarios, you playacted yourself and your speech through a variety of motivational appeals: Is the *fear* of rejection worth the possibility of mutual declarations of *love?* Will *aggressiveness* work better than quiet appeals to *companionship?* By a process of intrapersonal visualization you thus assembled a group of motivational appeals potent enough to move your "audience," your beloved, and you organized those appeals into little stories you could tell.

At other times, instead of visualizing courses of action for yourself or your listener, you may simply try to attach motivational concepts directly to other concepts. Technically, this verbal process is called *attribution*.[3] Suppose, for example, that you had shunned going to church because you thought of churches as *conformist, authoritarian, dominating, repulsive, destructive* institutions. One night, however, you went to a religious meeting, one where the preacher talked about the *adventure* of living a God-based life, the *beauty* of God's creation, the *reverence* one must feel in living a full life, the *endurance* one must have in overcoming doubts. You decided, upon reflection, that you had misconstrued the church's motivation and even misanalyzed yourself. You became a devout churchgoer. What happened? You changed the attributes of "churchness" in your own mind. Instead of attributing conformity/authority/dominance to that institution and ideal, you began attributing adventure/beauty/reverence to personal religion. Conversion was effected, and your behavior changed.

Motivational appeals, therefore, are verbal attempts to make salient and relevant a series of motives within an audience, within an idea or proposal under discussion, or within a countervailing force which you think is keeping listeners from accepting an idea or proposal. Such appeals work visually (through verbal depiction) or assertively (through verbal association).

Some Types and Examples of Motivational Appeals

Present in every listener and every audience, of course, is a near-infinite number of specific human wants and needs to which you could direct your appeals. Any attempt to enumerate them, therefore, must of necessity be incomplete and overlapping to some extent. However, we can assemble a list of motivational appeals which have been used by many successful speakers to win over audiences. By mastering the list and understanding the meaning and potential effect of each of the items, you can begin immediately to use them in your analysis of audiences and in your construction of speeches.

To open up just a few of the many possibilities, let us briefly examine a number of motivational appeals:

Achievement and display • Ordinarily, people want to do their best. They yearn to achieve success or distinction. They are willing to work hard to accomplish tasks in which they can display their skill and expertise, to *have*, to *do*, or to *be* something that sets them apart, that makes others willing to acknowledge their uniqueness.

Acquisition and savings • Most of us like to earn money, to keep it, and to spend only as much as necessary to acquire the other things we want. Discount stores are filled with people trying to get as much as possible at the lowest price. Advertisements for airlines and resort hotels frequently feature special "off-season rates." But this acquisitive or thrift-conscious motive extends to many things besides money. Stamp collecting, the keeping of photo albums, the gathering of art treasures or rare books, and similar hobbies reflect the same tendency.

Adventure and change • Nearly everyone likes the thrill of mild danger—the adventure of diving beneath the surface of the sea, of scaling a mountain, or of exploring strange lands and cities. Basic to a yen for adventure is the longing for *change*. Change is the impetus that drives us to seek out new and different things, to meet other people, to try new jobs, or participate in the latest fads.

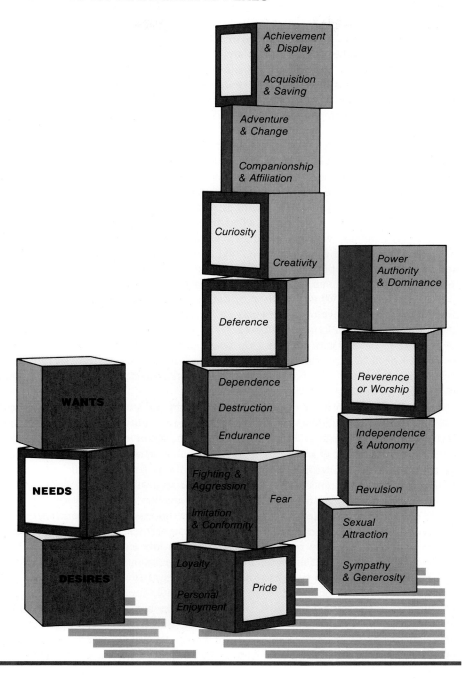

Companionship and affiliation • A few people prefer to be hermits, but most of us like company. We cross the street to walk with a friend rather than walk alone. We want to be a part of a group, to share, to make strong attachments. We go to parties, join clubs, write letters to absent relatives, and prefer to live in a dormitory or share an apartment with friends. Even the most tedious task becomes more bearable if others are sharing it with us.

Creativity • The urge to create shows itself in many ways: in inventions, books, buildings, business organizations, and empires. In addition to building with physical objects such as bricks, steel, or wood, we like to organize human beings into working units—political parties, business firms, athletic teams, and the like.

Curiosity • Children tear open alarm clocks to find out where the tick is, and adults crowd the sidewalks to gaze at a celebrity passing by. But curiosity is not mere inquisitiveness or nosiness, as is sometimes implied. It also provides the motivation for the experimenter, the scholar, and—when curiosity is coupled with the love for adventure—the explorer.

Deference • There are times when most of us recognize the advantage of deferring to someone whose wisdom, experience, and expertise are greater than our own. We sense the benefit of following instructions and doing what is expected of us. In the spirit of deference, we accept the leadership of others, conform to custom, and even learn to praise other people.

Dependence • When people *over*-defer, especially for extended periods of time, they tend to develop a dependence. Everyone is, of course, born dependent; and this is a feeling not altogether lost in adulthood. Whatever their age, people like to have others provide help when needed. In proper measure, dependence can be a healthy thing; overdone, it can quickly erode initiative and destroy other necessary drives and action tendencies. Indeed, many speakers appeal to its negative consequences in urging change.

Destruction • In most of us there seems to be an occasional impulse to tear apart, to break, to bulldoze over, to batter down, to cut to pieces—to destroy. Perhaps this urge springs from the desire to show our superiority, our dominance, over the object of our destruction and thus expand our ego. In any event, we are all destroyers at times. Build a house of blocks for a year-old boy, and he knocks it down. Let someone present a theory or an argument, and someone else delights in picking it full of holes and tearing it apart.

Endurance • Stick-to-itiveness in a highly mobile and impermanent age may seem something of an incongruity, but it is nevertheless a strong motivating force which tends to keep most of us steadily at a job until it is finished. On a larger scale, the motive of endurance is responsible for our sense of timelessness and institutional sanctity; people sometimes sacrifice their lives to guarantee that social institutions will endure.

Fear • If the other person is bigger than you are, you hesitate to attack him. Instead, you go home and put a lock on the door to keep him out. Physical injury, however, is by no means the only thing we fear. We are also afraid of losing our jobs, our property, our friends, our future. Especially do we fear the dangerous power of what is strange or hidden: *the unknown*. If the members of an audience are needlessly fearful, your first task is to reassure them—to allay their anxieties and dreads. If they are unaware of a danger that confronts them, your duty is to warn them.

Fighting and aggression • Much has been spoken and written in an effort to explain why human creatures fight one another—why they engage in acts of aggression and violence. Hence we shall concern ourselves with only two facets of this multifaceted manifestation of human conflict: *anger* and *competition*. We become angry at people who cheat or insult us, challenge our ideas or values, destroy our property, or interfere with our rights or efforts. The form in which we fight back against these intrusions may vary from physical attack to subtly destructive gossip, but normally it has for its purpose protecting our safety or restoring our self-esteem. The impulse to fight or to struggle also evidences itself in *competition*. Even though we are not angry with antagonists, we enjoy matching wits and muscles with them for the sheer pleasure of the struggle or for the sake of demonstrating our superiority. Participation in games is based on this tendency, and many people argue or debate for this reason. Business and scholastic rivalries are manifestations of the element of competition. The prevalent phrase "We *beat* them" suggests the combative nature of such efforts.

Imitation and conformity • Both consciously and subconsciously, people tend to imitate others. From earliest childhood, all of us try to emulate those whom we most greatly admire; and as we grow older, the range of the people, ideas, and behaviors we imitate steadily increases. We copy the garb, attitudes, actions, and even the pronunciations of other persons—especially of those we respect or envy. Do not suppose, however, that imitation is exclusively volitional; most of it is *imposed*. Often we feel compelled to imitate—to *conform*—because of subtle or overt pressures from peers, parents, and professors. "They say" and "Everybody's doing it" are clearly conformative in their motivation.

Independence and autonomy • In spite of the tendency to imitate or conform, we do not like to lose our independence, to be bossed about, to have to attend class, or to be prohibited from acting as we like. If you can influence your hearers to believe they are doing something of their own volition, they will be much more likely to do it than if the act is forced on them.

Loyalty • The feeling of loyalty, based on our tendency as individuals to identify with other persons or groups, sometimes provides strong motivation. The strength of the loyalty appeal will vary, however, with the degree to which the individual has become identified with a particular person or group of persons. Hence, a person's loyalty to family is usually stronger than loyalty to a college or a social club.

Personal enjoyment • Pleasures are many and varied, and people usually act to prevent their curtailment or to enhance their effect. Among the pleasures almost universally desired we find the enjoyment of comfort and luxury, beauty and order, sensory satisfactions, and relief from burdensome restrictions and restraints. Other pleasures are more personal in nature and vary from individual to individual.

Power, authority, and dominance • Most of us like to exert influence over others. In search of power, people have given up lucrative positions to enter government service at a much smaller salary, hoping thereby to increase their dominance over other human beings and to influence the course of events. If you can combine an appeal to increased power with an appeal to self-advancement in the form of a larger income or a higher social status, many of your listeners are likely to find your message exceedingly persuasive.

Pride • One of the most powerful single appeals that can be made is to pride, especially when you are dealing with young people. A varsity letter has little intrinsic value, but an unbelievable amount of work may be done to earn one. Election to an honorary society has more importance to most students than a cash award. But the influence of pride is not limited to the young; from childhood to old age, we are all extremely careful to protect our egos. Pride manifests itself in numerous ways, including intensive efforts to earn a *reputation, self-respect*, and recognition as a person of *sound judgment*.

Reverence or worship • There are times when all of us sense our own inferiority in relation to a superior person, idea, or thing. If we admire this sufficiently, we may grow to revere it. Reverence combines a feeling of humility and a willingness to subordinate ourselves. It takes three common forms: *hero worship*, or the deep admiration of another person or persons; *reverence for traditions and institutions;* and *worship of a deity*, whether it be conceived religiously or as a philosophical concept.

Revulsion • The fragrance of a flower garden attracts people; the odor of a refuse heap repels them. Just as pleasant sensory experiences evoke enjoyment, so unpleasant sensations and perceptions arouse disgust or loathing. By showing the unsanitary conditions in a city's slums, you may create sentiment to clean them up. By picturing the horrors of war in bloody detail, you may influence hearers who could not be reached by reasoned arguments alone. While doing these things, however, beware of rendering your descriptions so gruesome that your speech itself becomes revolting. Restraint is required to make a description of repulsive conditions vivid enough to be impressive without, at the same time, offending the sensibilities of the listeners.

Sexual attraction • Generally speaking, whatever promises to make listeners more attractive in the eyes of the opposite sex, or to remove obstacles to that attraction, is likely to gain attention and support. We all recognize that this appeal is used—and probably overused—in many forms of public communication, especially advertising. And the cultural changes of the past two decades have certainly raised our consciousness about the degree to which appeals to sexual attraction are used unethically and inappropriately and for purposes of manipulation rather than for legitimate advocacy. The larger issue is simply that all of us want to be liked by others. Properly used, then, appeals which highlight personal attractiveness are strong motivators, whether used by themselves or in conjunction with other appeals a speaker may employ.

Sympathy and generosity • Just as we are likely to identify ourselves with the groups to which we belong or aspire to belong, so we tend to see ourselves in the plight of those who are less fortunate than ourselves. This feeling of compassion for the unhappy or the unlucky, which we here call sympathy, makes us want to help them. We pause to aid a blind man or to comfort a crying child. Out of generosity we give money to feed people whose homes have been ravaged by flood, earthquake, or fire. As a speaker, you may influence your listeners by rousing in them the sentiment of sympathy or pity. To do so, however, remember that you must make it easy for them to identify themselves with the unfortunate ones, to put themselves in the other persons' shoes. You cannot accomplish this with statistics and abstractions; you must describe specifically, sympathetically, and compassionately the individuals to whom you refer, and you must depict their plight vividly.

Using Motivational Appeals

Using Appeals to Extend Audience Analysis

In the previous chapter we presented a step-by-step analysis of a speaking situation in which a speaker proposed to get an athletic board to expand women's competitive sports programs on her campus (see p. 95). Here, we use the same speech, "From Spectator to Participant: Athletics for Women," to suggest more precise ways of using motivational appeals (see Point VIII and its subpoints A, C, and E).

VIII. Proposed Adaptation to Audience and Occasion
    A. Introduce speech with thanks for fine intramural program now available to women (*appeal to previous generosity*). Make reference to surrounding facilities and equipment (*appeal to current achievements*).
    C. Stress primarily the *theoretical* values of intercollegiate competition for women. (*Such an appeal to professionals often ridiculed as "jocks" and anti-intellectuals can emphasize personal worth, adventure, creativity, competiton, or pride.*) Mention—but with this predominantly male audience, do not over-emphasize—the matter of equality between the sexes (*allay fears, and only gently move into questions of dominance*).
    E. Be prepared to answer Board's possible questions concerning number of women interested (*indirect appeal to political power*), neighboring schools which could furnish competition (*appeal to competition*), estimated cost of proposed program (*appeal to ease in acquisition*), available locker-room facilities (*visualization of proposal's workability*), and other questions that might be raised.

Overall, this speech stresses a theoretical (that is, psychological) value, with secondary appeals aimed at political and economic value-orientations. As an initial proposal, it maintains a firm, but conciliatory, stance. If the proposal were unreasonably rejected, of course, the next speech might make the political and economic values more important, especially if the speaker believes a confrontation is the only route to persuasion.[4]

Using Appeals in Your Speeches

It is important to develop skill, tact, and good judgment in your use of motivational appeals. Such attributes are the products of a technically sound audience analysis, some thoughtful reflection on what has worked (or not worked) in speeches you have heard or given, and just plain common sense. Over the years certain general communication rules regarding motivational appeals have evolved. Examples of such rules include the following:

1. *Avoid being blatant, objectionably obvious, or overly aggressive in your employment of motivational appeals.* Do not say, as extreme examples, "Mr. Harlow Jones, the successful banker, has just contributed handsomely to our cause. Come on, now. *Imitate* this generous man!" Or, "If you give to this cause we will print your name in the paper so that your *reputation* as a generous person will be known by everyone." Such appeals produce what is called in psychological theory a *boomerang effect*—an attitude or action that goes in a direction opposite to the one you want.[5] Instead, in making an appeal of this sort, respect the intelligence and sensitivities of your audience and suggest—through the use of what we earlier described as visualization—that contributors will not only be associated with others in a worthwhile and successful venture, but will also have the sincere appreciation of many who are less fortunate than they. In other words, let the members of your audience "think" of the motive, while you descriptively talk about or around it in this kind of situation.

2. *Use motivational appeals in combination, especially when some of them are socially suspect.* Appealing to self-centered interests—private fears, monetary gain or acquisition, and self-pride—can be an excellent persuasive strategy; however,

This young speaker, addressing a city council meeting, might be using some of the communication rules regarding motivational appeals. Generally her use of appeals should be subtle; she should know the level at which to focus her appeals. In addition, the speaker's use of the various combinations of appeals must remain ethically sound.

people, especially in groups, are often reluctant to acknowledge that they are acting for selfish reasons. This sometimes creates a dilemma for a speaker: although person-centered appeals might work well, audience members might not wish to surrender to their own interests in front of others. For example, at the end of the year many people contribute to charitable causes to increase their income tax deductions, but a speaker can hardly tell a group of people that the main reason they should give to a fund drive is to make some personal financial gains. Similarly, many people who are persuaded to join an exercise group because they have deep-seated fears of heart attacks, when asked why they exercise, are likely to say, "Oh, because it makes me feel so good." The response conceals their specific fears. Thus, as a speaker you may need to combine appeals to seemingly self-centered motives with more *publicly acceptable* motives. Even though people give to some causes for selfish reasons, you must suggest they are doing it for socially valued reasons like sympathy and generosity, loyalty, adventure, or change. The more self-centered motives can be mentioned, but they probably should not dominate your speech.

3. *Use motivational appeals in combination when you face a heterogeneous audience.* The analysis of social and cognitive structures offered in Chapter 5 can help you select an array of motivational appeals for a particular speech. Think about the range of ages, occupations, ethnic groups, fixed beliefs, valuative orientations, and so on represented in your audience, and then try to select motivational appeals that will be attractive to auditors in each of those categories. Suppose you were speaking to an Optimist Club on the need for a trauma center at the local hospital. In an Optimist Club you are likely to find doctors, storekeepers, members of social service agencies, old people, young persons, minority businesspeople, and the like. This should suggest that you will want to appeal to the financial interests of the business community (as more people will be brought to town, the number of consumers will increase); to the self-pride of doctors (who presumably will be able to treat severely injured patients more successfully); to the fears of older citizens (who now will have greatly improved chances of surviving heart attacks); to the innovativeness of younger persons (who usually value progress highly); to the humanitarian orientation of the social service agents (who always approve of ways to increase care for others); and to the medical plight of low-income minorities (who as a group often are denied quick treatment of the type offered by trauma centers). "Something for everyone"—within reason and good taste—should mark the motivational appeal in your speech.

4. *Think through Maslow's "hierarchy" as you settle on your motivational emphases in speeches.* Suppose you were giving a speech in favor of a urban renewal project to members of a ghetto. Appeals to higher-level needs (esteem needs such as achievement, prestige, or status) are likely to fall on deaf ears, for you would be addressing folks primarily concerned with such basic physiological needs as food and shelter and such safety needs as security, protection, and freedom from harassment. A speech on that topic to that audience probably ought not spend much time discussing beautification; instead it could emphasize increased access to goods and services, improved housing, better streetlighting, controlled

traffic, and better opportunities for community-centered law enforcement. The time-honored truism of public speaking, "Hit 'em where they are," deserves your attention when you are selecting motivational appeals.

5. *Think of ways to organize your motivational appeals effectively.* In Chapters 8 and 9 we will discuss organizational patterns and ways of choosing one appropriate to your purpose, your audience, and your materials. But for now, we can note that it also is possible to select an organizational pattern appropriate to the motivational appeals you settle upon. Your motivational appeals can control the entire structure; Chapter 8 will offer such a pattern, called the "Motivated Sequence." Read that chapter carefully.

6. *Finally, use motivational appeals in ethically sound ways.* Even in a free and open society, there are ethical bounds which, when crossed by the overzealous speaker, produce public condemnation or even retribution. Communication ethics are more than a matter of not lying or not misrepresenting yourself to an audience. They also impinge on motives and motivational appeals. Urging an audience to take a course of action because it will make them rich at the expense of others who have less power or knowledge, for example, is an ethically suspect motivational appeal; so is an intense, sustained fear appeal that finds hidden conspiracies to destroy the world under every rock and bush. The demagogue may win a battle now and then, but seldom wins the war. Think carefully about your own ethical limits, and about what kinds of appeals outrage you when *you* are a member of an audience. The social penalties for overstepping moral boundaries in your appeals can be relatively severe, and you must decide to what degree you are willing to risk social censure for what you advocate and how you advocate it.

In summary, think of motives as springs—as wants or desires tightly coiled and waiting for the "right" appeal or verbal depiction to set them off. Those springs, when worked by the skillful speaker, can convert the individuals in an audience into a cohesive group ready to think and act in ways consistent with your purpose. One of your jobs as a speaker is careful pre-planning, so that your motivational appeals can release those powerful springs to thought and action.

A Sample Speech

The following speech, delivered to a joint session of Congress on December 8, 1941, was President Franklin Delano Roosevelt's message requesting a declaration of war against Japan. Prior to that date, the United States had been negotiating around the clock with that nation to keep the peace; and, seemingly, all was going well. Then suddenly, on Sunday morning, December 7, the Japanese launched a massive, surprise attack on Pearl Harbor, Hawaii, sinking eight American battleships and other smaller craft and leveling planes and airfields.

The nation was numbed; Congress was indignant, and the President moved quickly. The joint session was held in the House chamber; the galleries were overflowing, and the speech was broadcast worldwide.

Notice the President's strategies, particularly his use of supporting materials and motivational appeals. Paragraphs 2 and 3 are cast in narrative form, so that background information could be presented in an easy-to-comprehend manner. Paragraph 4 offers the only comparatively detailed illustration; he obviously felt that short, quick specific instances—constructed in parallel fashion in Paragraphs 5 through 10—would have greater impact, especially as they could be molded into a reinforcing summary of American beliefs and attitudes in Paragraph 11. The President then was in a position to call for a solution to the problem—the declaration of war—via a series of motivational appeals to power, pride, patriotism, fear, and reverence. Few speeches have ever more efficiently used such a variety of supporting materials and motivational appeals.

● For a Declaration of War Against Japan*

Franklin Delano Roosevelt

Introduction

TO THE CONGRESS OF THE UNITED STATES: Yesterday, December 7, 1941—a date which will live in infamy—the United States of America was suddenly and deliberately attacked by naval and air forces of the Empire of Japan. /1

Body

Background orientation—Narration of the problem

The United States was at peace with that nation and, at the solicitation of Japan, was still in conversation with its government and its Emperor, looking toward the maintenance of peace in the Pacific. Indeed, one hour after Japanese air squadrons had commenced bombing in Oahu, the Japanese Ambassador to the United States and his colleague delivered to the Secretary of State a formal reply to a recent American message. While this reply stated that it seemed useless to continue the existing diplomatic negotiations, it contained no threat or hint of war or armed attack. /2

Statement of the problem

It will be recorded that the distance of Hawaii from Japan makes it obvious that the attack was deliberately planned many days or even weeks ago. During the intervening time the Japanese government had deliberately sought to deceive the United States by false statements and expressions of hope for continued peace. /3

Illustration

The attack yesterday on the Hawaiian Islands has caused severe damage to American naval and military forces. Very many American lives have been lost. In addition, American ships have been reported torpedoed on the high seas between San Francisco and Honolulu. /4

Specific instances

Yesterday the Japanese government also launched an attack against Malaya. /5

Last night Japanese forces attacked Hong Kong. /6

Last night Japanese forces attacked Guam. /7

---

*Originally printed in the *Congressional Record*, 77th Congress, 1st Session, Volume 87, Part 9, pp. 9504–9505, December 8, 1941.

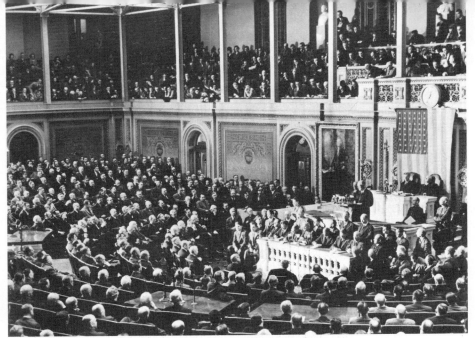

On the day after the Japanese attack on Pearl Harbor, President Franklin D. Roosevelt addressed a joint session of Congress to ask for a declaration of war against Japan. The text of his speech is a classic example of the use of motivational appeals.

Last night Japanese forces attacked the Philippine Islands. /8
Last night the Japanese attacked Wake Island. /9
This morning the Japanese attacked Midway Island. /10

Reinforcing summary

Japan has, therefore, undertaken a surprise offensive extending throughout the Pacific area. The facts of yesterday speak for themselves. The people of the United States have already formed their opinions and well understand the implications to the very life and safety of our nation. /11

Solution

As Commander-in-Chief of the Army and Navy I have directed that all measures be taken for our defense. /12
Always will we remember the character of the onslaught against us. /13

Appeal to power and pride

No matter how long it may take us to overcome this premeditated invasion, the American people in their righteous might will win through to absolute victory. /14

Appeal to patriotism

I believe I interpret the will of the Congress and of the people when I assert that we will not only defend ourselves to the uttermost but will make very certain that this form of treachery shall never endanger us again. /15

Overcoming fear

Hostilities exist. There is no blinking at the fact that our people, our territory, and our interests are in grave danger. /16

Reverence for strength, nation, and God	With confidence in our armed forces—with the unbounded determination of our people—we will gain the inevitable triumph—so help us God. /17
Conclusion	I ask that the Congress declare that since the unprovoked and dastardly attack by Japan on Sunday, December 7, a state of war has existed between the United States and the Japanese Empire.★★ /18

REFERENCE NOTES

[1]Data based on Hierarchy of Needs in "A Theory of Human Motivation" in *Motivation and Personality*, 2nd Edition, by Abraham H. Maslow. Copyright © 1970 by Abraham H. Maslow. Reprinted by permission of Harper & Row, Publishers, Inc.

[2]In the 1970 revision of his book, *Motivation and Personality*, Maslow identified two additional needs—the needs to know and understand and aesthetic needs—as higher need states which frequently operate as part of self-actualization needs.

[3]For a fuller discussion of "attribution," see Philip G. Zimbardo, Ebbe B. Ebbesen, and Christina Maslach, *Influencing Attitudes and Changing Behavior*, 2nd ed. (Reading, MA: Addison-Wesley Publishing Company, 1977), especially pp. 72–80.

[4]For an interesting attempt to rank-order, in terms of rhetorical sophistication, possible strategies for proposers of significant change, see John Waite Bowers and Donovan J. Ochs, *The Rhetoric of Agitation and Control* (Reading, MA: Addison-Wesley Publishing Company, Inc., 1971), esp. Chapter 2.

[5]For some illustrations of the boomerang effect, see Zimbardo, Ebbesen, and Maslach, pp. 163, 168, and 224.

 PROBLEMS AND PROBES

CHAPTER REPORT   Motive appeals form the heart of the advertising game; for even a single product, a great many different motive appeals can be used. Select a particular product—automobiles, liquor, tobacco, fast-food chains, laundry soaps—and collect a group of magazine and, if possible, radio and television ads. Then, (1) identify the motive appeals in each ad, (2) think about why those appeals are used in advertisements of that sort of product, and (3) write an essay, "Motive Appeals in Ads for [your product]," discussing both the appeals and why they are thought to be effective.

1.   Bring to class three examples of speeches which incorporate motivational appeals as discussed in this chapter. Explain what kinds of appeals are used in each, and why. Do these motive appeals add to or detract from the speaker's persuasive effort? What other appeals could the speakers have utilized? Combine your examples and your analysis in a brief written report and hand it to your instructor.

★★For a fuller analysis of this speech, see Hermann G. Stelzner, " 'War Message,' December 8, 1941: An Approach to Language," *Speech Monographs*, 33 (November 1966), 419–37. Also reprinted in Robert L. Scott and Bernard L. Brock, *Methods of Rhetorical Criticism; A Twentieth-Century Perspective*, 2nd ed. (Detroit: Wayne State University Press, 1980), pp. 298–320.

2. Clip and bring to class ten magazine advertisements which contain one or more motivational appeals. In preparing this assignment, identify each appeal, write a brief statement telling why you think it was selected to sell this particular product, and evaluate its effectiveness. Note that a motivational appeal may be used both in an illustration and in the printed text to reinforce each other and the motivational appeal(s) of the advertisement as a whole. Hand your analyses to your instructor, and be ready to talk about them informally in class if that should be requested.

3. Prepare a list of the motivational appeals you would employ when trying to persuade *(a)* a stranger to buy a subscription to a magazine; *(b)* an instructor to raise a grade; *(c)* an audience of college students to donate blood; *(d)* a smoker to give up smoking; *(e)* your parents to buy you a car. In each instance, which of the following methods do you deem the more persuasive: impressing your listeners with a motive for believing what you want them to believe or, showing them the logic of your proposal by presenting well-supported information and well-reasoned arguments? Develop and defend your analysis by considering alternative approaches.

4. Using the examples of speeches you gathered for Problem 1, determine whether the motivational appeals employed constituted ethical and legitimate means of persuasion. How do you distinguish between appeals that are ethical and legitimate and those that are not? Can you specify a few universal principles which allow us to make future distinctions between ethical and unethical motivational appeals? In answering these questions consider the subject matter of the speeches analyzed and the situation in which they were made, as well as the nature of the appeal itself.

 ORAL ACTIVITIES

1. Present a three- or four-minute speech in which, through the combined use of two or three related motivational appeals, you attempt to persuade your audience to a particular belief or action. (For example, combine appeals to *adventure, companionship,* and *personal enjoyment* to persuade them to take a conducted group tour of Europe; or combine *sympathy* and *pride* to elicit contributions to a charity drive.) At the conclusion of your speech, ask a classmate to identify the motive appeals you used. If other members of the class disagree with that identification, explore with the class as a whole the reasons why your appeals did not come through as you intended, and what you might have done to sharpen and strengthen them.

2. In a group discussion with other members of your class, attempt to construct a list of principles which help differentiate ethical from unethical appeals. In the course of discussion, answer the following questions: *(a)* Under what conditions would you consider a motive appeal to the wants or desires of listeners an entirely ethical and legitimate means of persuasion? *(b)* Under what conditions might such an appeal be unethical? *(c)* Where does the ethical responsibility rest: with the speaker? with the audience? or in adherence to a list of external criteria?

3. Assume you have a friend who is considering dropping out of school. What motivational appeal would you use to convince your friend to continue his/her ed-

ucation if you wanted to direct those appeals to your friend's *(a)* physiological needs; *(b)* safety needs; *(c)* belongingness and love needs; *(d)* esteem needs; *(e)* self-actualization needs? What factors help you to distinguish between those appeals? Illustrate your appeals with specific examples or statements. Then get into small groups to discuss your analyses with your classmates.

 ## SUGGESTIONS FOR FURTHER READING

Walter R. Fisher, "A Motive View of Communication," *Quarterly Journal of Speech,* 56 (April 1970), 131–39.

Charles U. Larson, *Persuasion: Reception and Responsibility,* 2nd ed. (Belmont, CA: Belmont Publishing Company, Inc., 1979), Chapter 5, "Cultural Premises in Persuasion."

Abraham Maslow, *Motivation and Personality,* 2nd ed. (New York: Harper & Row, Publishers, 1970), Chapter 4.

Gerald R. Miller and Murray A. Hewgill, "Some Recent Research on Fear-Arousing Message Appeals," *Speech [Communication] Monographs,* 33 (November 1966), 377–91.

Wayne C. Minnick, *Public Speaking* (Boston: Houghton Mifflin Company, 1979), Chapter 10, "Persuasive Speaking."

7

Finding and Using Supporting Materials

The effective communication of ideas depends on more than the selection of appropriate motivational appeals. If you are speaking on the values of state lotteries, the claim, "Lotteries provide funds for worthy causes," may be a good place to start. Now, how do you clarify the idea—to say nothing of justifying it as a good way to raise funds? Similarly, if you wish to justify your belief that nuclear plants should be closed down, you may need to go beyond the assertions: "Nuke plants are unsafe"; and "Everyone knows that the safe disposal of nuclear waste is impossible." An audience favorably disposed to your claims probably won't require much beyond your simple assertion as they can expand the statements with information they have in their possession. A neutral or hostile audience, on the other hand, probably will be unsatisfied with your general claims. These listeners will require additional, specific data on the safety question; they also will object to the vague allusion "everyone knows." Your task is to legitimize your claims by providing specific information relevant to both issues.

The *forms* of *supporting materials* identified in this chapter are the medium of exchange between your personal ideas and audience acceptance. Their function is to amplify, clarify, or justify the beliefs, attitudes, and values you wish to convey to your audience. They are the flesh and blood which bring your leading ideas to life and sustain them once they have been implanted in the minds of others. After the forms and the factors influencing their selection are identified, we will consider common sources of such materials and their uses in informative and persuasive contexts.

The Forms of Supporting Material

There are seven forms of supporting material (see figure, page 121) which you may use to develop or prove the major ideas in a speech:

1. Explanation
2. Analogy or comparison
3. Illustration (detailed example)
4. Specific instances (undeveloped examples)
5. Statistics
6. Testimony
7. Restatement

Sometimes two or more of these kinds of materials are combined, as when statistics are used to develop an illustration, or when the testimony of an authority is given to strengthen or verify an explanation. At other times they are used singly, the speaker's choice of materials depending upon the type of support needed. Comparisons and hypothetical illustrations, for example, can be especially helpful in making ideas clear and vivid. Specific instances, statistics, and testimony usually work effectively as proof. Factual illustrations and restatements serve both purposes.

Explanation

By definition, an explanation is an expository or descriptive passage which seeks (1) to make clear the nature of a term, concept, process, or proposal; or (2) to offer a supporting rationale for a contestable claim. Three types of explanations are especially useful to you as a speaker: *explanations of what, explanations of how,* and *explanations of why.*[1]

Explanations of what • Some explanations serve to delineate more specifically what a speaker is discussing; they make ideas clearer and more concrete, giving audiences enough details so that they can get their minds around the concept. For example, Scott Andrews, University of Iowa, offered this explanation of a type of literature called the *fantasy novel* in a speech on that subject:

> One of the most popular forms of literature in recent years is the fantasy novel. Like its first cousin, science fiction, "fantasy" is a difficult term to define. But usually the term is applied to a work which takes place in a non-existent and unreal world such as a fairyland or which concerns incredible and unreal characters, or which employs physical principles not yet discovered or even contrary to present existence. Tolkien's world in *The Hobbit,* Katherine Kurtz's "Deryni," and the vision of Arthurian England in Walter Munn's *Merlin's Ring* are universes with these characteristics.[2]

In clarifying her assertion that women's colleges need to address issues related to "family life," Elizabeth Tidball avoided possible misinterpretation by being explicit:

> Family living does not mean how to diaper the baby and bake a cake. Family living is making congruent and mutually constructive decisions about geographic mobility and work satisfaction; about competitiveness and priorities; about when and if to bear

children and how to rear them in the presence of dual careers; about loyalties and the boundaries of our capabilities; about legalities, finances, property; about professional growth and development for two people simultaneously; about isolation, mental and physical health, long-range planning and life goals.[3]

Explanations of how • A second class of explanations tells audiences "how"— how something came to be, or how something is done. Explanations of *how* frequently recount the processes or steps involved in carrying out an operation. P. Dorothy Gilbert used such an explanation in introducing a speech on chair-caning:

> The intricate patterns of cane or reed you see on chair seats make the process seem mysterious and all too artistic for most of us. On the contrary. As I will demonstrate to you today, anyone can learn to cane a chair in order to restore a valuable antique or to save a family heirloom. Chair-caning involves five easy-to-learn steps: First, soak the cane to make it pliable; then, clean out the holes through which the cane will be stretched; next, weave the cane or reed through the holes in four to seven operations; fourth, tie off the pieces of cane underneath the chair; and finally, lace a heavier piece of cane over the holes to cover them. Let me describe each step, one at a time.[4]

Explanations of why • Explanations which account for a thing's existence or present state can be called explanations of "why." They appear often in academic lectures, as when a history professor explains *why* a series of events caused a war or a revolution. Such explanations can lay the foundation for remedying problems—if we know why a problem or state of affairs persists, we can alter the situation with a solution that removes the "whys" or at least circumvents their harmful influence. After clearly outlining the inadequate foreign language preparation of American diplomatic officials, Charles W. Bray of the International Communication Agency accounted for the existence of the problem in this manner:

> The roots of these troubling facts are not hard to trace. *On the one hand*, a 1979 Rand Corporation report on international studies and the marketplace found that government foreign affairs agencies do not make effective use of the specialists they recruit. Career incentives encourage people to become generalists, not specialists. *On the other hand*, our educational system is not producing enough graduates, well enough trained, for government to hire.[5]

Explanations such as these can effectively clarify your meaning or justify your position on an issue. Keep your explanations brief and to the point; adding detail upon detail or making ideas too complex may lose audience attention and involvement. In addition, speak in specific, concrete terms. Abstract language or general propositions may be necessary in initiating a theme or an issue, but a speech replete with such statements will not draw audiences to your message. Finally, combine explanations with other forms of supporting material to assist in conveying ideas that are clear, interesting, and relevant to your purpose in speaking.

MATERIALS FOR VERBALLY SUPPORTING AN IDEA

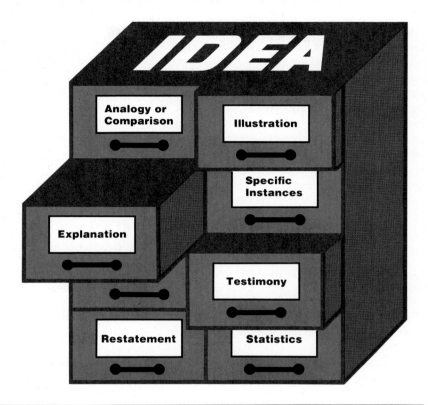

Analogy or Comparison

In an analogy or comparison, similarities are pointed out between something that is already known, understood, or believed by the listeners and something that is not. Thus, you might explain the game of cricket to an American audience by comparing it with baseball, or tell how a thermostat works by comparing it with a simple thermometer. Analogies or comparisons may be either *figurative* or *literal*.

Figurative analogies • Figurative analogies involve phenomena which, though basically different in nature, exhibit comparable properties or relationships. They are used principally to make ideas or distinctions clear to an audience. Dr. Louis Hadley Evans, minister-at-large for the Presbyterian Church, drew these figurative analogies to distinguish between the terms *deist* and *theist:*

> To you the world is what: a clock or a car? Is it a huge clock, that God once made, that He wound up at the beginning and left it to run of itself? Then you are a *deist*.

Do you believe that it is rather a car that God once made, but that does not run without His hand on the wheel, without His ultimate and personal control? Then you are a *theist*.[6]

Literal analogies • Although analogies which compare things that are unlike—the world with a clock or a car, for example—may be excellent means of clarifying a point or making it vivid, they generally are of limited value as proof. For this purpose it is always more effective to employ comparisons of *like* phenomena—to argue, for example, that a system of one-way traffic on the downtown streets of City X would relieve congestion and promote safety because such a system has had these effects in City Y. Note how a comparison of like phenomena—in this case, two state universities—was used to prove one of the claims advanced in a student speech by George Gruner:

> To show that an active and effective student government would help to reduce disciplinary problems at Iowa, we may refer to the experience of the university I attended before transferring here last fall—a school which, like Iowa, has between 15,000 and 16,000 students and which is a publicly supported state institution.
>
> Prior to reconstituting student government as a vital responsible force, the office of the dean at my former university handled more than 600 disciplinary cases each year. After putting new responsibility and authority into the hands of the students themselves, however, this number was cut by more than half, and the number of merely trivial or nuisance offenses decreased by about two thirds. The dean himself attributed this reduction chiefly to the new sense of pride which a revitalized student government had given the students in their school.[7]

Because it attempts to base a conclusion on a single parallel instance, an analogy used as proof must meet a rigid test: *the instances compared must be closely similar in all essential respects*. Clearly, you could not infer that what worked in a small denominational college also would work in a large state university or that an effect achieved in a select private school also would be achieved in an institution whose student body is more varied. Do the similarities between the items or classes compared outweigh any differences that might be relevant to the conclusion you are drawing? This is the question that needs to be asked—and answered—when you try to use an analogy as proof for a contention or claim.

Illustration

An illustration is a detailed example in narrative form. It may be used to picture the results that would flow from adopting the proposal you advocate, or to describe in detail conditions as they now exist. An illustration has two principal characteristics: (1) narrative form—recounting a happening or telling a story; and (2) vividly described details. There are two types of illustrations—*hypothetical* and *factual*. The one describes an imaginary situation; the other, an actual happening.

Hypothetical illustration • A hypothetical illustration, although it is an imaginary narrative, is believable if consistent with the known facts; it must seem probable or likely. In discussing the learning problems of the bilingual child, Mary Neagley of Clarion State College pictured for her audience the pupil whose family speaks little or no English:

> But imagine a child whose English is only a second language. Never spoken at home, this language must be absorbed from the outside—a piecemeal of key phrases; a vocabulary based on acquisition, not comprehension.
>
> Schooling becomes a disadvantage in itself. Forced to use a foreign language, the child can worry about mastery of material covered in class only after comprehending the web of its delivery. He is marked as "slow," unable to comprehend questions directed at him, and too afraid and uncertain to ask. He has been relegated to a position that may very well defy his intellectual capacities. This small, future resource has been dealt the beginnings of its demise.[8]

Because in a hypothetical illustration aspects of the situation can be manipulated at will, this form of support is an especially valuable means of clarifying an idea or of stimulating interest. Also, it provides a good way to explain a complicated process. Instead of talking in general terms, the speaker may take a person, perhaps herself or a member of the audience, and picture that person going through the various steps which the process entails. As proof, however, the hypothetical illustration is at best of doubtful value. The very fact that the details can be manipulated by the speaker may justifiably cause the audience to withhold credence.

Factual illustration • A well-chosen factual illustration is one of the most telling forms of support a speaker can use. Because details are brought into the story, the present or projected situation is made clear and vivid to the listeners; because the incident actually occurred, it frequently has high persuasive value. Kathy Weisensel of the University of Wisconsin used her personal knowledge of two retarded persons in removing beliefs that such individuals are "ineducable" and are "incapable of leading happy and productive lives." With reference to her brother, David, she noted:

> Under Wisconsin law he was entitled to school until age twenty-one, and he spent all those years in a separate special class. There he learned the basic skills of reading, writing, and mathematics. After graduation he was employed by the Madison Opportunity Center, a sheltered workshop for the retarded. He leaves home each morning on a special bus and returns each evening after eight hours of simple assembly line work. While he is by no means self-supporting and independent, he loves his work, and he is a happy man and a neat person with whom to share a family.[9]

With this illustration and others, Kathy was able to show that common misconceptions about the retarded can be easily removed—many such persons can be trained and can lead happy lives.

Keep three considerations in mind when choosing a factual illustration to explain or support an idea. First, *is the illustration clearly related to the idea that is to be clarified or proved?* If you have to labor to show its connection, the illustration will be of little use. Second, *is it a typical example?* An audience is often quick to notice unusual circumstances in an illustration; and if you seem to have picked an exceptional case, your description of it will not prove convincing. Third, *is it vivid and impressive in detail?* The primary value of an illustration is the sense of reality it creates. If this quality is absent, the advantage of using an illustration is lost. Be sure, then, that your illustrations meet the tests of relevance, fairness, and vividness of detail.

Specific Instance

A specific instance is an *undeveloped* illustration or example. Instead of describing a situation in detail, you merely refer to it in passing. Such references normally serve one of two purposes: (1) To make an idea *clear* and *understandable*, a passing reference to an event, person, place, or process your audience already is familiar with may be effective. Jane Scott of the University of Iowa opened a speech on architecture in this way: "You all are familiar with Old Capitol, the beautiful pillared building you pass each day walking from class to class. It's a perfect example of federal-period Georgian architecture, the subject of my speech this morning."[10] Her brief reference to a familiar building enabled the audience to orient itself to the speaker's topic. (2) Specific instances also are useful in *proving a proposition*. In this case, instances may be piled one upon the other until you have firmly established the impression you wish to create. Note, for example, how James K. Wellington demonstrated the serious nature of his claim that "creative and imaginative students often are not recognized by their teachers":

> We should remember that the following persons were all identified as low achievers or misfits:
>
> Einstein—4 years old before he could speak; 7 before he could read.
>
> Issac Newton—was rated a poor elementary school student.
>
> Beethoven—music teacher said, "As a composer, he is hopeless."
>
> Thomas Edison—teacher told him he was too stupid to learn anything.
>
> F. W. Woolworth—worked in a dry goods store at 21, employers would not let him wait on customers; "didn't have enough sense."
>
> Walt Disney—fired by a newspaper editor; "no good ideas."
>
> Winston Churchill—failed 6th grade.[11]

With these accumulated data, there could be little doubt that teachers may err in their judgment of a child's ability. In similar fashion, Charles Gould, Executive Director of the Hearst Foundation, offered proof for his claim that government departments were "playing fast and loose with our tax dollars":

> A Medicare study, for example, showed health benefits being paid to thousands of men and women who had died.

One dentist who handled hundreds of welfare patients charged for extracting 36 teeth from one patient. That's four more than God bestowed.

A midwestern doctor charged for 33 abortions in one week. One involved a woman who was 62 years old.[12]

If the names, events, or situations you cite are well known to your listeners, specific instances can aid comprehension or generate support for a claim or contention. On subjects with which the listeners are not familiar, however, or on which there are marked differences of opinion, specific instances can be supplemented with more fully developed illustrations to help create a strong argument.

Statistics

Not all figures are statistics; some are used merely for counting. Statistics are figures that *show relationships among phenomena*—that emphasize largeness or smallness (magnitudes), describe sub-classes or parts (segments), or establish trends. Because statistics reduce great masses of information into generalized categories, they are useful both in *making clear* the nature of a situation and in *substantiating* a potentially disputable claim.[13]

Magnitudes • We often use statistics to describe a situation or to indicate in a relatively short space the scope or seriousness of a problem. Statistical description of magnitude, especially when complemented by an analogy, helps an audience grasp the dimensions of a problem clearly. This is what Representative Tom Steed of Oklahoma did in a speech on governmental red tape and paperwork, delivered in the House of Representatives on January 17, 1977:

> Government agencies print about 10 billion sheets of paper to be filled out by U.S. businessmen—enough to fill more than 4 million cubic feet. Paperwork stemming from federal, state, and local governments averages about 10 forms for every man, woman, and child in the United States. Official records stored around the country total 11.6 million cubic feet, or an amount 11 times larger than the volume of the Washington Monument. Paperwork generated by Washington alone in one year would fill Yankee Stadium from the playing field to the top of the stands 51 times.[14]

Donald L. Baeder, President of the Hooker Chemical Company, employed the same approach in conveying how chemical proportions—*parts per billion* and *parts per trillion*—can more easily be grasped:

> One part per *billion* is the equivalent of one drop—one drop—of vermouth in two 36,000 gallon tank cars of gin—and that would be a very dry martini even by San Francisco standards!
>
> One part per *trillion* is the equivalent of one drop in *two thousand* tank cars.[15]

Note, however, that although Baeder's description of magnitude effectively conveys the proportions involved, it may not work equally well as an item of proof.

Is one drop of vermouth in 72,000 gallons of gin the same as one drop of pesticide in the same quantity of drinking water? If not, the description does not reasonably justify the safe use of any particular chemical treatment.

Segments • Statistics can be used to isolate the parts into which a problem can be subdivided or to show aspects of a problem caused by discrete factors. This descriptive approach is especially helpful when you wish to break down a complex topic into its component parts. A case in point is the amount of contributions by Political Action Committees to political campaigns. By illustrating, in dollar figures and in percentages, the amounts contributed by these PAC's, you can illustrate their spending patterns and preferences. In a speech before a Public Affairs Council, Federal Elections Commissioner Joan Aiken divided the number of PAC's into segments and proceeded to dispel the belief that corporate PAC's gave more readily to political *parties* than to individual *candidates:*

> The FEC statistics show that there are 2,728 non-party political committees. Of that number, 1,245 are corporate-sponsored and 332 are labor-connected. Obviously, the corporate-sponsored PACs constitute approximately 47 percent of the total non-party PAC universe. . . .
>
> The statistics for 1980 would seem to indicate that corporate PACs are looking at the candidates rather than at their Party labels and that is all to the good, in my opinion.
>
> In the 1980 election, there were 2,266 candidates running for the Senate and House. They raised a combined total of $240.1 million, $37.6 million of which came from non-party PAC sources. Corporate-sponsored PACs contributed 4.9 percent of the money received by Democratic candidates and 6.4 percent of the money received by Republican candidates. Organized labor gave 9.62 percent of the money received by Democratic candidates and only 0.65 percent of the money received by Republican candidates. Obviously, the overwhelming majority of the money raised for House and Senate candidates came from *individuals!*[16]

Trends • Finally, statistics often are employed to describe a trend across time. Statistical trends indicate where we have been and where we are going. Daniel Rose of Rose Associates, in a speech delivered at Cornell University, used a trend analysis to show the growth in this country's elderly population and to predict severe housing problems in the near future:

> In 1900, those over 65 constituted some 4 percent of the nation's population; by 1940, the percentage reached 6.8 percent; today the 23 million men and women over 65 make up over 10 percent of the nation and, significantly, 16 percent of the voting age population. Every day of the year, about 3,000 persons over 65 die, while some 4,000 enter the age group, for a total increase in the aged population of nearly 400,000 per annum. And if actual physical quarters appropriate for this group are in short supply, housing managers with necessary skills, knowledge, and techniques are even scarcer.[17]

When you use statistics to indicate magnitude, divide phenomena into segments, or describe trends, keep in mind the following cautions: (1) *Translate difficult-to-comprehend numbers into more immediately understandable terms.* In a speech on the mounting problem of solid waste, Carl Hall pictured the immensity of 130,000,000 tons of garbage by indicating that trucks loaded with that amount would extend from coast to coast.[18] (2) *Don't be afraid to round off complicated numbers.* "Nearly 400,000" is easier for auditors to comprehend than "396,456"; "over 33 percent" is usually preferable to "33.4 percent" and "over one third" probably is better than either of them. (3)*Whenever possible, use visual materials to clarify complicated statistical trends or summaries.* Hand out a mimeographed sheet of numbers; draw graphs on the chalkboard; prepare a chart in advance. This will allow you to concentrate on explaining the significance of the numbers, and not spend your time merely trying to report them. (4) *Use statistics fairly.* Arguing that professional women's salaries increased 12.4 percent last year may sound impressive to listeners—until they realize that women still are generally paid almost a quarter less than men for equivalent work. In other words, be sure to provide *fair contexts* for your numerical data and comparisons.[19]

Testimony

When speakers cite the opinions or conclusions of others, they are using *testimony.* As a form of support, testimony may serve to heighten the impact of an idea, to underscore or clarify a point that is being advanced; as an item of proof, testimony may help justify an assertion or claim that the speaker is advancing.

David Mahoney utilized testimony to serve the first purpose, to dramatize the need for a new civility in a presentation before the Anti-Defamation League of B'nai B'rith in New York City:

> There is another fundamental way to control the conflict between the thirst for equality and the hunger for uniqueness. It is to recognize the many sources of bitterness and defamation now spreading through our world and to consciously adopt a new civility.
>
> A generation ago, Walter Lippman said: "There is such a thing as the public philosophy of civility. It does not have to be discovered or invented . . . but it does have to be revised and renewed."
>
> I do not see the new civility as any goody-goody excess of politeness. I see it as the willingness to avoid patronization.[20]

In a speech to the National Management Association, Bette Ann Stead used specific instances of verbatim expressions to support her point about opportunities for women:

> There are still managers who seem to be blatantly against giving women equal opportunity. . . . For example, during the past few years, these incidents have really happened in major organizations: (1) A recruiter has told a female honor student, "Frankly, we consider women inferior." (2) Another recruiter has told a female applicant, "Women aren't any good at sales, and it would take you ten years to get where it would take a man six years to get in our company." (3) A vice president has

said (seriously), "The first mistake we made was giving women the right to vote fifty years ago."[21]

As public speakers, we often find it necessary to supplement our experience or analyses of the available information with testimony from *experts*—persons whose background and training qualify them as respected sources of information. Jim Elleson, in a speech presented in an introductory public speaking class at the University of Wisconsin, used this means to support his claim that American military might is falling behind that of the Soviet Union:

> Barry M. Blechman, Senior Fellow and head of the Defense Analysis Staff at the prestigious Brookings Institution, said in the January 3, 1976 issue of *New Republic,* "In 1965, the U.S. held a roughly 7:1 edge in total equivalent megatonnage—the best static measure of the destructive potential of nuclear weapons. The ratio is now 1.3:1 in favor of the Soviet Union and is likely to increase in the years ahead."[22]

As this brief excerpt illustrates, Jim Elleson did not depend solely on his own knowledge, nor did he base his testimonial support solely on those who have a vested interest in the outcome of expenditures for military hardware—the military or their service industries. By citing the person's credentials and the source of the material, Elleson improved his chances for being perceived as a credible speaker—one who knows what he is talking about.[23]

In some cases, it may not be necessary to quote the person directly. The governor of Wisconsin, Lee Sherman Dreyfus, used paraphrase rather than direct quotation in speaking on the role of special interest groups in the financing of political campaigns:

> There are those who argue that the special interests add up to a total of the state interest. David Broder of the *Washington Post,* who also predicted this situation in his book, *The Party's Over,* said the narrow objectives of the special interest do not all add up this way. There's no free market in political influence, he wrote. Some interests are more powerful—so powerful they can almost rig the game to assure a favorable outcome for themselves.[24]

So long as the allusion is an accurate representation of the person's position, paraphrasing is an acceptable and often useful shorthand way to add support for a position.

When you judge the acceptability of the testimony you might use in supporting your position, or assess the worth of a position addressed to you, consider the following criteria:

1. *The person quoted should be qualified by training and experience as an authority.* He or she should be an expert in the field to which the testimony relates.

2. Whenever possible, *the statement of the authority should be based on first-hand knowledge.*

3. *The judgment expressed should not be unduly influenced by personal interest.* An authority with a strong vested interest is suspect.

4. *The hearers should realize that the person quoted actually is an authority.* They should respect his or her opinion.

If the persons—or in some instances, organizations—satisfy these criteria, their opinions should meet the dual requirements of *authoritativeness* and *audience acceptability*. The best testimony comes from those persons whose qualifications your listeners will recognize and respect.

Restatement

Restatement is reiteration of an idea in different words. Therefore, it is to be distinguished from mere repetition, in which the words remain the same.

Although they provide no real proof, restatement and repetition often have subconscious persuasive impact. Advertisers realize this, and spend millions of dollars annually repeating essentially the same message in magazines, on billboards, and over radio and television. "Catch that Pepsi Spirit," "Nobody can do it like McDonald's can," "Budweiser—The King of Beers," "Oldsmobile—We've had one built for you." "Mazda—The more you look the more you like." Slogans such as these have been repeated until they are familiar to everyone.

Up to a certain point, of course, repetition of the same words or restatement of the same ideas may persuade the listener; beyond that point, however, they become monotonous and boring. Be careful to avoid this danger. Plan your restatements so that they reformulate the phrasing of the original idea as clearly and precisely as possible.

Walter F. Mondale, speaking at the 1980 Democratic National Convention, incorporated repetition of a phrase in heightening the impact of his view of the Democratic party and those who speak on its behalf:

> When we speak of peace, the voice is Ed Muskie's. When we speak of workers, the voices are Lane Kirkland's and Doug Fraser's. When we speak of freedom, the dream is Coretta King's. When we speak of compassion, the fire is Ted Kennedy's. And when we speak of courage, the spirit is Jimmy Carter's. When we in this hall speak for America—it is America that is speaking.[25]

Later, in the same speech, Mondale elicited a strong vocal response from the audience with his successive use of twin repetitions/restatements in reference to the types of actions Ronald Reagan was likely to commit:

> He'd have to be a person who believes, and I quote . . . Now who would say something like that? Ronald Reagan would.

> He'd have to be a person who calls the weak . . . Who on earth would say something like that? Ronald Reagan did.[26]

By the time he finished his eighth specific instance, the audience was chanting "Ronald Reagan" with him in response to his questions. In this fashion, Mondale aroused the weary delegates and reawakened their partisan spirit.

In an effort to make clear the kind of leader he thinks is required in present-day America, Dr. Ralph Eubanks of the University of West Florida employed a somewhat different kind of restatement or redefinition of his concept of the "new leadership." Notice how he has rephrased the essential idea in four different ways:

> We must, among other things, create a new leadership in America . . . .The leader I shall define as one who can help his group conduct well the ancient search for the "good life in the good society." Put another way, a good leader for our times is one who can hold ever before the members of his group a truly human vision of themselves. In slightly different terms, he is one who can help his group find their way to honorable, human goals and can teach them how to "care for persons" in the process. In still different terms, he is one who can help us live up to the ancient definition of ourselves as *Homo Sapiens*, or Man the Wise.[27]

Use these seven forms of supporting material—singly or in combination—to clarify or justify your assertions. Express *your* views, but seek to amplify and develop them further through the judicious addition of restatement, testimony, statistics, specific instances, detailed illustrations, analogies or comparisons, and explanations.

Sources of Supporting Materials

A good way to begin your search for speech materials is to jot down on a piece of paper everything you already know about your subject as a result of personal experience or observation. You always speak best about the people, ideas, and events that you know best; and you know best those things you have actually seen, heard, touched, tasted, smelled, or done. Even when materials of this kind cannot appropriately be cited in your message, they will sharpen your perspective or provide insights into the subject—something which almost invariably makes for greater clarity and vividness of expression. Whenever possible, make personal experience and observation your first "port of call" when searching for speech materials.

At times, however, you will be called upon to speak about matters which fall entirely outside the range of your own experience or observation. When this is the case, there are several sources of information open to you: interviews with experts, letters and questionnaires, publications of all kinds, and radio and television broadcasts. Let us consider how each of these sources can be used to best advantage in accumulating substantive materials for your speeches.

Interviews

Beginning speakers often fail to recognize that much useful and authoritative information may be gathered merely by asking questions of the right persons. If, for example, you expect to talk about interplanetary navigation, what better-informed and more convenient source of information could there be than a member of your college's astronomy department? Or, if you are interested in the growth of and diversity within the T-shirt industry, talk with the proprietor of a local shop. Brief interviews, properly arranged and scheduled, frequently yield invaluable factual data and authoritative interpretations and opinions.

To set up such an interview, select an informant who you think will approach the subject with reasonable objectivity and knowledge. Make an appointment in advance, stating your purpose and explaining why you think he or she can be of help. Acquaint yourself with the informant's background—current position, previous jobs, books or articles written, for example—to help you frame pertinent and penetrating questions and evaluate the responses you receive. Develop an interview plan—goals you seek to achieve, specific questions that will aid you in reaching those goals—so that you do not wander through the conversation unsure of yourself and of the precise information you are seeking.

When actually conducting the interview, be on time, restate your purpose, keep the interview moving at a lively pace, and carefully record the information and opinions you receive. A tape recorder, if you have one, will be a valuable aid, but be sure you have permission from the informant before turning it on. Finally, do not overstay your welcome. Respect the other person's time, and leave graciously. Avoid arguing or disagreeing with the informant (you can do that later in your speech!) and don't parade your own knowledge. Use the interview for what it is—a way of acquiring supporting materials to clarify, amplify, or prove a point in your speech.

Letters and Questionnaires

If you cannot talk directly with an expert, you can sometimes obtain the information you need through correspondence. You might, for example, write to your senator for information regarding a pending bill in the legislature, or to a cereal company for data relative to the amounts of sugars in its products. Be sure that you make clear exactly what information you want and why you want it. Moreover, be reasonable in your request. Do not expect a busy individual to spend hours or days gathering facts for you. Above all, do not ask for information that you could find yourself if you searched for it.

On other occasions, you may wish to discover what a group of people knows or thinks about a subject. If, for example, you wanted to give a speech on a proposed nuclear power plant, you could sample public opinion in the vicinity with a questionnaire. You might send it to people randomly chosen from the town's phone directory, circulate it through a dorm or classroom, or even administer it in person to passersby on a street corner. With the results, you could construct your own statistical segments and magnitudes, right out of your own school and community. When developing a questionnaire, be sure it has an introduction which explains the exact purpose and the procedures to be followed in answering the questions. Keep it short, or people will throw it away. If you mail it, include a self-addressed, stamped envelope to help guarantee returns to you. And, when conducting the survey in person, be polite and ask for only a small amount of time.

Printed Materials

The most common source of supporting materials is the printed word—newspapers, magazines, pamphlets, and books. Through the careful use of a library—and with the help of reference librarians—you can discover an almost overwhelming amount of materials relevant to your speech subject and purpose.

Newspapers • Newspapers obviously are a useful source of information about events of current interest. Moreover, their feature stories and accounts of unusual happenings provide a storehouse of interesting illustrations and examples. You must be careful, of course, not to accept as true everything printed in a newspaper, for the haste with which news sometimes must be gathered makes complete accuracy difficult. Your school or city library undoubtedly keeps on file copies of one or two highly reliable papers such as *The New York Times, The Observer,* or the *Christian Science Monitor,* and probably also provides a selection from among the leading newspapers of your state or region. If your library has *The New York Times,* it is likely to have the published index to the paper. By using this resource, you can locate accounts of people and events from 1913 to the present. Another useful and well-indexed source of information on current happenings is *Facts of File,* issued weekly since 1940.

If your topic deals with state or local issues, do not overlook the small town weeklies or the specialty weeklies that may cover important events in your immediate area. In Maine, for example, *Maine Times,* published weekly, covers environmental, social, and political issues in depth. Although its stories reflect the editorial bias of the writer, the information may be useful in supporting claims about the hazards of chemical spraying or the disposal of hazardous wastes in area landfill sites—to cite two topics recently covered by this newspaper.

Finally, your local newspaper also publishes syndicated columns. Even though *The New York Times* may be unavailable to you or difficult to obtain, you can locate commentary by nationally known columnists on significant national and international issues in most city dailies. Newspapers can be used for more than chronicles of who did what when.

Magazines • An average-sized university library subscribes annually to hundreds of magazines and periodicals. Among those of general interest, some—such as *Time, Newsweek,* and *U.S. News and World Report*—summarize weekly events. *The Atlantic* and *Commentary* are representative of a group of monthly publications which cover a wide range of subjects of both passing and permanent importance. Such magazines as *The Nation, Vital Speeches of the Day, Fortune,* and *The New Republic* contain comment on current political, social, and economic questions. Discussions of popular scientific interest appear in *Popular Science, Scientific American,* and *Popular Mechanics.* For other specialized areas, there are such magazines as *Sports Illustrated, Field and Stream, Ms., Psychology Today, Better Homes and Gardens, Today's Health, National Geographic Magazine,* and *Country Journal.*

This list, of course, merely suggests the wide range of materials to be found in periodicals. When you are looking for a specific kind of information, use the

Readers' Guide to Periodical Literature, which indexes most of the magazines you will want to refer to in preparing a speech. Look in this index under various topical headings that are related to your subject.

Professional and trade journals • Nearly every profession, industry, trade, and academic field has one or more specialized journals. Such publications include: *Annals of the American Academy of Political and Social Science, American Economist, Quarterly Journal of Speech, Journal of the American Medical Association, Journal of Afro-American Studies, AFL-CIO American Federationist, Trade and Industry, Coal Age, Educational Theatre Journal,* and others. In conducting research, you might consult such indexes as the *Education Index, Social Sciences Index, Humanities Index,* or *Psychological Abstracts.* These publications index most of the professional journals you may find helpful in supporting your ideas.

Yearbooks and encyclopedias • The most reliable source of comprehensive data is the *Statistical Abstracts of the United States,* which covers a wide variety of subjects ranging from weather records and birth rates to steel production and election results. More unusual data on Academy Award winners, world records in various areas, the "bests" and "worsts" of almost anything, can be found in the *World Almanac, The People's Almanac, The Guinness Book of World Records, The Book of Lists,* and *Information Please.* Encyclopedias such as the *Encyclopaedia Britannica* and *Encyclopedia Americana,* which attempt to cover the entire field of human knowledge, are valuable chiefly as an initial reference source or for background reading. Refer to them for important scientific, geographical, literary, or historical facts, for bibliographies of authoritative books on a subject, and for ideas you will not develop completely in your speech.

Documents and reports • Various governmental agencies—state, national, and international—as well as many independent organizations publish reports on special subjects. Among governmental publications, those most frequently consulted are the hearings and recommendations of congressional committees or those of the United States Departments of Health and Human Services, of Education, and of Commerce. Reports on issues related to agriculture, business, government, engineering, and scientific experimentation are published by many state universities. Such endowed groups as the Carnegie, Rockefeller, and Ford Foundations, and such special interest groups as the Foreign Policy Association, the Brookings Institution, the League of Women Voters, Common Cause, and the United States Chamber of Commerce also publish reports and pamphlets. Though by no means a complete list of all such pamphlets and reports, *The Vertical File Index* does offer you a guide to some of these materials.

In addition, check to see if a library in your area has been designated as a "government depository." These libraries regularly receive government publications of all types—senate committee hearings, the *Weekly Papers of the President,* the *Congressional Record,* and specialty reports. The *Public Affairs Information Service Bulletin* and the *Monthly Catalog of United States Government Publications* are useful guides to such documents and reports. Most state legislatures have a "legislative reference bureau" or other office which can be contacted for material related to state and local concerns.

Books on special subjects • There are few subjects suitable for a speech upon which someone has not written a book. As a guide, use the subject-matter headings in the card catalog of your library.

Collections of quotations • A wide range of quotations useful for illustrating an idea or supporting a point may be found in such works as Bartlett's *Familiar Quotations*, H. L. Mencken's *A New Dictionary of Quotations on Historical Principles from Ancient and Modern Sources*, Arthur Richmond's *Modern Quotations for Ready Reference*, George Seldes' *The Great Quotations*, and Burton Stevenson's *The Home Book of Quotations*.

Biographies • *The Dictionary of National Biography* (deceased Britishers), the *Dictionary of American Biography* (deceased Americans), *Who's Who* (living Britishers), *Who's Who in America, Current Biography*, and similar collections contain biographical sketches especially useful in locating facts about famous people and in finding the qualifications of authorities whose testimony you may wish to quote.

Radio and Television Broadcasts

Lectures, discussions, and the formal public addresses of leaders in government, business, education, and religion are broadcast frequently over radio or television. Many of these talks later are mimeographed or printed by the stations or by the organizations that sponsor them. Usually, as in the case of CBS's *Meet the Press*, copies may be obtained on request for a small fee. If no manuscript is available, you may audiotape the program (as long as you make no public use of that tape) or take careful notes. When taking notes, listen with particular care in order to get an exact record of the speaker's words or meaning. Just as you must quote items from printed sources accurately and honestly, so are you obligated to respect the remarks someone has made on a radio or television program and to give that person full credit.

Recording Information

When you find the information you have been looking for, either make a photocopy of it or take notes on the material. Whether you keep your notes on 4 x 6 note cards or in a notebook, it is helpful to have an accurate and legible record of the facts you wish to retain for your speech. An incomplete source citation may make it impossible to locate the source again; hurried scribbles may be difficult to decipher at a later time. Note cards are easier to use than a notebook because they can be classified as to topic area or type of support. However, if you are using a notebook, try to record each item on half of each page. Since most of your items of information will not fill a page, this will save paper; cutting the sheets in half will make it easier to sort your data or adopt a classification scheme and record information in accordance with particular themes or subpoints of your speech.

RECORDING INFORMATION

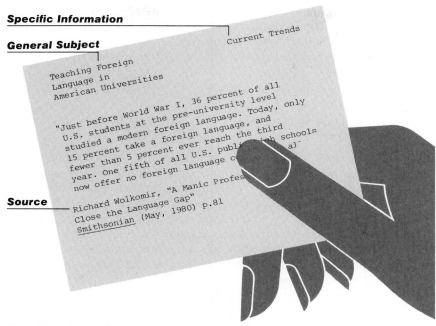

Specific Information

General Subject

Current Trends

Teaching Foreign
Language in
American Universities

"Just before World War I, 36 percent of all
U.S. students at the pre-university level
studied a modern foreign language. Today, only
15 percent take a foreign language, and
fewer than 5 percent ever reach the third
year. One fifth of all U.S. publi___ ___gh schools
now offer no foreign language c___ ___ al-

Source

Richard Wolkomir, "A Manic Profes___
Close the Language Gap"
Smithsonian (May, 1980) p.81

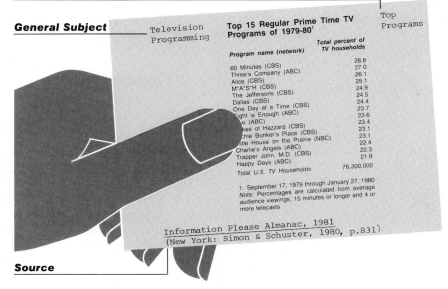

Specific Information

General Subject

Television
Programming

Top
Programs

Top 15 Regular Prime Time TV Programs of 1979-80[1]

Program name (network)	Total percent of TV households
60 Minutes (CBS)	28.8
Three's Company (ABC)	27.0
Alice (CBS)	26.1
M*A*S*H (CBS)	25.1
The Jeffersons (CBS)	24.9
Dallas (CBS)	24.5
One Day at a Time (CBS)	24.4
___ight is Enough (ABC)	23.7
___xi (ABC)	23.6
___kes of Hazzard (CBS)	23.4
___chie Bunker's Place (CBS)	23.1
___ttle House on the Prairie (NBC)	23.1
Charlie's Angels (ABC)	22.4
Trapper John, M.D. (CBS)	22.3
Happy Days (ABC)	21.9
Total U.S. TV Households	76,300,000

1. September 17, 1979 through January 27, 1980
Note: Percentages are calculated from average
audience viewings, 15 minutes or longer and 4 or
more telecasts

Information Please Almanac, 1981
(New York: Simon & Schuster, 1980, p.831)

Source

The illustrated note cards (page 135) indicate common features of note taking that will help you to recall or use specific information.[28] Place the appropriate subject headings at the top of the card and the complete source citation at the bottom. This way, the card can be classified by general subject (top left heading) and by specific information presented (top right heading). Also, if you need to return to the same article or document, the complete citation will enable you to find the material with ease. You can avoid losing "just perfect" information by taking the time to record the material on the spot and by carefully noting the source of the data.

Using Supporting Materials

Thus far in this chapter we have considered the forms of supporting materials, the influences that guide their selection, and the common sources for information. In this concluding section we shall try to demonstrate how particular types of materials may be packaged to expand on or to verify the *central idea* or *proposition* of a speech. Although a speech normally contains multiple ideas or themes, it is more likely to succeed when it conveys one single overriding idea to the audience. The remaining themes serve to supplement, round out, or otherwise support the central idea. In some cases the central idea may be the *only* point that is being conveyed, as when you are involved in classroom presentations, oral reports, or conference sessions where you need to make one concept or suggestion clear, or justify one simple point. The single-point speech is a good place to begin working with supporting materials. As subjects grow more complex, you will discover that the units of a longer speech—developed in the service of a central idea—are essentially a succession of single points. The examples in the discussions that follow illustrate the process of expanding on a central idea or proving a proposition.

Expanding a Central Idea

If the purpose of your speech is to explain an idea, proceed as follows:

1. State the idea or point in a short, simple sentence.
2. Make it clear
   a. by explanations, comparisons, and illustrations;
   b. by using diagrams, pictures, models, or maps.
3. Restate the idea you have explained.

In the clarification (step 2 above), you may present the verbal and nonverbal supporting materials either separately or together. That is, you may tell your listeners and *then* show them; or you may show them *while* you are telling them. The following outline for a central-idea speech illustrates how supporting materials may be assembled to explain an idea and make it clear.

HOW WE BREATHE

Explanation

I. The human breathing mechanism may be likened to a bellows which expands to admit air and contracts to expel it.
   A. When we inhale, two things happen.
      1. Muscles attached to the collarbone and shoulder bones pull upward and slightly outward.
      2. Muscles in the abdominal wall relax, allowing the diaphragm—a sheet of muscle and tendon lying immediately below the lungs—to fall.
   B. This permits the spongy, porous material of which the lungs consist to expand.
      1. A vacuum is created.
      2. Air rushes in.
   C. When we exhale, two things happen also.
      1. Gravity causes the rib cage to move downward.
      2. Muscles in the abdominal wall contract, squeezing the diaphragm upward.
   D. The space available to the lungs is thus reduced.
      1. The lungs are squeezed.
      2. Air is emitted.

Comparison

   E. The similarity between the breathing mechanism and a bellows is represented in this diagram:

Restatement

   F. In summary, then, to remember how the human breathing mechanism works, think of a bellows.
      1. Just as increasing the size of the bellows bag allows air to rush in, so increasing the space available to the lungs allows them to admit air.
      2. Just as squeezing the bellows bag forces air out, so contracting the space the lungs can occupy forces air to be emitted.

Visual Aid

HOW WE BREATHE

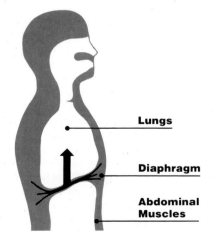

Lungs

Diaphragm

Abdominal Muscles

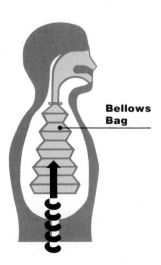

Bellows Bag

Supporting a Proposition

If your purpose is to obtain audience approval of an idea or proposition, follow these steps:

1. State your point.
2. Make it clear by explanation, comparison, or illustration.
3. Prove it by specific instances, testimony, statistics, or additional factual illustrations.
4. Restate your point as an established conclusion.

If your audience is hostile towards your idea, it may be wise to withhold the direct statement of your purpose until you can develop information leading to acceptance of your proposition. This strategy may be more persuasive if the audience is led to the conclusion during the course of your speech rather than allowing it to assess your supporting materials as you seek to justify an already announced claim. Because the sample speech in the following outline does not presume a hostile audience but does require verification, it follows the steps suggested above.

CABLE TELEVISION
WILL REVOLUTIONIZE YOUR LIFE

Statement of central idea or claim.

I. Cable television soon will revolutionize your everyday life.

First supporting statement.

A. Suppose, on a rainy day a few years from now, you decide to "run" your errands from your living room.

Hypothetical illustration— developed by a succession of specific instances.

   1. You turn on your two-way communication unit, and begin your round of errands:

     a. On Channel 37, your bank's computer verifies the amount of a recent withdrawal.

     b. On Channel 26, you ask the telephone company to review last month's long-distance charges.

     c. On Channel 94, a supermarket lets you scan products, prices, and home-delivery hours.

     d. On Channel 5, you study a list of proposed changes in the city charter.
       (1) You can call in for further information
       (2) You can vote from your own home.

     e. Channel 115 gives you access to resource personnel at the public library.

Restatement of first supporting statement.

   2. Thus—with "cable television at your service"— you have accomplished your day's errands with minimum expenditure of time, gas, and parking-meter money.

Second
supporting
statement.

II. The vast possibilities of cable TV, once thought of only as dreams, are becoming actualities across the United States.

Specific
instances.

    A. New York City has a channel which gives citizens direct access to city officials.

    B. San Francisco's "public-access channels" are filled with local talent and ethnic programming.

    C. Ann Arbor, Michigan, has been leasing channels to private firms and public-utility companies.

Third
supporting
statement.

III. Cable television soon will be available to virtually every household in the U.S. at a reasonable cost.

    A. Because the cost is shared by licensee and householder alike, no one bears an excessive burden.

Statistics.

        1. Studio facilities for the public-access channels are made available at cost in most cable television contracts—normally about $30 per hour.

        2. Monthly rental fees per household seldom exceed $12.

        3. Current installation charges for necessary home equipment range from $15 to $50.

Explanation
combined with
specific
instances.

    B. The technical characteristics of cable television render it inexpensive.

        1. Some existent telephone lines and equipment can be used.

        2. The conversion box mounts easily on a regular television set.

Restatement of
central idea or
claim.

IV. Given actual and potential uses, plus the positive cost-benefit ratio, cable television will revolutionize your daily life.

Analogy or
comparison.

    A. Just as the wheel extended our legs and the computer our central nervous system, so will cable television extend our communicative capabilities.

Testimony
used to
support
restatement
and summarize
the central
idea of the
speech.

    B. In the words of Wendy Lee, communication consultant to new cable-television franchises: "We soon will be a nation wired fully for sight and sound. We will rid ourselves of the need for short shopping trips; we will cut the lines in doctors' offices; and we will put the consumer and the constituent into the front offices of his or her corporate suppliers and political servants. The telephone and the motor car will become obsolete."

    Not all central-idea speeches require as many different forms of supporting materials as were used in these sample outlines, but they do show how you may combine a number of different materials to achieve a single purpose and to reach a variety of audiences.

REFERENCE NOTES

[1]For an informative analysis of explanation, see W. V. Quine and J. S. Ullian, *The Web of Belief* (New York: Random House, Inc., 1970). Chapter 8 "Explanation." These authors also have helpful chapters on "Testimony" (Chapter 4) and "Analogy" (Chapter 6).

[2]From a speech given at The University of Iowa, winter term, 1978. Reprinted with the permission of Mr. Andrews.

[3]From "To Use All Their Talents" by M. Elizabeth Tidball from *Vital Speeches of the Day*, 46, April 1980. Reprinted by permission of Vital Speeches of the Day.

[4]From a speech given at The University of Iowa, fall term, 1979. Reprinted with the permission of Ms. Gilbert.

[5]From "Ascendancy and Decline" by Charles W. Bray, III from *Vital Speeches of the Day*, 46, June 1980. Reprinted by permission of Vital Speeches of the Day.

[6]Excerpt from "Can You Trust God?" by Dr. Louis Hadley Evans. Reprinted by permission of the author.

[7]"Let's Revitalize Student Government," delivered in an advanced course in public speaking at The University of Iowa, March 14, 1966.

[8]From "Un Hombre Que Habla Dos Idiomas Vale Por Dos" by Mary Neagley. Reprinted from *Winning Orations* by special arrangement with the Interstate Oratorical Association, Larry Schnoor, Executive Secretary, Mankato State University, Mankato, Minnesota.

[9]Kathy Weisensel, "David: And a Whole Lot of Other Neat People," in *Contemporary American Speeches*, 4th ed., Wil Linkugel, R. R. Allen, and Richard Johannesen. Eds., (Dubuque, Iowa: Kendall-Hunt, 1978), p. 74.

[10]From a speech given at The University of Iowa, fall term, 1976. Reprinted with the permission of Ms. Scott.

[11]From "A Look At The Fundamental School Concept" by James K. Wellington from *Vital Speeches of the Day*, January 15, 1977. Reprinted by permission of Vital Speeches of the Day.

[12]From "Stop Tampering With the Machinery" by Charles Gould from *Vital Speeches of the Day*, 46, February 1980. Reprinted by permission of Vital Speeches of the Day.

[13]For a technical yet rewarding introduction to statistical analysis generally, see Frederick Williams, *Reasoning with Statistics* (New York: Holt, Rinehart & Winston, Inc., 1968.)

[14]Representative Tom Steed. *Congressional Record*, 95th Congress, 1st Session, Volume 123, Part 8. Washington, D.C.: U.S. Government Printing Office, 1977, H379–H380.

[15]From "Chemical Waste" by Donald L. Baeder from *Vital Speeches of the Day*, 46, June 1980. Reprinted by permission of Vital Speeches of the Day.

[16]From "Working with the Federal Election Commission" by Joan D. Aikens from *Vital Speeches of the Day*, 47, February 1981. Reprinted by permission of Vital Speeches of the Day.

[17]From "Our Aging Population: Housing and the Elderly" by Daniel Rose from *Vital Speeches of the Day*, 44, August 1, 1978. Reprinted by permission of Vital Speeches of the Day.

[18]From "A Heap of Trouble" by Carl Hall. Reprinted from *Winning Orations* by special arrangement with the Interstate Oratorical Association, Larry Schnoor, Executive Secretary, Mankato State University, Mankato, Minnesota.

[19]To protect yourself from the unscrupulous uses of statistics, read Darrell Huff, *How to Lie with Statistics* (New York: W. W. Norton & Company, Inc., 1954).

[20]From "The New Civility" by David Mahoney from *Vital Speeches of the Day*, 46, April 1980. Reprinted by permission of Vital Speeches of the Day.

[21]From "Women and Men in Management" by Betty Ann Stead from *Vital Speeches of the Day*, 46, October 1979. Reprinted by permission of Vital Speeches of the Day.

[22]Jim Elleson, "The Imbalance of Power," in *Contemporary American Speeches*, 4th ed., see note 9 for full citation, pp. 136–37.

[23]Helen Fleshler, Joseph Ilardo, and Joan Demoretcky, "The Influence of Field Dependence, Speaker Credibility Set, and Message Documentation on Evaluations of Speaker and Message Credibility," *The Southern Speech Communication Journal*, 39 (1974): 389–402.

[24]From "People or Money . . . Which Will Rule the State?" by Lee Sherman Dreyfus from *Vital Speeches of the Day*, 46, April 1980. Reprinted by permission of Vital Speeches of the Day.

[25]Walter F. Mondale, "Vice Presidential Acceptance Address," *Vital Speeches*, 46 (August 15, 1980): 711.

[26]Mondale, p. 712.

[27]From a speech before Annual Leadership Conference by Dr. Ralph Eubanks, from *Vital Speeches of the Day*, 29, May 15, 1963. Reprinted by permission of Vital Speeches of the Day.

[28]Sources for the note cards are: From "A Manic Professor Tries to Close the Language Gap" by Richard Wolkomir, *Smithsonian*, May 1980. Reprinted by permission of the author. "Top 15 Regular Prime Time TV Programs of 1979–1980." Copyright © 1980 by A. C. Nielsen Company. Reprinted by permission.

PROBLEMS AND PROBES

CHAPTER REPORT   Read the essays by Harte and Kellerman listed in the Suggestions for Further Reading at the end of this chapter. Write a 500-750 word essay in which you briefly summarize the principal conclusions reached by the authors and, on the basis of your review, evaluate the significance of evidence as a means of supporting ideas. In your evaluations, consider two questions: Should you always use evidence? Does evidence make a difference in your effort to affect beliefs, attitudes, or values?

1.   Read three recent public addresses in *Vital Speeches of the Day* or some other suitable source, and tabulate the supporting materials employed by the speakers. Considering the subjects with which these speeches deal and the purposes at which they are aimed, try to explain why some forms of supporting material appear more frequently than others. For anthologies of recent speeches, see Carroll C. Arnold, Douglas Ehninger, and John Gerber. *The Speaker's Resource Book,* 2nd ed. (Scott, Foresman, 1966); Glenn Capp. *The Great Society* (Dickenson, 1968); Wil A. Linkugel, R. R. Allen, and Richard L. Johannesen, eds., *Contemporary American Speeches,* 4th ed. (Kendall-Hunt, 1978).

2.   Review a transcript from the Carter/Reagan debate, or listen to a tape of the actual proceedings. What kinds of supporting materials were employed by these presidential candidates? Did the materials substantiate the claims that were made? Did one candidate have better supporting material than the other? Did this affect the outcome of the debate and your perception of which speaker did the better job of debating?

3.   Arrange to meet classmates in the Reference Room of your college library. Work in groups of five. Each member will locate two of the items in the left-hand column of the following list. First, determine which of the sources listed in the right-hand column contains the material you need. When you locate your items, show your group the source and indicate where it is shelved.

a. Weekly summary of current national news	*Book Review Digest*
b. Brief sketch of the accomplishments of Henry Ford	*Congressional Record*
c. Description of specific traffic accident	*Encyclopedia Americana*
d. Explanation of major Indian tribes	*local newspaper*
e. Text of Ronald Reagan's Inaugural Address	*New York Times*
f. Comprehensive data on oil production in U.S. in 1980 and 1981	*Oxford English Dictionary*
	Statistical Abstracts
g. Daily summary of stock prices	
h. Origin of word "rhetoric"	*Time*
i. Critical commentary on Christopher Lasch's *The Culture of Narcissism,* published in 1978	*Vital Speeches*
	Who's Who
j. Current status of national legislation on gun control	

4.   Editorials generally present an abbreviated argument supporting or opposing an issue of current local, national, or international interest. Find a recent editorial in a newspaper or magazine and identify the major premises in the argument. In addition to the supporting materials offered by the author, find three original pieces of support for each point. Consider what kinds of evidence are appropriate to the particular premise and to the argument in general. Does the author provide sufficient and adequate evidence? Using the editorial as the basis for a speech to persuade, construct an outline for the speech that uses your supporting materials.

5.   Interview a friend, family member, or classmate regarding some attitude, belief, or value he or she holds strongly. Tape the conversation if possible; if not, simply take notes. Ask the person to state the attitude, belief, or value, to explain why he or she holds it, and to defend the view. Assume the role of a somewhat skeptical observer. Later, analyze the response in terms of the kinds and quality of supporting materials employed. Were they sufficient and adequate? Would the evidence supplied in the interview be sufficient and adequate in a speech? What other supporting materials might strengthen the response?

 ORAL ACTIVITIES

1.   Present to the class a five-minute, central-idea speech, the purpose of which is either to explain or clarify a term, concept, process, or to verify or prove a point. Use at least three different forms of supporting material in developing your idea. To formulate an evaluation of the effectiveness of your speech, the instructor and the other students will consider the following: *(a)* adequacy of supporting material; *(b)* appropriateness of supporting material, both as to type and to substance; and *(c)* the insight and skill with which the supporting material is developed.

2.   Following the suggestions offered in this chapter, prepare to present in class a two- or three-minute central-point speech to inform, to convince, or to actuate. For a subject, consult entries in your Personal Speech Journal, the list of subject categories at the end of Chapter 4, or both.

SUGGESTIONS FOR FURTHER READING

Pearl Aldrich, *Research Papers: A Beginner's Manual* (Cambridge, MA: Winthrop Publishers, 1976).

Douglas Ehninger, *Influence, Belief, and Argument* (Glenview, IL: Scott, Foresman and Co. 1974), Chapter 5.

B. Thomas Florence, "An Empirical Test of the Relationship of Evidence to Belief Systems and Attitude Change," *Human Communication Research,* 1 (1975): 145–58.

Thomas Harte, "The Effects of Evidence in Persuasive Communication," *Central States Speech Journal,* 27 (1976): 42–46.

Kathy Kellerman, "The Concept of Evidence: A Critical Review," *The Journal of the American Forensic Association,* 16 (1980): 159–72.

Charles J. Stewart and William B. Cash, Jr., *Interviewing: Principles and Practices,* 2nd ed. (Dubuque, IA: Wm. C. Brown, 1978).

Adapting the Speech Structure to Audiences: The Motivated Sequence

In preceding chapters we considered how to select the basic appeals and support the principal ideas comprising your speeches. It is now time to discuss ways in which those materials should be structured or organized to form the speech as a whole. You cannot simply ram ideas down people's throats, nor can you usually get away with stringing them together in a random manner; ideas must be digested and then shaped into a sensible, coherent whole, so that people will voluntarily and easily follow them to your conclusions.

Because different organizational patterns serve different audience needs and emphasize different aspects of topics, speakers should have a thorough knowledge of various structures or patterns and the uses to which each can be put on occasion. In this chapter we will examine the psychological bases underlying the need for structure generally, and then discuss in detail a common, highly useful pattern—the Motivated Sequence—so called because it is based on the kind of motivational analysis we reviewed in Chapter 6. Then, in Chapter 9, we will define and exemplify the more traditional patterns which speakers have used for centuries.

The Psychological Bases of Speech Organization

Human beings, like all other animals, learn quickly in life to react to stimuli in their environments; we learn to sort out stimuli (experiences) into various categories of things or events, in order to predict consequences. But, unlike most other animals, humans can go beyond sorting, even beyond understanding consequences—they can seek *coherence* in their environments. (1) We can *generalize and anticipate*. A baby who burns its hand on a hot stove, a match, and a metal sheet sitting in the sun quickly learns that "hot objects produce pain"; the baby can remember past instances of pain and anticipate future pain when it notices even previously unexperienced "hot objects" in its surroundings. (2) We search for *coherent structures* in our environments. Young children soon learn to seek relationships between and among items in their environment. They learn early that one set of furniture comprises a bedroom, another set, a kitchen, and another set, a playroom; they soon learn that living and dead objects are treated differently. By early elementary school, children can determine what is "foreground" or "figure" in a picture, and what is "background" or supporting detail. An important part of environmental control is understanding relationships between and among the environmental elements. (3) Structures become so important to us psychologically that we even learn to *fill in or complete* missing elements. If someone says to you, "One, two, three, four," you almost automatically continue, "five, six, seven, eight." Cartoonists can draw a minimum number of features of a famous person, and most members of their reading public will be able to identify the person in question. This is because we all have what Gestalt psychologists term the "drive to complete," the need to complete missing elements and thus "make sense" out of some stimulus.[1]

Speakers and others who work with ideas publicly have an even more importan quality of coherence to consider: (4) *People can make ideas coherent in a number of different ways*. Sometimes, people make sense out of their experiences by arranging them chronologically, as when describing the high points in their lives. Occasionally they will discuss something they are looking at by moving from left to right or top to bottom. When they want to understand what events led to what consequences, they may try to relate "causes" to "effects." And sometimes they simply seek "natural" divisions in objects or events—inside vs. outside, the three branches of government, body vs. soul, night vs. day—in order to talk intelligibly about them. All these ways of relating two or more aspects of objects, places, and events to each other form the bases for most of the organizational patterns we will examine in Chapter 9.

Finally, however, there is one especially important way individuals come to grips with the environment and their own thoughts or actions within it—they systematically examine and then follow up on *their own motivations*. This is a natural tendency, for we all seek not only to rationalize our surroundings but also to find our own place within them. We tend to follow our own motives-to-act in one of two ways:

1. We may tend toward a *world-* or *problem-orientation*. The American philosopher John Dewey early in this century recognized this tendency when he devised his "psycho-logic"—a pattern for thought he called "reflective thinking." In Dewey's view, individuals tend to (and sometimes do) follow a systematic procedure for solving problems. First, said Dewey, people become aware of a specific lack or disorientation—some situation with which they are, for one rea-

son or another, dissatisfied. Second, they examine this difficulty in their world to determine its nature, scope, causes, and implications. Third, they search for new orientations or operations that will solve the problem or satisfy the need. Fourth, they compare and evaluate the possible solutions that have occurred to them. And, fifth, they select the solution or course of action which, upon the basis of their foregoing reflections, seems most likely to put their minds at rest and to handle the real-world dimensions of the problem.[2] Dewey, in other words, adapted the so-called "scientific method" to individual and group problem-solving.

2. Our other tendency is to be more *self-centered*, more *motivation-centered*. Salespersons and advertisers began recognizing this principle in the 1920s. They realized that you and I buy a particular automobile, not simply to get from here to there, but also to create a certain image; we buy this or that style of clothes to identify ourselves with others who wear certain sorts of trousers and coats; we buy furniture that is both functional and decorative. In other words, our personal motivations, hopes, fears, and desires often control the ways we act and the goods we consume.

Alan Monroe (1903–1975), the original author of this textbook, knew Dewey's work well and had himself worked in the 1920s training sales personnel. As he thought about Dewey's "psycho-logic" and the various sales techniques he had taught people to employ, Monroe discovered he could unite both sets of procedures—one set based on the personalized scientific method, and the other rooted in an understanding of human motivation—to form a highly useful organizational pattern. Since 1935, that structure has been called "Monroe's Motivated Sequence."[3] We will devote the rest of this chapter to it.

The Motivated Sequence: Its Five Basic Steps

The motivated sequence derives its name partly because it follows Dewey's problem-solution format for thinking and partly because it makes attractive analyses of those problems and their solutions by tying them to human motives. That is, in terms of our preceding discussion, the motivated sequence is simultaneously problem-oriented and motivation-centered.

There are five basic steps in the motivated sequence: (1) To begin with, you must get people to attend to some problem, or to feel disorientation or discomfort strongly enough to want to hear more. (2) Then, you can create more specific wants or desires, a personal sense of need. (3) Third, when wants or needs are created, you can attempt to satisfy them by showing what can be done to solve the problem or relieve the sense of discomfort. (4) Simply describing a course of action, however, may not be enough, so in the fourth place you can visualize the world as it would look if the actions were carried out (and often what it might be like if they were not). (5) With that, if the speaker has done the preceding four tasks well, audience members should be ready to act—to put into practice the proposed solution to their problems.

Thus, the motivated sequence is composed generally of five basic steps in the presentation of verbal materials (see figure, page 148):

1. *Attention.* The creation of interest and desire.
2. *Need.* The development of the problem, through an analysis of things wrong in the world and through a relating of those wrongs to individuals' interests, wants, or desires.
3. *Satisfaction.* The proposal of a plan of áction which will alleviate the problem and satisfy the individuals' interests, wants, or desires.
4. *Visualization.* The verbal depiction of the world as it will look if the plan is put into operation.
5. *Action.* The final call for personal commitments and deeds.

The motivated sequence can be used to structure many different sorts of speeches on many different kinds of topics. It could be used, for example, in a speech urging your classmates to join a blood donors' association: (*Attention*) "If you had needed an emergency blood transfusion in Johnson County on December 17, 1981, you probably would not have gotten it." (*Need*) "Blood drives seldom produce enough blood of all types to meet emergency needs in an area such as this one." (*Satisfaction*) "A blood donors' association guarantees a predictable, steady supply of blood to the medical community." (*Visualization*) "Without a steady supply of blood, our community will face needless deaths; with it, emergencies will be met with prompt treatment." (*Action*) "You can help by filling out the blood donors' cards I am passing out."

Or, you could use the motivated sequence to sell a friend insurance: (*Attention*) "For pennies a day, you can pick up considerable peace of mind and a solid background for future financial security." (*Need*) "Life insurance can protect your family from the impact of an untimely death, guarantee you future security, give you a source of emergency loans, educate your children, and supplement other forms of investment." (*Satisfaction*) "Here's how we can tailor your insurance coverage to meet particular aspects of your own situation." (*Visualization*) "Consider the following situations and what a life insurance program can do to get you out of them." (*Action*) "Get a routine physical examination today, and tomorrow we can start your coverage for as small or as large an investment as you care to make."

The motivated sequence also can be used to talk about larger, more pervasive aspects of social problems. The following speech was prepared by Ms. Jan Bjorklund of Mankato State College, Mankato, Minnesota, and was presented in one of the annual contests sponsored by the Interstate Oratorical Association. As you read the speech, note how Ms. Bjorklund (1) calls *attention* to her subject by piquing curiosity; (2) points out—with statistics, specific instances, authoritative testimony, and comparisons—the crucial *need* to bring venereal disease under control; (3) demonstrates—by offering a three-way solution—that this need can be *satisfied;* (4) briefly *visualizes* the results of carrying out the proposed solution; and (5) concludes with an appeal for direct and immediate *action* in the form of a concerted drive against the disease.

THE MOTIVATED SEQUENCE

1 *Attention*

Getting attention

Vote for Clean Air

I want to listen

2 *Need*

Showing the need: describing the problem

Something needs to be done

3 *Satisfaction*

Satisfying the need: presenting the solution

This is what to do to satisfy the need

4 *Visualization*

Visualizing the results

I can see myself enjoying the benefits of such an action

5 *Action*

Requesting action or approval

Clean Air ☒ Yes ☐ No

I will do this

Nice People[4]

Jan Bjorklund

Attention Step

What I am about to say, I have said before; so have many others in many other ways. And that's about it. A great deal has been said, but very little has been done; so this problem remains a problem. For this reason, I'd like to emphasize the words and the meaning of this speech, hoping that you will react from an understanding of these words. /1

Need Step

An epidemic of contagious disease is threatening the United States at this very minute: one so massive that a new case occurs every 15 seconds, for a total of 7,500 a day.[1] /2

All age levels are being victimized by this disease, but most selectively young people, ages 16 to 30. This epidemic is capable of spreading undetected inside the bodies of over 700,000 women, allowing them to continue a normal life, causing them no discomfort, no disability, no pain, while robbing them of their ability to bear children.[2] /3

All the while this disease continues to strike, to spread, and to slay, the means to cure it not only exist, but are relatively inexpensive, relatively simple to administer, and painless to the receiver. /4

Isn't it strange that our nation, one of the healthiest in the world, should allow such a disease to continue, to multiply into an uncontrollable epidemic? One would think that the halls of government would be echoing with the debate and discussion of possible courses of action to eradicate this festering blight. Yes, one could think that—until realizing this is not the case, due to the small and medically irrelevant fact that the disease in question is *venereal* disease. /5

In 1936, the Surgeon General of the United States Public Health Service, Thomas Parran, stated that the great impediment to the solution of the VD problem was that "nice" people don't have it.[3] Since then, the basis for this statement has disappeared. Oh, Freaks have it, and Blacks, and Jesus People, and urban disadvantaged, and poverty-stricken, and people on welfare: *they* all have it, all right! It's been called "their" disease. But is it theirs alone? /6

Berkeley, California, is a "nice" place to live. Within the city's limits, we find the University of California and many of its prominent faculty and students. Last year, 2,000 cases of gonorrhea were reportedly found there, too.[4] /7

Houston, Texas, is a "nice" place, too. Nice enough to attract attention and become the headquarters for our national space program. Last year it also attracted 1,266 cases of gonorrhea for every 100,000 inhabitants.[5] Atlanta, Georgia, the cultural and commercial capital of the South, also leads the nation in the reported number of cases of gonorrhea. Last year it reported 2,510 cases for every 100,00 inhabitants.[6] /8

These are only the *reported* cases, estimated to be 25 percent of all cases, for only 1 out of every 4 cases is ever reported.[7] /9

This would mean that of the 100,000 inhabitants of Berkeley, California, approximately 8,000 contracted VD; that would be 1 out of 12! /10

This ratio isn't so crucial, though, when you compare it to that in some San Francisco high schools where a student has 1 chance in 5 of contracting syphilis or gonorrhea before he graduates.[8] /11

Why? People neglect to get the proper treatment; or when they do, they don't name all their contacts, so the disease continues to spread. /12

According to *Today's Health* magazine, of the 4 out of 5 cases that are treated by private physicians, only 1 out of 9 is reported.[9] And of the many, many that go by unreported, I'd guess that 90 percent involve nice people. /13

Syphilis and gonorrhea are infectious diseases outranked in incidence only by the common cold.[10] /14

Venereal disease is especially rampant among young people. As reported in *Newsweek*, January 24, 1972, at least 1 of every 5 persons with gonorrhea is below the age of 20.[11] Last year, over 5,000 cases were found among children between the ages of 10 and 14. Another 2,000 cases were found among children below the age of 9. Dr. Walter Smartt, Chief of the Los Angeles County Venereal Disease Control Division, states that the probability of a person acquiring VD before he reaches the age of 25 is about 50 percent. This would mean that of the number of us here in this room, one half of us have already or shortly will come in contact with VD. Where does that put you? Or me? It's always easy to say it can only happen to someone else, to the other person, but there is only one guarantee that it can't strike me or you. /15

And that one guarantee is abstinence. But in this day and age, that's hardly a likely possibility. We wouldn't think of stopping tuberculosis by stopping breathing, so how could we think of stopping venereal disease by stopping sex? /16

Satisfaction Step
What is the solution? A number of suggestions have been made. First of all, in the opinion of many experts, syphilis could be brought under control by case-finding. However, in the last few years the number of case-finders has been reduced. The federal government is not supporting this effort. /17

Secondly, there is a deplorable inadequacy in both teaching and courses of instruction concerning VD. We need an educational effort at the earliest feasible age group. Looking at the ages of the patients coming into the clinics, we see we almost have to beat puberty. /18

Another possibility has been suggested by Dr. John Knox of Houston's Baylor College of Medicine. He predicts that a vaccine for syphilis could easily be developed in 5 years, but at the rate the government is putting out money, it will probably take 105 years.[12] A vaccine for gonorrhea, on the other hand, seems almost impossible at this point. There is a crying need for more research. /19

Visualization Step
I thought for sure that such a complex problem would require a complicated cure. However, I became aware of my mistaken thinking during a visit with my college physician, Dr. Hankerson. He informed me that syphilis and gonorrhea can be brought under control and cured by simple treatments of penicillin or similar antibiotics. If every American would have a regular checkup, and receive treatment if necessary, by 1973 we could begin to send venereal disease the way of typhoid, measles, polio, and the bubonic plague. If each of us would begin with a regular checkup, now. /20

Action Step

As you can see, it is a complex problem, and no one solution can completely eliminate it. What we need is a concerted drive that will encompass case-finding, support for an educational effort, and the search for a vaccine, along with the use of penicillin and other similar antibiotics. /21

But even if this does happen, the effort cannot be successful, for venereal disease will continue to spread as long as it is thought of as dirty and shameful. Dr. McKenzie-Pollock, former director of the American Social Health Association, made the following statement: "Once the public is aware and notified that syphilis and gonorrhea are serious factors in our everyday lives right now, the rest will follow."[13] /22

Very well, consider yourself *notified* . . . or are you one of those "nice people"? /23

Reference Notes (for the Speech)
[1]VD Fact Sheet—*1971, U.S. Department of Health, Education, and Welfare, Public Health Service, page 9.* [2]Today's Health, *April 1971, page 16.* [3]Today's Health, *April 1971, page 16.* [4]VD Statistical Letter, *DHEW, February 1972, page 11.* [5]Ibid., *page 4.* [6]Newsweek, *January 24, 1972, page 46.* [7]Minneapolis Tribune, *Wednesday, April 5, 1972, page 2A.* [8]Newsweek, *January 24, 1972, page 46.* [9]Today's Health, *April 1971, page 69.* [10]Sex and the Yale Student, *Student Committee on Human Sexuality, 1970, page 51.* [11]Ibid., *page 46.* [12]Ibid., *page 49.* [13]Today's Health, *April 1971, page 69.*

The Structure and Development of the Steps in the Motivated Sequence

Now that we have viewed the motivated sequence as a whole, let us look more closely at the *individual steps*, noting in particular their internal structuring, the methods of their development, and the kinds of materials that may be used with good effect in each. The five basic steps in the motivated sequence are illustrated in the diagram on page 148.

The Attention Step

As a speaker, your first task is to *gain attention*. Attention may be thought of as a focusing on one element in a given field, with the result that other elements in that field fade, become dim, and for all practical purposes momentarily cease to exist.[5] In other words, gaining attention is a matter of causing listeners to focus tightly on you and your ideas—rather than on a knocking radiator, tomorrow's dental appointment, or the person down the row. You capture people's attention in part, of course, by the way you deliver your speech—the vigor and variety of your gestures and bodily movements, the flexibility and animation of your voice. Your credibility or *ethos* with the audience also help you secure a degree of attention, as will the color and impressiveness of your language or style. *Fundamentally, however, you will capture—and hold—attention through the types of ideas you present to your listeners*. Your ideas must tap their sense of interest and personal motivation to "force" them to listen.

The types of ideas that have high attention value are sometimes called the *factors of attention,* and include the following: (1) activity or movement; (2) reality; (3) proximity; (4) familiarity; (5) novelty; (6) suspense; (7) conflict; (8) humor; and (9) the vital. These terms, of course, overlap; and, in an actual speech the qualities they represent often are combined. For purposes of explanation, however, let us consider them separately.

Activity • If you were at the theater and one actor was standing motionless while another was moving excitedly about the stage, which one would you look at? The moving one, more likely. Ideas that "move" likewise tend to attract attention. Narratives in which something happens or in which there are moments of uncertainty and crisis nearly always have attention value. Similarly, expository talks hold attention when, for instance, the parts of a machine are described as being in motion or when aspects of a process are introduced.

In addition, your speech as a whole should "move"—should, as someone has said, "march" or press forward. Nothing is so boring as a talk that seems to stand still. For this reason, it is important to make the progress of your speech apparent to your audience by indicating when you have finished one idea and are ready to tackle the next, or by previewing the ground yet to be covered. Instructions and demonstrations, particularly, demand orderly, systematic "marching." Do not spend too much time on any one point, and do not elaborate the obvious; constantly push ahead toward a clearly defined goal.

Reality • The earliest words a child learns are the names of "real" objects and of tangible acts related to them. This interest in reality—in the immediate, the concrete, the actual—persists throughout life. The proposition $2 + 2 = 4$ when unrelated to any specific events, persons, or circumstances holds little interest. Instead of talking in abstractions, talk of real-life people, places, and happenings. Use pictures, diagrams, and charts, especially in reports. Tell not what happened to "a certain prominent physician of this city," but to Dr. Fred Smith, who lives at 418 Paine Street. Remember always that actual cases are more real to a listener than general trends or broad classifications; particular names and places more interesting than impersonalized, vague allusions.

Proximity • A direct reference to someone in the audience, to some object near at hand, to some incident that has just occurred, or to the immediate occasion on which the speech is being made usually will command attention. A reference to a remark of a preceding speaker or of the chairperson creates a similar effect. If attention lags, call a member of the audience by name or make him or her the central character in a hypothetical illustration. Not only will this awaken anyone who happens to be dozing (heaven forbid!), but it will also tend to increase the attention-level of the other members. As psychologists Floyd L. Ruch and Philip G. Zimbardo point out, "Individuating listeners is one of the most effective means of getting—and holding—attention. When you are talking to a single individual, looking him straight in the eye increases the likelihood that he will look back at you and listen to what you have to say."[6]

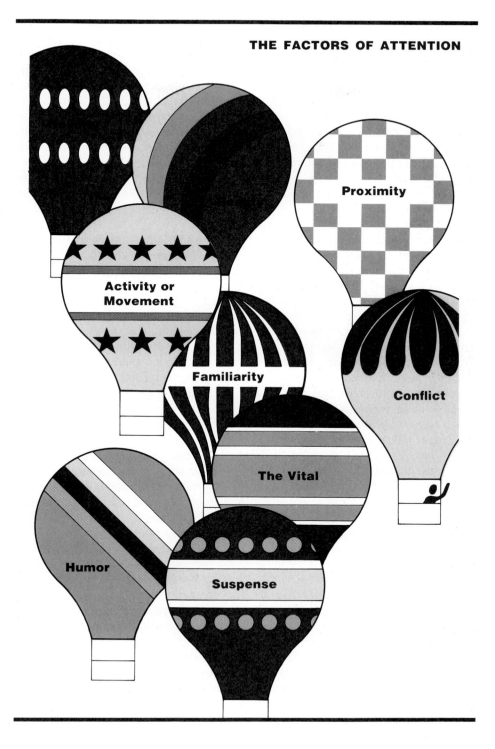

Familiarity • Many things are familiar to us because of the frequency with which we meet them in our daily lives. Knives and forks, rain, automobiles, toothbrushes, classes, and a host of other common objects and events are closely built into our experiences. Because they are so much a part of us, these familiar things catch our attention. We say, "Ah, that is an old friend"; oral instructions almost always profit from references to the familiar. But, as with old acquaintances, we become bored if we see too much of them and nothing else. In a spoken message, the familiar holds attention primarily when the speaker introduces it in connection with something unfamiliar or when some fresh or unknown aspect of it is pointed out. Stories about Lincoln and Washington, for example, are interesting because we are familiar with their characters; but we don't like to hear the same old railsplitter or cherry-tree tales unless they are given a new twist or application.

Novelty • As an old newspaper adage has it, when a dog bites a man, it's an accident; when a man bites a dog, it's news. Perhaps we should marvel that airplanes make countless flights across the oceans every day, but we take this for granted. Even missile launchings and space travel command less attention than they did a few years ago. Routine occurrences are not news; only novel happenings, dramatic advances, or unusual developments attract wide notice.

Two special types of novelty are *size* and *contrast*. Insofar as *size* is concerned, especially large or especially small objects or amounts attract attention. Reference to a $7,500 automobile or to a $75,000 home would not stand out as unusual; but reference to a $30,000 automobile or to a $300,000 home would. In a speech on the high cost of national defense, a speaker caught the attention of his listeners with this sentence: "Considering that it costs more than $5,000 to equip an average soldier for combat, it is disquieting to learn that in a year his equipment will be 60% obsolete."[7]

Although attention-arousing in themselves, large and small figures become even more compelling when thrown into *contrast* with their opposites. Here is how Henry W. Grady, in an address at the University of Virginia, used novel or startling contrasts to focus attention on the gap between the rich and the poor:

> A home that cost three million dollars and a breakfast that cost five thousand are disquieting facts to the millions who live in a hut and dine on a crust. The fact that a man . . . has an income of twenty million dollars falls strangely on the ears of those who hear it as they sit empty-handed with children crying for bread.[8]

In utilizing the materials of novelty be careful, of course, not to inject elements that are so different or unusual that they are entirely unfamiliar. As we have emphasized, your listeners must at least know what you are talking about, or their attention will soon waver. They must be able to relate what you say to things they know and—preferably—have a degree of experience with. Best results are achieved by the proper combination of the new and the old, of the novel and the familiar. Note, too, that novelty may gain attention, but will not necessarily hold it.

Suspense • A large part of the interest that people have in a mystery story arises from uncertainty about its outcome. When you give a speech, create uncertainty by pointing out results which have mysterious or unknown causes or by calling attention to forces which threaten uncertain effects. Introduce suspense into the stories you use to illustrate your ideas, especially in lectures or even in demonstrations. Mention valuable information you expect to divulge later in your talk that requires an understanding of what you are now saying. Use the factor of suspense, but observe two cautions: (1) Do not make the information seem so difficult or mysterious that your listeners lose all hope of comprehending it; and (2) make sure that the information you finally reveal is important enough to warrant the suspense you have created.

Conflict • The opposition of forces compels attention—especially if the listeners identify themselves with one of the contending sides. Conflict, like suspense, often suggests uncertainty; but even when there is little doubt of the outcome, the combat itself draws attention. Football games, election contests, the struggle against disease and the adverse elements of nature—all these have an element of conflict within them; and people become interested when the conflict is vividly described. For the same reason, controversy is more interesting than concurrence. A vigorous attack upon some antisocial force—be it organized crime, graft, or child abuse—will draw more immediate attention than an objective analysis of it, although the analysis might—in the long run—prove more effective or enduring. Describe a fight, show vividly the opposition between two factions, or launch a verbal attack on somebody or something, and people usually will listen to you. Be cautious, however, of sham battles. If you set up straw men and knock them down, the reality—and hence the effectiveness—of your message may be largely destroyed. Nevertheless, communicating a sense of conflict can vitalize a report or lecture, especially when you want listeners to visualize a decision they must make in the future.

Humor • Laughter indicates enjoyment, and people pay attention to that which they enjoy. Few things, in fact, will hold an audience as well as the speaker's judicious use of humor. It provides relaxation from the tension often created by other factors of attention—conflict and suspense, especially—and thus reduces fatigue while still exercising a measure of control over the perceptions of the listener. When using humor, however, remember that its attention-holding power is likely to be much stronger if you keep two guidelines in mind: (1) *Be relevant*. Beware of wandering from the point under discussion. Any joke or anecdote you use must reinforce rather than detract from the central ideas of your speech. (2) *Use good taste*. Avoid humor on occasions where it would be out of place, and refrain from using those types of humor which might offend the sensitivities of your listeners.

The vital • Finally, people nearly always pay attention to matters that affect their health, reputation, property, or employment. If you can show your audience that what you are saying concerns them in one or more of these ways, the chances are good that they will consider your message vital and will listen to it closely. Pointing out how your subject concerns persons close to them also will command your listeners' attention because people tend to identify themselves with family, friends, and associates. If the other factors of attention are important, an appeal to the *vital* is indispensable.

The vital, humor, conflict, suspense, novelty, familiarity, proximity, reality, and activity or movement—these nine attention-attractors should be your constant guides when you are assembling, sorting out, and presenting ideas for a speech. They have special importance for the Attention Step in the Motivated Sequence, of course, because they can be used to draw listeners into the world of your topic and purpose. But, because they allow you to achieve clarity and concreteness as well as engage listeners' minds when people must relate what is new or unknown to experiences which are old or known, the factors of attention likewise can be employed throughout any speech. They should help you keep hearers motivated and interested in what you are saying.

The Need Step

Ideally, a good need step should contain four parts or elements:

1. *Statement*—a clear, concise statement or description of the need.
2. *Illustration*—one or more detailed examples which illustrate the need.
3. *Ramification*—additional examples, statistical data, testimony, and other forms of support to show the extent of the need.
4. *Pointing*—a convincing demonstration of how the need directly affects the people addressed: their health, happiness, security, or other interests.

When dealing with a simple problem or with one the audience knows a good deal about, you may not find it necessary to use all four of these parts or structural elements. But regardless of whether you use the complete fourfold development, only a part of it, or some other structure, you will find that the need step is one of the most important in your speech. *It is here that you relate your subject to the vital concerns and interests of your audience.*

The Satisfaction Step

The purpose of the satisfaction step, as we have suggested, is to enable your hearers to understand the information you are presenting or to get them to agree that the belief or action you propose is the correct one. The structure of this step differs somewhat, however, depending on whether your major purpose is primarily informative or persuasive. For this reason, the satisfaction step for informative or instructive speeches and the satisfaction step for persuasive and actuative speeches must be considered separately.

The satisfaction step in speeches to inform • When your purpose is to inform—to give your audience a clear understanding of some subject—the satisfaction step usually will constitute the bulk of your speech and will present the information that was specified as necessary in the need step. The development of the satisfaction step as used in informative speeches customarily includes:

1. *Initial summary*—briefly state in advance the main ideas or points you intend to cover.
2. *Detailed information*—discuss in order the facts or explanations pertaining to each of these ideas or points.
3. *Final summary*—restate the main points or ideas you have presented, together with any important conclusions you have drawn from them.

The satisfaction step in speeches to persuade • When the purpose of your speech is to persuade or to actuate, these four elements are usually included in the satisfaction step:

1. *Statement*—briefly state the attitude, belief, or action you wish the audience to adopt.
2. *Explanation*—make sure your proposal is understood. Diagrams or charts are often useful here.
3. *Theoretical demonstration*—show how this belief or action logically meets the problem pointed out in the need step.
4. *Practical experience*—give actual examples showing that this proposal has worked effectively or that this belief has been proved correct. Use facts, figures, and the testimony of experts to support your claims.

Here again, probably, you will find that you do not need to include all of these elements or parts in the satisfaction step of every persuasive speech. Nor will it be necessary that they always appear in the same order. For instance, you can sometimes meet objections best by distributing answers strategically throughout the step, at whatever point questions are likely to arise. When developing the satisfaction step in speeches to persuade or to actuate, however, the first four elements—*statement, explanation, theoretical demonstration,* and *practical experience*—offer a convenient and effective sequence, thus: *(a)* Briefly state the attitude, belief, or action you propose. *(b)* Explain it clearly. *(c)* Show how, in theory, it will meet the need. *(d)* Give actual examples of how the proposal or plan is working.

Parallel development of the need and satisfaction steps • In some speeches of a persuasive nature, the need step may have two or more important aspects. To give each of these aspects sufficient emphasis and to make your discussion clear, you may decide to develop the need and satisfaction steps in a *parallel* order. That is, you first present one aspect of the need and show how your proposal satisfies it; then you follow this same procedure in treating the second aspect, the third aspect, and so on. This method weakens the cumulative effect of the motivated sequence, but the additional clarity often makes up for the loss.

The *normal order* and the *parallel order* for developing the need and satisfaction steps of a speech to actuate are illustrated in the following skeletal outlines:

OUTLINE I: NORMAL ORDER

Attention Step

I. While working on the construction of the new state highway last summer, I witnessed a number of automobile accidents in which the driver was severely injured.
   A. Vivid description of how the accident occurred.
   B. Vivid description of the injuries sustained by the driver.

Need Step

I. In each case the driver was injured either because he or she was driving too fast or failed to wear a seat belt.
   A. The driver was unable to stop in time.
   B. The driver was thrown through the windshield or against the steering post.

Satisfaction Step

I. In order to reduce your chances of serious injury or even death, you must do two things above all others.
   A. You must slow down.
   B. You must wear your seat belt at all times.

Visualization Step

I. You will actually enjoy driving more when you have the assurance these actions bring.

Action Step

I. Resolve right now to do two things when you drive.
   A. Go slower.
   B. Always wear your seat belt.

OUTLINE II: PARALLEL ORDER

Attention Step

I. While working on the construction of the new state highway last summer, I witnessed a number of automobile accidents in which the driver was severely injured.
   A. Vivid description of how the accident occurred.
   B. Vivid description of the injuries sustained by the driver.

Need and Satisfaction Steps (First phase)

I. In some cases the driver was unable to stop in time.

II. To assure yourself a safe stopping distance you must slow down.

Need and Satisfaction Steps (Second phase)

   I.   In some cases the driver was thrown through the windshield or against the steering post.

  II.   To guard against such an eventuality, you must wear your seat belt at all times.

Visualization Step

   I.   You will actually enjoy driving more when you have the assurance these actions bring.

Action Step

   I.   Resolve right now to do two things when you drive.
     A.   Go slower.
     B.   Always wear your seat belt.

Whether you use the normal order or the parallel order in the satisfaction step, you will, of course, always need to develop support for your statements by supplying an abundance of illustrations, statistics, quotations, and comparisons.

The Visualization Step

The visualization step, as we have said, is commonly used only in the speeches to persuade or to actuate. (See the chart on page 162.) The function of the visualization step is *to intensify desire:* to help motivate the listeners to believe, feel, or act. In order to do this, it projects them into the future. Indeed, this step might also be called the "projection" step, for its effectiveness depends in large part upon the vividness with which it pictures the future or potential benefits of believing or acting as the speaker proposes. Accordingly, the visualization step may be developed in one of three ways: (1) by projecting a picture of the future that is *positive,* (2) by projecting a picture that is *negative,* or (3) by projecting first a negative and then a positive picture in order to show *contrast.*

The positive method of developing the visualization step • When using the positive method, describe conditions as they will be in the future if the belief you advocate is accepted or the action you propose is carried out. Provide vivid, concrete descriptions. Select some situation which you are quite sure will arise in the future, and in that situation picture your audience actually enjoying the safety, pleasure, pride, etc., which the belief or proposal will produce.

The negative method of developing the visualization step • When using the negative method, describe the adverse conditions that will prevail in the future if the belief you advocate is *not* adopted or the solution you propose is *not* carried out. Graphically picture for your audience the danger or unpleasantness which will result. Select the most striking problems or deficiencies you have pointed out in the need step and demonstrate how they will continue unless your recommendations are adopted.

The contrast method of developing the visualization step • The method of contrast combines the positive and negative approaches. Use the negative development first, visualizing the *bad* effects that are likely to occur if your listeners fail to follow your advice; then introduce the positive elements, visualizing the *good* effects of believing or doing as you urge. By means of this contrast, both the bad and the good effects are made more striking and intense.

Whichever method you use, however, remember that the visualization step always must stand the test of *reality*. The conditions you picture must seem probable. In addition, you must to the fullest extent possible *put your listeners into the picture*. Use vivid imagery: make them actually see, hear, feel, taste, or smell the things and benefits you describe. The more real you make the projected situation seem, the stronger will be their reaction.

The following visualization step, in a speech advocating planned and orderly urban growth, illustrates the method of contrast:

> Whether we like it or not, then, as these facts show, nearly all of our towns and cities are going to continue to grow and expand in the years ahead. *How* your town grows, however, is going to be entirely up to you.
>
> As new suburbs are developed and annexed, one of two policies can be followed. First, this growth may be haphazard and unplanned, and may occur without strict zoning ordinances to regulate it. In this case, it is likely that paved streets, if they are present at all, will be cheaply constructed without storm sewers or attention to traffic flow. Houses will be crowded together on tiny lots and will vary widely in value and in architectural style. Filling stations, business establishments, and even light industries—with their odors and noises—may appear in the middle of residential neighborhoods. In short, if you were to buy a home in such an area, it is altogether likely that you would soon be faced with huge bills for new streets and sewers, and that your property, instead of appreciating in value, would decline rapidly in the years ahead. As a home buyer you would be a loser all around—a loser not only because of the poor quality of life you and your family would experience, but a loser, and a big loser, in hard dollars and cents.
>
> On the other hand, if additions to your town are properly planned and zoned, as a home owner you will be assured of clean air and adequate living space, will enjoy a house that increases rather than decreases in value, and will be assured that you are not paying for new streets and sewers a few years after you move in. Isn't it worthwhile requiring that your town annex only subdivisions that have been properly planned and zoned—that it insist on orderly responsible growth? Remember, buying a home is very probably the largest single purchase you will make during the course of your entire life. Remember, too, that a healthy, attractive environment is perhaps the greatest gift you can give to your family.

The Action Step

As the chart on page 162 indicates, only the speech to actuate *always* requires an action step. At times, however, as a speaker you may use something resembling an action step to urge further study of the topic dealt with in an informative speech or to strengthen the belief or attitude urged in a persuasive one.

There are many methods for developing the action step, but most commonly these methods employ one or more of the following devices: *(a)* challenge or appeal, *(b)* summary, *(c)* quotation, *(d)* illustration, *(e)* statement of inducement, *(f)* statement of personal intention—materials which are considered in detail in Chapter 10, pages 190–193.

Whatever method or material you use, be sure to keep the action step *short*. Someone has given the following rule for effective public speaking: "Stand up, speak up, shut up!" Insofar as the action step is concerned, modify this admonition to read: *Clinch your major ideas, finish your speech briskly—and sit down.*

Applying the Motivated Sequence

As we conclude this chapter, let us now see how the motivated sequence can be used to organize your speeches regardless of their general purposes. Because we will discuss it further in later chapters (especially Chapter 17), we here will offer only short outlines, to give you a basic sense of the coherence which can be achieved when you use this organizational pattern.

The Motivated Sequence and Speeches to Inform

Generally, an informative speech concentrates on only three of the five steps. As always, you need to catch your listeners' *attention* and direct it to the substance of your remarks. You must also motivate them by pointing out why they *need* to know what you are about to tell them. And, of course, you have to *satisfy* this need by supplying the information. Here, however, your speech terminates since the purpose for which you are presenting it has been fulfilled. Note how these three steps are applied in an informative speech on how to rescue drowning persons:

ROW—THROW—GO

Attention Step

    I.   Holiday deaths by drowning are second in number only to automobile accidents.

Need Step

    I.   Every person should know what to do when a call for help is heard.
        A.   This information may help you save a friend.
        B.   This information may help you save a member of your family.

Satisfaction Step

    I.   Remember three important words when someone is drowning: *row, throw, go.*
        A.   *Row:* Look for a boat.
            1.   You can well afford to take a little time to look for a means of rowing to the rescue.

ADAPTATION OF THE MOTIVATED SEQUENCE TO THE GENERAL ENDS OF SPEECH

General End	TO INFORM	TO PERSUADE	TO ACTUATE
Reaction Sought	UNDERSTANDING CLARITY	BELIEF INTERNAL	SPECIFIC ACTION OBSERVABLE
1 Attention Step	Draw attention to the subject.	Draw attention to the need.	Draw attention to the need.
2 Need Step	Show why the listeners need a knowledge of the subject; point out what problems this information will help them meet.	Present evidence to prove the existence of a situation which requires that something be decided and upon which the audience must take a position.	Present evidence to prove the existence of a situation which requires action.
3 Satisfaction Step	Present information to give them a satisfactory knowledge of the subject as an aid in the solution of these problems; begin and end this presentation with a summary of the main points presented. (Normal end of the speech.)	Get the audience to believe that your position on this question is the right one to take, by using evidence and motivational appeals.	Propose the specific action required to meet this situation; get the audience to believe in it by presenting evidence and motivational appeals (as in the speech to persuade).
4 Visualization Step	Sometimes: briefly suggest pleasure to be gained from this knowledge.	Briefly stimulate a favorable response by projecting this belief into imaginary operation. (Normal end of the speech.)	Picture the results which such action or the failure to take it will bring; use vivid description (as in the speech to persuade).
5 Action Step	Sometimes: urge further study of the subject.	Sometimes: arouse determination to retain this belief (as a guide to future action).	Urge the audience to take definite action proposed.

        a.   Look for a boat.
        b.   Look for a canoe.
        c.   Look for a raft.
    2. Rowing to the rescue is always the wisest way.
  B. *Throw:* Look for a life buoy.
    1. See if you can locate something buoyant to throw
       to the person in distress.
        a.   Look for a life buoy.
        b.   Look for an inflated inner tube.
        c.   Look for a board.
        d.   Look for a child's floating toy.
    2. You can throw an object faster than you can swim.
  C. *Go:* As a last resort, swim out to the drowning person.
    1. Approach the victim from the rear.
    2. If you are grabbed, go underwater.
    3. Clutch the person's hair.
    4. Swim for shore.

II. Remember, when you hear the call for help:
  A. Look first for something in which to row.
  B. Look for something buoyant to throw the victim.
  C. Swim out only as a last resort.

The Motivated Sequence and Speeches to Actuate

In speeches to actuate, as we have said, the entire sequence is used. Here, in abbreviated outline form, is how a relatively simple speech on fire prevention could utilize the structure:

FIRE PREVENTION IN THE HOME

Attention Step

I. If you like parlor tricks, try this:
  A. Place a blotter soaked in turpentine in a jar of oxygen.
  B. The blotter will burst into flames.

II. If you do not have a jar of oxygen around the house, try this:
  A. Place a well-oiled mop in a storage closet.
  B. In a few days the mop will burst into flames.

Need Step

I. Few homes are free from dangerous fire hazards.
  A. Attics with piles of damp clothing and paper are combustible.
  B. Storage closets containing cleaning mops and brushes are fire hazards.
  C. Basements often are filled with dangerous piles of trash.
  D. Garages attached to houses are danger spots.

Satisfaction Step

I. To protect your home from fire requires three things:
  A. A thorough cleaning out of all combustible materials.

      B.   Careful storage of such hazards as oil mops and paint brushes.
           1.   Clean them before storing.
           2.   Store them in fireproof containers.
      C.   A regular check to see that inflammable trash does not accumulate.
  II.   Clean-up programs show practical results.
      A.   Clean-up campaigns in Evansville kept insurance rates in a "Class 1" bracket.
      B.   A clean-up campaign in Fort Wayne helped reduce the number of fires.

Visualization Step

   I.   You will enjoy the results of such a program.
      A.   You will have neat and attractive surroundings.
      B.   You will be safe from fire.

Action Step

   I.   Begin your own clean-up campaign now.

The Motivated Sequence and Speeches to Persuade

Finally, study the following outline for a persuasive speech arguing that students be given greater voice in the management of their college. This outline is somewhat longer than the two previous ones, so that you can see more clearly ways in which you can develop each of the five steps.

CITIZENS WITHOUT VOTES

Specific Purpose:	To urge students to secure a greater voice in the decisions affecting their college lives.

Attention Step	I. "Taxation without representation" was the rallying cry of our Revolutionary forebears.
	    A. It epitomized the plight of the voteless citizens of the American colonies.
	    B. It stirred them to action against "the mother country."

Need Step
Statement
Illustration
	I. Today as students at Old Ivy College, we are voteless citizens of our academic community.
	    A. We have no voice in determining the fees that are assessed against us.
	       1. Tuition is set by the Board of Trustees.
	       2. Other charges are fixed by the Business Office.

Illustration	B. We have no voice in determining academic requirements.
	       1. Degree programs are established by the Faculty.
	       2. Grading policies are determined by the Dean.

Illustration	C. We have no voice in the government of our residence halls.

	1.	Rooms and roommates are assigned arbitrarily by the Director of Dormitories.
	2.	Policies affecting visiting privileges and study periods are set by the hall counselors.

Ramification   D. We are therefore not only voteless but also powerless.

Satisfaction Step

I. This state of affairs must end.

Statement   A. We students should be given a voice in determining the fees we are charged.

Explanation
     1. We should be allowed to make recommendations to the Board of Trustees.
     2. We should have student representatives who are allowed to meet regularly with officials in the Business Office.

Statement   B. We students should be given a voice in determining the establishment of academic policies.

Explanation
     1. We should have a voting representative on the Committee on Curriculum.
     2. We should be consulted whenever a change in grading policies is contemplated.

Statement   C. We should be granted complete control of our residence halls.

Explanation
     1. Democratically elected dormitory councils should assign rooms and roommates.
     2. All residents should vote on policies affecting visiting privileges and study periods.

Practical experience

II. Fair and just policies of a similar nature already have been successfully instituted at many other colleges.
    A. At Mountain Top College, representatives of the Student Senate sit on all faculty committees.
    B. At Seaside College, students have complete control of their residence halls.

Meeting the main objection

III. In all cases where students have been given such authority, they have proved responsible.
    A. They have discharged their duties faithfully and fairly.
    B. They have acted conscientiously and with consistently good judgment.

Visualization Step

Positive projection

I. The proposed reforms would bring two important benefits to Old Ivy.
    A. They would provide important new inputs and insights into solving the many serious problems our college faces.
    B. They would heal the misunderstandings and breaches now developing between students and faculty/administration.

Action Step

I. Begin action here and now to secure adequate student representation in college affairs.
   A. You owe it to yourself as a student.
   B. You owe it to the college community of which you are a member.

II. Raise your voices loud and strong in a modern-day variation of that old revolutionary war cry: "No relaxation until we get representation!"

The motivated sequence is a time-tested, flexible organizational pattern, one based on a speaker's two fundamental communicative concerns—a concern for creative problem-solving and a concern for the audience's motives. We will return to the motivated sequence at several other points, but, for now, let us examine other organizational patterns you will want to think about when it comes time to package your ideas for others.

REFERENCE NOTES

[1] Classical "Gestalt" perception theory, which forms the basis for many of these remarks, is reviewed usefully in Ernest R. Hilgard, *Theories of Learning*, Hawthorn Books (New York: Appleton-Century-Crofts, 1956). There also is an emerging body of literature on "visual literacy"—on the ways we learn to process and codify elements in our perceptual fields. See, e.g., Doris A. Dondis, *A Primer of Visual Literacy* (Cambridge, MA: The MIT Press, 1973), and Leonard Zusne, *Visual Perception of Form* (New York: Academic Press, Inc., 1976).

[2] John Dewey, "Analysis of Reflective Thinking," *How We Think* (Boston, MA: D. C. Heath & Company, 1910), p. 72.

[3] Anyone interested in how Alan Monroe conceived of and first used the motivated sequence—then a revolutionary idea—should see the first edition, Alan H. Monroe, *Principles and Types of Speech* (Chicago: Scott, Foresman and Company, 1935), esp. pp. vii–x.

[4] "Nice People" by Jan Bjorklund. Reprinted from *Winning Orations* by special arrangement with the Interstate Oratorical Association, Larry Schnoor, Executive Secretary, Mankato State University, Mankato, Minnesota.

[5] Psychologist Floyd L. Ruch, University of Southern California, describes attention more precisely as, "The process of psychological selectivity by which we select from a vast number of potential stimuli, only those which are related to present interests and needs." He explains: "From among the many stimuli which are within range physiologically, we select—and consciously react to—only those that are related to our present needs and interests. . . . Most psychologists regard attention as having three interrelated aspects, all of which are part of a single complex act. Attention is (1) an adjustment of the body and its sense organs, (2) clear and vivid consciousness, and (3) a set toward action." In *Psychology and Life*, 7th brief ed. (Glenview, IL: Scott, Foresman and Company, 1967), pp. 295, 572.

[6] Floyd L. Ruch and Philip G. Zimbardo, *Psychology and Life*, 8th ed. (Glenview, IL: Scott, Foresman and Company, 1971), p. 268.

[7] Neal Luker, "Our Defense Policy," a speech presented in a course in advanced public speaking at the University of Iowa.

[8] From an address by Henry W. Grady, presented to the Literary Societies of the University of Virginia, June 25, 1889.

PROBLEMS AND PROBES

1. Examine the following list of suggested proposals or statements of belief for persuasive and actuative speeches, and choose one that is of special interest to you personally. Or, if that is not feasible, devise one of your own liking and ask your instructor to approve it.

> Strict gun-control laws should be enacted.
> Legalize marijuana.
> Go to church every Sunday.
> Exercise to benefit your heart.
> All college students should take at least three years of science (or mathematics, foreign language, etc.).
> We should have a national repertory theater.
> Good books are a permanent source of satisfaction and pleasure.
> Solve the problem of race relations.
> Improve the quality of television programs.
> We can conquer urban blight.
> Give a fair deal to the farmer.
> We should have a national system of health insurance.
> Reform college teaching.

Assuming that the members of your class will be your audience for a speech on this topic or thesis, devise an appropriate *specific purpose* for a speech either to persuade or to actuate. Set this purpose down in writing. Then prepare a five-sentence plan or structure designed to elicit the response you desire—*one carefully written sentence for each step in the motivated sequence.* Develop a strong need step directly related to the interests and desires of your prospective listeners. Show through careful reasoning and vivid examples how your proposal or idea will satisfy this need. Use the positive, negative, or contrast method to build the visualization step. Close with a direct appeal for belief or action relative to your specific purpose.

2. Choose a social controversy as a topic for a speech and specify two audiences, one opposing the issue and one supporting it (for example, a speech on the Equal Rights Amendment to be given to a meeting of the Moral Majority and a convention of the National Organization for Women). Using the motivated sequence as a pattern, construct outlines for a speech to be given before each of these audiences. Detail the specific purpose, and what information you would use in each case. Specify how you would develop the information at each step in the sequence so that your speech serves the five functions of the motivated sequence. Consider the needs of each audience and adapt your appeals at each step accordingly.

3. Find in *Vital Speeches of the Day* or elsewhere a speech to inform developed according to the steps in the motivated sequence. In writing, analyze the speech structurally, pointing out where each step begins and noting its method of development. Look in particular at the conclusion of the speech. Does the speaker suggest the pleasure or advantages to be gained from a study of the subject or urge further attention to it? That is, does he or she add to the three basic steps (attention, need, satisfaction) an optional visualization and/or action step? If not, how is the speech terminated?

4. Find in *Vital Speeches of the Day* or elsewhere a speech to persuade or to actuate that is *not* developed according to the steps in the motivated sequence. Without altering in any material way the ideas presented, rewrite the speech so that it conforms to the motivated sequence.

5. Defend (orally or in writing, as your instructor may require) the *logical* validity and the *psychological* effectiveness of the motivated sequence. That is, point out why—both logically and psychologically—the attention step must *begin* the sequence, why need must *precede* satisfaction, why action appropriately *follows* visualization, and so on. Would any other ordering of these five steps have equal logical and psychological validity?

ORAL ACTIVITIES

1. After your instructor has divided the class into small groups of four, five, or six members, meet with your group and discuss your plans for a six-minute persuasive or actuative speech. As a basis for the discussion, each member of the group will read aloud the proposal or belief selected in Problem 1 of Problems and Probes, the statement of the specific purpose evolved for it, and the five-sentence, motivated-sequence plan or structure designed to influence audience belief in and/or acceptance of the idea or proposal. Other members of the group will then respond to these matters analytically, suggesting clarifications and improvements. Afterward, revise or reconstruct your speech plan, making it as effective as you can.

2. Present a five-minute speech to the class, employing one of the outlines constructed in Problem 2 of Problems and Probes. Tell the class in advance which of the two audiences your speech is directed toward. After the speech the class will evaluate the effectiveness of your choices at each step in the motivated sequence. Discuss with the class what alternate strategies you might have used, the needs and nature of the particular audience, and how a speaker might appeal to that audience.

SUGGESTIONS FOR FURTHER READING

Winston L. Brembeck and William S. Howell, *Persuasion: A Means of Social Influence,* 2nd ed. (Englewood Cliffs, NJ: Prentice-Hall, Inc., 1976), Chapter 6, "Attitudes and Attitude Change: Theory and Practice."

John Dewey, *How We Think* (Boston: D. C. Heath & Company, 1910).

Alan H. Monroe, *Principles and Types of Speech* (Chicago: Scott, Foresman and Company, 1935), Preface.

Joseph T. Plummer, "A Theoretical View of Advertising Communication," *The Journal of Communication,* 21 (December 1971), 315–25. Reprinted in Ronald C. Applbaum, Owen O. Jenson, and Richard Carroll, *Speech Communication: A Basic Anthology* (New York: The Macmillan Company, 1975), pp. 268–76.

Irving J. Rein, *The Public Speaking Book* (Glenview, IL: Scott, Foresman and Company, 1981), Chapter 2, "Audience Analysis."

9

Adapting the Speech Structure to Audiences: Traditional Organizational Patterns

In the preceding chapter, we considered in some detail the *motivated sequence,* a pattern of speech organization based on the thought processes that listeners often follow when called upon to receive new information or to consider how a problem may be solved. Moreover, we showed how this pattern may be adapted so as to fit each of the three basic types of speeches. Because of its versatility, the motivated sequence provides the speaker with an option that should be considered.

There may be occasions, however, on which it seems best to organize your speeches in other ways. Therefore, in this chapter we present a number of alternative patterns for structuring the substance or body of a speech and suggest some of the factors that should guide you in choosing among them.

Types of Organizational Patterns

If a speech, whatever its type or purpose, is to communicate your thoughts effectively, it must satisfy at least five general criteria relative to its structure: (1) *The plan of the speech as a whole must be easy for the audience to grasp and remember.* As we noted in the previous chapter, if listeners have difficulty seeing how your ideas fit together or cohere, attention will be distracted from the matters you wish considered and comprehension will be lost. (2) *The pattern must provide for a full and balanced coverage of the material under consideration.* You must find a pattern which allows you to work in the ideas, supporting materials, images, and notions you need to clarify or defend your central idea or major proposition.

(3) *The structure of a speech should be appropriate to the occasion.* As we noted in Chapter 1, there are some occasions or settings where speakers are expected to observe group traditions. Presidential inaugural addresses, for example, tend to follow a particular format originally created by our first presidents.[1] Likewise, eulogies and even speeches of introduction normally are delivered in patterns members of our culture have come to expect. (See Chapter 18.) An occasion, therefore, may almost dictate your organizational pattern. (4) *The structure of a speech should be adapted to the needs and/or level of knowledge of the audience.* The motivated sequence, as well as other patterns we will consider shortly, tends to focus on particular audience needs. Some of the patterns we will describe are particularly well-suited to times when listeners have little background on some subject, while others are useful for situations in which the audience is particularly interested in special aspects of topics on which they have a good deal of information. Select structures with audience needs and informational backgrounds in mind. (5) *The speech must move forward steadily toward a complete and satisfying termination.* You must always structure your speech so as to create a sense of forward motion—of "marching" through a series of sub-topics and ideas that culminate in the ideas and attitudes with which you want to leave your audience. If you repeatedly backtrack to mention points you forgot, if you seemingly throw out facts and figures in a random fashion, or if you get bogged down on one point to the exclusion of other equally important ones, your listeners will surrender to the temptation to ignore you and your message.

Holding these criteria in mind, let us consider some of the organizational options other than the motivated sequence. These options are usefully grouped into four major types: (1) *chronological patterns;* (2) *spatial patterns;* (3) *causal patterns;* and (4) *topical patterns.*

Chronological Patterns

The defining characteristic of chronological patterns is their adherence to the order in which events actually occurred. They are useful for either offering orienting background to listeners who know little about some topic, or showing how a particular situation should cause an audience to hold some set of attitudes toward that situation. In the first case, the sequence is called *temporal;* in the second, *narrative.*

Temporal sequence • When employing a temporal sequence, you begin at a certain period or date and move forward (or backward) in a systematic way so as to offer background on some topic about which the audience knows little. For example, you might describe the methods for refining petroleum by tracing the development of the cracking process from the earliest attempts down to the present time; or the manufacture of an automobile, by following the assembly-line process from beginning to end. Your goals are to create an interest in an area you think your audience should know more about and to present basic information in a clear manner. When talking to a photography club on the history of that art, for example, you might use the following temporal sequence:

THE EARLY HISTORY OF PHOTOGRAPHY

I. In 1839 the French painter Daguerre introduced the daguerreotype.
II. In 1851 the wet-plate process was discovered by Frederick Archer.
III. The moderan era of dry-plate photography begin in 1878.
IV. Roll film first came on the market in 1883.

Narrative sequence • If you want to do more than merely offer background information, however, you are better advised to use a chronological pattern which makes a point. Narratives are "stories"—stories that allow you to draw some conclusions about the series of events. Aesop's fables are narratives with a "moral" about human motivation and action; the series of events surrounding a crime are usually reviewed chronologically by lawyers to point the finger of guilt or innocence at a defendant. In narrative sequences, therefore, speakers review events or actions to persuade audiences to accept some proposition or point-of-view.[2] Suppose you wanted an audience to understand why the modern civil rights question is such a multi-faceted and complex issue. A narrative format would allow you to achieve that purpose:

THE COMPLEXITIES OF MODERN CIVIL RIGHTS

I. Immediately after World War II, civil rights became a political question, starting with the 1948 Democratic National Convention debate over Hubert Humphrey's platform plank.
II. The national judiciary system entered the debate in the 1954 Supreme Court decision in *Brown vs. The Board of Education in Topeka, Kansas.*
III. The late 1950s saw the development of grass roots efforts, particularly with such actions as the Montgomery, Alabama, bus boycott of 1956 and the "sit-ins" and "freedom rides."
IV. Even as grass roots organizations grew, the federal government in the early 1960s took its first major steps, in the form of court-ordered injunctions and national legislation in 1964 and 1965.
V. 1966 saw the birth of the "black power" movement, stressing particularly the use of economic means for bringing about change.
VI. The black cultural awareness aspect of the civil rights movement came to the fore in the "black is beautiful" theme of 1968.
VII. Affirmative action legislation and court orders became the hallmark of the 1970s, thus institutionalizing many of the political, legislative, judicial, economic, and social gains of the previous twenty-five years.
VIII. Thus, the modern civil rights movement, unlike its predecessors, has permeated every major institution and aspect of American society in its development over the past thirty-five years.

Spatial Patterns

Generally, spatial patterns for a speech arrange ideas or sub-topics in terms of their physical proximity or relationships one to the other. Some of these patterns, those normally called *geographical patterns*, organize materials according to well-defined regions or areas so as to visualize physical movement and development. A common talk of this type can be seen in the evening weather forecast: a meteorologist will first discuss today's high pressure dome over your area, then the low pressure lying over the Midwest which will produce tomorrow's overcast sky, and finally next week's cold snap which will result from the Arctic air mass coming in from northern Canada. The idea of "geography" need not be taken so grandly, however. If you wish to orient your fellow students to the campus library, you might use a geographical pattern to set in their minds various library services:

THE CAMPUS LIBRARY

I. As you enter the main doors, you will find the check-out counter.
II. Immediately past that counter you will find displays of newly acquired books, to help you keep up on publications of interest to you.
III. In the next room you will find the information desk, the serials department, the card catalogue, and the reference room, so you can obtain the information you need to find what you are looking for.
IV. The second floor houses three more specialized functions—the reserved book reading room, the newspaper collection, and the magazine and journal collection.
V. The third and fourth floors are devoted to the book collection.

Other organizational patterns have some of the qualities of a spatial pattern, but without the sense of geographical movement or development. For example, a speaker may want to deal with comparative *magnitude or size*; If you wanted to talk about the comparative advantages of using a small-town vs. a metropolitan bank, or seeking medical treatment at an out-patient rural medical center vis-à-vis a large university medical complex, you still would be using essentially a spatial pattern but one without "maps." Also, a spatial pattern often, as is also true of a chronological pattern, can be successfully combined with other patterns. A speech on the effects of nuclear fallout, for example, could be organized spatially by talking about the effects on farmland, small towns, and large cities.

In any case, spatial patterns have the virtues of visualization and hence conceptual clarity, and are most useful in giving listeners a sense of growth, development, and dynamism.

Causal Patterns

As their name implies, causal patterns of message organization move either (1) from an analysis of present causes to a consideration of future effects, or (2) from a description of present conditions to an analysis of the causes which appear to have produced them. When employing the cause-effect arrangement, you might, for instance, first point out that a community's zoning ordinances are outdated or ineffective, and then predict that as a result of this situation fast-food chain

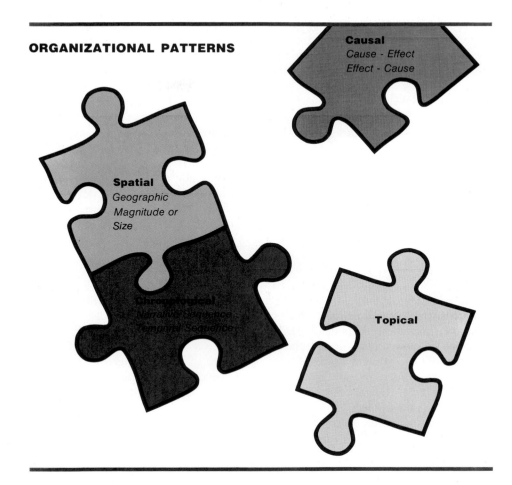

ORGANIZATIONAL PATTERNS

Causal
Cause - Effect
Effect - Cause

Spatial
Geographic
Magnitude or
Size

Chronological
Narrative Sequence
Temporal Sequence

Topical

establishments and gas stations soon will invade prime residential areas. Or, reasoning in other direction (from effect to causes), you could argue that the continued spread of fast-food outlets and small businesses into prime residential areas is the result of ineffective zoning ordinances. Compare the following outlines:

PRODUCTION COSTS

   I. Each year the cost of manufacturing goods goes up.
     A. Labor costs rise an average of nine percent annually.
     B. Costs of raw materials advance five to twelve percent each year.
     C. Transportation fees increase five to seven percent yearly.

  II. The effects upon an economy can be disastrous—increased consumer prices, soaring interest rates, and double-digit inflation.

. . .

I. We all know that hamburger prices rose forty percent a pound more this year than last—but why?
   A. There is less open-range land for grazing.
   B. The cost of feed for pen-fed stock has increased dramatically because of export markets and because of last spring's drought.
   C. Butchering, storage, and shipping costs have risen along with everything else.

II. The resulting inflation, therefore, must be attributed to widely diversified causes which must be dealt with separately.

Note a characteristic of both these outlines: each starts with the aspect of the situation *better known* to audience members, and then proceeds to develop the *lesser known* facets of the problem. You will find a cause-effect pattern useful if the causes are more familiar to the listeners than the effects, and an effect-cause sequence preferable if the opposite is true.

Topical Patterns

Some speeches on familiar topics are best organized in terms of subject-matter divisions which over a period of time have become more or less standardized. For example, financial reports customarily are divided into assets and liabilities; discussions of government, into legislative, executive, and judicial functions; and comparisons of different kinds of telescopes, into celestial and terrestial models. Topical patterns, thus, are most useful for speeches that *enumerate* aspects of persons, places, things, or processes. Occasionally, a speaker tries to discuss all the aspects of a subject, as in a speech on the three branches of government. More often, however, a partial enumeration of the possible topics or areas is sufficient. For example, a speech on where to read about starting a garden probably would deal with only a few sources of information.

READING UP ON GARDENING

I. Although there are innumerable printed materials on starting a garden, let me tell you about three sources that are inexpensive and easily available.
   A. Pamphlets put out by seed and fertilizer manufacturers provide you with important information on seed characteristics, hardiness, yield, and cost.
   B. Pamphlets put out by the federal and state governments—available from your local county extension office—provide you with simple step-by-step directions for planting and caring.
   C. Magazines such as *Better Homes and Gardens* and *Organic Gardening*, which are available in our downtown public library, allow even beginners to specialize in particular kinds of gardening.

Topical patterns certainly are among the most popular and the easiest to use. Only take care, especially when doing a partial enumeration of topics, that you justify to your audience members the aspects of the situation or problem you choose to discuss. If someone asks, "But why didn't you talk about X?", then perhaps you have not made your range of topics seem coherent and commonsensical.

Arranging the Subpoints in the Structure

After you have selected a pattern of organization and arranged the major ideas of your speech accordingly, you must determine how to organize the subpoints and supporting materials that fall under them. Unless you do this thoughtfully, with due attention to the principles of proper subordination and coordination, you will lose much of the effectiveness of your speech. Here are five standard ways in which the subpoints within a speech may be systematically arranged:

Parts of a Whole

If a major idea concerns an object or a process which consists of a series of component parts, the subpoints may treat those parts in order. For example, you may describe a golf club by discussing the grip, the shaft, and the head. Or you may cite the number of churches in England, Scotland, Ireland, and Wales as subtotals of the aggregate number of churches in the British Isles.

Lists of Qualities or Functions

If the main point suggests the purpose of some mechanism, organization, or procedure, the subpoints may list the specific functions it performs. Thus timbre, pitch, and loudness are qualities under which the nature of sound may be discussed; or the purpose of a police department may be made clear by citing its various responsibilities or functions.

Series of Causes or Results

If you use the cause-effect sequence to arrange your major ideas, you will often find that neither cause nor effect is single. Each of the several causes or results may then constitute a subpoint. Even when another type of sequence is used for the major ideas, a list of causes and results often forms the sub-items under these points. The causes of highway accidents, for instance, might be listed as excessive speed, poor roads, and improperly maintained vehicles. The results of a balanced diet could be given as greater comfort, better health, and longer life.

Items of Logical Proof

In a speech to persuade or to actuate, the subpoints often provide logical proof for the idea they support. When this is the case, you should be able to connect the major idea and subpoints with the word "because" (the major idea is true *because* subpoints a, b, c, etc., are true); and, conversely, you should be able to use the word "therefore" when reasoning from the subpoints to the major head (the subpoints are true; *therefore* the main point is true). Here is an example of this type of subordination: Strikes are wasteful because *(a)* workers lose their wages; *(b)* employers lose their profits; and *(c)* consumers lose the products they might otherwise have had.

Illustrative Examples

Many times the main point consists of a generalized statement for which the subpoints provide a series of specific illustrative examples. This method may be used both in exposition and in argument, the examples constituting clarification or proof, respectively. Thus, the general statement that fluoride helps reduce tooth decay might have as it subpoints a series of examples citing the experience of those cities which have added fluoride to their drinking water.

You may decide to use one of the foregoing sequences for the items under one major idea and a different sequence for those under another, but do not shift from one sequence to another *within* the same coordinate series since this is likely to confuse your listeners. Above all, be sure that you do employ some kind of systematic order; don't throw items together haphazardly just because they are subordinate points. The following outline illustrates how the spatial and chronological sequences may be combined in ordering the main and subordinate points of a speech:

INDUSTRIAL DEVELOPMENT IN THE UNITED STATES

   I. New England
      A. The first industries.
      B. Expansion following the War between the States.
      C. Present conditions.
      D. Future prospects.

  II. The South
      A. The first industries, . . . (*Developed chronologically as above.*)

 III. The Middle West
      A. . . . (*Developed as above.*)
                     · · ·

Organizing speeches may seem, at times, like a near-impossible chore, as you sit in your study surrounded by hundreds of ideas, facts, analogies, quotations, and possibilities. As we noted in the beginning of Chapter 8, however, the task of building utilitarian structures for those speeches is crucial, for unless listeners see and comprehend a pattern, they will be unable to make sense out of what you are trying to do with verbal-visual symbols. As long as you remember that the organizational pattern you ultimately select, no matter which one of the many we have suggested, must be adapted to your speech purpose, your auditors' needs, and the occasion, you ought to be able to structure those speeches in clear and compelling ways.

REFERENCE NOTES

[1] See, for example, Donald L. Wolfarth, "John F. Kennedy in the Tradition of Inaugural Speeches," *Quarterly Journal of Speech,* 47 (April 1961), 124–32.

[2] For further discussions of narratives and their use in persuasive speeches, see Bruce E. Gronbeck, *The Articulate Person: A Guide to Everyday Public Speaking* (Glenview, IL: Scott, Foresman and Co., 1979), esp. pp. 193–94, and Donovan J. Ochs and Ronald J. Burritt, "Perceptual Theory: Narrative Suasion of Lysias," in *Explorations in Rhetorical Criticism,* ed. G. P. Mohrmann et al. (University Park, PA: Penn. State Univ. Press, 1973), pp. 51–74.

PROBLEMS AND PROBES

1. Select from *Vital Speeches of the Day* or some other suitable source four speeches for close organizational analysis. Comment critically on the order in which the speaker's major ideas were arranged in view of the subject dealt with and the audience addressed. Study also the arrangement of the subpoints which fell under the major ideas. Were they presented in a systematic, orderly fashion? Can you describe the patterns of organization which they followed? Give each of the speeches you study a letter grade (A, B, C, D) on organization, and be prepared to defend your evaluation of it. If some of your classmates studied the same speeches, see how closely your evaluations agree with theirs.

2. Look back in your speech journal for topics that interest you. Using five of these topics, decide which organizational pattern is best suited for each one. Be prepared to defend your choice of pattern in terms of your general and specific purposes for each subject.

ORAL ACTIVITIES

1. Before coming to class, briefly outline a message in two different organizational patterns, noting a general and specific purpose for each organization. Remember that a variety of organizational patterns can be used, depending on what you wish to accomplish. In class, your teacher will divide you into small groups so that group members may share their messages and discuss which organizational pattern best serves their purposes.

2. Prepare a four- to six-minute speech on a controversial topic. Assume that you will be addressing a hostile audience, and plan your message accordingly. How would a message directed to a favorable audience differ?

3. Prepare a five- to seven-minute speech on a subject of your choice for presentation in class. After you've delivered it, and without receiving critical comments from your instructor or classmates, write and give to the instructor a short paper titled "If I Had It to Do Over." In this paper, either defend the pattern of organization you employed in arranging the major heads and developing the subpoints; or suggest how, after the experience of actually presenting your material to an audience, you see now where you could make improvements. See if your instructor and the other members of the class agree with your critical perceptions of your own work.

4. With the whole class participating, hold a general discussion in which you consider how each of the following topics might be most effectively arranged for a short speech to be delivered to your speech class:

Why many small businesses fail.

Developments in automotive engineering.

The "hot spots" of world politics.

Digging for diamonds.

Eat wisely and live long.

How the world looks to your dog.

The "new math."

Bridge for the beginner.

Appreciating contemporary art.

The metric system.

Making out your income tax return.

 ## SUGGESTIONS FOR FURTHER READING

Ernest G. Bormann and Nancy C. Bormann, *Speech Communication: A Comprehensive Approach,* 2nd ed. (New York: Harper & Row, Publishers, 1977), Chapter 7, "How to Organize a Public Speech."

James Gibson, *Speech Organization: A Programmed Approach* (New York: Holt, Rinehart & Winston, Inc., 1971).

Jim D. Hughey and Arlee W. Johnson, *Speech Communication: Foundations and Challenges* (New York: Macmillan Publishing Co., Inc., 1975), Unit 10, "Verbal Outputting."

Robert C. Jeffrey and Owen Peterson, *Speech: A Text With Adapted Readings,* 3rd ed. (New York: Harper & Row, Publishers, 1980), Chapter 8, "Methods of Dividing Speech Materials."

Roselyn L. Schiff, Harry J. Kone, Juanita Moseley, and Ricardo Gutierrez, *Communication Strategy* (Glenview, IL: Scott, Foresman and Company, 1981).

10

Beginning and Ending the Speech

Your listeners' receptiveness to your ideas and their understanding of what you are asking of them hinges on an effective beginning and ending to your presentation. Well-thought out, creative beginnings heighten audience interest in what you are about to say; they provide a reason for listening to the remainder of your speech. Because your audience may not clearly understand your proposal or the importance of your information, you should begin by establishing a context for the substance of your remarks. In closing your speech, an effective ending ties the threads of your talk together into a cohesive unit; it provides your final opportunity to leave the audience with a clear understanding of your central idea or proposition, your reasons for presenting it, and your concern for its acceptance. In this chapter we will consider the functions of beginnings and endings and elaborate on methods and materials to secure audience involvement in the transmission of your ideas.

Beginnings: Initial Considerations

Before settling on an opening strategy for your presentation, ask yourself the following questions:

1. Is the audience likely to be interested, or must I arouse interest through some attention-getting approach?
2. Is the audience sufficiently aware of my qualifications or must I establish my expertise?
3. Does my speech fulfill or depart from the expectations of the audience or occasion? If the speech is not consonant with expectations, should I clarify my reasons for the direction I am taking?

4. How important is it to create an atmosphere of good will?

5. Does the audience have prior knowledge of the scope of my speech, or should I forecast the major themes before delving into the substantive portion?

Each of these initial considerations allows you to analyze what functions the beginning of your speech should serve to adapt your message effectively to the audience and the occasion.

Gaining Attention

In most settings your listeners are likely to appreciate an overt effort on your part to focus their attention on you and your subject. Even if they have an initial interest in your talk, various distractions may impede their willingness to attend fully to your ideas. You can use the *factors of attention,* discussed in detail in Chapter 8, to arouse the interest of your listeners. Apply these factors to illustrate *why* the audience should listen to you—why your topic is important, significant, and deserving of study or action. If the audience is not already convinced that your topic is *vital* and *real,* you may help your case by offering reasons for believing—at the very beginning of your speech—that the problem is indeed one of critical importance.

Stating Qualifications

Your listeners are probably unaware of the depth and breadth of your knowledge, or of the time you have spent in becoming knowledgeable about your subject. They may not know of your involvement with a local anti-nuclear or pro-life group, or your attendance at a recent political convention. They may not know that you spent the last ten years working in the family ice-cream shop, or that you spent four hours interviewing environmentalists, scientists, and politicians in preparing a speech on a local controversy over polluted waterways. Although you probably should not take seven of your allotted ten minutes to extoll your experiences as a family helper or an industrious researcher, a brief reference to your qualifications may allay audience concerns over the extent of your expertness.

Satisfying Demands of Audience and Occasion

A third function of the speech beginning is to speak directly to the audience's expectations of what the speech should cover. You may satisfy these expectations at the outset by noting the relationship of your theme to the purpose of the meeting or the ceremonial thrust of the occasion. In some instances, however, a speaker may wish to move in a direction different from that expected by the audience or strongly suggested by the occasion. The keynote speech at a political convention, for example, usually combines a hard-hitting attack on the opposition with the affirmation of the virtues of the speaker's party. Barbara C. Jordan, keynote speaker at the 1976 Democratic National Convention, chose to alter these expectations. In so doing, she noted in her opening remarks what such an occasion called for, and how her approach would differ (see her speech, pp. 378–382).

Creating Good Will

Audiences appreciate speakers who take a few moments to create good will. Recognizing the efforts of the group being addressed, expressing appreciation for being invited, or taking a humorous approach to the beginning of the speech are ways to foster a relaxed atmosphere—one in which your views will be respected because you have recognized and shown your respect for the audience. When you face a hostile audience, you may need to recognize explicitly the differences that exist. Giving credit to your opponents for having thoughtfully considered an issue may go a long way toward creating a more responsive atmosphere for your own address. On other occasions, you may find yourself in the midst of personal acquaintances or fellow workers gathered to hear you speak on a subject of mutual interest. In this instance, good will already permeates the setting and extensive time devoted to furthering it would be at the expense of the development of your ideas.

Clarifying the Scope of Your Speech

Because the audience is unlikely to know how you plan to develop the topic of your speech, what points you will cover, and whether you will deal briefly with many points or treat a few in depth, you may find it useful to *forecast* the development of the speech. You can accomplish this by enumerating your major ideas or themes—by telling the people in your audience what you will be speaking about—thus helping to guide them through the development of your speech.

Beginning the Speech: Methods and Materials

Not every introduction will require specific development of *all* the functions described in the preceding section. Nevertheless, the speech you are to present is sure to need at least one. To satisfy that function, and any others that may be required or helpful in attaining your purpose, speakers frequently employ one or more of the following methods:

1. Refer to the subject or problem.
2. Refer to the occasion.
3. Extend a personal greeting or make a personal allusion.
4. Ask a rhetorical question.
5. Make a startling statement of fact or opinion.
6. Use an apt quotation.
7. Relate a humorous anecdote relevant to a topical point.
8. Cite a real or hypothetical illustration.

Reference to the Subject or Problem

If the audience already has a vital interest in the subject you are to discuss, you may need only to *state* that subject before plunging into your first main point. The very speed and directness of this approach suggest alertness and eagerness to come to grips with your topic. Thus, public relations counsel Harold Knoll began a speech on business communications this way:

> Today, let's zero in on one problem in communication that affects business as it deals with an increasingly hostile public. We can symbolize that problem as the arrow or the ring, a choice we have between two ways of communicating.[1]

Although a reference to the subject is a good way to begin a speech with an audience already friendly or interested in the subject, if the listeners are skeptical, such a beginning lacks the elements of *common ground* and *ingratiation* upon which acceptance often depends. When used in the latter situation, therefore, it should be combined with material specifically designed to arouse interest. This is well illustrated by the opening of a speech delivered by Father Theodore M. Hesburgh, then President of the University of Notre Dame:

> I wish to address you this evening on the subject of science and man. It is a fair assumption that the majority of this audience knows much more about science and technology than I do. This being so, one might wonder why I do not drop the first part of my title of science and man. This is why: I shall not pretend to make any startling revelations in the field of science and technology; but I do want to consider this twin reality in conjunction with man and his actual world. What I have to say may not be popular, but then I never have found this to be a good reason for not saying something that should be said. Anyway, most statements that are popular and safe are also generally dull. This you should be spared.[2]

Reference to the Occasion

In some circumstances you may begin your speech by referring to the occasion that brings you and the audience together. A direct reference to the occasion is illustrated in the beginning of Elizabeth B. Bolton's commencement address to women graduating from Virginia Commonwealth University's "Focus on Choice" program:

> It is a pleasure for me to be with you today. I am very honored at being asked to speak to the graduating class of Focus on Choice for a number of reasons. First of all, because I consider you to be the representative of perhaps a new breed of women who have taken a look at their lives and have decided that life is full of choices and options and that you are among those who want to know what your options are. Secondly, because it takes courage to examine one's choice of goals, those of the past—and perhaps to foresee new goals for the future. Thirdly, because I think it is women like yourselves who will become the standard bearers for other women who will also make choices in their lives beyond the traditional roles and become models for other women such as yourselves and most importantly for your daughters seeking examples to follow.[3]

The beginning moments of a speech are extremely important in clarifying your scope and purpose and in gaining the attention and good will of your audience. Personal references, anecdotes, and illustrations are among the various methods you may wish to use at the outset to establish interest and provide reasons for the audience to listen to the remainder of your speech.

Personal Reference or Greeting

At times, a personal word from the speaker serves as an excellent starting point because it can establish a common bond between the person talking and the people listening. Walter F. Mondale, then Vice-President of the United States, used this technique well when addressing the citizens of the People's Republic of China:

> I am honored to appear before you. And I bring you warm greetings and friendship of the President of the United States and the American people.
>
> For an American of my generation to visit the People's Republic of China is to touch the pulse of modern political history. For nearly three decades our nations stood separate and apart. But the ancient hunger for community unites humanity. It urges us to find common ground.
>
> As one of your poets wrote over a thousand years ago, "We widen our view three hundred miles by ascending one flight of stairs." We are ascending that flight of stairs together.
>
> Each day we take another step. This afternoon, I am privileged to be the first American political figure to speak directly to the citizens of the People's Republic of China.[4]

The way a personal reference may be used in an introduction to gain a hearing from a suspicious or skeptical audience was shown by Anson Mount, Manager of Public Affairs for *Playboy* magazine, in a talk he presented to the Christian Life Commission of the Southern Baptist Convention:

I am sure we are all aware of the seemingly incongruity of a represenative of *Playboy* magazine speaking to an assemblage of representatives of the Southern Baptist Convention. I was intrigued by the invitation when it came last fall, though I was not surprised. I am grateful for your genuine and warm hospitality, and I am flattered (though again not surprised) by the implication that I would have something to say that could have meaning to you people. Both *Playboy* and the Baptists have indeed been considering many of the same issues and ethical problems; and even if we have not arrived at the same conclusions, I am impressed and gratified by your openness and willingness to listen to our views.[5]

A personal reference should, of course, be modest and sincere. Otherwise, it may gain the attention of the audience, but is unlikely to establish rapport and good will. Beware, however, of being *overly* modest or apologetic. Avoid saying, "I don't know why your organization picked me out to talk on this subject when others could do it so much better," or "The person who was scheduled to address you couldn't come, and so at the last minute I agreed to speak, but I haven't had much time to prepare." To introduce yourself and your message with self-denigrating allusions of this sort defeats your communicative purpose by suggesting that neither you nor your message is worthy of attention. Be cordial, sincere, and modest—but not apologetic.

In the three types of speech openings we have just analyzed—reference to the subject or problem, reference to the occasion, and personal greeting or self-allusion—you probably noticed that establishing a *common ground* is a predominating concern. In the remarks offered, the speaker attempts to tie his or her experience or interests to those of the hearers. This thread of common ground runs throughout the fabric of all effective speech communication, and can be a powerful force in winning a favorable response to your message.

Rhetorical Question

To ask a rhetorical question—a question to which no immediate and direct answer is sought—is another effective means of introducing the central ideas of a speech. One or more such questions, especially if they are well phrased and strike swiftly and cleanly at the core of your subject, will prompt hearers to seek an answer in their own minds and stimulate them to think about the matters you wish to deal with.

In beginning his discussion of fire hazards in campus buildings, a student pointedly asked: "What would you do if a fire should break out downstairs while I am talking and the stairway collapsed before you could get out?" Rhetorical questions of this kind are especially effective if they impinge on some immediate interest of the listener or deal with a problem of widespread concern. Indeed, if you are following the need-satisfaction or problem-solution approach by posing a series of rhetorical questions, you may lead your audience to formulating an answer or series of answers by which they themselves will arrive at the solution you advocate. Charles W. Bray, then Deputy Director of the International Communication Agency, effectively employed rhetorical questions in focusing audience attention on the purpose of his speech:

Since early November the endless chants of "Death to America" emanating from crowds at our embassy in Tehran and the attacks on our properties in Islamabad, Tripoli, and elsewhere have led many of us to believe that anti-American feeling is rampant at least in the Middle East and perhaps by extension elsewhere in the world.

How accurate is this picture? And why does it seem that we have become the villains of the international community?

I should like to try to address these questions this morning. My goal is to de-mystify anti-Americanism.[6]

Startling Statement

Another method of opening a speech consists of jarring the audience into attention by a startling statement of fact or opinion. An example of this type of introduction is provided in a student speech by Connie Eads, titled "Subliminal Persuasion: Mental Rape":

Man's most precious possession is his mind. Our ability to reason is what distinguishes us from lower forms of life. We look down on those who have lost their ability to reason: call them crazy, loony, retards. Today, in our country, our powers of reasoning have been undermined; our minds have been raped. Everyone of us has been victimized and manipulated by the use of subliminal or subconscious stimuli directed into our unconscious minds by the mass merchandisers of the media.[7]

Whether you use a startling statement as the sole method of beginning a speech or combine it with one or more other methods, keep in mind that to rivet your listener's attention, you will have to phrase your assertions with special care and as strikingly as possible. In both the phrasing and the selecting of ideas to be presented, avoid obvious sensationalism—shock solely for the sake of shock. Such materials may, because they are questionable factually, overexaggerated, or in poor taste, impair the listeners' respect for your integrity and good judgment. The objective is to invite and attract their *favorable* attention, not to alienate them.

Pertinent Quotation

A properly chosen and presented quotation may be an excellent way to introduce a speech. Here, however, the qualities of simplicity and succinctness are highly desirable. Observe, for example, how a student at the University of Iowa, Alicia Becker, began a speech on crises in higher education:

"It was the best of times, it was the worst of times; it was the age of foolishness, it was the age of reason; it was the epoch of belief, it was the epoch of incredulity; it was the season of light, it was the season of darkness; it was the spring of hope, it was the winter of despair." With those words Charles Dickens described the era of the French Revolution, nearly 200 years ago. But he could just as well have been talking about today and tomorrow. We live in a similar age of contradiction and turbulence, in an atmosphere which threatens to destroy every institution, including this school. Today, I would like to discuss with you some ways in which contradictory forces from the government, the people of this state, the faculty of the university, and the students who attend it are threatening the basic purpose of your education.[8]

Humorous Anecdote

Another often-used—and often-abused—way to begin a speech is to tell a funny story or relate a humorous experience. A word of caution is in order here, however: be sure that the story or experience you recount will amuse the audience and that you can tell it well. If your opening falls flat (and an unfunny or irrelevant story may do just that), your speech will be off to a poor start. If the story has no apparent connection with the circumstance or context of the message, at the very least your audience will be perplexed; if your story is off-color and offends their sensibilities, you will have alienated them at the outset. It is imperative, therefore, that an introductory anecdote be relevant and appropriate to your *subject,* your *purpose,* and your *audience.* A joke or a story that is unrelated to these important concerns wastes valuable time and channels the attention and thoughts of your listeners in the wrong direction. Resist the temptation to tell a funny story just to get a "good laugh." Instead, exercise your ingenuity and imagination in the search for a humorous start to your speech that is clearly related either to your subject or your reason for speaking.

Economist Paul W. McCracken, speaking before the Economic Club of Detroit, deftly interwove an old story with the point of his message to the audience:

> All of us recall variants of that old Irish story about the man who was asked to sit up all night at a wake. Unknown to him he was being set-up by some practical joking friends, and in the dead of the night the presumed corpse sat up in the coffin screaming the fellow's name. Whereupon the man carrying out this somber vigil walked over to the coffin, pushed the very-much-alive cadaver back down into the coffin, and exclaimed sternly: "If you're dead, lie down and act like it!"
>
> Some such sentiment as this must have occurred to many of you as you have read forecast after forecast of the forthcoming recession, each forecast followed by another month's data reflecting no clear recedence. . . . In spite of the doctors' (of economists,' that is) insistence that the expansion underway since 1975 is supposed to be dead, long enough for signs of rigor mortis to be showing, the economy has persisted in showing a good deal of life as it has sat very much upright in the recessionary coffin our economic models have tried to construct for it.[9]

When considering the use of a humorous anecdote, ask yourself whether you can handle it. The speaker who "*tries* to be funny" rarely is. Few people enjoy listening to a smart aleck, fewer still enjoy the person who pre-plans a "joke" and then obviously waits for the hilarious reaction of the audience. Instead, tell your tale simply and clearly, letting a quiet sense of humor and enthusiasm shine through. Take the general attitude: "I myself enjoyed the humor and good fun of this joke, and I'm hoping you will share a measure of that enjoyment with me." Above all, if you cannot help laughing at your own jokes, at least give the audience a chance to laugh first.

Real or Hypothetical Illustration

A vivid narrative, whether drawn from real events, fable, or myth, is another way to arouse audience interest in the subject of your speech. As with the humorous anecdote, the illustration should be related clearly to the central idea you are trying to communicate to your audience. It also should possess strong interest value in itself, or you may find that it does little to advance your purpose. Gail Bauer, a student at Wisconsin State University, effectively employed a hypothetical illustration in highlighting her central idea:

> Picture this: a husband comes to the hospital to pick up his wife and new baby. As he passes the nursery door, he reads a sign which says: "Parents: No infants released until satisfactory answers can be given to these questions—Are you Catholic, Protestant, or Jew? Do both parents share the same faith? Do you belong to a church? Please name. Will the child receive religious training? Note: Non-believers need not apply."
>
> An actual sign? Of course not. Incredible? Yes, for couples lucky enough to conceive and bear their own children. But for those who seek a child through adoption these questions are no laughing matter. For in this land of religious freedom, the wrong religion, or—even worse—no religion, can be the bar between the happy union of a child who needs parents and a couple who want a baby to love.[10]

Combining Methods

These eight methods can be used singly or in combination to arouse interest, gain the good will of your audience, focus their attention on the central idea of your message, or to fulfill other functions of your opening remarks. Observe, for example, how one student combined several methods—startling statement, rhetorical question, and personal reference—to arouse attention, to establish his qualifications, and to orient his listeners to the substance of his argument:

> Busing—a word that can silence a room full of people as neatly as a pistol shot—a word that vividly recreates images of parents picketing and children traveling to school with police escorts—a word that divides communities.
>
> When people talk about busing they're talking about court-ordered or forced busing of students. Ostensibly undertaken to desegregate schools and thus improve their racial balance, forced busing means that blacks are physically transported to predominantly white schools, and vice versa. It is a "tool" that has become ever more popular with the courts, and it is a "tool" that has been met by hostile reaction and turmoil in many of our nation's communities.
>
> What is the value of this program? Does it work? After carefully weighing the evidence, I have reached the conclusion that busing for the purpose of achieving deseg-

regation should be ceased. My conclusion is based on two arguments: first, that busing does not improve the quality of education; and second, that it does not actually alter the racial balance within the schools.[11]

The use of the various methods we have been discussing is not limited to the beginning of speeches. Humorous anecdotes, rhetorical questions, and other methods are effective ways to relieve an otherwise dry and technical discussion of issues, or to dramatize a subordinate idea within the context of your speech. Employed judiciously, they invite audience attention to the principal ideas and thereby assist you in accomplishing your purpose in speaking.

Ending the Speech: Initial Considerations

The principal function of any method used to close a speech is to *leave your listeners with a clear understanding of what you want them to know, how you want them to feel, or what you want them to do.* As you reflect on the substance of your speech—main ideas and supporting materials—ask yourself the following questions:

1. Is the speech developed in a simple or a complex fashion?
2. Does the content lead naturally to a "so what?" question?
3. What mood do I wish the audience to be in as I conclude?
4. Should I signal the ending of the speech?

Adapting to Complexity

A speech that advances but one idea, fully developed through clear, relevant supporting materials, needs only a simple restatement of the central point to ensure audience understanding. A speech that advances ten propositions about the effects of a particular bill or governmental action needs a summary that synthesizes the different ideas into a condensed, unified form. The complexity of your ideas thus affects the choice of an appropriate ending.

Answering the "So What?" Question

Speeches that address the significance of a problem, such as the rising crime rate or the effects of inflation on college-bound students, often leave the members of the audience wondering what they can or should do to alleviate or counteract the indicated condition. Although your purpose may be simply to make people aware of the situation, you may lead them to an action step you did not intend in your more limited purpose. To handle this potential problem, you need to note explicitly that your purpose is to lay the foundation for action through accurate information, and suggest that possible corrective action will be the subject of a later address. Another approach may be to indicate your willingness to discuss ways the audience can help in a question-answer session following the speech, or

BEGINNING AND ENDING THE SPEECH

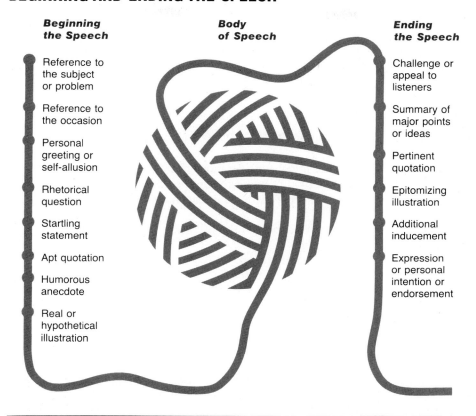

Beginning the Speech

- Reference to the subject or problem
- Reference to the occasion
- Personal greeting or self-allusion
- Rhetorical question
- Startling statement
- Apt quotation
- Humorous anecdote
- Real or hypothetical illustration

Body of Speech

Ending the Speech

- Challenge or appeal to listeners
- Summary of major points or ideas
- Pertinent quotation
- Epitomizing illustration
- Additional inducement
- Expression or personal intention or endorsement

through individual contacts at a later time. If your presentation is directed toward some type of overt response, your conclusion is the final chance to clarify what you want that response to be.

Creating the Appropriate Mood

The ending of your speech should leave the audience in a mood that is appropriate to your purpose. If you expect your listeners to express vigorous enthusiasm, you must stimulate that feeling by the way you close. If you want them to reflect thoughtfully on what you have said, your conclusion should encourage a calm, judicious attitude. Decide whether the response you seek requires a mood of serious determination or good-humored levity, of warm sympathy or cold anger, of objective deliberation or vigorous action. Then plan to conclude your speech in such a way as to generate that mood or create that frame of mind.

Signaling the Ending

A successful speech also conveys a sense of *completeness* and *finality*. You can signal the end with transition phrases: "In summary, . . . "; "As I conclude this address, let me reiterate . . . "; "The eminent poet, Robert Frost, best summarizes what I have been saying. . . . " However you signal the final moments of your speech, avoid giving the audience a false sense of when you will finish. Few things annoy an audience as much as thinking a speech is over, only to have the speaker go on, and on, and on.

Ending the Speech: Methods and Materials

Thoughtful attention to the initial considerations noted previously will enable you to select an appropriate method of ending your speech. Speakers frequently employ one or more of the following methods in concluding their addresses:

1. Issue a challenge or an appeal to the listeners.
2. Summarize major points or ideas.
3. Provide an appropriate quotation.
4. Epitomize with a thematic illustration.
5. Offer an additional inducement for accepting or acting upon the proposal advocated.
6. Express their own intention or endorsement.

Challenge or Appeal to Listeners

When using this method, appeal openly for belief or action, or remind your listeners of their responsibilities in achieving a desirable goal. Phrase the appeal in vivid language; strive to make it a compelling reason for the action you desire. The challenge or appeal will be stronger if it contains a suggestion of the principal ideas or arguments presented in the speech. Robert E. Thomas, President of MAPCO, used such an appeal in concluding a speech on the energy crisis:

> Collectively, we are on a collision course with economic disaster. Unless some drastic changes occur, unless Congressmen from the heavy oil-consuming states in particular stop playing games, our country is headed for lower business activity, lower standards of living, lower employment, and other unpleasant consequences.
>
> It is so sad and so completely unnecessary. We do have vast quantities of energy; we have the manpower, talent, expertise, and money—in short, we have the foundation for energy independence in our time—provided—and this proviso is a must—clear-cut guidelines are established by the Congress, and Congress ceases its political vendetta directed at destroying our energy companies. Only if you and other concerned citizens become aroused, only if you and other concerned citizens across this great land of ours maintain steady pressure on your Congressmen and Senators, can we hope to accomplish such a result. Many connected with energy are belatedly doing their best—but we badly need the help of every concerned American.[12]

Summary of Major Points or Ideas

A summary conclusion reviews the main ideas that have been presented and draws whatever inferences may be implicit in the speech as a whole. In a speech to inform, a summary ending is nearly always appropriate because it restates and helps impress upon the listeners the points you especially want remembered. In a speech to persuade, a summary conclusion provides a final opportunity to re-iterate your principal arguments and appeals.

In concluding his presentation to a group of accountants, Donald Rogers combined an explicit recognition of the action his audience would be taking with a concise summary of his argument:

> Many of you will be responsible for making disclosure decisions, many of you will participate in making disclosure decisions, and many of you will be called upon to advise your clients on disclosure decisions. I hope you will consider the points I've discussed tonight:
>
> 1. The effects of disclosure are not as terrible as we fear,
> 2. Public attitudes strongly support disclosure, and
> 3. Public policy will promote more disclosure in the future.
>
> After you have considered these points, I think you will decide that the best disclosure strategy is one of deliberate, voluntary disclosure and aggressive, honest communication.[13]

An effective ending to your speech will tie it together into a cohesive unit. It will leave your audience with an understanding of your central idea, your reasons behind it, and your hope for their acceptance of it. An enthusiastic response such as the one pictured here indicates that the speaker probably achieved the purpose of his or her speech.

Pertinent Quotation

A quotation, either in poetry or prose, may be used to end a speech if it bears directly on the central idea you have been trying to communicate, or if it strongly suggests the attitude or action you wish your listeners to take. A few lines of poetry, for instance, may provide in figurative, climatic language the theme or essence of your message. A few words of quoted prose may encapsulate your speech purpose and lend color and authority to your conclusion. Lisa Hartman used this in concluding a speech on television titled "Hope for the Medium":

> Television can never begin anew. We cannot erase what has happened to our medium in the last three decades. The effects of television are too well-rooted in the foundations of this nation and of nations abroad. We can only hope that through the processes of adaptation and change, television will evolve into a source of enlightenment for the 20th Century. In the words of the late Edward R. Murrow: "This instrument can teach; it can illuminate; yes, it can even inspire. But it can do so only to the extent that humans are determined to use it to those ends. Otherwise, it is merely lights and wires in a box."[14]

Epitomizing Illustration

Just as an illustration which epitomizes your leading ideas may be used to open a speech, so may it be offered at the close of your discourse. A speech-ending illustration should be both *inclusive* and *conclusive:* inclusive of the main focus or thrust of your speech, conclusive in tone and impact. In exhorting speech communication majors to take a more active role in governing their department and in setting professional goals for themselves, Speech Club President Sandra Marks achieved both ends in this way:

> There's a wonderful story about a six-year-old in Sunday School which captures the spirit of what I've been trying to say tonight. The child was busily drawing a picture, and the teacher asked what it was. The six-year-old replied, "It's a picture of God." "But," protested the teacher, "nobody knows what God looks like." "They will when I'm done," came the reply. It's that sort of self-assurance, creativity, and naive willingness to take on big projects I'm talking about. I hope your professional work, both here at the university and later in your careers in communication, will be marked by those same qualities.[15]

Additional Inducement

Sometimes you may conclude a speech by quickly reviewing the most important ideas presented in the body of the talk and then supplying one or two additional reasons for accepting the belief or taking the actions proposed. A speech urging the importance of an annual medical checkup might, for example, be concluded as follows:

> All in all, then, you will find an annual checkup by a competent physician to be a wise investment, no matter what your age or how well you may feel at the moment.

As I have pointed out, in their early stages a number of potentially serious diseases have no symptoms of which the victim is in any way aware. Many other illnesses if caught in time can be eliminated or brought under control. Finally, the time and money a good checkup will cost you are only a tiny fraction of the time and expense a serious illness entails.

Here, as in other aspects of life, be guided by the old but still pertinent adage, "A stitch in time saves nine." Remember that even though you may be foolish enough to take chances with your own well-being, you owe it to your loved ones and to those dependent on you to take no chances with the most precious of all things—your own good health. Make an appointment for a checkup today!

Expression of Personal Intention or Endorsement

A statement of personal feeling or of intention to act as your speech recommends is another common way to conclude a talk. This method is particularly valuable when your prestige with the audience is high, but may also be employed with good effect in other circumstances. Perhaps the most famous example of this method of closing a speech is the declaration attributed to Patrick Henry: "As for me, give me liberty or give me death!"

Donald Baeder, President of Hooker Chemical Company, concluded his presentation on the disposal of hazardous chemicals by referring to an earlier illustration—his experience with Mike Wallace and the television program, "60 Minutes"—and then offering a personal statement of his philosophy as a businessman and human being:

> I want to close by repeating something I said to Mike Wallace last fall when "60 Minutes" came to Houston. I am a businessman and the head of a chemical company, but first I am a human being. I am also a father and I don't want my children and grandchildren to be exposed to unnecessary hazards any more than you do. I also want my children and grandchildren to enjoy a safe and high standard of living that our free enterprise system and the development of advanced technology—including chemistry—make possible.

> I give you my pledge that our company will continue to make products that are as free from hazards as we can possibly make them; that we will continue to work to eliminate risks from our places of business; and that we will seek constantly to maintain our careful stewardship of the environment that we all share.[16]

As these illustrative examples suggest, the various ways to end a speech can be used alone or in combination. In ending your message, don't overlook the possibility of recalling the opening anecdote, quotation, or rhetorical question to highlight your central idea and to unify your message.

The methods and materials reviewed in this chapter suggest ways the opening and closing of your speech can aid the effective transmission of your ideas. Plan in advance the kind of introduction and conclusion you will use, carefully consider the functions of openings and closings in your speech, and adopt those techniques that seem to fit best your own purposes in communicating to your audience.

REFERENCE NOTES

[1]From "The Arrow or the Ring? The Art of Communicating to the Public," by Harold Knoll, from *Vital Speeches of the Day*, 44, January 1978. Reprinted by permission of Vital Speeches of the Day.

[2]Excerpt from a speech by Father Theodore M. Hesburgh from *Representative American Speeches: 1962–1963*, published by the H.W. Wilson Company. Reprinted by permission of the author.

[3]From "Have it Your Way: Mid-Career Women and Their Options," by Elizabeth B. Bolton, from *Vital Speeches of the Day*, 44, July 1978. Reprinted by permission of Vital Speeches of the Day.

[4]Walter F. Mondale, "Strengthening Sino-American Relations," *Representative American Speeches: 1979–1980*, ed. Waldo W. Braden (New York: W.W. Wilson Company, 1980), p. 29.

[5]Excerpt from a speech by Anson Mount from *Contemporary American Speeches*, 4th ed., ed. Wil A. Linkugel, R.R. Allen, and Richard Johannesen (Dubuque, IA: Kendall-Hunt, 1978). Reprinted by permission of the author and the Christian Life Commission.

[6]Charles W. Bray, III, "De-mystifying Anti-Americanism," from *Representative American Speeches: 1979–1980*, p. 39.

[7]Connie Eads, "Subliminal Persuasion." Reprinted from *Winning Orations* by special arrangement with the Interstate Oratorical Association, Larry Schnoor, Executive Secretary, Mankato State College, Mankato, MN.

[8]From a speech given at The University of Iowa, spring term, 1979. Reprinted with the permission of Ms. Becker.

[9]From "Is There Hope for the 1980s?" by Paul W. McCracken, from *Vital Speeches of the Day*, 46, April 1980. Reprinted by permission of Vital Speeches of the Day.

[10]Gail Bauer, "Religion and Adoption." Reprinted from *Winning Orations* by special arrangement with the Interstate Oratorical Association, Larry Schnoor, Executive Secretary, Mankato State University, Mankato, MN.

[11]John Kitslaar, "Is Busing the Answer?" in *Contemporary American Speeches*, 4th ed., ed. Wil A. Linkugel, R.R. Allen, and Richard Johannesen (Dubuque, IA: Kendall-Hunt, 1978), p. 295.

[12]From "Can We Solve the Energy Crisis?" by Robert E. Thomas, from *Vital Speeches of the Day*, 41, July 1975. Reprinted by permission of Vital Speeches of the Day.

[13]From "The Disclosure of Information," by Donald P. Rogers, from *Vital Speeches of the Day*, 46, May 1980. Reprinted by permission of Vital Speeches of the Day.

[14]Lisa Hartman, "Hope for the Medium." Reprinted from *Winning Orations* by special arrangement with the Interstate Oratorical Association, Larry Schnoor, Executive Secretary, Mankato State College, Mankato, MN.

[15]From a speech given at The University of Iowa Speech Club, October 4, 1980. Reprinted with the permission of Ms. Marks.

[16]From "Chemical Waste" by Donald L. Baeder, from *Vital Speeches of the Day*, 46, June 1980. Reprinted by permission of Vital Speeches of the Day.

 PROBLEMS AND PROBES

CHAPTER REPORT   Read at least five other public speaking textbooks which discuss various methods of beginning and ending speeches (see Suggestions for Further Reading). Which methods are "new" or different from those mentioned in this text? Summarize your findings in a brief paper. Why is it important to vary introductions and conclusions as the audience for your speech changes?

1.   This probe is designed to promote your understanding of the importance of adapting the introduction and conclusion to the audience. Assume you have been asked to speak on the topic "The pros and cons of advertising" (or some other topic that interests you) in the following situations: *(a)* a classroom lecture; *(b)* a large audience who favors the pro side of your argument; *(c)* a large audience who favors the con side and is hostile to the pro side of your argument; *(d)* a televised address which exposes you to an audience with a variety of attitudes on the topic.

What factors influence the way you prepare the introductions and conclusions for the different audiences? Which techniques explained in the chapter would be most beneficial to utilize? Least beneficial? Why?

You may find it helpful to write a brief introduction and conclusion for each of the above situations as an illustration of your analysis.

2.   Some television stations produce programs where speakers discuss items relevant to the particular viewing area. Watch one of these programs, or "60 Minutes," or "Face the Nation," and then discuss the format. If a speaker is allowed a set time for opening and closing statements (usually separated by questions and responses) evaluate the effectiveness of the introduction and conclusion. If there is no provision for set introductions or conclusions, how does the speaker gain attention, initially secure good will, set the tone for what is to follow; and how does the speaker leave the audience in a specific mood to convey a sense of completeness and finality? How does the moderator introduce and close the program as a whole? Overall, then, how effective is the format? What improvements, if any, need to be made?

3.   After listening to one or more of the following types of speeches, evaluate the introduction and conclusion which the speaker used in *(a)* a classroom lecture; *(b)* a sermon; *(c)* an open hearing at a meeting of the city council; *(d)* remarks made at a club or dormitory council meeting; and *(e)* a formal address, "live" or televised, made by a political candidate. In reporting your evaluation, supply sufficient information about the speaker and speaking situation so that someone who was not present could understand why you evaluated a particular beginning or ending as you did.

 ORAL ACTIVITIES

1.   To emphasize the different ways to introduce and conclude a speech, choose a topic and prepare two different one-minute introductions and conclusions to be delivered in an impromptu round of classroom speeches. The class should analyze the varying approaches, and compare their benefits and disadvantages.

2.   Assume that you have been asked to speak on the topic "The Importance of Self-Confidence." This speech is to be given to the following three audiences:
   a. the graduating class of a local high school
   b. a regularly scheduled meeting of the Parent-Teachers Association
   c. the local Rotary Club luncheon
Write a brief introduction for the speech that you think would be appropriate for each audience and identify those factors that would influence the way in which you prepared the three introductions. Be prepared to present your introductions orally in class.

3. Participate in a class discussion concerning introductions and conclusions to public speeches. The discussion might be structured as follows: One student leads off by suggesting a topic for a possible speech to this class. A second student then suggests an appropriate type of introduction and conclusion, justifying those choices. A third student, in turn, challenges that selection, proposing alternative introductions and/or conclusions. Continue this discussion until everyone has proposed and defended the different types of introductions and conclusions that would be appropriate for the speech topics discussed.

 SUGGESTIONS FOR FURTHER READING

Aristotle, *Rhetoric,* 1414b–15a, "The Proem or Introduction"; and 1419b–20b, "The Epilogue."

Bert E. Bradley, *Fundamentals of Speech Communication: The Credibility of Ideas,* 3rd ed. (Dubuque, IA: Wm. C. Brown Company, Publishers, 1981), Chapter 6, "Beginning and Ending the Speech."

Donald C. Bryant and Karl R. Wallace, *Fundamentals of Public Speaking,* 5th ed. (Englewood Cliffs, NJ: Prentice-Hall, Inc., 1976), pp. 277–87, "Introductions" and "Conclusions."

Larry A. Samovar and Jack Mills, *Oral Communication. Message and Response,* 4th ed. (Dubuque, IA: Wm. C. Brown Company, 1980), pp. 116–123, "Preparing the Introduction" and "Preparing the Conclusion."

Herbert W. Simons, *Persuasion: Understanding, Practice, and Analysis* (Reading, MA: Addison-Wesley Publishing Company, 1976), Chapter 10, "Orienting Receivers."

11

Outlining the Speech

An outline for a speech serves the same function as a blueprint for a building: when the major structural components of the speech are clear—the main ideas selected and the general pattern identified—you are ready to move to the drawing board. By laying out the structure of your speech in advance, you can determine whether the major sections fit together smoothly, whether each main idea receives its proper emphasis, and whether all the important areas of the subject are covered. Just as a blueprint identifies the building materials that will be essential, so will an outline highlight relationships between main points and supporting material. If you have failed to substantiate any of your leading ideas, your speech blueprint will show this. If information that is obviously needed to support your main idea is missing—statistical data, or specific instances, for example—you will notice this too in a careful review of your completed outline. Finally, just as careful analysis of a finished blueprint fixes the overall structure in the minds of those concerned, so can a thorough study of your outline help you to recall its pattern as you speak. A visual map of your speech can be a valuable aid to remembering what comes next in your presentation.

Requirements of Good Outline Form

The amount of detail and type of arrangement you use in an outline will depend on the simplicity or complexity of your subject. It also will depend on the speaking situation, and your prior experience in composing outlines. To be useful as an aid in building your speech, a good outline satisfies four basic requirements.

1. Each item in the outline should contain only one unit of information • Outlines that combine a series of phrases or run together several statements under one heading cannot show relationships between and among ideas. The following example shows each unit of information separately:

I. Athens, Greece should be the permanent site for the Olympic Games.
   A. The Games have become more and more politicized in recent years.
      1. The U.S. decision to avoid the 1980 Summer Olympics in Moscow is an example.
      2. The African decision to boycott the 1976 Summer Olympics is an example.
   B. Costs for building sites in new locations each four years are becoming prohibitive.
   C. Returning the Games to their homeland would place renewed emphasis on their original purpose.

2. The items in the outline should be properly subordinated • Subordinate ideas *rank below* others both in scope and importance. In the preceding example, A, B, and C are extensions of the main head—they explain the reasoning for the major claim. The following outline is an additional illustration of how subordinate ideas are arranged:

I. The theft of antiques is a growing problem.
   A. Summer homes in resort areas are broken into with increasing frequency.
   B. Year-round residences are not immune from potential losses.
II. Present means of combating this type of crime are ineffective.
   A. Police protection is inadequate.
   B. Home owners fail to provide sufficient protection.
III. Recovery of stolen antiques is virtually impossible.
   A. Antiques are difficult to trace once they have been passed from thieves to dealers.
   B. There is a sizable foreign market for antiques.

3. The logical relation of items in an outline should be shown by proper indentation • The greater the importance or scope of a statement, the nearer it should be placed to the *left-hand margin*. If a statement takes up more than one line, the second line should be indented the same as the first.

I. Choosing edible wild mushrooms is no job for the uninformed.
   A. Many wild species are highly toxic.
      1. The angel cap (*amanitas verosa*) contains a toxin for which there is no known antidote.
      2. Hallucinogenic mushrooms produce short-lived euphoria, followed by convulsions, paralysis, and possible death.
   B. Myths abound regarding methods for choosing "safe" mushrooms.
      1. Mushrooms with easily peeled skins are not necessarily safe.
      2. Mushrooms eaten by animals are not necessarily safe.
      3. Mushrooms that do not darken a silver coin (placed in a pan of hot water containing mushrooms) are not necessarily safe.
      4. Mushrooms that do not produce a reaction in one person are not necessarily safe for others to consume.[1]

4. A consistent set of symbols should be used • One such set is exemplified in the outlines printed in this chapter. But whether you use this set or some other, be consistent; do not change systems in the middle of an outline. Unless items of the same scope or importance have the same type of symbol *throughout,* the mental blueprint you have of your speech will be confused, and the chances of a smooth and orderly presentation impaired. The following examples demonstrate the right usage of this set of symbols.

I. Our penal system should be reformed.
    A. Many of our prisons are inadequate.
        1. They fail to meet basic structural and safety standards.
        2. They lack facilities for effective rehabilitation programs.
    B. The persons who manage our prisons are ill equipped.
        1. All too often they have had little or no formal training for their jobs.
        2. Low rates of pay result in frequent job turnovers.

Types of Outlines

There are two principal types of outlines, each of which fulfills a different purpose—the *full-content* outline and the *key-word* outline. The former helps make the process of speech preparation more systematic and thorough; the latter serves as a memory aid in the early stages of oral practice.

The Full-Content Outline

As its name implies, a full-content outline represents the complete factual content of the speech in outline form. Whether you use the traditional divisions of the speech (introduction, body, conclusion) or the steps in the motivated sequence (attention, need, satisfaction, visualization, action), each division or step is set off in a separate section. The principal ideas are stated as main heads, and subordinate ideas—properly indented and marked with correct symbols—are entered in their appropriate places. *Each major idea and all of the subordinate ones are written down in complete sentences.* In this manner, their full meaning and their relation to other points within the speech are clearly established. Sources for supporting material may be placed in parentheses at the end of each piece of evidence, or combined in a bibliography at the end of the outline. Once the outline has been completed, you or any other person can derive a clear, comprehensive picture of the speech as a whole. The only features missing are the specific wording you will use in presenting your speech, and the visible and audible aspects of your delivery. By bringing together all the material you have gathered and by phrasing it in complete sentences and in detail, you ensure thoroughness in the preparation of your speech. The outline that follows, which forecasts material in the next section of this chapter, is an example of a full-content outline.

STEPS IN PREPARING A GOOD OUTLINE

I. Determine the general purpose of the speech for the subject you have selected.
  A. Limit the subject.
    1. Limit the subject to fit the available time.
    2. Limit the subject to ensure unity and coherence.
  B. Phrase the specific purpose in terms of the exact response you seek from your listeners.

II. Develop a rough draft of your outline.
  A. List the main ideas you wish to cover.
  B. Arrange these main ideas according to one of the methods discussed in Chapters 8 and 9.
    1. You might use the steps in the motivated sequence.
    2. You might use one of the traditional patterns of organization.
  C. Arrange subordinate ideas under their appropriate main heads.
  D. Fill in the supporting materials to be used in amplifying or proving your ideas.
  E. Review your rough draft.
    1. Does it cover your subject adequately?
    2. Does it carry out your specific purpose?

III. Put the outline into final form.
  A. Write out the main ideas as complete sentences.
    1. State main ideas concisely, vividly, and—insofar as possible, in parallel phraseology.
    2. State the major heads so that they address directly the needs and interests of your listeners. (Instead of saying "Chemical research has helped improve medical treatment," say "Modern chemistry helps the doctor keep you well.")
  B. Write out the subordinate ideas either as complete sentences or as key phrases.
    1. Be sure they are subordinate to the main idea they are intended to develop.
    2. Be sure they are coordinate to the other items in their series.
  C. Fill in the supporting materials.
    1. Be sure they are pertinent.
    2. Be sure they are adequate.
    3. Be sure to include a variety of types of support.
  D. Recheck the entire outline.
    1. It should represent good outline form.
    2. It should adequately cover the subject.
    3. It should carry out your speech purpose.

The Key-Word Outline

The key-word outline has the same indentation and the same symbols as the full-content outline, but it boils down each statement to a key word, phrase, or—at most—a brief sentence that can be more easily remembered. By reading a key-word outline through several times from beginning to end, you will be able to fix the ideas of your speech firmly in mind and to recall them readily as you stand before the audience. Thus, it is an excellent aid to memory in the oral practice of your speech. Of course, to ensure accuracy you may want to read specific quotations or figures from notecards.

The preceding sample outline, if developed as a *key-word* outline, might look like this:

    I.   Determine general purpose.
        A.   Limit subject.
            1.   Fit available time.
            2.   Assure unity and coherence.
        B.   Phrase in terms of listener response.

   II.   Develop rough draft.
        A.   List main ideas.
        B.   Arrange main ideas.
            1.   Motivated sequence.
            2.   Traditional pattern.
        C.   Arrange subordinate ideas.
        D.   Add support materials.
        E.   Review rough draft.
            1.   Adequacy?
            2.   Meet specific purpose?

 III.   Final outline form.
        A.   Complete sentences.
            1.   Concise, vivid, parallel phrasing.
            2.   Address needs and interests of listeners.
        B.   Subordinate ideas—complete sentence or key word.
            1.   Under appropriate main head.
            2.   Coordinate with subordinate ideas of equal weight.
        C.   Add support materials.
            1.   Pertinent.
            2.   Adequate.
            3.   Variety.
        D.   Review outline.
            1.   Good form.
            2.   Adequate coverage.
            3.   Meets purpose.

To put this process to the test, let us now flesh out the outlines in a discussion of the major steps involved.

Steps in Preparing a Good Outline

Three major steps in outlining—selecting and limiting the speech subject, developing a rough draft, and preparing an outline in final form—are essential in constructing your speech.

Selecting the Subject and Determining the Purpose

Suppose your instructor has asked you to prepare an informative speech on a subject in which you are interested. You decide that you will talk about Cardiopulmonary Resuscitation—or CPR—because you recently have gone through the training program and because you think everyone can profit from knowledge of these lifesaving techniques. Your broad topic area, therefore, is:

CARDIOPULMONARY RESUSCITATION

In the eight-to-ten minutes you have to speak, however, you obviously will not be able to cover everything you might say about this subject, nor could you possibly teach your audience how to use CPR techniques. Therefore, recalling what you learned in Chapter 3 about adapting your material to your listeners and to time-limits, you decide to focus your discussion on some background on lifesaving and CPR and on a brief description of the procedures and techniques involved. Consequently, you limit your topic as indicated below:

Cardiopulmonary Resuscitation

(A brief description of where the techniques came from and what they involve.)

Developing the Rough Draft of the Outline

In determining the limits of your subject, you already have made a preliminary selection of some of the principal ideas to be dealt with in your speech. Now you jot these points down to see how they may be modified and fitted into a suitable sequence. Your list may look something like this:

- Kinds of accident victims
- Previous methods of lifesaving
- Organizations which support CPR training
- Sources of CPR training
- Costs of CPR training
- Steps in using CPR techniques

This list covers a number of points you want to be sure to include, but the order appears random. As you think about organizing these items, you successively review various arrangement patterns: A *chronological* pattern will enable you to organize the history of CPR and the steps involved in administering it to someone, but it really would not give the speech as a whole a sense of coherence. Either of the *causal* patterns might work well for a persuasive speech, but, since this is primarily an informative discourse, you do not really want to spend time on describing how CPR as a "cause" affects the operations of the human body.

So, you settle upon a *topical* order, because you really want to bring to your listeners two kinds of information—the background of CPR and a description of CPR techniques:

- *Background of CPR*—previous methods of lifesaving, and organizations which support and sponsor CPR training;
- *Description*—steps in using CPR techniques.

As you think about this pattern, another thought occurs to you: You could announce these two subtopics, and then further subdivide each of them chronologically, in this manner:

I. Background of CPR
   A. Previous methods of lifesaving
   B. Organizations which supported its development
   C. Organizations which currently provide training
II. Steps in using CPR techniques
   A. Clear the airways of a victim
   B. Restore breathing for a victim
   C. Restore circulation for the victim

You now have prepared a *rough outline*. You have identified your topic, clarified your purpose, considered various subtopics and settled on a reasonable number of them, and decided on a coherent method for organizing and developing your speech. Notice in the resulting rough outline that the main points of the speech follow one method of arrangement (topical) and the subordinate ideas follow another, parallel pattern (each main point being developed via chronology). As we mentioned previously, this combination is perfectly acceptable. When mixing patterns as we have done here, however, be sure one predominates and that the other is clearly presented as well.

When you have thus chosen and arranged the major points, or "heads," of your speech, proceed to phrase them more precisely, then to place under each major head the subordinate ideas by which it is to be explained and amplified. This additional development enables you to sketch in the necessary supporting materials in the form of examples, statistics, comparisons, and the like.

Developing the Full Technical Outline

You now are ready to assemble a full-content outline. This normally is done in two steps: First, you draft the speech as completely as possible, using standard outline form. You may have to combine or rearrange certain of the points as they appear in your rough draft, or perhaps even drop several of them because of overdevelopment or of time pressures. Cast all of the items as complete sentences—sentences which convey your meaning clearly and exactly. Arrange the sentences so that they adhere to the following principles of good outline form we have just discussed.

Second, in analyzing the completed outline to discover possible gaps or weaknesses, it frequently is helpful to work out a *technical plot* of your speech. To make such a plot, lay the completed outline beside a blank sheet of paper; and on this sheet, set down opposite each unit a statement of the materials or devices used in developing it. Where you have used statistics in the outline, write the word *statistics* in the technical plot, together with a brief statement of their function. In like manner, indicate all of the forms of support and methods of development you have employed.

Used as a testing device, a technical plot can help you determine whether your speech is structurally sound, whether there is adequate supporting material, whether you have overused one or two forms of support, and whether the appeals you plan are adapted to the audience and occasion. Many speeches, of course, do not need to be tested this thoroughly; and experienced speakers often can make an adequate analysis without drafting a complete technical plot. For the beginner, however, there is no more effective way of checking the structure of a speech and testing the methods used to develop it.

A Sample Full-Content Outline

The following example shows both the complete content of an outline and its technical plot. For illustrative purposes, all items in the outline are stated as complete sentences. Such completeness of detail may be desirable if the occasion is an especially important one or if you sometimes have difficulty framing thoughts extemporaneously. Usually, however, it may be sufficient to write out only the main ideas as complete sentences and to state the subordinate ideas and supporting materials as key phrases.

THE A-B-C'S OF CPR[2]

TECHNICAL PLOT	Full-Content Outline
First topic: background	I. To understand the importance of CPR techniques, one needs to know something about its background.
[Optional topic: develop only if there is time]	A. Let's review some of the ancient methods of resuscitation—flagellation and heat in the Middle Ages; fumigation, inversion, and the barrel methods of the 18th century; the Russian and trotting-horse methods of the 19th century; and artificial respiration as taught in the 20th century.
Beginning of the idea	B. In 1966, the National Academy of Sciences-National Research Council sponsored a Conference on Cardiopulmonary Resuscitation.
Details on recommendations	1. It recommended that medical, paramedical, and allied health personnel be trained in CPR.
	2. Its recommendations resulted in widespread profes-

sional acceptance of CPR and related training programs.

Second phase

C. That conference was followed, in 1973, by the National Conference on Standards for CPR and Emergency Cardiac Care sponsored by the American Heart Association and the National Academy of Sciences-National Research Council.

Authoritative testimony

1. Participating in the 1973 conference were over thirty-five national medical, governmental, and service organizations; American Heart Association chapters from thirty-seven states; and representatives from thirty medical schools.

Details on spreading the idea

2. In part, the 1973 conference urged that:
    a. Professional and public educational programs to increase awareness of heart attack symptoms and emergency treatment be opened immediately;
    b. The public, particularly, become more involved in basic life-support training; and,
    c. Communities integrate emergency cardiac care as part of a comprehensive medical services program, making them available throughout entire communities.

Details on how the idea was phased into the country

3. To carry out the recommendations, the 1973 conference argued that:
    a. Professionals such as police, firefighters, lifeguards, and the like be trained in CPR immediately;
    b. High-risk industry workers and families of cardiac patients be trained next; and,
    c. Then, the training be extended to school children and the general public.

Transition

D. And, that's where I—and I hope you—come in.

Second topic: steps in CPR technique

II. What, then, *is* CPR?

Explanation—what

A. Technically, CPR is a series of actions for basic life-support, wherein one recognizes airway obstruction, respiratory arrest, and cardiac arrest, and then properly applies—singly or with another person—a series of measures for alleviating those problems.

Comparison (analogy)

B. CPR can be compared to procedures used by traffic controllers when they are faced with a blocked interstate highway.
    1. First, they must open sideroads or remove vehicles blocking the highway.
    2. Second, they must signal the stopped vehicles to get moving.
    3. Third, they must bring in rescue or tow trucks to restore cars which have become disabled during the stoppage.

Use of a mnemonic
device to aid recall

C.   Likewise, CPR is as simple as A-B-C.

Develop the details
in chronological
order, offering an
explanation—how

    1.   "A" stands for "airways."
       a.   If you come upon a collapsed person, first shake the person, shouting "Are you all right?"
       b.   If there is no answer, put the person on his or her back.
       c.   Then, lift the neck or chin to open the airway, looking for chest and stomach movement, listening for sounds of breathing, and feeling for breath on your cheek.
    2.   "B" stands for "breathing."
       a.   If opening the airway does not start spontaneous breathing, you must provide rescue breathing.
       b.   The best method is the mouth-to-mouth technique.

(Generally
demonstrate these
techniques)

          (1)   Pinch off the nose with one hand, holding the head in a tilted position with the other.
          (2)   Immediately give four quick, full breaths in rapid succession.
       c.   Then check for a pulse along the carotid artery.
    3.   "C" stands for "cardiac compression."
       a.   Pressing on the person's chest in the right place will start to provide artificial circulation.
       b.   To force the heart to pump, you must set up a rhythmical, rocking motion to ensure the proper amount of pressure and relaxation.

(Hold up card—it
saves you a lot of
technical
descriptions)

       c.   You then begin a procedure whereby you alternate chest compressions and mouth-to-mouth breaths, in ratios which you will find on the card I have given you.
    4.   Continue these techniques until help comes, until you are exhausted, or until there are unmistakable signs that the person will not recover.

Restatement and
reinforcement
with visual aid

III.   I have outlined the basic A-B-C's: A—open airways; B—start rescue breathing; C—initiate cardiac compression. This poster should help you remember them. These comprise the CPR techniques to use when coming upon a victim.

Warning

A.   Remember, though, that there are variations in techniques when dealing with a child rather than an adult, a drowning or electrical shock victim, or someone with a fractured neck.

Reiteration of
speech purpose

B.   My job today is *not* to teach you CPR; that can only be done in an authorized CPR training class. My job is, rather, to tell you what it is, to let you know it can and ought to be learned by everyone in this room.

The A · B · C's of CPR

Open
Airways

Start Rescue
Breathing

Initiate Cardiac
Compression

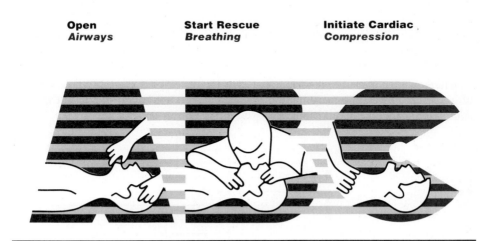

Developing a Speaking Outline

As you probably realize, however, the outline just built would be difficult to work from were you to actually deliver a speech on CPR. Because it is a full-sentence outline, it is "too dense" to be manageable from a lectern. Moreover, because all of the details are included, you probably would be tempted simply to read it to your auditors. If you did that, you would lose vital audience contact or visual bonding.

Normally, therefore, you must compress the technical outline into a form more convenient for use during the presentation of the message. This may involve rewording the main heads in phrase or key-word form on a sheet or notecard, putting statistics or quotations on other notecards, and the like. The actual method you use, of course, will depend upon your personal habits; some people like to work from sheets of paper, others, from notecards. Whatever your preferences are in these matters, your actual speaking outline should serve two functions while you are addressing the audience: (1) it should provide you with reminders of the direction of your speech—main points, subordinate ideas, etc.; and (2) it should record material of a technical or specific nature which must be carefully or precisely worded.

There are four characteristics of the key-word outline: (1) Most points are noted only with a key word or phrase. If you have practiced the speech from the full, technical outline, a word or two should be enough to trigger your memory at these points. (2) Use a full sentence when you want to say something in a precise way, as in the case of formally defining "cardiopulmonary resuscitation." (3) You even may wish to include some directions to yourself, such as a reference to "SHOW POSTER!" at the appropriate point in your outline. (4) Emphasis can be indicated in any number of ways—all capital letters, underlining, indentation patterns, etc. Find a method of emphasis that will catch your eye easily and will help you remember what is subordinated and/or related to what.

Fitting the Beginning and Ending to the Body of the Speech

In Chapter 9 we considered various patterns for developing the body or substance of a speech. When the introduction and conclusion are added to the outline the completed structure should look something like this:

Introduction	I.	_____.
	A.	_____.
	B.	_____.
Body	I.	_____.
	A.	_____.
	B.	_____.
		1. _____.
		2. etc. _____.
	II.	_____.
	III.	_____.
Conclusion	I.	_____.
	A.	_____.
	B.	_____.

In summary, arranging and outlining may seem to involve a lot of useless busywork. That undoubtedly is true in some situations. For an impromptu speech, for example, you probably will do no more than jot a few notes on a scrap of paper. Yet, in the case of longer speeches, arranging the points carefully will allow you to structure your discourse clearly and vividly, and outlining the entire speech will force you to assess its soundness. Arranging and outlining, therefore, helps you check on your speech's *form*, its *coverage* of the subject, and its *suitability* to your purpose and the needs of the audience.

REFERENCE NOTES

[1]Information taken from Vincent Marteka, "Words of Praise—and Caution—about Fungus Among Us," *Smithsonian*, May 1980, pp. 96–104.

[2]Information for the CPR outline has been taken from "Standards for Cardiopulmonary Resuscitation (CPR) and Emergency Cardiac Care (ECC)," Supplement to *Journal of the American Medical Association*, February 18, 1974. Copyright 1974, © the American Medical Association. Reprinted with permission from the American Heart Association.

PROBLEMS AND PROBES

1. To develop your skill in outlining, select two speeches from a recent issue of *Vital Speeches of the Day,* or some other likely source. Or if you wish, use Jimmy Carter's Farewell Address (see *The New York Times,* January 15, 1981, page 12), and Ronald Reagan's Inaugural Address (*The New York Times,* January 21, 1981, page 13). Half the class should prepare a full-content outline of Carter's speech and a key-word outline of Reagan's speech, while the other half of the class prepares a full content outline of Reagan's speech and key-word outline of Carter's speech. Append to each a technical plot on which you indicate the forms of support, attention factors, and motive appeals which the speakers employed. An in-class discussion of the outlines would be a useful exercise. Compare your outlining skills with other members of your class and contrast the text of the two speeches.

2. For a speech entitled "The Investigator as Resource," discussing why a lawyer may want to hire a private detective on a case-by-case basis, rearrange the following points and subpoints in proper outline form:
    a. Investigative services can save the lawyer time.
    b. Investigative reports indicate areas where the lawyer should concentrate in building a case.
    c. It's advantageous for a lawyer to employ an investigator on a case-by-case basis.
    d. The investigator performs two basic services.
    e. Known witnesses must be interviewed and other witnesses sought out.
    f. The detective examines reports from the FBI or other governmental and private agencies and evaluates them for reliability and to determine what has to be done.
    g. The investigator examines, collects, preserves, and analyzes physical evidence.
    h. The investigator compiles information in an effort to reconstruct an incident.
    i. Lawyers may need only occasional detective assistance on especially critical cases.
    j. Investigative reports can be used in out-of-court settlements.

3. Using speeches in this textbook, recent issues of *Vital Speeches of the Day,* or other sources suggested by your instructor, select three speeches for organizational analysis, and make a complete outline of each. Which of the three was easiest to outline? Which was the most difficult? How do you account for these differences? Would you want to rework the most difficult outline if you gave a speech on the same topic? Why, or why not? How would you alter the speech?

 ORAL ACTIVITIES

1. Prepare a five- to seven-minute speech on a subject of your choice for presentation in class. As part of your preparation, draw up a full-content outline and technical plot in accordance with the sample form provided in this chapter. Hand your speech outline in to your instructor at least one week before you are scheduled to speak. The instructor will check this material and return it to you.

2. During the next round of classroom speeches, your instructor will ask each student to outline several talks as they are given. Listeners should identify the organizational patterns that are used; and, after each speech, they should compare their outlines with a main-point outline that the speaker will then write on the chalkboard.

3. Prepare a four- to six-minute speech on a controversial topic. Assume that you will be addressing a hostile audience, and plan your message accordingly. How would a message directed to a favorable audience differ?

 ## SUGGESTIONS FOR FURTHER READING

Bert E. Bradley, *Fundamentals of Speech Communication: The Credibility of Ideas,* 3rd ed. (Dubuque, IA: Wm. C. Brown, 1981), Chapter 6, "Structuring the Speech."

Donald C. Bryant and Karl R. Wallace, *Fundamentals of Public Speaking,* 6th ed. (Englewood Cliffs, NJ: Prentice-Hall, Inc., 1980).

Richard Heun and Linda Heun, *Public Speaking: A New Speech Book* (St. Paul, MN: West Publishing Co., 1979), Chapter 6, "Developing Organizational Skills."

Charles S. Mudd and Malcolm O. Sillars, *Speech: Content and Communication,* 4th ed. (New York: Harper & Row, 1979), Chapter 13, "Preparing the Outline."

Gerald M. Phillips and J. Jerome Zolten, *Structuring Speech. A How-to-Do-It Book About Public Speaking* (Indianapolis: The Bobbs-Merrill Company, Inc., 1976), Chapter 5, "Structuring: Putting It Together."

Otis M. Walter, *Speaking Intelligently: Communication for Problem Solving* (New York: The Macmillan Company, 1976), pp. 239–43, "Outlining."

PART THREE

PUBLIC SPEAKING

Modes
of Communication

12

Using Language to Communicate

In Part Two we focused on the process of creating speeches: preparing, organizing, and adapting messages to their intended audiences. Here, in Part Three we shall turn our attention to the *modes of creating (encoding) and interpreting (decoding) messages*. These modes—language, bodily and vocal behaviors, and visual reinforcement—are the means by which public speakers communicate ideas, beliefs, attitudes, and values to listeners. We begin the discussion with language—the word choices that you as a speaker must make when you encode your ideas and feelings.

There are two major reasons for systematically examining language choices. First, language communicates the *meaning* or sense of your message. Second, language communicates your *feelings* and *values*. In fulfilling these functions, language choices reveal *what* is important to you and *why*.

Using Language to Communicate Meaning

Communicating meaning with precision and clarity is not always easy. Choosing words that increase both listener *comprehension* and *retention* is a major aim of speakers who seek to enable their audiences to "make sense" of their messages and to recall the information or proposal after the speech is completed. Maximizing comprehension and retention has been a concern of rhetorical theorists and practitioners in both ancient and modern times; the virtues of *accuracy, simplicity, reiteration,* and *coherence* in achieving these aims are now widely recognized.

Accuracy

Careful word choice is an essential ingredient in transmitting your meaning to an audience. The man who tells a hardware store clerk that he has "broken the hickey on my hootenanny and needs a thingamajig to fix it" had better have the hootenanny in his hand to procure the right thingamajig; the ambiguity of his message is only a little greater than that of the orator who proclaims that "we must follow along the path of true Americanism." The sentiment being expressed is undoubtedly a noble one, but just what does the speaker mean? Political campaigns are notorious for the ambiguity of the candidates' pronouncements.[1] In the 1980 presidential campaign, for example, Carter never explicitly stated that "Reagan is for war" or "Reagan will lead us into a nuclear holocaust." Nevertheless, his use of expressions such as "the choice is between war and peace" and "there is a disturbing pattern to the statements of the Republican candidate" allowed him to leave the impression that Reagan was not to be trusted in matters of war and peace; moreover, they also allowed him to deny that he had called Reagan a warmonger. In this case, precision was sacrificed so that Carter could "say something without having to say it."

When you speak, your goal should be precision. Leave no doubt as to your meaning. Words are symbols that stand for the concepts or objects they represent; thus, your listener may attach to a symbol a meaning quite different from the one you intend to convey. *Democracy*, for example, does not mean the same thing to a citizen of the United States as it does to a citizen of the Soviet Union, or, in fact, to one American citizen and another. The term *democracy* will elicit different meanings in those belonging to the Moral Majority and those belonging to the American Communist Party.

It is also imprecise to discuss people or objects in a particular class as though they were no different from other members of the same class. Franco-American A differs from Franco-American B and C; one Oldsmobile may be an excellent car and another may be a lemon. Students of general semantics continually warn us that many errors in thinking and communication arise from treating words as if they were the actual conditions, processes, or objects and—as such—were fixed and timeless in meaning. From their perspective, the phrase "once a thief, always a thief" is an imprecise and inaccurate reference to apply to all persons convicted of theft; a person is more than a label.[2]

To avoid vagueness in definition and elsewhere, choose words that express the exact shade of meaning you wish to communicate. Although dictionary definitions are not infallible guides, they do represent commonly accepted usages stated as precisely as possible. Observe, for example, the distinctions a good dictionary makes among related words, such as *languor, lassitude, lethargy, stupor,* and *torpor.* In a book of synonyms (such as Roget's *Thesaurus*) among those listed for the verb *shine* are *glow, glitter, glisten, gleam, flare, blaze, glare, shimmer, glimmer, flicker, sparkle, flash, beam.* The English language is rich in subtle variations. To increase the precision of your expression, make use of this range of meaning in your choice of words.

Simplicity

Words such as "gobbledygook" and "doublespeak" have become common terms in our political vocabulary precisely because of the failure of bureaucrats and politicians to communicate ideas in simple terms.[3] *Euphemisms*—words that convey a more pleasant sense of an object, person, or act than the expressions they replace—such as "pacification of the enemy infrastructure"[4] for the obliteration of a Viet Cong village—hide from view the simple, clear event they purport to describe. During the days of the Watergate scandal, White House Press Secretary Ron Zeigler's penchant for clouding events in "denial" language (e.g., calling Nixon's early statements on Watergate "inoperative") prompted newspaper columnist Sydney J. Harris to suggest disclaimers of other wrongdoers as they might have been written if Zeigler had been the person's press agent:

> Jack the Ripper: I regret that my sexual anomalies, stemming from a repression in childhood, led me to indiscreet violation of the persons of some ladies.

> John Dillinger: Within the time frame of my youth, it was my proclivity toward derring-do that led to further acts of doubtful legitimacy.

> Attila the Hun: Perhaps it was excessive zeal, but I sincerely felt that the welfare of Western barbarism made it imperative to halt the spread of civilization by any means within my power.

> Judas Iscariot: In extenuation, may I remind you that the man was a troublemaker, an outside agitator from Nazareth, and obviously trying to subvert law and order.[5]

"Speak," said Lincoln, "so that the most lowly can understand you, and the rest will have no difficulty." This advice is as valid today as when Lincoln offered it; and because modern audiences as created by the electronic media are vaster and more varied than any Lincoln dreamed of, there is even more reason for contemporary speakers to follow it. Say "learn" rather than "ascertain," "after-dinner speech" rather than "postprandial discourse," "large" rather than "elephantine." Never use a longer or less familiar word when a simpler one is just as clear and accurate. Billy Sunday, the famous evangelist, gave this example:

> If a man were to take a piece of meat and smell it and look disgusted, and his little boy were to say, "What's the matter with it, Pop?" and he were to say, "It is undergoing a process of decomposition in the formation of new chemical compounds," the boy would be all in. But if the father were to say, "It's rotten," then the boy would understand and hold his nose. "Rotten" is a good Anglo-Saxon word, and you do not have to go to the dictionary to find out what it means.[6]

Simplicity does not mean that your language must be simplistic or that you should "talk down" to your audience; it does suggest that you consider the advantages of short, easily understandable words that convey precise, concrete, specific meanings. The able speaker, regardless of experience, pays close attention to these qualities because they contribute vividness and interest to the speech.

Reiteration

Were accuracy and simplicity your only resources as an oral communicator wishing to convey meanings clearly, messages might resemble the famous bulletin of World War II: "Sighted sub, sank same." But because you are working with your listeners face-to-face, in oral and not written language, a third stylistic factor becomes important: reiteration. Reiteration, as we use the term, is intentional repetition of two kinds: (1) *rephrasing* of ideas or concepts in more than one set of words or sentences, and (2) *re-examination* of ideas or concepts from more than one point of view. Because words literally disappear into the atmosphere as soon as you speak them, as an oral communicator you do not have the writer's advantage when transmitting ideas to others. Instead, you must rely heavily upon the linguistic techniques of rephrasing and re-examination.

Rephrasing • The effect of skillful rephrasing to clarify a message and make it more specific can be seen in the following passage from John F. Kennedy's inaugural address:

> Let the word go forth from this time and place, to friend and foe alike, that the torch has been passed to a new generation of Americans—born in this century, tempered by war, disciplined by a hard and bitter peace, proud of our ancient heritage—and unwilling to witness or permit the slow undoing of those human rights to which this nation has always been committed, and to which we are committed today at home and around the world.

> Let every nation know, whether it wishes us well or ill, that we shall pay any price, bear any burden, meet any hardship, support any friend, oppose any foe to assure the survival and the success of liberty.[7]

Re-examination • Re-examining an idea from a number of perspectives usually can be achieved by reformulating its constituent elements or by redefining the basic concept. You can see this principle of re-examination at work in the following excerpt from a student speech. Note how the speaker defines and redefines "political image" in a variety of ways, thereby providing metephorical, psychological, and sociological perspectives:

> A "politician's image" is really a set of characteristics attributed to that politician by an electorate [*formal definition*]. A political image, like any image which comes off a mirror, is made up of attributes which reflect the audience's concerns [*metaphorical definition*]. An image is composed of bits and pieces of information and feelings which an audience brings to a politician [*psychological definition*], and therefore it represents judgments made by the electorate on the bases of a great many different verbal and nonverbal acts a politician has engaged in [*sociological definition*]. Therefore, if you think of a political image only in terms of manipulation, you are looking only at the mirror. Step back and examine the beholder, too, and you will finds ways of discovering what a "good" image is for a politician.

If carefully handled, reiteration in the form of rephrasing or re-examination may help you clarify ideas and help your listeners remember these ideas more readily. Be careful, however, of mindless repetition—too many restatements, especially restatements of ideas already clear to any alert member of your audience, are sure to be boring.

Coherence

Transmitting ideas orally requires attention to the perceived *coherence* of your message. Audiences do not have the luxury of going back over your points as they do in reading an essay; nor do they have punctuation marks to help them distinguish one idea from another. Hence, speakers use *signposts* in the form of carefully worded phrases and sentences to enable listeners to follow the movement of ideas within a speech and to perceive the overall message structure.

Summaries are useful signposts in ensuring that your audience is able to see the overall structure: *preliminary* and *final summaries* are especially helpful in laying out or pulling together the major divisions or points of the speech:

Preliminary Summaries	*Final Summaries*
Today I am going to talk about three aspects of . . .	I have talked about three aspects of . . .
There are four major points to be covered in . . .	These four major points—(restate them)—are the . . .
The history of the issue can be divided into two periods . . .	The two periods just covered—(restate them)—comprise the significant . . .

In addition to these summarizing strategies, signposts may be *connectives* which move an audience from one idea to another within the speech. The following are typical *transition* statements you might employ:

- In the first place . . . The second point is . . .
- In addition to . . . notice that . . .
- Now look at it from a different angle . . .
- You must keep these three things in mind in order to understand the importance of the fourth . . .
- What was the result? . . .
- Turning now . . .

Expand this list, especially to include phrasings adapted to your own speaking style; and use them to make easy, smooth transitions from one point to another.

The preceding signposts are *neutral*—they tell the audience that another idea is coming, but do not indicate the more subtle relationships that exist between the points being made. You can improve the clarity and coherence of your message by being precise about such relationships as *parallel/hierarchical, similar/different,* and *coordinate/subordinate.* Expressing these relationships requires *connectives* or *transitions* such as:

- Not only . . . but also . . . [*parallel*]
- More important than these . . . [*hierarchical*]
- In contrast . . . [*different*]
- Similar to this . . . [*similar*]

- One must consider X, Y, and Z . . . [*coordinated*]
- On the next level is . . . [*subordinated*]

The use of preliminary or final summarizing statements to capture the holistic structure of your speech, and more specific signposts to distinguish ideas and indicate their relationship to each other will help ensure that your message is perceived as a coherent whole by the audience.

Using Language to Create Feelings and Reactions

The second major function of a speaker's linguistic choices is to give the audience cues to his or her feelings, attitudes, and values. A given idea can be phrased in a variety of words, all of which have the same *denotative* or dictionary meaning, but each of which *connotatively* conveys a positive or negative valuation of the speaker's idea. In addition to transmitting meaning, speakers often seek to share their feelings to heighten the impact of the message and to arouse similar feelings in their audiences. Although there are several ways to use these *affective* dimensions of language, we shall concentrate on three: *imagery*, *metaphor*, and *language intensity*.

Imagery

We receive our impressions of the world around us through the sensations of sight, smell, hearing, taste, and touch. One effective way to elicit reactions to your ideas is to clothe them in language which appeals to the senses. You can, for example, reach your listeners *directly* through visual and auditory senses: they can see you, your movements, your facial expressions, and any objects you use as visual aids; moreover, they can hear what you say.

Although you cannot use the remaining senses in as literal a fashion, you can *indirectly* stimulate all of the senses of your listeners by using language that has the power to produce imagined sensations, or which causes them to recall images they have previously experienced. Through image-evoking language, you can help your hearers create many of the sensory "pictures" and "events" that you yourself have experienced or encountered. Through vivid words, you can project the desired image swiftly into the "mind's eye" of your listeners. The language of imagery is divided into seven classes, or types, each related to the particular sensation that it seeks to evoke. The seven types of imagery are:

1. Visual (*sight*)
2. Auditory (*hearing*)
3. Gustatory (*taste*)
4. Olfactory (*smell*)
5. Tactual (*touch*)
   a. Texture and shape
   b. Pressure
   c. Heat and cold
6. Kinesthetic (*muscle movement*)
7. Organic (*internal sensations*)

The examples of imagery that follow are offered as suggestions—the demands of your own message may differ, but the central concept will remain the same. Choosing words which, taken as an extended thought unit, create an image of the thing, person, or idea will increase the likelihood that listeners will feel and react as you do.

Visual Imagery

Try to make your audience actually "see" the objects or situations you are describing. Mention *size, shape, color,* and *movement.* Recount events in vivid visual language. For example, in a time of "cold war" between the United States and Russia, General of the Army Douglas MacArthur knew he had to steel the cadets of the United States Military Academy for their uncertain future. His central theme—"duty, honor, and country"—was a refrain through the speech. To give that theme life, General MacArthur relied upon a variety of visual images in his view of the dedicated soldier stressing size, shape, color, and movement.

> In twenty campaigns, on a hundred battlefields, around a thousand campfires, I have witnessed that enduring fortitude, that patriotic self-abnegation, and that invincible determination which have carved his statue in the hearts of his people.

> From one end of the world to the other, he has drained deep the chalice of courage. As I listened to those songs in memory's eye I could see those staggering columns of the First World War, bending under soggy packs on many a weary march, from dripping dusk to drizzly dawn, slogging ankle deep through mire of shell-pocked roads; to form grimly for the attack, blue-lipped, covered with sludge and mud, chilled by the wind and rain, driving home to their objective, and for many, to the judgment seat of God.

> . . . Always for them: Duty, honor, country. Always their blood, and sweat and tears, as they saw the way and the light. And twenty years after, on the other side of the globe, again the filth of dirty foxholes, the stench of ghostly trenches, the slime of dripping dugouts, those boiling suns of relentless heat, those torrential rains of devastating storms, the loneliness and utter desolation of jungle trails, the bitterness of long separation of those they loved and cherished, the deadly pestilence of tropical disease, the horror of stricken areas of war.

> Their resolute and determined defense, their swift and sure attack, their indomitable purpose, their complete and decisive victory, always through the bloody haze of their last reverberating shot, the vision of gaunt, ghastly men, reverently following your password of duty, honor, and country.[8]

Auditory Imagery

All of us are acquainted with how poets often use words to make us actually "hear" what they are describing. In his translation of Homer's *Iliad,* for example, Alexander Pope has the following lines:

> Loud sounds the air, redoubling strokes on strokes;
> On all sides round the forest hurls her oaks

Headlong. Deep echoing groan the thickets brown,
Then rustling, crackling, crashing, thunder down.

In prose passages and in speeches, also, auditory imagery may frequently be used to project an audience into a scene, as Tom Wolfe does in the following example, where he is describing the opening of a "demolition derby":

Then the entire crowd, about 4,000 started chanting a countdown, "Ten, nine, eight, seven, six, five, four, three, two," but it was impossible to hear the rest, because right after "two" half the crowd went into a strange whinnying wail. The starter's flag went up, and the 25 cars took off, roaring into second gear with no mufflers, all headed toward that same point in the center of the infield, converging nose on nose.

The effect was exactly what one expects that many simultaneous crashes to produce: the unmistakable tympany of automobiles colliding and cheap-gauge sheet metal buckling.[9]

Gustatory Imagery

Sometimes you may even be able to help your audience imagine the *taste* of what you are describing. Mention its saltiness, sweetness, sourness, or its spicy flavor.

An animated and dynamic speaker conveys to the audience the meaning of his or her message through the use of words. In addition, the speaker must share feelings and beliefs in such a way that similar feelings are aroused in the listeners. Language, used in an affective manner, through imagery, metaphor, and intensity, can help create these desired reactions.

Observe how Jane Bochman, a student at the University of Iowa, describes the taste of granola not only to stimulate the imagination of her listeners, but also to appeal to their aesthetic values:

> Few people forget their first taste of homemade granola. Unlike the commercial varieties, which are so heavily sugar-coated that they are almost indistinguishable from the usual Kellogg's products, homemade granola provides you with confusing sensations. The sweetness of honey is mixed with the saltiness of nuts. The rolled oats have a mealiness which contrasts sharply with the firmness of whole grain wheat. Your tongue bravely battles both stringy coconut and small, firm flax seeds. Overall, the first impression of sweet treats is followed by a lingering sourness. Your system as well as your taste buds are pleasantly awakened as you do early morning encounter with nature's best. If you have not had these experiences, then you obviously have not been making use of the health food store down the street.[10]

Olfactory Imagery

Help your audience smell the odors connected with the situation you describe. Do this not only by mentioning the odor itself, but also by describing the object that has the odor or by comparing it with more familiar ones, as shown in this example:

> As he opened the door of the old apothecary's shop, he breathed the odor of medicines, musty, perhaps, and pungent from too close confinement in so small a place, but free from the sickening smell of stale candy and cheap perfume.

Such associations also allow your audience to make positive or negative judgments about the experience.

Tactual Imagery

Tactual imagery is based on the various types of sensation that we get through physical contact with an object. Particularly, it gives us sensations of *texture* and *shape*, *pressure*, and *heat* and *cold*.

Texture and Shape • Enable your audience to feel how rough or smooth, dry or wet, or sharp, slimy, or sticky a thing is.

Pressure • Phrase appropriate portions of your speech in such a way that your auditors sense the pressure of physical force upon their bodies: the weight of a heavy trunk borne upon their backs, the pinching of shoes that are too tight, the incessant drive of the high wind on their faces.

Heat and Cold • These sensations are aroused by what is sometimes called "thermal" imagery.

Review the excerpt from Douglas MacArthur's speech on page 220 for some vivid examples of tactual imagery. Effective use of tactual imagery also is well demonstrated by the blind Helen Keller in explaining how the sense of touch enabled her to experience the world about her:

When water is the object of my thought, I feel the cool shock of the plunge and the quick yielding of the waves that crisp and curl and ripple about my body. The pleasing changes of rough and smooth, pliant and rigid, curved and straight in the bark and branches of a tree give the truth to my hand. The immovable rock, with its juts and warped surfaces, bends beneath my fingers into all manner of grooves and hollows. The bulge of a watermelon and the pulled-up rotundities of squashes that sprout, bud, and ripen in that strange garden planted somewhere behind my finger tips are the ludicrous in my tactual memory and imagination.[11]

Kinesthetic Imagery

Kinesthetic imagery describes the sensations associated with muscle strain and neuromuscular movement. Phrase suitable portions of your speech in such a way that your listeners may feel for themselves the stretching, tightening, and jerking of muscles and tendons, the creaking of their joints.

Jason Elliot, a student at the University of Iowa, makes skillful use of kinesthetic imagery to describe the experience of jogging:

Even if you've gone through a brief warmup, early morning jogging can be a jolt to both mind and body. As you start, you first notice tiny cramps in your lower legs. Then, small, shooting pains begin to work their way upward, and you soon realize your knee sockets are literally pounding with each step. The muscles in your thighs complain bitterly about having to bear the brunt of the effort. Just when you think you're starting to get your legs under control, you notice that your chest is not happy about the whole affair, either. You feel like you have two cement blocks resting squarely on it; the arteries leading from your heart threaten to burst; your lungs seem to search in vain for a little more oxygen. Your breathing comes in gulps and gasps. But then almost magically, something happens: your legs feel like they could keep going forever, and your breathing becomes regular and painless. Serenity and tranquility set in, and you finally can occupy your mind with the landscape, the sunrise, the day's activities. You remember why you started jogging in the first place.[12]

Organic Imagery

Hunger, dizziness, nausea—these are a few of the feelings organic imagery calls forth. There are times when an image is not complete without the inclusion of specific details likely to evoke these inner feelings in listeners. Be careful, however, not to offend your audience by making the picture too revolting. Develop the sensitivity required to measure the detail necessary for creating vividness without making the resultant image so gruesome that it becomes either disgusting or grotesque. Observe how H. G. Wells has made use of organic imagery to create a desired effect:

That climb seemed interminable to me. With the last twenty or thirty feet of it a deadly nausea came upon me. I had the greatest difficulty in keeping my hold. The last few yards was a frightful struggle against this faintness. Several times my head swam, and I felt all the sensations of falling. At last, however, I got over the well-mouth somehow and staggered out of the ruin into the blinding sunlight.[13]

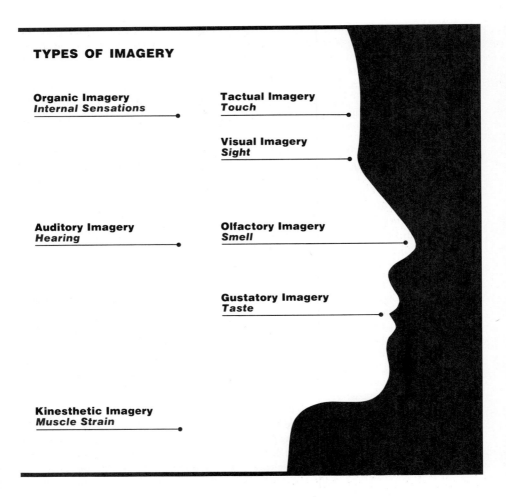

TYPES OF IMAGERY

Organic Imagery
Internal Sensations

Tactual Imagery
Touch

Visual Imagery
Sight

Auditory Imagery
Hearing

Olfactory Imagery
Smell

Gustatory Imagery
Taste

Kinesthetic Imagery
Muscle Strain

The seven types of imagery we have considered—*visual, auditory, gustatory, olfactory, tactual, kinesthetic,* and *organic*—may be referred to as "doorways to the mind."[14] They function to open the audience to new levels of awareness in understanding and believing speakers and acting on their messages. Because people differ in their degrees of sensitivity to different types of imagery, you should try to build into your messages as many of these perceptual "doorways" as possible. In the following example, note how the speaker has *combined* various sensory appeals to arouse listener interest and reaction:

The strangler struck in Donora, Pennsylvania, in October of 1948. A thick fog billowed through the streets enveloping everything in thick sheets of dirty moisture and a greasy black coating. As Tuesday faded into Saturday, the fumes from the big steel mills shrouded the outlines of the landscape. One could barely see across the narrow streets. Traffic stopped. Men lost their way returning from the mills. Walking through the streets, even for a few moments, caused eyes to water and burn. The thick fumes grabbed at the throat and created a choking sensation. The air acquired a sickening bittersweet smell, nearly a taste. Death was in the air.[15]

In this example, college student Charles Schaillol uses vivid, descriptive phrases to affect the senses of his listeners: *visual*—"thick sheets of dirty moisture"; *organic*—"eyes to water and burn"; *olfactory, gustatory*—"sickening bittersweet smell, nearly a taste."

To be effective, such illustrations must appear *plausible:* the language must convey an impression that what is being described did or could happen in the way the speaker chooses to tell about it. The "strangler" that struck Donora offers a plausible account of the event. More importantly, it does so in a fashion that arouses feelings. Audiences would not be as likely to share the experience if the speaker had simply said, "Air pollution was the cause of death in Donora."

Metaphor

The images created by appealing to the various senses often use *metaphors*—words which suggest a comparison between two dissimilar things. Charles Schaillol's "fog . . . thick sheets" is one example of a metaphor used to illuminate the image he wished to create of the fog's effect. To be successful, as Michael Osborn notes, the metaphor should "result in an intuitive flash of recognition that surprises or fascinates the hearer."[16] Furthermore, good metaphors should extend our knowledge or increase our awareness of a person, object, or event. A reference to a table's "legs" may illuminate the object, but it lacks any fascination. When they are fresh or vivid, metaphors can be powerful aids to the evoking of feelings in listeners (e.g., "balanced on four obese toothpicks, the antique table swayed under the heavy load"). Their potency cannot be discounted, nor can their prevalence as descriptive labels for people or events be ignored. Often, several metaphors may be classed together under a single label. Alleen Pace Nilsen's sarcastic, even caustic, critique of sexist language provides an illustration:

> The chicken metaphor tells the whole story of a girl's life. In her youth she is a *chick*, then she marries and begins feeling *cooped up*, so she goes to *hen parties* where she *cackles* with her friends. Then she has her *brood* and begins to *henpeck* her husband. Finally, she turns into *an old biddy.*[17]

In this illustration each term functions as an alleged descriptive metaphor for the life of a female; taken together, the derivatives of this animal metaphor illuminate the negative status accorded females in a male-dominant language structure.

Archetypal Metaphors

The potency of the "chicken" metaphor derives from its status as *archetypal:* a word or phrase that has enduring popularity and usage throughout the ages.[18] An analysis of several speeches suggests that there are many different archetypes: references to *light and darkness, water and sea, the human body, animals, war, structures, family,* for example, recur throughout time. The constancy of these and other such classifications shows their lasting strength and appeal as each generation embraces them in giving meaning and sense to events. The archetypes, *light and darkness* and *water and sea,* are two of the most common; the following examples suggest their usage in public speeches:

> *Light and darkness:* Tarnished as the glory of this nation is, and as far as it has waded into the shades of an eclipse, some beams of its former illumination still play upon its surface, and what is done in England is still looked to as argument, and as example.[19]
>
> —*Edmund Burke*

> With this faith in the future, with this determined struggle, we will be able to emerge from the bleak and desolate midnight of man's inhumanity to man, into the bright and glittering daybreak of freedom and justice.[20]
>
> —*Martin Luther King, Jr.*

> *Water and sea:* When the mariner has been tossed for many days in thick weather, on an unknown sea, he naturally avails himself of the first pause in the storm, the earliest glance of the sun, to take his latitude, and ascertain how far the elements have driven him from his true course. Let us imitate his prudence, and, before we float farther on the waves of this debate, refer to the point from which we departed, that we may at least be able to conjecture where we are now.[21]
>
> —*Daniel Webster*

> We travel together, passengers on a little space ship, dependent on its vulnerable reserves of air and soil; all committed for our safety to its security and peace; preserved from annihilation only by the care, the work, and, I shall say, the love we give our fragile craft.[22]
>
> —*Adlai Stevenson*

In this last example, the metaphor shifts from sea to space, perhaps an indication of our growing preoccupation with realms beyond our own world. In each case, whether from the words of the British politician, Edmund Burke, or from our own time, the expressions draw upon archetypes that have relevance for our daily existence. Archetypes breathe energy and force into listless speeches.

Thematic Metaphors

Metaphors may be used within descriptive passages, to create images, or structure archetypes. They also can be used as the central or unifying theme of an entire speech. Vernon Jordan adopts the metaphor of the "hammer" in characterizing the plight of blacks in our society:

> Black people are under the hammer of inflation . . .
>
> Black people are under the hammer of unemployment . . .
>
> Black people are under the hammer of income disability . . .
>
> Black people are under the hammer of bad health.[23]

In each case, he uses parallel phrasing to focus attention on the difficulty under review. At the conclusion of his speech, Jordan returns to the same theme, quoting from the Pete Seeger song, "If I had a Hammer," and claiming that "Yes, black people are asking for the hammer of freedom, the hammer of justice, the hammer of decency; for with that hammer we can build wonders. We can hammer out love and peace, justice and fairness . . . all over this great land of ours."[24] The "hammer" theme is in the context of a structural archetype, particularly in the conclusion—hammers can be used to hold down, destroy, or to build. Developing a speech around a single metaphor or a series of related ones is an effective way to engender in audiences the positive or negative reactions you intend them to have.

Ideological Metaphors

Just as a single term can function as the organizing principle for a speech, a word or phrase can act—metaphorically—for a larger set of ideas, values, or propositions. In education, for instance, the phrase "Back to Basics" surfaced in many discussions of the scholastic disciplines in the mid-1970s. It referred—metaphorically—to a complex set of propositions: basic, concrete skills are more important than abstract, esoteric perspectives on knowledge. Hard-cord learning, usable in many contexts, is preferable to fragmented-by-situation education. The "old math" is better than "new math," and so on. The adoption of "Back to Basics" as a catch phrase represents all of these and other equally specific value assumptions about the nature of a quality education. Pulled together, these assumptions imply a particular *ideological* stance—an inclusive or comprehensive *system* of *attitudes* and *values* that comprise your habitual world view or outlook on life. Within American culture, terms such as "liberty," "freedom," "rule of law" and others function as shorthand expressions for an entire set of values or an orientation to the world.[25] These and similar terms thus involve much more than the single metaphor or phrase itself. Because they call to mind more than they can ever fully express, such terms are potent rhetorical symbols for speakers who seek to persuade audiences. They reveal your ideological inclinations as well as those of others who use them. Each time you address a controversial topic, on which you take a position and urge others to think about and possibly adopt, you consciously or subconsciously select a vocabulary that reflects a certain ideological framework. Phrases such as the following are typical of those you have used or heard from others:

- The feminist perspective on . . .
- The humane thing to do . . .
- If you want to play hard ball . . .
- For my money . . .
- The beauty of it all is . . .

All of these expressions contain implicit but nonetheless potent value orientations; all of them express ideological stances adopted by the speaker.

If, as the rhetorical critic Kenneth Burke suggests, words not only arise out of such inclinations or orientations, but in turn help to *shape* events and values,[26] it is clear that language has a potent effect on people's willingness to believe and to act. As a student of communication, learn to monitor carefully your own word choices and those of others. Try to become increasingly aware of unstated value systems, and critically examine proposals and claims in light of both implicit and explicit ideological stances.

Language Intensity

Words do more than create images and provide suggestive metaphors for the ideas you wish to communicate. In his lecture, "Mind and Language," Dr. Robert T. Oliver, Professor Emeritus of Speech at Pennsylvania State University, reminds us:

> The labelling function of words . . . is only a part of their service and of their influence. What language does to us and what we can do with it extends far beyond the simple process of identifying objects by naming them.
>
> Words are also *incitements;* they are stimulants. Words are used much as a red flag is used to arouse the anger of bulls or as bait is used to attract fish. In the heat of a presidential campaign, the words "Democrat" and "Republican" are used less as labels than as inducements to loyalty or to enhance antagonism. "I love you" is not only a label for an emotion but also an invitation to reciprocity. "Communist" and "Nazi" are words used to arouse dislike; "patriotism" and "duty" are used to stir up loyal devotion. Much of our use of words is aimed less to define meanings than to create or magnify attitudes. And attitudes are not attributes of fact-items as they exist in the exterior world but are personal preferences. They assume forms and serve functions determined by the mind rather than prescribed by the fact-items to which they refer.[27]

As a speaker, your choice of a label often is determined by the way you feel about the object to which you attach it and the strength or *intensity* of that feeling. That is, by the chosen word or phrase you communicate your *attitude* toward it. Consider, for example, the following "attitudinally weighted" terms:

RELATIVELY POSITIVE	"men in blue" "safety officials" "officers of the law"
RELATIVELY NEUTRAL	"traffic officials" "police personnel" "cops"
RELATIVELY NEGATIVE	"the brass" "the fuzz" "pigs"

These nine terms are roughly rank-ordered according to their intensity, ranging from the highly positive "men in blue" to the highly negative "pigs." For some examples of attitudinally weighted statements with highly positive, relatively

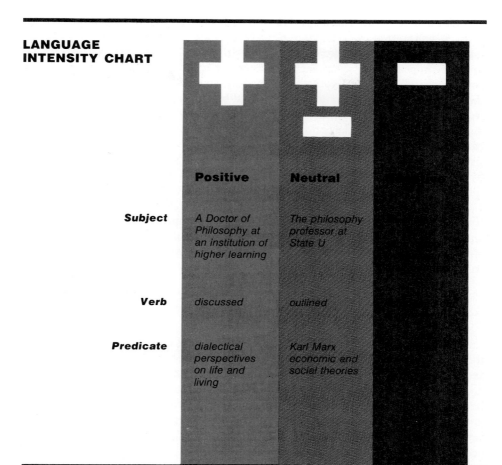

LANGUAGE INTENSITY CHART

	Positive	Neutral
Subject	A Doctor of Philosophy at an institution of higher learning	The philosophy professor at State U
Verb	discussed	outlined
Predicate	dialectical perspectives on life and living	Karl Marx economic and social theories

neutral, or highly negative language intensity, examine the language intensity chart above.

Such language choices make apparent to your listeners the particular intensity of the attitudinal language you are using. Some of these decisions are, of course, out of your precise control because of the limitations on your experience and vocabulary. And only on rare occasions can you hope to choose each word in an entire speech with perfect care, for this would very likely produce stilted or artificial oral discourse. Yet, the key ideas you develop do deserve careful attention to the intensity of the language with which you express them. Equally deserving of careful thought is the material you wish to quote from others.

How intense should your language be? This will depend, in large part, on the issue position of your listeners, their perception of your credibility, and their expectations of your intensity. Professor John Waite Bowers has suggested a useful rule of thumb: Let your language be, roughly, one step more intense than the position or attitude of your audience.[28] If your audience seems generally neutral toward your idea or proposal, make your key pieces of language slightly positive or slightly negative in the degree of intensity you employ. If your audience already is committed, say, to your positive position on reform, then you can afford to make your language quite intense. In general, audiences that are hostile to your proposal will reject highly intense language; audiences sympathetic to your views will not be negatively affected by your use of "loaded" language. If the audience perceives you as a highly credible source, intense langauge will be reacted to more favorably than would be the case if your credibility is low. During the 1980 presidential campaign, Carter's "mean" language threatened to backfire, especially with people for whom Carter's credibility was low already. In situations where an "intense" response is expected, speakers may actually gain by adopting a moderate language.[29] Thus, Reagan's restrained language in response to Carter's strident rhetoric worked to the Governor's advantage.

In sum, as you select precise wording for important ideas in your speeches, try to employ different degrees of intensity. By this means, you will be able not only to reflect your own attitudes more accurately and judiciously, but you will often be able to control to a considerable extent the way in which your audience will respond.

Adopting an Appropriate Oral Style

Language choices that adequately reflect meaning and convey feelings depend on the preceding strategies to create effective messages for your audience. You should also ask yourself such questions as those which follow.

How formal is the occasion? Language appropriate in one social context may be inappropriate in another. Does your audience expect colloquial or slang language or more formal language? Sensitivity to these and other concerns will convey to your audience your respect for their perception of the formality of the occasion.[30]

How assertive or qualified should your language be? Semanticists have noted the "static" nature of the use of *is* and other forms of the verb *to be*. When we assert that "He is a communist" or "He is a thief," we may think that we have identified someone completely and finally. By qualifying our phrases, "His political philosophy is communistic," "He was once a thief," we convey a less dogmatic and "certain" view of the lasting quality of the attributes we attach to people or events. Similarly, our use of such *modal verbs* as could/should, can/must, or might/will, varies the force of our language. *Could* implies tentativeness; *can* means you have the capacity to do something; *might* is a soft, unsure prediction; *should* admonishes or offers advice; *must* is a direct order; and *will* makes a strong prediction. The simple choice of one of these modals can give an audience different impressions of your assertiveness or willingness to qualify your prediction.[31]

Speakers who do not consider the assertiveness of their language may tend to use many ideological metaphors, "all or nothing" categorizations, and frequent "is" expressions.[32] Such language choices reflect an *absolute* or certain view of the relations between people, objects, and events. Employing qualifiers, perhaps, when you are less than sure is an honest and forthright appraisal of the information you have and your degree of certainty respecting that information. Being tentative in highly controversial situations is highly desirable, lest later assessments prove your certainty to be rash and unfounded.

Finally, what degree of emotionality is appropriate to the speech topic and situation? To arouse feelings of sadness, happiness, frustration, or disgust, use vivid imagery and intense language. However, the subject and occasion should justify your linguistic choices. Highly intense language and descriptive imagery may be appropriate in advocating an end to the slaughter of baby seals, but would be out of place in an informative speech on existentialism. Similarly, "human interest" stories of misery and suffering may be very helpful in creating the emotional responses you desire when the subjects themselves deal with the same general conditions. However, if the speech is to be delivered to fourth graders rather than to adults, your attempt at emotionalism may be too strong for such an audience, or even missed entirely by the younger set.

Language, as we have emphasized throughout this chapter, must be an all-pervasive concern of the effective oral communicator. Some two hundred years ago, the French critic Count Buffon observed: "The style is the man himself." *Your* language "style," certainly, reveals much about you, your concern for accurate and coherent meaning, your feelings about the beliefs and attitudes of your listeners, and the hopes that you have for your messages. As you prepare your speeches, therefore, think through those linguistic choices carefully. Language is not only one of the most prevalent modes of public communication; often it can also be one of the most potent.

A Speech of Acceptance

William Faulkner (1897–1962) presented the following speech on December 10, 1950, in accepting the Nobel Prize for Literature. Since he had no reputation as a lecturer, the public might well have expected a lesser speech filled with the kind of pessimism so characteristic of his novels. Instead, he greeted his listeners with a positive and stirring challenge to improve humankind.

Notice that Mr. Faulkner uses organic imagery and archetypal metaphors in depicting what it feels like to write of the human condition. Note too, the series of contrasts, the simplicity and clarity of language as he emulates the advice offered in this chapter. These qualities of style make his speech worthy of our attention.

● On Accepting the Nobel Prize for Literature[33]
William Faulkner

I feel that this award was not made to me as a man, but to my work—a life's work in the agony and sweat of the human spirit, not for glory and least of all for profit, but to create out of the materials of the human spirit something which did not exist before. So this award is only mine in trust. It will not be difficult to find a dedication for the money part of it commensurate with the purpose and significance of its origin. But I would like to do the same with the acclaim too, by using this moment as a pinnacle from which I might be listened to by the young men and women already dedicated to the same anguish and travail, among whom is already that one who will some day stand here where I am standing. /1

Our tragedy today is a general and universal physical fear so long sustained by now that we can even bear it. There are no longer problems of the spirit. There is only the question: When will I be blown up? Because of this, the young man or woman writing today has forgotten the problems of the human heart in conflict with itself which alone can make good writing because only that is worth writing about, worth the agony and the sweat. /2

He must learn them again. He must teach himself that the basest of all things is to be afraid; and, teaching himself that, forget it forever, leaving no room in his workshop for anything but the old verities and truths of the heart, the old universal truths lacking which any story is ephemeral and doomed—love and honor and pity and pride and compassion and sacrifice. Until he does so, he labors under a curse. He writes not of love but of lust, of defeats in which nobody loses anything of value, of victories without hope and, worst of all, without pity or compassion. His griefs grieve on no universal bones, leaving no scars. He writes not of the heart but of the glands. /3

Until he relearns these things, he will write as though he stood among and watched the end of man. I decline to accept the end of man. It is easy enough to say that man is immortal simply because he will endure: that when the last ding-dong of doom has clanged and faded from the last worthless rock hanging tideless in the last red and dying evening, that even then there will still be one more sound: that of his puny inexhaustible voice, still talking. I refuse to accept this. I believe that man will not merely endure: he will prevail. He is immortal, not because he alone among creatures has an inexhaustible voice, but because he has a soul, a spirit capable of compassion and sacrifice and endurance. The poet's, the writer's, duty is to write about these things. It is his privilege to help man endure by lifting his heart, by reminding him of the courage and honor and hope and pride and compassion and pity and sacrifice which have been the glory of his past. The poet's voice need not merely be the record of man, it can be one of the props, the pillars to help him endure and prevail. /4

REFERENCE NOTES

[1]See Lance Bennett, "The Ritualistic and Pragmatic Bases of Political Campaign Communication Discourse," *Quarterly Journal of Speech*, 63 (1977): 219–38.

[2]For a more extended treatment of this subject, see Irving J. Lee, *Language Habits in Human Affairs* (New York: Harper & Row, Publishers, 1941); Wendell Johnson, *People in Quandaries* (New York: Harper & Row, Publishers, 1946); Doris B. Garey, *Putting Words in Their Places* (Glenview, IL: Scott, Foresman and Company, 1957); and Roger Brown, *Words and Things* (Glencoe, IL: The Free Press, 1968).

[3]See Paul Eschholz, Alfred Rosa, and Virginia Clark, eds., *Language Awareness*, 2nd ed. (New York: St. Martin's Press, 1978), esp. Part II, "Politics and Doublespeak."

[4]"Telling it Like it Isn't," *Time*, Sept. 19, 1969. Quoted from Eschholz, et al., *Language Awareness*, p. 56.

[5]From *Strictly Personal* by Sydney J. Harris. Copyright Field Enterprises, Inc. Courtesy of Field Newspaper Syndicate.

[6]Quoted in John R. Pelsma, *Essentials of Speech* (New York: Crowell Collier and Macmillan, Inc., 1934), p. 193.

[7]From *Public Papers of the Presidents of the United States: John F. Kennedy*. Washington, D.C.: U.S. Government Printing Office, 1961.

[8]Excerpts from "Duty, Honor and Country" by Douglas MacArthur in *The Dolphin Book of Speeches*, edited by George W. Hibbitt. Copyright © 1965 by George W. Hibbitt. Reprinted by permission of Doubleday & Company, Inc.

[9]Reprinted with the permission of Farrar, Straus & Giroux, Inc., and International Creative Management, from *The Kandy-Kolored Tangerine-Flake Streamline Baby* by Tom Wolfe. Copyright © 1963, 1964, 1965 by Thomas K. Wolfe, Jr., Copyright © 1963, 1964, 1965 by New York Herald Tribune, Inc.

[10]From a speech given at the University of Iowa, winter term, 1978. Reprinted with the permission of Ms. Bochman.

[11]Helen Keller, *The World I Live In* (New York: The Century Company, 1908), p. 11.

[12]From a speech given at the University of Iowa, spring term, 1978. Reprinted with the permission of Mr. Elliot.

[13]H. G. Wells, "The Time Machine," *The Complete Short Stories of H. G. Wells* (London: Ernest Benn, Ltd., 1927), p. 59.

[14]Victor Alvin Ketcham, "The Seven Doorways to the Mind," in *Business Speeches by Business Men,* ed. William P. Sandford and W. Hayes Yeager (New York: McGraw-Hill Book Company, 1930).

[15]From "The Strangler" by Charles Schaillol. Reprinted from *Winning Orations* by special arrangement with the Interstate Oratorical Association, Larry Schnoor, Executive Secretary, Mankato State College, Mankato, Minnesota.

[16]Michael Osborn, *Orientations to Rhetorical Style* (Chicago: Science Research Associates, 1976), p. 10.

[17]Alleen Pace Nilsen, "Sexism in English: A Feminist View," in *Language Awareness*, p. 224.

[18]Osborn, *Orientations to Rhetorical Style*, p. 16. The discussion of archetypes is based on Osborn's research. See Michael Osborn, "Archetypal Metaphor in Rhetoric: The Light-Dark Family," *Quarterly Journal of Speech*, 53 (1967), 115-26; Osborn, "The Evolution of the Archetypal Sea in Rhetoric and Poetic," *Quarterly Journal of Speech*, 63 (1977), 347–63.

[19]Edmund Burke, "Previous to the Bristol Election," in Chauncey Goodrich, *Select British Eloquence* (1852; rpt. New York: Bobbs-Merrill Co., Inc., 1963), p. 305. Quoted from Osborn, "Archetypal Metaphor in Rhetoric," p. 122.

[20]Martin Luther King, Jr., "Love, Law, and Civil Disobedience," in *Contemporary American Speeches*, p. 85.

[21]Daniel Webster, "Second Speech on Foote's Resolution: Reply to Hayne," in *American Speeches*, ed. W. M. Parrish and M. Hochmuth (New York: Longmans, Green, 1954), pp. 179–80. Quoted from Osborn, "The Evolution of the Archetypal Sea," p. 355.

[22]Adlai Stevenson, "Strengthening International Development Institutions," in *Speeches in English,* ed. Bower Aly and Lucille F. Aly (New York: Random House, 1968), p. 301. Quoted from Osborn, "The Evolution of the Archetypal Sea," p. 363.

[23]From "Under the Hammer" by Vernon E. Jordan, Jr. from *Vital Speeches of the Day*, June 15, 1974. Reprinted by permission of Vital Speeches of the Day.

[24]Jordan.

[25]Several studies examine the ideological import of symbol usage. In particular, see Michael Calvin McGee, "The 'Ideograph': A Link Between Rhetoric and Ideology," *Quarterly Journal of Speech,* 66 (1980), 1–16; McGee, " 'Not Men, But Measures': The Origins and Import of

an Ideological Principle," *Quarterly Journal of Speech*, 64 (1978), 141–54; and Bruce E. Gronbeck, "The Rhetoric of Political Corruption: Sociolinguistic, Dialectical, and Ceremonial Processes," *Quarterly Journal of Speech*, 64 (1978), 155–72.

[26]Kenneth Burke, *Philosophy of Literary Form* (Baton Rouge: Louisiana State Univ. Press, 1941), p. viii. A comprehensive analysis of political metaphors illustrates how symbols help shape our interpretation of events—see Jane Blankenship, "The Search for the 1972 Democratic Nomination: A Metaphorical Perspective," in *Rhetoric and Communication*, ed. Jane Blankenship and Hermann G. Stelzner (Urbana, IL: Univ. of Illinois Press, 1976), pp. 236–60.

[27]From "Mind and Language" by Robert T. Oliver, *Vital Speeches of the Day*, 31 (Oct. 15, 1964). Reprinted by permission of Vital Speeches of the Day.

[28]John Waite Bowers, "Language and Argument," in *Perspectives on Argumentation*, ed. G. R. Miller and T. R. Nilsen (Glenview, IL: Scott, Foresman, 1966), esp. pp. 168–72.

[29]The research on language intensity is reviewed in James Bradac, John Waite Bowers, and John Courtright, "Three Language Variables: Intensity, Immediacy, Diversity," *Human Communication Research*, 5 (1979), 257–69. Also see Michael Burgoon, S. Jones, and D. Stewart, "Toward a Message-Centered Theory of Persuasion: Three Empirical Investigations of Language Intensity," *Human Communication Research*, 1 (1975), 240–56.

[30]For an analysis of social context and other linguistic variables involved in the production and execution of speech, see Herbert H. Clark and Eve V. Clark, *Psychology and Language* (New York: Harcourt Brace Jovanovich, 1977), esp. Chapters 6 and 7. For studies of the differences between oral and written style, see Jane Blankenship, "The Influence of Mode, Sub-Mode, and Speaker Predilection on Style," *Speech Monographs*, 41 (1974), 85–118; Lois Einhorn, "Oral Style and Written Style: An Examination of Differences," *Southern Speech Communication Journal*, 43 (1978), 302–11. Also see R. Bostrom, J. Basehart, and C. Rossiter, "The Effects of Three Different Types of Profane Language in Persuasive Communication," *Journal of Communication*, 23 (1973), 461–75; A. Mulac, "Effects of Obscene Language Upon Three Dimensions of Listener Attitude," *Communication Monographs*, 43 (1976), 300–307.

[31]To pursue these subjects, see Irving J. Lee, *Language Habits in Human Affairs* (New York: Harper, 1941); Julian Boyd and J. P. Thorne, "The Semantics of Modal Verbs," *Journal of Linguistics*, 5 (1969), 62; Stephen E. Toulmin, *The Uses of Argument* (Cambridge: Cambridge University Press, 1964), esp. Chapters 1 and 2; Stephen Toulmin, Richard Rieke, and Allen Janik, *An Introduction to Reasoning* (New York: Macmillan, 1979); Jerry Feezel, "A Qualified Certainty: Verbal Probability in Arguments," *Speech Monographs*, 41 (1974), 348–56.

[32]These categories are developed by Roderick Hart, "Absolutism and Situation: Prolegomena to a Rhetorical Biography of Richard Nixon," *Communication Monographs*, 43 (1976), 204–28.

[33]"On Accepting the Nobel Prize for Literature" by William Faulkner. Reprinted from *The Faulkner Reader*. Copyright 1954 by William Faulkner, Random House, Inc.

PROBLEMS AND PROBES

CHAPTER REPORT   Read at least two studies which explore the relationship between *language and politics* or two which focus on *language intensity* (for resources, see notes 25, 26, and 29 above). Write a brief summary of your reading and offer your own views on either topic. Specifically, what major themes are presented in the essays? Do the authors' conclusions seem adequately developed and supported? Are there major questions which the essays leave unresolved?

1.   Make a list of ten neutral words or expressions. Then for each word in this list find *(a)* an attitudinally weighted synonym which would cause listeners to react

favorably toward the object or idea mentioned, and *(b)* an evaluative synonym which would cause them to react unfavorably toward the same object or idea. (Example: *neutral word*—"old"; *complimentary synonym*—"mellow"; *uncomplimentary synonym*—"senile.")

2. What connective phrase might you use to join *(a)* a major idea with a subordinate one, *(b)* a less important idea with a more important one, *(c)* two ideas of equal importance, *(d)* ideas comparable in meaning, and *(e)* ideas that stand in contrast or opposition?

3. Using varied and vivid imagery, prepare a written description of one of the following:

Sailboats on a lake at sunset
Goldfish swimming about in a bowl
Traffic at a busy intersection
Sitting in the bleachers at a football game in 15° weather
The hors d'oeuvre table at an expensive restaurant
The city dump
A symphony concert

4. In your speech journal compile a list of at least ten slogans or phrases employed by social or political movements such as: "Back to Basics," "Pro-choice," "Pro-life," or "Black is beautiful." For each slogan analyze the kind of imagery it evokes, and the variety of metaphors used by the movement. Does a particular type of image or metaphor dominate each movement? Are some images more persuasive than others? What do you think makes an image or slogan effective?

5. Find a speech in *Vital Speeches of the Day* or the *Congressional Record,* e.g., a presidential address to Congress, whose tone is very formal. Rewrite the speech for a different audience in a less formal setting. What changes must be made in the speech? How might the wording be changed? What stylistic changes can be made? How does the audience affect the language used? Does the message remain the same in both versions of the speech? These considerations should help you to adapt your speeches to their audiences.

 ORAL ACTIVITIES

1. Describe orally to your class a mundane object, such as paper clip, brick, or pen, and the purposes to which it might be put. Employ vivid imagery in describing this object to help your audience visualize it.

2. Write a three- to four-minute speech narrating your feelings about a particular location. For instance, you might describe the town in which you grew up, a building you always dreamed of seeing, or a place made famous by one of your favorite authors. Present the speech from manuscript. Carefully revise your manuscript to take advantage of the suggestions made in this chapter. In particular, make generous use of varied and vivid imagery, appropriate words with connotative affect, and clear and graceful connective phrases.

3. Prepare a description of some process with which you are familiar, such as how to ride a bicycle, how to operate a machine, how to prepare a meal, or some

other process of your choosing. Prepare and deliver a speech for each of the following audiences: *(a)* a group of first graders, *(b)* your peers, *(c)* a group of college graduates. How does your choice of language differ for each group? How did your word choice, sentence structure, and overall approach differ? For example, do you need to repeat more for younger audiences? Does your language need to be more vivid?

4.   Divide into small groups and analyze the importance of language selection as you prepare a speech for varying audiences. In addition to age differences, what are the challenges for gender, racial, or class differences?

 ## SUGGESTIONS FOR FURTHER READING

Kenneth Boulding, "Introduction to 'The Image,' " in *Dimensions in Communication: Readings,* 2nd ed., ed. James H. Campbell and Hal W. Hepler (Belmont, CA: Wadsworth Publishing Company, Inc., 1970), pp. 26–35.

Gary L. Cronkhite, *Public Speaking and Critical Listening* (Menlo Park, CA: The Benjamin-Cummings Publishing Co., Inc., 1978), Chapter 10, "Language and Style."

Abne M. Eisenberg, *Living Communication* (Englewood Cliffs, NJ: Prentice-Hall, Inc., 1975), pp. 149–180.

Dan P. Millar and Frank E. Millar, *Messages and Myths: Understanding Interpersonal Communication* (Port Washington, NY: Alfred Publishing Co., Inc., 1976), Chapter 6, "Openness and Self-Disclosure."

Michael Osborn, *Orientations to Rhetorical Style* (Chicago: SRA, 1976).

R. R. Allen and Ray E. McKerrow, *Pragmatics of Public Communication,* 2nd ed. (Dubuque, IA: Kendall/Hunt, 1981), Chapter 3, "Language."

13

Using the Body to Communicate

In a story that has come down through the centuries, the Greek orator Demosthenes, when asked for the most important ingredient of effective public speaking, replied, "Delivery." When asked for the second and third most important ingredients, his answer remained the same. *Delivery,* as we have been using the term in this textbook, refers to the manner in which a speaker presents a message to others, including the use of the voice and of gestural actions.

In the nineteenth century, great attention was devoted to delivery skills. The minutest adjustments of gesture, body, and voice were thought to communicate subtle shifts of meaning and feeling. Elaborate systems were developed for coordinating meaning- and feeling-states with physical and vocal shifts, and the "refinements" of delivery behaviors came to constitute a kind of rule-governed, universal language or code. Students of public speaking spent many hours working with instructors or before mirrors, trying to perfect the tiniest movements of the hands or body. Because of these and other extremes to which the study of "delivery" went, *elocution*—as it then was called—fell into a period of neglect and disgrace at the beginning of this century.

Within the last thirty years or so, however, we have witnessed a renewed interest in the subject among scholars, teachers, and students of oral communication. Once we discarded the innumerable "rules" for delivery which the elocutionists followed and began to explore anew the kinds of meanings and feelings which are communicated *nonverbally,* we found that the nineteenth-century teachers were on the right track. They merely had jumped too quickly to the setting forth of innumerable *do's* and *don't's*. In this chapter, therefore, you will not find a list of predetermined rules or directions. Rather, you will find discussions of those aspects of your physical behavior which affect the reception of your message by an audience. You also will find some help in deciding how to handle yourself in the speaking situation.

Delivery and Nonverbal Message Systems

If it is true (as we suggested in Chapter 12) that your *words* communicate your thoughts or ideas, it is equally true that your *non-words* often communicate your feelings and attitudes. In support of this view, sociologist Erving J. Goffman says that your words "give," but your body "gives off"—that is, reflects most accurately your *feelings* toward yourself, your message, your audience, and your situation.[1] Extending and reinforcing this notion of the verbal/nonverbal duality of delivery is communications scholar Dale G. Leathers, who notes: "Feelings and emotions are more accurately exchanged by nonverbal than verbal means. . . . The nonverbal portion of communication conveys meanings and intentions that are relatively free of deception, distortion, and confusion."[2] In view of such statements, it seems sensible to conclude that delivery represents a system of communicative cues, a kind of "language" every bit as important to communication as are words. There are four primary nonverbal message systems which affect public communication: *proxemics, bodily movement and stance, gestures,* and *facial expression.*

Proxemics

One of the most important but perhaps least recognized aspects of nonverbal communication is proxemics, or the use of space by human beings. Two components of proxemics are especially relevant to public speakers:

1. *Physical Arrangements*—the layout of the room in which you are speaking, including the presence or absence of a podium, the seating plan, location of chalkboards and similar aids, and physical barriers between you and your audience.
2. *Distance*—the extent or degree of separation between you and your audience.[3]

Each of these components has a bearing on how you communicate publicly. Most public speaking situations include a designated speaking area—a podium at a head table, a lectern in the center of an auditorium stage, or a comfortable chair from which you can deliver your message while seated. In each case, the physical arrangement helps determine the formal nature of the situation and serves to set you apart from your listeners. This "setting apart," you should remember, is both *physical and psychological.* Literally as well as figuratively, objects such as podiums, tables, and chairs can stand in the way of an open and free communicative exchange. If you want to reduce the psychological sense of separation between you and the audience, you must reduce the impact of the physical barriers. This can be accomplished by achieving a more relaxed and informal atmosphere—talk beside the podium instead of behind it, stand in an open area away from the head table but still in clear view of the audience, or sit at the edge of a table. There is no single rule for using space. Consider the formality of the occasion (working from behind a podium is more formal and is

CLASSIFICATION OF INTERHUMAN DISTANCE

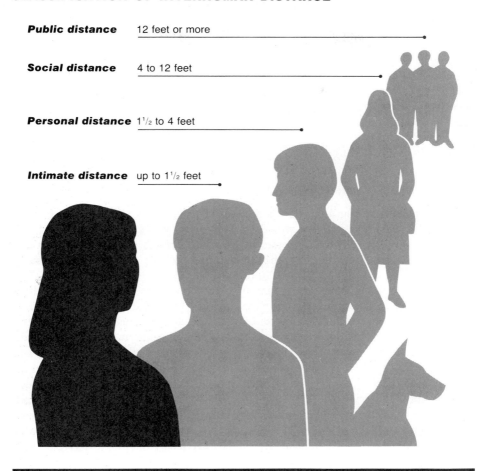

Public distance   12 feet or more

Social distance   4 to 12 feet

Personal distance 1½ to 4 feet

Intimate distance up to 1½ feet

therefore better suited to lectures, presentations, or prepared reports); the nature of the material you are offering (you may need a podium to read from if you are dealing with statistics or extensively quoted material); and your personal characteristics (some speakers need the "protection" provided by a podium, while others feel much more comfortable speaking beside or in front of it). (But remember that the podium is for your convenience in referring to manuscript or notes; you should not use it as a physical prop while you speak.)

Edward T. Hall's study of the effect of distance on communicative behaviors adds a second set of considerations. Hall divided inter-human distances into four segments: *intimate distance*—up to 1½ feet apart; *personal distance*—1½ to 4 feet; *social distance*—4 to 12 feet; and *public distance*—12 feet or more. On the basis of these distinctions he carefully noted how people's eye contact, tone of voice, and ability to touch and observe change from one distance to another.[4]

For our purposes, the most important of Hall's findings are those having to do with the characteristics of *public distance*—particularly as it affects communicating over an expanse of 25 feet or more. To communicate with people that far away, you obviously cannot rely upon your normal speaking voice or minute changes in posture or muscle tone. Instead, you must *compensate* for the distance by relying more heavily upon relatively large gestures, gross shifts from place to place, and increased vocal energy. Perhaps this urgent necessity to communicate *more in the large*, with bigger-than-usual movements, is one of the things which makes public speaking such a strange experience to some. Once understood and knowledgeably applied, however, the proxemics of nonverbal message systems can greatly enhance your delivery.

Bodily Movement and Stance

How you move and stand provides a second set of nonverbal cues for your audience. *Bodily movement* includes shifts you make from one spot to another during the delivery of a speech; *posture* refers to the relative relaxation or rigidity of your body, as well as to your overall stance (erect, slightly bent forward or backward, or slumping).

Purposive bodily movements can, in a very real sense, communicate ideas about yourself to an audience. The speaker who stands stiffly and erectly may, without uttering a word, be saying either (*a*) "This is a formal occasion" or (*b*) "I am tense, even afraid, of this audience." The speaker who leans forward, physically reaching out to the audience, is saying silently but eloquently: "I am interested in you. I want you to understand and accept my ideas." A head cocked to the right or left, drawn slightly back and with an appropriate facial expression, communicates incredulity. Sitting casually on the front edge of a table and assuming a relaxed posture communicates informality and a readiness to engage in a dialogue with the listeners.

Bodily movement and adjustment in posture also function to *regulate communication*. As a public speaker you may, for instance, move from one end of a table to the other to indicate a change in topic; or you may accomplish the same purpose simply by changing your posture. At other times, you may move toward your audience when making an especially important point. In each case, you are using your body to signal to your audience that you are making or are about to make a change or transition in the subject matter of your speech, or are dealing with a matter of special concern. An equally important point to remember is that your posture and bodily movements can not only work for you, but also against you. Aimless and continuous pacing back and forth is distracting. A nervous bouncing up and down or swaying from side to side will make the audience tense and uneasy. If you adopt an excessively erect stance, you may lose rapport with your listeners. Your movements, in other words, should be *purposive*. Only then will stance and movement aid in your communicative effort, and produce the sense of self-assurance and control you desire to exhibit.[5]

Rather than standing behind a podium, this professor has chosen to communicate with his students from an informal, seated position. Through relaxed posture and spontaneous gestures, he is narrowing the psychological distance between himself and his listeners.

Posture and bodily movement, therefore, are far more than matters of "standing straight," "looking your audience in the eye," and "avoiding random movements" of your body in order to "look poised on the platform." They are important aspects of *communication,* matters that provide you with one of your most potent means of "telling" an audience what your ideas are and how they ought to be taken or interpreted.

Gesture

Gestural communication involves *purposeful movements* of the head, shoulders, arms, hands, or some other part of the body (as distinguished from movements of the *whole* body). Fidgeting with your jacket buttons or aimlessly rearranging notecards on the podium are not gestures because they are *not* purposeful, and they detract from rather than support or illustrate the ideas you are expressing. The public speaker commonly employs three kinds of gestures:

1. *Conventional gestures*—signs or symbols which have specific meanings assigned to them by convention or custom. The raised-hand "stop" gesture of the policeman directing traffic, the hand-and-finger language of deaf-mutes, the arm signals of football referees are examples of conventional gestures.

2. *Descriptive gestures*—signs or symbols which depict or describe more or less directly the idea to be communicated. Speakers, for example, often

These speakers are enhancing their verbal communication with effective nonverbal behaviors through the utilization of direct eye contact, descriptive gestures, and intense facial expressions.

describe the size, shape, or location of an object by movements of hands and arms. They may extend an upraised arm to indicate the height of a stranger. They may make hand-and-finger motions to help describe what a punch press looks like and to demonstrate the successive steps in its manipulation.

3. *Indicators*—movements of the hands and arms, often in combination with the rest of the body, which represent feeling-states or emotions. Thus, speakers may throw up their arms when disgusted, pound the podium when angry, or point a threatening finger when issuing a warning. In using such indicators, speakers are in a sense trying to transmit, even "transplant," their own feelings and emotional states to their listeners.[6]

As should be obvious from the foregoing, gestural communication functions in three important ways for the speaker: (1) *Pictorialization.* Gestures can "draw pictures" for your audience, especially to indicate sizes, shapes, and relationships between, as well as the motions of, objects. Such pictures depend primarily on what we have called descriptive gestures. (2) *Condensation.* Gestures, particularly conventional gestures, may take the place of words in many instances. They may function as shorthand terms for things it would take many words to describe fully. (3) *Arousal.* Gestures often work in concert with facial expressions to communicate your state of mind to the audience. Indicators are especially important in affecting audiences because they usually scan your body as well as your face for cues concerning how to interpret your message.

Facial Expression

Your face is another important nonverbal message channel. On the one hand, it can work in congruity with the feelings you have at the moment (e.g., smiling when happy, frowning when confused, stern when angry). Your facial expressions also can "hide" or mask your actual feelings—putting on a "happy face" when you are depressed or sad, appearing attentive in class when you are day-dreaming. At other times, you may try to mask your feelings by appearing cheerful, but your facial expression will give you away.[7]

Communicating—voluntarily or not—your feelings is a major function of facial expression. What Paul Ekman and Wallace V. Friesen call *affect displays* are given to your audience via your face.[8] That is, the listeners scan your face to see how you feel about yourself and how you feel about them. Second, facial details provide listeners with cues that help them *interpret the contents* of your message: Are you being ironic or satirical? How angry are you? Are you sure about some conclusion you have stated, or haven't you really put yourself on the line with the assertion? Do you like this audience, or are you afraid of it? As a nonverbal message channel, your face provides audiences with partial answers to these questions of interpretation. And, third, the "display" elements of your face—your eyes especially—establish a *visual bonding* between you and your listeners. The speaker who looks down at the podium instead of at listeners, who reads excessively from notes or manuscript, or who delivers a speech to the back wall has severed visual bonding. Our culture has come to expect eye-to-eye contact from speakers who are deemed "earnest," "sincere," "forthright," or "self-assured."[9] In the familiar adage "The eyes have it," there is a good deal of cultural truth.

Of course, you cannot control your face completely—which is probably why people search it so carefully for both "meaning" and "feelings"—but you can attempt to make sure that your facial messages do not belie your verbal messages. In practical terms this means that when you are uttering angry words, your face should be communicating anger; when you are uttering key assertions or points that members of your audience may consider controversial or at odds with their belief systems, your eyes will be seeking out theirs for feedback indicating disagreement, rejection, or contempt.

Using Nonverbal Behaviors Effectively

Let's begin with two assumptions. First, you cannot completely control *every-thing* that you "say" with your body. Some of your facial expressions, your hand-and-arm gestures, your bodily movements, and even your posture may be so ingrained—so habituated—by previous experience and social conditioning that you are unaware of their very presence or effect on others. Second, it should be equally clear to you that you *can* gain some skill in orchestrating your nonverbal behavior in ways that complement or supplement your verbal message. You can consciously make some decisions about how you will use your body to communicate effectively. The following principles may guide your decisions.

Begin with "You" as Communicator

Know what kind of person you are—whether, for example, you are basically quiet and reticent or excitable and extroverted; whether you are prone to vigorous physical activity or like to "take things easy and relax"; whether you talk easily and well on your feet or prefer to sit while talking. Once you think through the kind of person you are, then you can work more purposefully. Find ways to stimulate and activate yourself during the delivery of your message, for if you do not move, an audience will notice and judge you as apathetic, indifferent, or listless. Choose the mode of self-motivation that is best for you.

This process of self-awareness will help you identify your strengths and weaknesses as a nonverbal communicator. Whether as a result of sex-role stereotyping or other variables, women tend to be more adept than men at creating facial expressions which can be accurately interpreted by viewers. Men, on the other hand, tend to communicate feelings of "positive liking" more clearly than their female counterparts. Persons who are conscious of their own behavior—and of the effects of social conditioning on their ability to transmit nonverbal messages—are more effective users of space, movement, and stance.[10]

Determine Formality of Setting

Create a proxemic relationship with your audience that reflects your needs and attitudes toward your subject as well as your audience's expectations about the degree of formality that should be present. If you feel more at home behind a podium, plan to have it placed accordingly. If you want your whole body to be visible to the audience, but feel the need to have notes at eye level, stand beside the podium and arrange your notecards on it. If you want to relax (and are sure you can compensate for the resulting loss of bodily action by increasing your vocal volume), sit behind a table or desk. If you feel free physically and want to be wholly "open" to your audience, stand in front of a table or desk. These actions will affect both the physical distance and the sense of separation your audience feels is present. As you consider these or other adjustments, you must consider what the audience is accustomed to—will your changes make them uneasy or uncomfortable? If so, it may be wiser to place the interests of the audience ahead of your own, if only to ensure that they will hear your ideas without being distracted unduly by your violation of the expected formality of the occasion.

Assess Effects of Physical Distance

Aside from the impact on formality, physical distance also may affect the audience's ability to see and hear you. *The farther away you are from your listeners, the more important it is for them to have a clear view of you and your visual aids.* The speaker who crouches behind a podium in an auditorium of three hundred people soon loses contact with them. The farther away your audience is, the harder you must work to project your words, and the broader your physical movements must be. Keeping in mind what Edward Hall noted about *public distance* in communication, you should realize that subtle changes of facial expression or small movements of the fingers do not communicate clearly when you are twenty-five or thirty feet away from your listeners. Although many of the auditoriums in this country have a raised platform and a slanted floor to allow a speaker to be seen more clearly, you should, nevertheless, adjust by making your body movements and gestures larger. In addition, if you are going to use such visual aids as a chalkboard, flipchart, working model, or process diagram, remove the tables, chairs, and other objects which cut off the listeners' view and therefore impair their understanding of your message. Review in your own mind large lecture classes you have attended, sermons you have heard in large churches, or political rallies you have attended. Recall the behaviors of speakers who worked effectively in such situations, choosing and adapting those that might also work for you.

Establish Direct Eye Contact

Scan your audience from side to side and from front to back, looking specific individuals in the eyes. This does not mean, of course, that your head is to be in a constant state of motion; "scanning" does not imply rhythmical, nonstop bobbing. Rather, it implies that you must be aware—and must let an audience know you are aware—of the entire group of human beings in front of you. Take them all into your field of vision periodically; establish firm visual bonds with most of them occasionally. The visual bonding that results from direct eye contact is good for both you and the audience: it enhances your *credibility* and it keeps the auditors' attention from wandering.

Let Your Feelings Show

Use your body to communicate your feelings about what you are saying. When you are angry, do not be afraid to gesture vigorously. When you are expressing tenderness, let the message come across your face. In other words, when you are communicating publicly, use the same affective responses you do when you are talking to another individual on a one-to-one basis.

Supplement Your Verbal Message with Gestures

Use your full repertoire of descriptive and conventional gestures while talking publicly. You probably do this in everyday conversation without even thinking about it; so recreate that same set of mind when addressing an audience. Here, physical readiness is the key concern. Keep your hands and arms free and loose enough so that you can call them easily, quickly, and *naturally* into action when you need them. Let them hang comfortably at your sides, relaxed, but in readiness. Occasionally, rest them on the lectern. Then, as you unfold the ideas of your speech, use descriptive gestures to indicate size, shape, or relationship, making sure the gestures are large enough to be seen in the back row. Use conventional gestures also to give visual dimension to your spoken ideas. Keep in mind, of course, that there are no "right" *types* of gestures, just as there are no "right" *number* of gestures that you ought to use. As you prepare your speech, and especially as you practice it orally, however, think carefully through your purpose, your topic, and your plan of development—all the while thinking of the kinds of bodily and gestural actions that would most appropriately and effectively contribute to your delivery of it.

Signal Changes in Content

Use your body to regulate the pace of your presentation and to control transitions. Change positions or shift your weight as you move from the beginning of your speech to the main point. Increase the amount of nonverbal movement when speaking rapidly; decrease bodily and gestural action when verbally slowing down to emphasize particular ideas. Arbitrarily pre-planning *all* such movements never works, but we do urge you to give careful thought to pacing and regulating by nonverbal means those portions of your speech that could benefit from them. You will thus make it much easier for the audience to follow content changes, to know which points you believe are important or crucial, and to increase its interest in hearing what you have to say.

Although much more could be said about using your body to communicate, and more advice obviously could be generated, we have tried to provide at least a basis on which you can build. What happens from here on is up to you. Engage in careful, systematic self-analysis and study, examining your own and other speakers' use of nonverbal communication systems as means for transmitting messages to an audience. Capture a vision of your communicative behaviors as *others* see them, utilizing videotapes, diagnoses from instructors, and feedback from friends. With this enlarged understanding of your speaking behavior, you will be better prepared to form necessary personal decisions on ways to make your body work better for you. Above all, *keep at it.* It takes much practice to ensure that your visual and verbal messages are congruent, and that you are using your total *self* with maximum effectiveness to transmit messages in situations where words alone may fail.

REFERENCE NOTES

[1]Erving Goffman, *The Presentation of Self in Everyday Life* (New York: Doubleday & Company, Inc., 1959), pp. 2–4.

[2]Dale G. Leathers, *Nonverbal Communication Systems* (Boston, MA: Allyn & Bacon, Inc., 1976), pp. 4–5.

[3]For a fuller discussion of each of these components, see Leathers, pp. 52–59.

[4]Hall introduces these discussions of distances in his *The Hidden Dimension* (New York: Doubleday & Company, Inc., 1969), Chapter X, "Distances in Man."

[5]See F. Deutsch, "Analysis of Postural Behavior," *Psychoanalytic Quarterly,* 16 (1947): 195–213; W. James, "A Study of the Expression of Bodily Posture," *Journal of General Psychology,* 7 (1932): 405–36; Albert Mehrabian, "Significance of Posture and Position in the Communication of Attitude and Status Relationships," *Psychological Bulletin,* 71 (1969): 359–72.

[6]For a useful system for classifying gestures, see "Hand Movements" by Paul Ekman and Wallace V. Friesen, *Journal of Communication, 22* (December 1972): 360.

[7]An excellent review of research on facial communication can be found in Leathers, Chapter 2. Those wishing a larger treatment should see Paul Ekman, Wallace V. Friesen, and P. Ellsworth, *Emotion in the Human Face: Guidelines for Research and an Integration of Findings* (New York: Pergamon Press, Inc., 1972).

[8]Paul Ekman and Wallace V. Friesen, "The Repertoire of Nonverbal Behavior—Categories, Usage and Coding," *Semiotica,* 1 (1969): 49-98.

[9]For a difficult but rewarding essay on the management of demeanor, see Erving Goffman, *Interaction Ritual; Essays on Face-to-Face Behavior* (New York: Doubleday & Company, Inc., 1967), "On Face-Work," pp. 5–46.

[10]For a review of research on the abilities of senders of nonverbal communication cues, see Robert Rosenthal and Bella M. DePaulo, "Expectancies, Discrepancies, and Courtesies in Nonverbal Communication," *Western Journal of Speech Communication,* 43 (Spring, 1979): 76–95; Marianne La France and Clara Mayo, "A Review of Nonverbal Behavior of Women and Men," *Western Journal of Speech Communication,* 43 (Spring, 1979): 96–107; and Mark L. Knapp, *Nonverbal Communication in Human Interaction,* 2nd ed. (New York: Holt, Rinehart & Winston, 1978), pp. 411–28.

PROBLEMS AND PROBES

CHAPTER REPORT "Body language" is a term often used to describe much of what is considered in this chapter. Drawing upon the Suggestions for Further Reading, (page 249), enlarge your understanding of this subject, and prepare a short report on some aspect of nonverbal message systems for your instructor or your class.

1. Listen to some speaker on the campus or in your community, and write a brief report on your observations regarding his or her platform behaviors. Before you attend, make a short outline of the suggestions and warnings contained in this chapter, and use it as a checklist against which to compare the speaker's physical behavior. Your commentary on both strong and weak qualities in the speaker's physical contact with the audience can be centered on two important questions: *(a)* Did the speaker's use of proxemics, facial details, gesture, posture, and bodily movement reinforce or detract from the emotional impact of his or her verbal mes-

sage? *(b)* Did the speaker's use of those aspects of delivery reinforce or detract from your comprehension of the message? Observe particularly patterns of emphasis, body tension, and gestures which depicted qualities or shape, and—in general—movement which seemed to draw in or repel an audience.

2. Watch someone who "signs" for the deaf. If possible, listen for a while to what is being said as well as watching the sign language. Then, remove the hearing aspect. What nonverbal cues do you get from the "speaker" other than hand and finger movements? How important are body movements? Facial expressions? Describe your observations in your journal.

3. Watch but do not listen to several television commercials. What nonverbal messages do you receive? Pretend you are from another country and imagine what conclusions you would draw about American people from commercials. In your personal speech journal, outline composites of "The American Man, Woman, and Child." Note your own impressions of the commercial's perspective. How do you feel about the images which are projected?

 ORAL ACTIVITIES

1. Much has been written about the necessity of proper dress for the interview situation. (See, for example, *Dress for Success,* by John Molloy, [Wyden, 1975].) Have several members of the class individually draw up a list of "approved" clothing for both the male and female interviewee. Then share lists. What items of clothing are mentioned most often? Is there a classic business "costume" for the interviewee?

2. Divide the class into teams and play "charades." (Those needing rules for classroom games should read David Zauner, "Charades as a Teaching Device," *Speech Teacher,* 20 [November 1971]: 302.) A game of charades not only will loosen you up physically, but also should help sensitize you to the variety of small but perceptible cues—both descriptive and conventional gestures—you "read" when interpreting messages.

3. Make a two- or three-minute speech explaining to the class how to do something: driving a golf ball, bowling, performing a sleight-of-hand trick, cutting out a shirt, tying some difficult knots, or playing a musical instrument. Use movement and gestures to help make your ideas clear. Do not use the chalkboard or previously prepared diagrams.

4. Prepare and present a short speech describing some exciting event you have witnessed—an automobile accident, a political or campus rally, a sporting event. Use of movement and gestures to render the details clear and vivid. That is, the audience should be able to "see" and "feel" the event as you seek to integrate words/ideas and movements/actions for maximum impact. Successful completion of this assignment should demonstrate to you your ability to employ all of the available message systems.

5. Five or six members of the class will participate in a brief impromptu discussion of a controversial topic. The participants should sit in an arrangement of their choice at the front of the classroom. During the discussion the rest of the class

should watch carefully and take notes about nonverbal communication. Afterward, the class as a whole should discuss proxemics, bodily movements and stance, facial expression, and gestures. Participants may want to comment on their levels of communication apprehension and ascertain how apprehension was transmitted nonverbally. In addition, the class may notice and wish to discuss differences in male and female use of nonverbal communication.

6.   The use of space to suggest power—where an office is located, where your secretary sits, how many windows you have—is a topic that frequently appears in how-to-be-a-corporate-success books. For instance, Michael Korda's *Power: How to Get It, How to Use It* (New York: Ballantine Books, 1976) and Betty Lehan Harragan's *Games Mother Never Taught You: Corporate Gamesmanship for Women* (New York: Rawson Associates, 1977) include chapters on using space. Read one or both sources, and prepare to discuss the principles of using space. After the class discussion, make arrangements to visit a firm or offices in one of the departments on your campus. Take careful notes as you tour the surroundings so that you can relay your findings in a class report.

 SUGGESTIONS FOR FURTHER READING

Judee K. Burgoon and Thomas Saine, *The Unspoken Dialogue* (Boston: Houghton Mifflin Co., 1978).

Paul Ekman and Wallace V. Friesen, *Unmasking the Face* (Englewood Cliffs, NJ: Prentice-Hall, Inc., 1975).

Edward T. Hall, *The Hidden Dimension* (New York: Doubleday & Company, Inc., 1969).

Randall P. Harrison, *Beyond Words: An Introduction to Nonverbal Communication* (Englewood Cliffs, NJ: Prentice-Hall, Inc., 1974).

Mark L. Knapp, *Nonverbal Communication in Human Interaction,* 2nd ed. (New York: Holt, Rinehart & Winston, Inc., 1978).

Dale G. Leathers, *Nonverbal Communication Systems* (Boston: Allyn & Bacon, Inc., 1976).

Rhetorica Ad Herennium, III. 26–27, "Physical Movement."

14

Using the Voice to Communicate

Reflect for a moment, and you will realize that you have more than one way of speaking. You speak one way to your parents, another to your dear old Aunt Matilda, another to your college instructors, and still another to the person you encounter by chance in a local cafe. You talk one way when despondent, another when overjoyed, another when reticent, and still another when confidently assertive. Add to these possibilities all the potential *combinations* of your vocal characteristics, and you will find that you have more ways of communicating orally— more *vocal styles*—than you could ever hope to catalog. One of your tasks as a public communicator, therefore, is to select from this large repertoire of oral communication styles those most consistent with your habitual modes of expressing yourself and which, at the same time, best fit the demands of the particular situation in which you will be speaking publicly.

The characteristics of communication that combine to produce your personal style may be approached from both *physiological* and *psychological* perspectives. Understanding the physiological aspects of sound production and reception (see the diagram on page 258) is the concern of *speech scientists:* audiologists, speech and language pathologists, and voice therapists. These specialists work closely with individuals whose ability to produce or receive sound requires remediation.[1] Accordingly, they ask such questions as:

1. Does the speaker or hearer have physiological problems in producing and receiving speech sounds?
2. Are the speaker's vocal cues loud enough to be heard?
3. Is the communicator speaking too loudly or too softly?
4. Are there enough pauses or "breaks" in the stream of sound to maximize comprehension by the hearer?

5. Is the speaker articulating sharply enough to allow for discrimination between similar words (for instance, "hair" and "heir," "slobber" and "slaughter")?
6. Does the speaker's vocal variety—emphasis and stress pattern, changes in pitch and duration—aid listeners' comprehension?

The concerns identified by these questions are not limited to professional interests in measuring or interpreting sound transmission and reception. They also are highly important concerns of the student of speech communication who desires to understand the workings of the speech mechanism. Such study can create a greater awareness of the flexibility of the human voice and the almost infinite combinations of its characteristics in producing unique vocal styles.

The characteristics of vocal communication also have important *psychological* dimensions which cannot be ignored. In recent years researchers have concentrated their study on the *effects* which various vocal characteristics have upon listeners in a variety of situations. Through their research they are finding that to a significant extent listeners judge a speaker's *background* (age, sex, race, education, geographical origin), *personality, emotional state, stock of information,* and *degree of authority* on how they perceive his or her vocal delivery.[2] Persons interested in the *psychological* aspects of oral communication are interested in answering such questions as:

1. How do such vocal cues as loudness, stress patterns, pitch variation, tempo, and the like affect an audience's judgment of a speaker's background, personality, or emotional state?
2. How do members of this culture *expect* a doctor, a teacher, a mechanic, or a president to "sound"? That is, what kind of and how much "vocal stereotyping" is likely to be at work in a given communication transaction?
3. To what degree do regional or ethnic dialects control an audience's perception of expertness and authority?

Answers to such questions involve an exploration, not so much into the ways in which vocal sounds are produced and absorbed, but of the impact or effects they are likely to have upon receivers' perceptions and judgments. Those who seek answers to such questions are often termed *paralinguists:* persons interested in how *vocal sounds* interact with *words* to produce *meaning.*

Because our intent in this chapter is to explore how vocal communication contributes to the creation of meaning, we shall adopt, for the most part, the perspective of the paralinguist. As a result, we shall consider relevant aspects of the physiological perspective only in defining essential terms. Students interested in developing a more flexible and effective voice should consult Appendix A (p. 412) for exercises to improve normal vocal patterns.

Characteristics of Effective Vocal Communication

Speakers try to combine vocal cues to achieve three simple goals: to be heard, to be understood, and to be endured. If you speak too softly in a 2,000-seat auditorium, if your speech is indistinct or sloppy, or if your monotonous pace of delivery causes people to "tune out," you have not achieved these objectives. The following discussion covers these and other features of communication under the headings *intelligibility, variety,* and *stress.*

Intelligibility

To ensure maximum intelligibility while you are speaking publicly, consider four independent but related factors: (1) *the overall level of loudness at which you speak;* (2) *the rate at which you speak;* (3) *the care with which you enunciate important words;* and (4) *the standard of pronunciation you observe.*

Loudness • "Loudness," as we use the term here, refers to the amount of energy or pressure a sound exerts on your eardrum. The amount of that pressure is affected by (*a*) the *energy* level of the sound produced by the speaker, (*b*) the *distance* the sound has to travel from speaker to listener, and (*c*) the amount of *noise* through which the sound must go. As an initial consideration, you must produce "something" to be heard by your listeners. If you approach the task in a listless, indifferent manner, you are likely to produce a sound that travels to the edge of the podium and drops from "sight." On the other hand, if you put yourself enthusiastically into the task, you are likely to be able to project in a manner required by the situation. Obviously, the farther away your listeners are, the louder you must talk for them to hear you well. Most of us make this loudness-level adjustment unconsciously when projecting our voices over extended distances. What we often forget is that a corresponding adjustment is required when the listeners are only a few feet away. You should realize also that your own voice will always sound louder to you than to your listeners because your own ears are closer to your mouth than theirs are.

In addition to distance, the amount of surrounding noise with which you must compete has an effect on the required loudness level. Even in normal circumstances some noise always is present. For example, the noise level of rustling leaves in the quiet solitude of a country lane (10 decibels) is louder than a whisper six feet away. The noise in empty theaters averages 25 decibels, but with a "quiet" audience it rises to 42. In the average factory, a constant noise of about 80 decibels is characteristic. This is just about the same level as very loud speaking at a close range. (Note that we are using the term "decibel" only to suggest *comparative* loudness levels. Actually, it is a technical term used by acoustic experts and voice scientists to mean "a unit for expressing the relative intensity of sounds on a scale from zero for the average least perceptible sound to about 130 for the average pain level."[3] Thus, the decibel is usually considered to be the smallest degree of difference in sound detectable by the human ear.)

Although you may be speaking with enough energy to hear yourself perfectly well, what is crucial is your auditors' perception of loudness: how easily can they hear you in the context of other background noises that compete for their attention? You will be helped by the fact that an audience *genuinely interested* in your oral message will force itself to listen closely even if you are speaking at a loudness level of only 50 decibels. Of course, if the background noise is constant—heavy equipment is operating just outside the window, the circulating fan in the ceiling has a nasty buzz—your hearers may tire in time and simply "drop out." Calling attention to the competition, asking if you can be heard in spite of it, or even moving to more suitable surroundings are some of the strategies that will help avoid this. Ignoring the difficulty and continuing to attempt to speak over it—or not even trying—will only hasten your audience's mental, if not physical, departure. Thus, although the audience will cooperate and struggle to attend to your words for a time, you cannot count on this "good behavior" for the entirety of your speech.

Finally, consider the value of *contrast* in loudness—speaking at the same decibel level without alteration also may put your listeners to sleep, or cause them to concentrate on things other than your message—the hot room, your droning voice, the wasp that just entered, or the quality of the meal they just completed. Continually yelling at your audience may seem a good way to gain their attention and display your energies as a speaker; it is likely to gain you little applause. Varying your loudness level will help maintain audience interest in your message as well as add emphasis to your important ideas.

Rate • The decision to use a fast or slow rate of speech may hinge on a variety of factors: the formality of the setting, the size of the room in which you are speaking, and the degree of emotional intensity that you wish to convey. In a highly informal situation, your animated conversation with friends may well clip along at 200–250 words per minute. This rate is specially characteristic of persons raised in the North, Midwest, Southwest, or West. Because the distance between you and other persons is short, such fast rates are normally intelligible. In large auditoriums or outdoors, rapid delivery can impede intelligibility and reduce the amount of material comprehended and retained by your audience. Echoes can often distort or destroy sounds in rooms, and in outdoor situations words often seem to drift and vanish into the open air. In addition, if the audience lacks incentive to listen closely—is not strongly motivated to listen—a fast rate (240 words) will lower their comprehension level.[4] When addressing large audiences, then, most of us must slow down to about 120–150 words per minute.

All of this is not to say, of course, that you never should speak rapidly. Undoubtedly, there are temperamentally excitable persons who tend to talk rapidly most of the time, and there certainly are situations when a quickened delivery will help you stir and intensify the emotions of your auditors. If you are such a person and if you talk in emotion-charged situations, you will have to learn to compensate. As your rate increases, for example, you must often adjust your volume and almost always you should take more care in your enunciation of sounds and words.

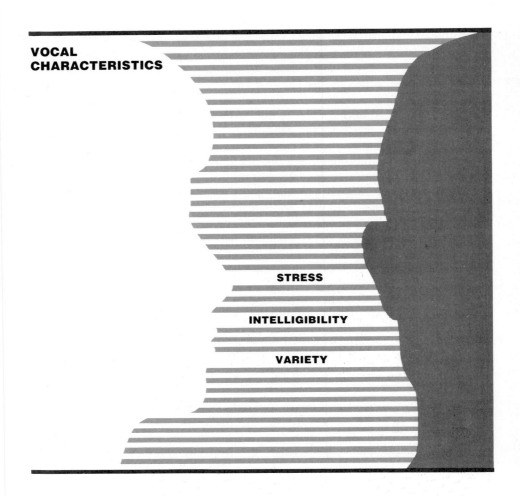

VOCAL CHARACTERISTICS

STRESS

INTELLIGIBILITY

VARIETY

Articulation • Technically, articulation refers to the shaping, joining, or separating of sounds produced by the vocal mechanism. Good articulation has a great deal to do with the distinctness of sounds you produce—the crispness and precision with which you form words vocally. Most of us are "lip lazy" in normal conversation: we tend to slur sounds, drop some syllables completely in enunciating words, or even skip over the beginnings and endings of words. Careless articulation or enunciation of sounds may not inhibit casual conversation with friends, but it can seriously undermine a speaker's intelligibility in front of an audience.

When speaking publicly, you may have to monitor your own enunciation consciously, forcing yourself to say "buy*ing*" instead of "buy*in*," "have to" instead of "hafta," "Quit your belly aching" instead of "Kwitcherbellyachin." Physiologically, this means moving your lips, tongue, and jaw with precision and energy to mold sounds into intelligible word units.

Pronunciation • Beyond the physiological problems of articulating sounds clearly are psychological problems that involve pronunciation and dialect. To be intelligible to your listeners, you must form sounds carefully *and* meet audience expectations of acceptable pronunciation. If you do not pronounce words acceptably, your listeners will not be able to grasp easily and quickly the meaning or significance of what you say. And, even if your words are recognized, any peculiarity of pronunciation is almost sure to be noticed by some of the people who hear you. Saying "To err (as in *air*) is human" instead of "To err (as in *cur*) is human" may reveal your lack of sensitivity to correct standards of pronunciation. Such a mistake may distract your listeners' attention from your line of thought and discredit your knowledge and authority as a speaker.

Standards of pronunciation, of course, differ from region to region. These differences we term *dialects*. A dialect is "a variety of language that is used by one group of persons and has features of vocabulary, grammar, and pronunciation distinguishing it from other varieties used by other groups."[5] Thus, your pronunciation of words, together with the ways in which you arrange them grammatically or syntactically, determines your dialect: a British or German "accent," a white Southern or black Northern dialect, a Detroit vernacular, or a New England "twang." Any given dialect has its own rules for pronunciation which may be quite different from the rules of another dialect. When a Midwestern American ear tries to interpret the sounds emitted by a cockney English mouth, noncommunicative confusion may result.

Unfortunately, dialects may produce not only misunderstandings between speakers and listeners, but they may also produce *negative judgments*—judgments which may seriously affect some auditors' perceptions of the speaker's credibility, education, reliability, responsibility, and capabilities for leadership.[6] This happens because dialects and even professional jargon contribute heavily to what paralinguists call "vocal stereotypes."[7] For example, the dialect of Midwesterners is generally perceived as more credible and competent than the dialect of Southerners or "Downeasters."[8] It is no accident that your nightly television fare is overpopulated with a single dialect—Midwestern. In addition, dialect stereotypes have racial overtones: "both blacks and whites rate speakers of standard English higher than speakers using a nonstandard dialect."[9] This means that, as a speaker, you may have to make some serious decisions regarding your accent: Should you learn to talk in the grammar, vocabulary, and vocal patterns of "middle America" when addressing such audiences? Many speakers of dialects are forced to become "bilingual," using the vocal patterns of their own background when talking with local audiences, and patterns we call Midwestern American when facing more varied audiences.

Variety

Whereas variety in loudness is important in determining the intelligibility of your message, other aspects of variety—rate, pitch, and extent or duration of sounds—are of great importance in controlling the degree of audience interest you are able to generate and sustain, and the subtle shades of attitude and feeling you can communicate.

Varying the rate • Earlier we discussed the effects of a fast or slow rate of speech on intelligibility. Just as a lack of change in loudness may dull audience sensibilities, so may an inflexible rate have a damaging effect on the interest level you wish to maintain. Varying the rate in accordance with the ideas you are expressing is a positive means of clearly communicating the significance or meaning of words. The emotional character of your subject matter can be reflected through subtle shifts in rate. A fast tempo helps to communicate feelings of anger, fear, happiness, and surprise; a slow pace, on the other hand, may help to convey feelings of sadness, disgust, or boredom.[10] In observing how other speakers use changes in rate to communicate thoughts, consider how television news analysts use pace to create a mood of somber reflection or urgent appeal, and how evangelists change pace in keeping with the emotional intensity of the message. A variable rate also may reflect the changing complexity of the subject matter: a rapid rate signifies that the material is easily grasped; a slower rate may be necessary in going over complicated statistics, in explaining a technical term, or in discussing an esoteric religious or philosophical belief. Whether to communicate feeling or otherwise reflect on the nature of the ideas, changing the rate of your speech helps to keep the audience's attention riveted on the speech.

Changing the pitch • Physically, pitch is a matter of vibrations or "waves" produced in air or other media by an energy source. The greater the number of vibrations produced in a given time, the *higher* the pitch; the fewer the number, the *lower* the pitch. As all stereo buffs know, the human ear can hear wide variations in pitch (measured in waves or cycles per second or *cps*), and those variations are important to the perception of sound by listeners.

As a public speaker you should concern yourself with three aspects of pitch: (1) *pitch level*—whether it is high or low or in between; (2) *pitch range*—nearly everyone, for example, can easily span an octave, and many people have voices flexible enough to vary more than two octaves without strain; and (3) *pitch variation*—how often you change the pitch level of your voice.

To begin with, everyone has a *habitual pitch level*. Whether high or low, this is your normal speaking level, and it is the essence of your everyday vocal communication. Unless you are doing impressions, you probably should not try consistently to alter the level, lest you slip and be perceived as "affected" or "phony" because of an unnatural pitch level. However, temporary changes in pitch level are of major importance when you wish to extend your *pitch range*. In normal conversation, you may use only a few notes—even less than an octave—and get away with it. If you try to talk in a limited range from a podium, however, you may seem monotonous. Given the distances sounds must travel between speaker and audience and the length of time speakers talk, you have to exaggerate, have to employ a larger than normal range. Your pitch "highs" should become higher and your "lows" lower. In this way you will be employing an effective variety and using vocal tones appropriate to the emotional content of your speech. Finally, the key to successful use of pitch lies in your ability to control *variations in pitch*. In essence, you should let the importance of a particular word or phrase, or the normal function of a sentence—question, command—determine the appropriateness of a pitch change. Moving your voice up at the end of a question, or changing to higher or lower "notes" to add emphasis within a particular sentence are ways of communicating your intent to an audience.

Psychologically considered, all three facets of pitch affect the audience's perception of your personality and emotional state. A low-pitched voice, for instance, is characteristically associated with pleasantness, serenity, or sadness; a high-pitched voice is frequently associated with fear, surprise, or anger. A narrow pitch range tends to be monotonous and usually communicates boredom or a lack of involvement, whereas an extremely wide-ranging pitch indicates enthusiasm, excitement, or—sometimes—fear. Extreme variations, in which the pitch "slides" rapidly up and down the scale, create impressions of happiness, surprise, and activity.[11] These indicators are, of course, suggestive rather than arbitrary, but should at least be taken into account when you are trying to analyze the effect of your voice upon others.

Altering duration of sound • By duration we mean the extent or amount of time you devote to the production of particular sounds within the syllables you utter. But merely slowing down is not enough. How well you are understood depends also upon "quantity" or—as we have termed it—duration. Talking at a moderate rate *while prolonging the sounds uttered* improves intelligibility markedly.[12] If you spend little time producing each sound, the overall effect is an enunciation that is "clipped," as in the dialogue in bad movies about stereotyped Germans, who usually speak in overly clipped English. If you spend a comparatively long time forming each sound, the result is an enunciation that is "drawled" or "rounded," as in equally bad movies about stereotyped hillbillies.

Duration of speech sounds is important psychologically because (1) almost every speaker has habitual patterns of duration which make up his or her regional or ethnic dialect, and (2) variations in syllable or sound duration indicate variations in mood or emotional state. For example, research has shown that a communicator who speeds up the speaking rate and decreases syllable duration is likely to be thought happy, surprised, or excited; a speaker who slows the rate and increases syllable duration is likely to be thought sad, disgusted, fearful, or bored.[13] In short, duration ought to *vary* with the thrust of your words: a "clipped" vocal delivery makes sense when you are communicating excited or angry thoughts, but it is hardly the voice of love.

Stress

A third significant aspect of vocal behavior is stress—the ways in which sounds, syllables, and words are accented. Without vocal stress, everything in a speech would sound the same, and the resulting message would be both incomprehensible and emotionless. Without vocal stress, you would sound like a computer.

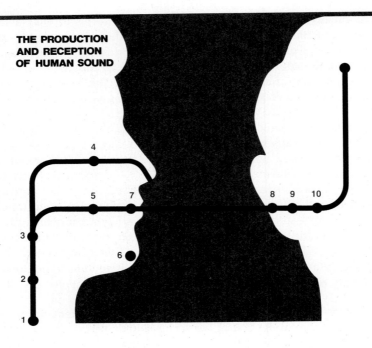

THE PRODUCTION AND RECEPTION OF HUMAN SOUND

1. A *stream of air* is sent from the lungs through the trachea to
2. the *vocal folds* ("voice box"), which in turn vibrate at various pitches, depending upon tension in the muscles. As the sound proceeds up the throat, it is shaped by
3. the *palate* and given resonance or additional tones by
4. the *nasal and sinus regions*. The sounds or phonemes which make up our language are formed primarily by
5. the *tongue,*
6. *jaw placement* and
7. the *lips*. The formed sound in "waves," travels through the air to an ear.

8. It enters the *outer ear* (concha), moves through
9. the *auditory canal* (external meatus), and strikes
10. the *tympanum* (eardrum). The eardrum "translates" the sound waves once more to physical vibrations, which, through the bones of the middle ear, send the vibrations via nerves to the brain.

Vocal stress is achieved in two ways—through vocal emphasis and through the judicious use of pauses.

Adding emphasis • By emphasis we refer to those points in a sentence where, principally through increased vocal energy (loudness) and intonation (pitch), you utter a sound or word more forcefully or "hit" it harder than normal. By emphasizing vocally the important or key words in your discourse, you are able to communicate meanings more clearly and accurately. If you regularly stress syllables—as in "MA-ry HAD a LIT-tle LAMB"—you are employing a *rhythmical* pattern in your speaking. If you irregularly accent words—for example, the first, fourth, fifth, and eleventh words in a sentence—you are using an *arrhythmical* or *non-rhythmical* pattern. Both rhythmical and arrhythmical stress patterns are useful to public speakers.

Consider, for example, the accent-and-stress pattern in these words of the Revolutionary War propagandist Thomas Paine: "THESE are the TIMES *(pause)* that TRY *(pause)* men's SOULS." When you read that statement aloud, evenly spacing the emphasized words, *these, times, try,* and *souls,* not only can you sense a kind of muffled drumbeat that helps to communicate the solemnity and seriousness of the crisis, but you see also how stress may be used to facilitate comprehension and heighten listeners' feelings.

Arrhythmical or non-rhythmical stress, too, can be important in helping an audience comprehend what you are saying. Consider the simple sentence: "Matt can use his axe today." Notice how the meaning varies with the word being emphasized:

1. MATT can use his axe today. (not someone else)
2. Matt CAN use his axe today. (he is allowed to)
3. Matt can use HIS axe today. (not mine)
4. Matt can use his AXE today. (not the splitting mallet)
5. Matt can use his axe TODAY. (permission does not extend to other days)

Without careful control of vocal force, a speaker is liable to utter messages subject to a great many possible meanings. A lack of vocal stress may not only create an impression of boredom, it may cause needless misunderstandings.

Emphasis also is fostered through changes in pitch and rate. Relatively simple changes in pitch, for example, can be used to "tell" an audience where you are in an outline, as when a speaker says,

"My final point is this: We must not forget handicapped workers."

In this sentence, the audience can hear that the speaker has completed one idea and moved on to the next, and that handicapped workers will be the principal concern of that section. Variations in rate can operate in the same way. Consider the following sentence:

"We are a country faced with . . . [moderate rate] runaway inflation, racial tensions, an energy crunch, a crisis of morality, unemployment, government waste . . . [fast rate] and-a-stif-ling-na-tion-al-debt." [slow rate]

This speaker has built a vocal freight train. The ideas pick up speed through the accelerating list of problems, and then come to an emphatic halt when the speaker's main concern—the national debt—is mentioned. Such variations in rate essentially communicate to an audience what is and what is not especially important to the speech. Emphasis has been achieved through the control of speaking rate.

Emphasis is an important characteristic of the flexible speaking voice. When talking informally to a friend on the street, we all emphasize "naturally," the way our culture has taught us to communicate. Many people, however, become so stiff when talking from a podium that they retreat to vocal patterns characterized by little force, a single pitch, and a steady rate. They become monotonous, especially when they try to read from a full manuscript. Remember that conversationality is your goal when standing before an audience. In that way, you probably will return to your normal emphasis patterns.

Pauses and intrusions • This aspect of stress involves (a) the silences and (b) the extraneous vocal noises you build into your utterances. *Pauses* are intervals of silence between or within words, phrases, or sentences. *Intrusions,* sometimes called vocalized pauses, include the "uhs," "ums," "ahs," and similar meaningless noises with which we so often fill our speech. These vocalized intrusions may serve to allow for more "thinking time" in the context of very difficult speech settings, and may be present with greater frequency when you are more anxious or nervous.[14] One or two intrusions may not harm your perceived competence and sureness, but a speech liberally sprinkled with them—"Today, ah, er, I would like, you know, to speak to you, umm, about a pressing, well-uh, like, a pressing problem facing this, uh, campus"—destroys any chance a speaker has of getting a firm, convincing message through to an audience. Thus, you should make a concerted effort to remove them from your speaking behavior.

Silent pauses, in contrast, may be either positive or negative in their effect, depending on their frequency, duration, and placement within the flow of spoken sounds. Such pauses *punctuate thought* by separating groups of spoken words into meaningful units. The silent pause placed immediately before a key idea or the climax of a story creates suspense; placed immediately after a major point or key idea, it adds emphasis. Introduced at the proper moment, a dramatic pause may express your feeling more forcefully than words. Clearly, silence can be a highly effective communicative tool if used intelligently and sparingly and if not embarrassingly prolonged.[15]

Vocal Control of the Emotional Atmosphere

A listener's judgment of a speaker's personality and emotional commitment often centers on that person's vocal quality—the fullness or thinness of the tones, whether or not it is harsh, husky, mellow, nasal, breathy, or resonant. On the psychological basis of voice quality listeners also make judgments about a speaker's attitude or state of mind: they characterize the speaker as being angry, happy, confident, fearful, sad, sincere, or insincere.

Fundamental to an audience's reaction to your voice quality are what G. L. Trager calls *emotional characterizers*—laughing, crying, whispering, yelling, moaning, whining, spitting, groaning, belching, marked inhaling or exhaling, etc.[16] Physiologically, such "characterizers" are produced by highly complex adjustments of your vocal mechanism: lips, jaw, tongue, hard and soft palates, throat, and vocal folds. Psychologically, what is important about emotional characterizers is that they combine in various ways with the words you speak to communicate different shades of meaning. Consider, for a moment, a few of the many ways you can say the simple sentence:

"Tom's going for pizza tonight with Jane."

First, say it as though you were only *reporting the fact* to a mutual friend. Now say it as though *you can't believe* Tom is going with Jane. Or, again, as though it is *impossible* Jane would go with Tom. Then indicate that you wish *you were going* instead of Tom or Jane. Next, say it as though you cannot believe Tom is *actually spending money* on pizza (when he could be purchasing something less expensive). Finally, say it as though you are *expressing doubts* about Tom's motive—indicate that you think he is after more than pizza on this trip.

As you said that sentence over and over, you not only varied your pitch and loudness, but you probably also made some strange and complicated changes in your emotional characterizers. Such changes are important determiners of how a message should be taken or interpreted by listeners.

In brief, the characterizing aspects of voice, or what David Crystal defines as "a single impression of a voice existing throughout the whole of a normal utterance,"[17] are of prime importance in determining the overall or general impression you make upon an audience. Although you cannot completely control your emotional characterizers, you can be alert to the effects they are likely to produce and try to make meaningful adjustments in your voice quality consistent with the demands of your spoken messages—as you have just done in repeating the simple statement about Tom, Jane, and pizza. We are not urging, of course, that you experiment over and over again with every sentence in a speech so as to achieve a "proper" emotional overtone. We are emphasizing, however, that key ideas—and more especially, key evaluations and expressions of your attitudes—will be interpreted more accurately by an audience if you consider such characterizers. In sum, keep your repertoire of voice qualities in the forefront of your mind as you decide whether to yell at, cry with, sneer at, plead with, harp on, or humble yourself before an audience.

Choosing an Appropriate Vocal Style

The facets of vocal style we have discussed—intelligibility, variety, and stress—significantly influence an audience's perception of you and your message. Some of these communicative effects are summarized in the table on page 263. As you mix all of these variables together into your own *vocal style*, it should be apparent that you make conscious choices between and among the alternative ways of speaking: fast, slow, loud, with stress, and so forth. In making these choices, consider questions such as the following.

Is your normal voice appropriate for the topic, audience, or physical setting? Although we are not suggesting that you adopt what is for you an unnatural vocal style, you may find it necessary to alter your normal style. If the topic is complex and unfamiliar to your listeners, rapid, slurred speech will leave them confused. Slowing down and articulating more carefully than is necessary in everyday conversation will enhance audience comprehension. If the audience is either lethargic or highly motivated, a low-key delivery will not be as effective as one which is energetic and lively—to jar dull listeners out of their doldrums or to match the interest level of an enthusiastic group. Similarly, the physical setting may require you to make an extra effort to project your voice so as to be heard. You can compensate for greater distance between yourself and the audience by increasing vocal intensity or loudness while exercising careful articulatory control. You also will need to pay close attention to pitch and pitch variation, and usually will find it helpful to slow your speaking rate.

Does the formality of the occasion affect your choice of vocal style? When you are presenting a speech in a formal setting, you will be acutely aware of social pressures that require you to pay more than casual attention to your presentation. You will find it helpful to speak more slowly than you do in conversation, to suit pitch and loudness variations to the dignity of the occasion, and exercise careful articulatory control. In contrast, when you are in an informal setting, you undoubtedly will feel free to use "street talk," to speak at an accelerated rate, and to pay less attention to careful articulation.

Are there traditions or customs which affect the choice of vocal style? Clergymen, for example, soon discover that tradition decrees that their formal addresses assume vocal patterns which identify them as preachers, priests, or rabbis in the audience's experience. Similarly, people hold stereotyped images of what college professors, professional athletes, or presidents of civic or social organizations traditionally sound like. Therefore, when you are called on to speak in situations where precedents and customs (e.g., communication rules) exert a significant influence, you must decide in what respects and to what degree you will adapt your characteristic vocal behaviors to the style demanded by tradition.

Does your purpose in speaking affect your choice of vocal style? Suppose, for example, that in giving an informative speech, Speaker X realizes that she will be presenting ideas which may be unfamiliar to her listeners. In terms of the vocal characteristics we have discussed, what choices might she make in projecting her sensitivity to audience needs? A composite picture of the vocal behaviors she might exhibit—and one which no two speakers would duplicate exactly—could include the following:

Voice Quality — (1) Employ a relatively matter-of-fact emotional characterizer.

Intelligibility — (1) Articulate precisely so that unfamiliar words or ideas can be understood; (2) use standard, community-based pronunciations, especially of

VOCAL CHARACTERISTICS AND THEIR COMMUNICATIVE EFFECTS*

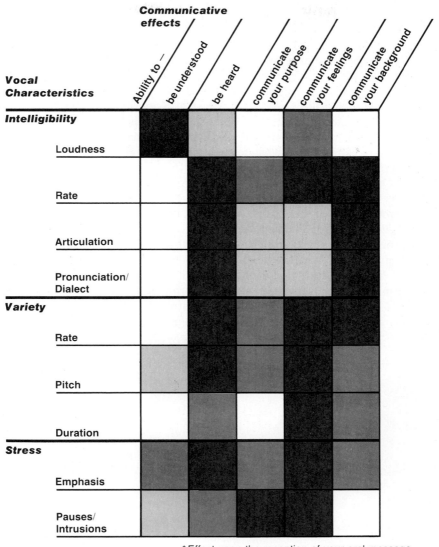

Vocal Characteristics	Ability to – be understood	be heard	communicate your purpose	communicate your feelings	communicate your background
Intelligibility					
Loudness	very important	mildly important		relatively important	
Rate		very important	relatively important	very important	very important
Articulation		very important	mildly important	mildly important	very important
Pronunciation/Dialect		very important	mildly important	mildly important	very important
Variety					
Rate		very important	relatively important	very important	very important
Pitch	mildly important	very important	very important	very important	relatively important
Duration		relatively important		very important	very important
Stress					
Emphasis	relatively important	very important	relatively important	very important	relatively important
Pauses/Intrusions	mildly important	mildly important	very important	very important	

*Effect upon the reception of your oral message

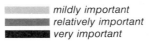

mildly important
relatively important
very important

(These judgments are based on the research reported in the footnotes to this chapter.)

technical terms, because some listeners may be hearing these words for the first time. Maintain moderate volume, neither extremely loud nor extremely soft.

Vocal Variety — (1) Sustain a normal pitch range and level, avoiding distracting extremes; (2) keep enough pitch variation, however, to maximize intelligibility and minimize monotones; (3) maintain a moderate rate, slowing down especially at points where the material is unfamiliar, but important.

Stress — (1) Emphasize words which express key concepts; (2) pause after key ideas, checking audience feedback to make sure that her information is getting through to her listeners.

Now, for the sake of contrast, let us suppose that Speaker X is aiming not at the intellectual and emotional detachment of a so-called informative speech, but rather at the reforming fervor of one bent on righting a wrong. In achieving what she considers an appropriate persuasive style, what vocal behaviors might she conceivably exhibit, and what related concerns might she have? As we observe her presentation this time, she might:

Voice Quality — (1) Employ a wide assortment of emotional characterizers which reflect the emotional states through which she and (she hopes) her audience are progressing, as she pleads, condemns, cajoles, exhorts, etc.

Intelligibility — (1) Articulate carefully to compensate for the fact that emotional fervor tends to make articulation somewhat hurried and possibly less distinct; (2) give careful attention to pronunciation of key words, especially those expressing highly positive and highly negative concepts, because her sense of urgency can cause her to rush or blur such pronunciations; use—within rather strict limits—somewhat altered pronunciations to heighten emotional effect; (3) utilize only as much dialect as is appropriate to herself as a concerned person and

An appropriate vocal style is important in effectively communicating your message to your listeners. The type of occasion, the physical setting, and your purpose in speaking, all shape your choice of vocal style.

to her audience as concerned listeners; (4) employ loudness levels that range from shouts to whispers if and when they are appropriate to her topic, her audience, and the occasion.

Variety — (1) Vary her pitch, giving it higher tops and bottoms than in her informative speech; (2) employ a greater pitch variation when excited; (3) take vocal duration into careful account, "clipping" words and phrases she feels she can afford to hurry by, but sustaining the appropriate syllables within words expressing key ideas; (4) allow for considerable variation in her rate of speaking, being careful only to avoid a rate so rapid and excited that it reduces listeners' comprehension.

Stress — (1) Seek to maintain, in conjunction with her phrasing of key ideas, an appropriate stress pattern, occasionally employing highly rhythmical patterns when trying to carry her audience along with her to an emotional pinnacle; (2) typically avoid "uhs," "ums," and other vocal intrusions, even though this is difficult when the speaker is highly emotional; and (3) employ pauses strategically to heighten message impact.

The Importance of Practice

In this chapter we have studied the characteristics of an effective speaking voice. We have suggested ways in which you can make your speech more intelligible and have reviewed the standard of pronunciation to which you should adhere. In addition, we have pointed out the importance of having a voice that is varied as well as clear, and have shown how variety depends upon a proper use of rate, force, and pitch. Do not assume that you will be able to master in a day or a week all the vocal skills that have been described. Take time to review and digest the ideas presented.

Above all, *practice*. Practice the exercises which are given in Appendix A. These have been designed to make more flexible your vocal apparatus—breathing, phonation, resonance, articulation, and control of rate, pause, and inflection. When you are able to control your vocal mechanism, to make it respond to your desires, you will be able to achieve vocal intelligibility, variety, and stress. Then you will be able to add the emotional coloring the well-tuned vocal instrument is capable of generating. Remember that any vocal skill, before it can be natural and effective with listeners, must be so much a habit that it will work for you with little conscious effort when you begin to speak and will continue to do so throughout the course of your oral message.

REFERENCE NOTES

[1]For an analysis of vocal communication, see W. Barnett Pearce and Bernard J. Brommel, "Vocalic Communication and Persuasion," *Quarterly Journal of Speech*, 58 (1972): 298–306.

[2]Much of the research on judgments people make about your voice is summarized in and comes from Mark L. Knapp, *Nonverbal Communication in Human Interaction*, 2nd ed. (New

York: Holt, Rinehart & Winston, Inc., 1978), especially Chapter 10; Judee K. Burgoon and Thomas Saine, *The Unspoken Dialogue* (Boston: Houghton Mifflin Co., 1978), Chapters 3 and 8; Randall P. Harrison, *Beyond Words: An Introduction to Nonverbal Communication* (Englewood Cliffs, NJ: Prentice-Hall, Inc., 1974), Chapter 6; and Dale G. Leathers, *Nonverbal Communication Systems* (Boston: Allyn & Bacon, Inc., 1976), Chapter 6.

[3]By permission. From *Webster's New Collegiate Dictionary*, copyright © 1981 by G. & C. Merriam Co., publishers of the Merriam-Webster dictionaries.

[4]Michael J. Beatty, Ralph R. Behnke, and Deirdre Froelich, "Effects of Achievement Incentive and Presentation Rate on Listening Comprehension," *Quarterly Journal of Speech*, 66 (1980): 193–200.

[5]By permission. From *Webster's Third New International Dictionary*, copyright © 1976 by G. & C. Merriam Co., publishers of the Merriam-Webster dictionaries.

[6]The effects of dialect are usefully summarized in Judee K. Burgoon and Thomas Saine, *The Unspoken Dialogue* (Boston: Houghton Mifflin Co., 1978), pp. 182–83; and Mark L. Knapp, *Nonverbal Communication and Human Interaction*, 2nd ed. (New York: Holt, Rinehart & Winston, Inc., 1978), pp. 333–35.

[7]Recent studies of vocal stereotyping may be found in W. E. Lambert, H. Frankel, and G. R. Tucker, "Judging Personality Through Speech: A French-Canadian Example," *Journal of Communication*, 16 (1966): 312–13; David W. Addington, "The Relationship of Selected Vocal Characteristics to Personality Perception," *Speech Monographs*, 35 (1968): 492–503; W. J. Weaver and R. J. Anderson, "Voice and Personality Interrelationships," *Southern Speech Communication Journal*, 38 (1973): 275–278; and B. L. Brown, W. J. Strong, and A. C. Rencher, "The Effects of Simultaneous Manipulations of Rate, Mean Fundamental Frequency, and Variance of Fundamental Frequency on Ratings of Personality from Speech," *Journal of the Acoustical Society of America*, 55 (1974): 313–18. (The last study is particularly interesting because it offers advice on ways of altering vocal stereotypes.)

[8]Judee K. Burgoon and Thomas Saine, *The Unspoken Dialogue* (Boston: Houghton Mifflin Co., 1978), p. 182.

[9]Ibid., pp. 182–83.

[10]From "Cue Utilization in Emotion Attribution from Auditory Stimuli," by Klaus R. Scherer and James S. Oshinsky, *Motivation and Emotion*, 1 (1977): 340. Adapted by Burgoon and Saine, *The Unspoken Dialogue*, p. 205.

[11]From "Acoustic Concomitants of Emotional Dimensions: Judging Affect From Synthesized Tone Sequences," by Klaus R. Scherer, presented at Eastern Psychological Association meeting, Boston, April 1972. Reprinted in *Nonverbal Communication; Readings with Commentary*, ed. Shirley Weitz. Reprinted by permission of the author.

[12]From "Effects of Duration and Articulation Changes on Intelligibility, Word Receptions, and Listener Preference," by Gilbert C. Tolhurst, *Journal of Speech and Hearing Disorders*, 22 (September 1957). Reprinted by permission of the American Speech and Hearing Association and Dr. Gilbert C. Tolhurst.

[13]From "Acoustic Concomitants of Emotional Dimensions: Judging Affect from Synthesized Tone Sequences," by Klaus R. Scherer, presented at Eastern Psychological Association meeting, Boston, April 1972. Reprinted in *Nonverbal Communication: Readings with Commentary*, ed. Shirley Weitz. Reprinted by permission of the author.

[14]Mark L. Knapp, *Nonverbal Communication and Human Interaction*, 2nd ed., p. 345. See M. Cook, "Anxiety, Speech Disturbances, and Speech Rate," *British Journal of Social and Clinical Psychology*, 4 (1965): 1–7.

[15]For further study of pauses and intrusions, see F. Goldman-Eisler, *Psycholinguistics: Experiments in Spontaneous Speech* (London and New York: Academic Press, 1968); M.C. Lalljee, "Disfluencies in Normal English Speech," unpublished Ph.D. Dissertation, Oxford Univ., 1971; and Richard L. Johannesen, "The Functions of Silence: A Plea for Communication Research," *Western Speech Journal*, 38 (1974): 25–35.

[16]For an analysis of emotional or vocal characterizers, see George L. Trager, "Paralanguage: A First Approximation," *Studies in Linguistics*, 13 (1958): 1–13.

[17]David Crystal, *Prosodic Systems and Intonation in English* (Cambridge: University Press, 1959), p. 123.

PROBLEMS AND PROBES

CHAPTER REPORT   What kinds of judgments do people make about you just by hearing your voice? In answering this question, review research cited in note 2 (pp. 265–266); write a brief essay listing the kinds of judgments likely to be made; also, discuss the general importance of voice based on your findings.

1.   To verify Edward T. Hall's conception of *intimate* distance, *personal* distance, *social* distance, and *public* distance *(a)* read the appropriate section of Hall's book, *The Hidden Dimension* (New York: Doubleday & Company, Inc., 1966); *(b)* then—in conducting your own investigation—purposely place yourself at the specified distances from others and carry on conversations, noting carefully the changing characteristics of voice quality, loudness, syllable duration, distinctness of articulation, vocal stress, variety, rate, force, and pitch; *(c)* finally, chart several of these characteristics and compare your conclusions with those of Hall.

2.   Listen to a successful speaker addressing a crowd—someone who, because of the extended distance involved, must project his or her voice to a large audience without a microphone. Chart the vocal characteristics listed in Problem 1 above. Then answer these questions: *(a)* What kinds of sentence structures are spoken easily by someone forced to project vocally? *(b)* What kinds of sentence structures are apparently difficult for listeners to understand in such circumstances? *(c)* Can you discern relationships between vocal quality, loudness, rate, pitch, etc., and the physical behavior of the speaker? Identify these relationships. *(d)* In general, describe some of the relationships among vocal, physical, and verbal characteristics of successful, large-scale, public communication.

3.   Are you sensitive to vocal dialects? Can you tell where a person is from by the way he or she speaks? Do you evaluate people on the basis of their speech? What associations do you make when you hear particular dialects? What factors make up a dialect?

   Vocal cues, and particularly regional dialects, are used to stereotype people. Think of television programs such as *Dallas* or *Welcome Back Kotter* that are set in specific geographical settings. What relation do those actors' dialects have with the real regional dialects? Do their dialects and vocal patterns help the audience to recognize certain types of character? Do you use vocal cues to decide what sort of personality a person has? Is that an accurate guide?

ORAL ACTIVITIES

1.   Your instructor will provide the class with a list of emotions. Each student is to choose one emotion and to decide on a number. Using only vocal cues and speaking only that number, each student is to try to express that emotion. The class

should try to guess what emotion is being expressed. After each attempt, the class should try to direct the speaker by suggesting additional cues that will help the speaker to express the emotion.

2.   Find the text of a short speech in *Vital Speeches of the Day,* or other appropriate sources. Using only the written text, prepare the speech for delivery in class by rehearsing the speech aloud a number of times. Each time you rehearse the speech, vary the rate, variety, and punctuation of your voice. Deliver the version that you think most clearly expresses the author's intentions.

 SUGGESTIONS FOR FURTHER READING

D. W. Addington, "The Relationship of Selected Vocal Characteristics to Personality Perception," *Speech Monographs,* 35 (1968): 492–503.

Bert E. Bradley, *Fundamentals of Speech Communication: The Credibility of Ideas,* 3rd ed. (Dubuque, IA: Wm. C. Brown Company, Publishers, 1981), "Pronunciation" and "Attitude Toward a Non-Standard Dialect," pp. 125–30.

J. R. Davitz, *The Communication of Emotional Meaning* (New York; McGraw-Hill, 1964).

M. R. Key, *Paralanguage and Kinesics* (Metuchen, NJ: Scarecrow Press, 1975).

Joseph A. DeVito, Jill Giattino, and T. D. Schon, *Articulation and Voice: Effective Communication* (Indianapolis: The Bobbs-Merrill Company, Inc., 1975).

Donald H. Ecroyd, Murray M. Halfond, and Carol C. Towne, *Voice and Articulation: A Handbook* (Glenview, IL: Scott, Foresman and Company, 1966), esp. Chapters 3–7 and 9.

15

Using Visual Materials in a Speech

In the mid-1960s, when Marshall McLuhan asserted that American culture was returning to a tribal state, he was recognizing the power of electronic, visual communication to integrate diverse peoples and ideas.[1] Humanity, we can safely assume, invented visual art long before it concocted the arbitrary system of signs we call language; and human beings, we are discovering through careful observation, become visually literate before they can be deemed verbally literate.

Visual communication, indeed, is an important area of scholarly and practical study. Based primarily on the principles of Gestalt psychology, scholars have conducted extensive research on the perception and integration of discrete visual experiences into unified wholes. In particular, interactions between visual media, learning, and attitude change have attracted attention in both academic and business worlds.[2] Such ongoing research is of vital importance to a world in which computers can reproduce information spatially and in which copying machines put faithful duplicates of originals in the hands of consumers almost instantly. Today the average person cannot escape the bombardment of visual messages—films, television, billboards, T-shirts, bumper stickers, handouts, mass-mailed advertising circulars, buttons, store-window displays, business signs, etc.—that come at us constantly.

The study of visual communication is especially important to the public speaker because it relates to oral communication in two significant ways. (1) As we noted in Chapter 13, the human body itself is a visual message, one which is "read" by an information-seeking audience; and (2) as a speaker you are frequently faced with questions concerning the use of so-called visual aids or visual supporting materials: Should I employ visual aids? If so, what kind? How big? When should I introduce a picture, a bar graph, or a working model? Should I look at the chalkboard or the audience? These are eminently practical questions about everyday speechmaking. Systematic research has not offered answers to all such questions, but it is far enough along to help you as a public communicator make some important decisions.

In this chapter we first will consider briefly how you learn to recognize and "read" four commonly used visual-message systems: shape, size, color, and complexity. Then we will examine two key functions of visual support—aiding comprehension and memory and increasing persuasiveness. Third, we will identify several useful types of visuals. And, finally, we will suggest some factors to consider when choosing among the several types of visual aids.

"Reading" Visual Symbols and Patterns

The phrase *visual literacy* refers to the idea that all people have been taught, in varying degrees, to "read" visual symbols and visualized configurations or patterns. Thus, you have learned that smoke is a visual sign for fire. You have learned that inverted yellow-hued clouds riding a southwest wind on a hot muggy day in southern Illinois portend a tornado. Some such patterns you learn through *personal experience*, as when children learn to identify friendly and unfriendly dogs by watching their tails, shoulders, teeth, and eyes. Other patterns you acquire from *institutions* and *instruction*, as when you were taught the meaning of certain conventional gestures by your family or friends and certain religious symbols by a church or synagogue. Overall, in a few short years you learned to discriminate among visual objects that differ only in the slightest detail, as when you distinguish among almost identical shades of red or between lines which are perfectly parallel and those which are slightly angular. And, of course, you may even be one of those rare people who have sharpened their visual acuity to a point where they are hypersensitively literate—for example, the experts who spot painting forgeries, or the standards-control inspectors who can see the tiniest ripple in an assembly-line paint job at five feet. Why are we able to make such subtle discriminations? Because what we are really perceiving are several discrete or separate *visual-message systems*, including *shape, size, color*, and *complexity*.[3]

Shape • You not only have been taught to identify certain shapes, forms, and configurations as significant to your life, but also your basic perceptual equipment seems designed to allow you to finish out or "complete" partial shapes and figures. A standard section on drivers' tests, for example, includes a number of geometric figures—a circle, a hexagon, a square, a wedge—which you know from road experience represent different highway warnings or directions. Psychologically, you *complete* shapes only partially formed, either by adding missing portions or items or by associating an incomplete shape with a complete object.[4]

Size • As a child, you probably were confused by the fact that objects at a distance appeared smaller than objects nearby. You soon learned, however, to estimate distance and adjust your perspectives accordingly, just as you learned to judge loudness, odors, etc. Now you are able to *focus* your perceptual equipment. Through a highly complex process of physiological adjustment and psychological training, you can perceive almost invisibly small objects (such as pins) and distinguish them from among a host of larger objects (such as the chairs, coffee table, and lamps in a room).

Color • As we have noted, you also are able to discriminate among a great variety of colors, hues, and shades. A farmer, by noting the color of a field of wheat, can judge the appropriate time to harvest it. A clothes designer makes decisions on hues based on the subtlest of differences. Homeowners determine when to water their lawns, often unconsciously, by observing the color of the grass. As a matter of fact, people even go so far as to react *attitudinally* to colors. Political commercials presented in color, for example, are perceived more favorably than when presented in black and white. Recent research also suggests that persons with moderate and conservative views respond more favorably to the color blue, whereas reform-minded persons prefer yellow and radicals prefer red.[6] The color of a person's political bumper sticker may have an effect on how the individual is perceived by various political groups. Film presentations in color, as opposed to black and white, also may enhance learning in the educational setting.[7]

Complexity • Finally, as you grow up, you are taught to process visual messages that have varying degrees of complexity. A child of four has difficulty verbally describing pictures that contain a number of objects, or abstract line drawings, whereas a child of eight or nine can do this with relative ease. You learn to scan visual objects and to rank elements in them hierarchically in order to determine what is most important, next-most important, and so on. Most significantly, perhaps, you learn to make judgments about *figure-ground relationships*. That is, you learn to identify the central figure or point of focus in a visual presentation. The makers of television commercials are among our culture's most careful students of figure-ground relationships. It makes a difference, for example, whether an oil company shows its derricks against the background of the North Sea (ruggedness, exploration, adventure) or against a bird sanctuary and bayou swamp (serenity, preservation, reverence); whether soda pop is being consumed on the family porch (hominess, day-to-day existence) or in a group of eighteen-year-olds having fun (excitement, peer approval).

In other words, we are learning much about the associations people make with shapes, sizes, colors, and varying degrees of complexity. This research has had considerable impact upon advertising, the preparation of materials for school-age children, and the like. It also can be put to practical use by public speakers in their day-to-day presentations. Before we can explore such applications, however, we must first understand the functions of visual materials in public communication settings.

The Functions of Visual Materials

Visual materials serve the speaker in two important ways: (1) they aid listener comprehension and memory; (2) they add persuasive impact to a message.

Comprehension and Memory • Well-executed visuals can aid significantly your auditors' comprehension of your message. If a picture is worth a thousand words, then it is useful principally because it adds important information that is more easily understood visually than aurally. Visual research has demonstrated that bar graphs, especially, make statistical information more accessible to an audience, that simple (as opposed to complicated) drawings enhance recall, and that charts and even "human interest" visuals (especially photographs) help an audience retain data.[8] In addition, pictures which accompany a story being read aloud to children have significant effects on listener recall and comprehension.[9] Thus, do not underestimate the value of such visual aids when your purpose is to inform or "teach" the audience.

Persuasiveness • In addition to enhancing comprehension and memory, visual aids may heighten the persuasive effects of speeches. Lawyers, for example, have taken advantage of the dramatic effects which attend the visual evidence of injuries or of crimes in eliciting a favorable response from juries. Some lawyers are experimenting with the use of video technology to create dramatic portrayals of events—the condition of a road, a person's evident sense of caring and loving in a custody battle—in order to bring visual materials to bear upon jury decisions. Undeniably, a speaker's credibility, as well as the credibility of an idea, is positively affected by appropriate visuals.[10]

Although we normally think of "supporting materials" (see Chapter 7) as verbal constructs or ideas, it is advantageous to consider visual aids as useful, even necessary, forms of support. Their function is not merely that of providing entertaining or aesthetically pleasing qualities to a speech. With care, they can be integrated into a public presentation and may play a major role in oral instruction and persuasion. Visual materials satisfy a culturally induced need to "be shown"—in this sense they often function as crucial means by which speakers can achieve their purposes.[11]

Types of Visual Support

There are several ways in which you can enhance the instructional or persuasive potential of your message. The following list is suggestive; your own experience may present other imaginative ways to clarify and dramatize your ideas.

The object itself • If it is portable and intricate, the object itself may be brought to the podium. Explaining the sonar principle of the new Polaroid SRX-70 Sonar camera can be facilitated by bringing the camera with you. The correct use of an optical microscope could hardly be explained without having an actual instrument at hand. The adjustment of focus, of the eyepiece, and of the illumination sources would not be clear unless the audience could see how to to it. Objects create a level of interest often impossible to generate with words alone, particularly if the object is "new" to the audience. Finally, audience participation can be fostered if you hand out pieces of paper for a speech on origami, or samples of "chocolate" chip cookies made with carob chips.

The use of yourself • Physical action is often essential in explaining a particular concept or movement. Speeches on yoga positions, ballet steps, or tennis strokes gain concreteness and vitality from speakers who illustrate their subjects personally. A speech on Little League baseball may be enhanced by your visual demonstration of how various youngsters hold the bat at the beginning of the year or how attentive they are on the field. The entire speech need not be devoted to a "physical" subject in order to employ your body in illustrating action.

Models • If an object is too large to bring into the room or too small to be seen easily, you will want to use a model. Small-scale models of geodesic domes, for example, could illustrate the home of the future for certain audiences; large-scale models of molecules could add specificity to something normally invisible. Explaining the complexity of micro-circuitry may be made easier by constructing a large scale model of the electronic schematic. Arguing for a ban on aerosol sprays may call for a model of an ozone molecule; illustrating how the molecule is physically altered may help the audience understand why their seemingly innocuous deodorant spray cans can have a harmful effect on the environment.

Slides • Although they require projection equipment and darkened rooms, slide projectors or overhead projectors give many speakers the added advantage of showing shape, color, texture, and relationships. A speech on the history of logging operations or on farming methods in the early 1900s can be made more interesting and informative if appropriate slides are used. The persuasive impact of a speech against the construction of a hydro-electric dam can be enhanced by slides depicting the wilderness waterway that will be destroyed if the dam is built. If you can't bring a Rembrandt or a Picasso painting to your audience, slides of both artists' work may be the best way to illustrate differences in technique or style.

Films and videotapes • By taking advantage of new video-technology, you can increase the interest and informational potential of your speech. Segments from previously aired television shows may dramatically underscore your point about the treatment of the elderly on today's "sit-coms." If the necessary equipment is available, you may be able to define "psychodrama" more clearly by having persons role-play a scene for you. The scene can then be used in the context of your presentation. Lawyers are finding "depovisions"—videotaped testimony from doctors or others who find it difficult to attend a trial in person—a convenient way to obtain needed information on behalf of their clients. These can be inserted at the appropriate moment in a trial, rather than having to place information out of context to accommodate professional schedules of witnesses.

Films add other dimensions to a talk—moving, changing relationships or vivid illustrations. A speech on the disintegration of families would gain considerable force if you showed a clip from *The Failing Marriage;* a discussion of creativity would profit immeasurably from showing a segment of *Why Man Creates.*

Chalkboard drawings • By now, you have been conditioned to "reading the board" in school. Chalkboards are often substituted for more permanent illustrators by lazy speakers, but, more important, they are especially valuable when you wish to "unfold" an idea, step-by-step, before an audience, or when you suddenly feel the need to depict an idea or process you thought would be clearly understood merely through words. So, supervisors often lay out next month's sales campaign step-by-step on the board, and a football coach occasionally discovers that the breakdown in trap blocking must be sketched out.

You need not be an accomplished artist to employ this means of visually communicating your ideas. A rough approximation of a state map may be helpful in orienting listeners to the location of proposed nuclear plants, or in illustrating the impact of a chemical spray program on adjoining communities (e.g., by indicating prevailing wind direction). Similarly, size differences or time lines can be displayed by quick chalk drawings. The size of a micro-dot might be indicated by comparison to a known object: "If a micro-dot were the size of a small pea, then the small pea would be . . ." Similarly, the relatively short history of human life-forms can be visually depicted by a quick time-line drawn on the blackboard, with rough approximations of when life began, when recorded history began, and the time elapsed since the fall of the Roman Empire.

Graphs • Graphs take several different forms. *Bar* graphs show the relationship of two or more sets of figures. Figures comparing the income of various professionals, for example, are well illustrated with bar graphs. *Line* graphs show relations between two or more variable facts. Economists are fond of showing the disparities between "real" and "actual" income by plotting across time average real and actual incomes of consumers. *Pie* graphs show percentages by a circle divided proportionately; for example, a charitable organization used a pie graph to point out how it spends its contributions (wages/salaries/campaigns/target projects, each being a "wedge" in the pie). And, *pictorial* graphs show relative amounts by size or number of symbols. A nutritionist will, for example, make concrete the amount of meat consumed per capita in various countries with a chart showing a "small" cow for India, a larger one for Sweden, and a still larger beast for the United States.

Your choice of *bar, line, pie,* or *pictorial* graphs will depend on the nature of the subject and the nature of the relationships you wish to convey. A pie graph will not illustrate how much two different groups vary in terms of a single item such as income. A bar graph, although it would work in this instance, would not be as effective as a pie graph in depicting how a finite amount of money is distributed. If you are contemplating graphs to communicate relationships, consider their potential limitations as well as their probable impact on audiences.

Diagrams • To avoid the problems of drawing on chalkboards, many speakers will prepare flipcharts or tagboard diagrams before delivering the speech. A *cutaway* diagram of an object—say, a four-cycle engine—can display the inner workings of an automobile. A *three-dimensional* diagram can illustrate complex relationships otherwise difficult to comprehend; posters available at your local planetarium are often of this variety.

Organizational charts or tables • Business executives and governmental representatives spend much of their time preparing and talking from organizational charts. Nor is the utility of such aids limited to the worlds of business and government. In forming a new club or civic association, or in explaining the operation of a new group to others, organizational charts provide a useful means of discussing duties of various officers, channels of communication, and interrelationships between people within the organization. The visualization of power relationships is a helpful way to unravel the mysteries of large bureaucracies or even small community organizations.

Copied or printed material • You certainly can hand out statistical information, suggestions for later actions, addresses of organizations or persons who should be written to, or stages in an intricate process. Such materials can be studied later, used to jog memories, and employed in follow-up actions. They are especially important when you want your audience to remember the seven danger signs of cancer, to write their congressional representatives, or to vote on a specific resolution or motion.

The Selection and Use of Visual Materials

As a resourceful speaker, you can effectively employ a number of different types of visuals, provided you make careful choices from among them. These choices usually should be based on three factors: (1) *your own personality and purposes*, (2) *the communicative potential of each type of visual material*, and (3) *the nature of the audience and the occasion*.

Start with Yourself

Visual materials may contribute in important ways to your audience's perception of you as a person—your concerns, your values, your feelings, and your ideas. A speech on scrimshawing, with examples of objects that you have carved from whalebones, not only tells an audience that you have certain skills and hobbies, but also indicates your attitudes toward the preservation of folk culture. The bar graphs you utilize in a speech on inflation not only demonstrate support for your proposition, but also represent your attitudes toward concrete, summary data. Visual aids, especially those you prepare in color and detail, communicate both your forethought (you cared enough for your audience to make something for them) and, perhaps, a measure of your ingenuity and flair for the artistic. Because visual supporting materials are presented as a *part* of the total communication process, you reveal much about yourself by what you show an audience. They "express" you and, at the same time, help to express and support your ideas.

Consider the Communicative Potential of Various Visual Materials

Keep in mind, of course, that each type of visual material has certain potentials for communicating particular kinds of information, and that each type interacts with your *spoken* presentation as well as your audience's state of mind. In preparing speech materials of this kind, remember that visuals primarily pictorial or photographic in nature have the potential for making an audience *feel* the way you do. Aids such as slides, movies, sketches, and photographs often may be used effectively to accompany travelogs or reports of personal experiences because they illustrate or reproduce in others the kinds of *feelings* you experienced in another place, situation, or time.

Visuals containing descriptive or verbal materials, on the other hand, can help an audience to *think* the way you do. In contrast to pictorial materials, such aids as cutaways, models, diagrams, charts, and dittoed summaries of statistical data frequently add *rational support* to propositions you are attempting to defend. The nature of your topic and your communicative purpose, therefore, play a large role in determining the kinds of visuals you ought to employ in a given circumstance. A speech informing listeners of your experiences in Indonesia should probably be accompanied by slides or films and even some household artifacts. A speech to persuade your listeners that the United States ought to sever all association with the Southeast Asia Treaty Organization probably should be supported by maps, charts, and chalkboard drawings.

Integrate Verbal and Visual Materials Effectively

As you make your decisions about the visual elements you will use to support and illustrate your speech, *choose only those objects and materials which are relevant to your speech topic and communicative purpose.* In other words, be sure that your visual materials will work *for,* and not *against,* you. Some visuals, if not selected carefully, may distract, frustrate, or actually anger an audience. You can guard against such negative and unintended effects by the following means:

1. *Painstakingly prepare all of your visual aids well in advance of your speech* • Exercise considerable care in conceptualizing them, using familiar shapes (for example, the pie) and contrasting colors (red on white, blue on yellow), and making sure that the image, concept, steps, or other constituent elements—the things you really wish to emphasize—are immediately and strikingly visible.

2. *Keep charts, diagrams, and other graphic aids clear and simple* • Research has demonstrated that plain bar graphs—probably because they offer not only numbers but also a visualization of numbers through the use of "bars"—are the single most effective method for displaying statistical comparisons.[12] To restate a point we emphasized earlier, make sure that the central element or "figure"—the essential information you want your audience to focus upon—stands out clearly from the background of your chart, diagram, or other visual depiction. Let simplicity be your watchword in the preparation of all visual aids. Cut away extraneous information, however interesting, and display your material in a clear simple form—bars, pies, and pictures.

3. *Make your visuals—especially those with materials which must be read or scrutinized closely—large enough to be seen clearly and easily* • Listeners—especially those in the back rows—get frustrated when, in the middle of the speech, they suddenly notice that they are having to lean forward and squint in order to see a detail on a sketch or diagram. Make your

figures and lettering large enough so that, as John Hancock noted in connection with the Declaration of Independence in 1776, they "can be seen by the King of England without his glasses."

4. In preparing to present visually the details of an object, device, or process, decide well in advance whether or not to bring in the object or device itself or a model of it • This is especially pertinent to the so-called "demonstration" speech. For instance, if you have practiced a particular craft or mastered a certain skill and wish to communicate the details or steps in the creative process, you probably will want to show a working sample or product of that process. This can be effective; but when you elect to do it, keep in mind throughout the demonstration speech that the *object* or *process model* is communicating at the same time and very possibly as much as you are. It is telling the audience: "Here's what it is." "Here's why it's worth your while." Take pains to ensure, therefore, that everyone in your audience can clearly see the object or device—perhaps even handle it. This latter possibility gives rise to a fifth precaution.

5. Be prepared to compensate orally for any distraction your visual aid may inadvertently create among your audience • If you do pass around a sample of your work—a leather purse you have made or a silver ring you have handcrafted—remember that an actual object or a detailed model is a complex, potent visual stimulus. This makes it a "message-maker" in its own right; and in a very real sense, you must compete with it for the listeners' attention. Very carefully tell your audience what aspects of it to examine closely, and which ones they may ignore. If, despite your precautions, the actual object or full-scale model is likely to prove unavoidably distracting, build enough reiteration into your speech to make reasonably certain your hearers can follow your train of thought even while they are studying the object and passing it around. As added insurance, you might also provide a schematic diagram or sketch of it on the chalkboard, visually reinforcing the verbal message you are trying to communicate.

6. When using slides, films, overhead projectors, or videotapes, be prepared to make the verbal and physical adjustments necessary to coordinate the visual materials with the spoken materials • With these aids, you often darken the room, thereby compelling your audience to concentrate upon a source of light: the "silver screen" in the case of slides and films, the 19-inch screen in the case of a TV set. At such times, you—the *oral* communicator—must compete with the *machine* or *electronic* communicator. If, as often happens, your audience begins to concentrate harder on the flow of light than on the flow of words, you defeat your own purpose. Therefore, when using projected materials as visual support, either *(a)* talk more loudly and move more vigorously when communicating simultaneously with the machine, or *(b)* refuse to compete with it at all. That is, show the film or the slides either *before* or *after* you comment on their contents. Whatever strategy you use, however, make sure that the projected visual materials are well integrated into the rest of your presentation.

Visual materials serve to aid the speaker in a number of ways—enhancing listener comprehension and memory, and adding persuasive impact to the speaker's message. If skillfully presented and integrated with verbal materials during the speech, visual material can be an effective communication tool.

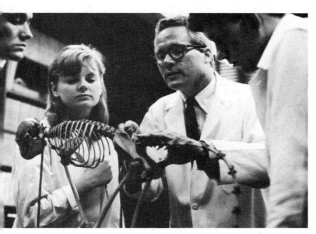

7. Hand to your listeners a copy of those materials you wish them to think back on or carry away from your speech • If, for example, you are making recommendations to a student council, you may provide copies of a proposal for the council's subsequent action. Or, if you are reporting in a speech the results of a survey, the most pertinent statistics will be more easily comprehended (and remembered later) if you give each listener a duplicate copy. Few people can recall the "seven warning signs" for cancer, but they could keep a list of them in a handy place if you presented each member of your audience with a notecard on which such a list appears. Remember that we are referring here only to speech material that is legitimately a *visual aid*. Obviously, you will not put everything you have to say on a ditto. Select only those elements or items bearing upon the information you have introduced in your speech, especially those having future or lasting value.

Although more could be said about choosing and using the various types of visual media to which we have referred, the foregoing suggestions should at least enable you—with some prespeech thought and planning—to take good advantage of their communicative potential. In any event, it should be apparent that by judicious selection, preparation, and handling of diagrams, charts, models, slides, and similar graphic aids, the conscientious speaker can increase listeners' comprehension. In sum, good visual material is not distracting. It "fits," it is essential to the verbal messages, and it leaves an audience with a feeling of completeness.

Consider the Audience and the Occasion

In choosing the types and contents of the visual supporting materials you will use, your common sense will tell you that you must also take into consideration the *status* of the subject in the minds of your audience. Ask yourself: Do I need to bring a map of the United States to an audience of American college students when discussing the westward movement of population in this country? Of, if I'm going to discuss offensive and defensive formations employed by a football team, should I or should I not bring in a "play book" showing such formations? And, can I really expect an audience to understand the administrative structure of the federal bureaucracy without an organizational chart?

How much an audience *already knows, needs to know,* and *expects to find out* about you and your subject are clearly determinants which must weigh heavily when you are faced with a choice as to the types and numbers of visual supports you will use in a speech. How readily that audience can comprehend *aurally* what you have to say is another. Granted, it is not always easy to assess any of these conditions or capabilities. It may be exceedingly difficult, in fact, to decide how much an audience of college freshmen and sophomores knows about college or governmental structures; and, certainly, you cannot judge easily how well acquainted a Rotary Club audience is with football plays. That being the case, probably the next-best thing you can do is to check out your speculations by "asking around" among your probable listeners well ahead of the time you are scheduled to deliver your speech. In other words, before making any final decisions about visual supporting materials, *do as much audience research and analysis as you possibly can.*

As a part of your advance planning for the use of visuals, also take into account the nature of the *occasion* or the uniqueness of the *circumstances* in which you will be speaking. You will find that certain kinds of occasions seemingly cry out for certain types of graphic supporting materials. The corporate executive who presents a projective report to the board of directors without a dittoed or printed handout and without diagrams and pictures probably would be drummed out of the firm. The military adviser who calls for governmental expenditure for new weapons without offering simultaneously pictures or drawings of the proposed weapons and printed technical data on their operations is not likely to be viewed as a convincing advocate. At halftime, an athletic coach without a chalkboard may succeed only in confusing team members—not helping them. In classroom settings, students who .give demonstration speeches without visuals frequently feel inadequate, even helpless—especially when they realize that most of the other speakers are well fortified with such supports. In short, if you are to speak in a situation which demands certain kinds of visual media, plan ahead and adapt your message to take full advantage of them. If the speech occasion does not appear to require visual supports, analyze it further for possibilities anyway. Use your imagination. Be innovative. *Do not overlook opportunities to make your speech more meaningful, more exciting, and more attention-holding in the eyes of your listeners.*

REFERENCE NOTES

[1]Marshall McLuhan, *Understanding Media: The Extensions of Man* (New York: McGraw-Hill Book Company, 1965).

[2]The general theories of Gestalt psychology are reviewed understandably in Ernest R. Hilgard, *Theories of Learning* (New York: Appleton-Century-Crofts, 1956). Their applications in areas of visual communication can be found, among many other places, in Rudolph Arnheim, *Visual Thinking* (Berkeley: University of California Press, 1969); John M. Kennedy, *A Psychology of Picture Perception* (San Francisco: Jossey-Bass, Inc., Publishers, 1974); Sol Worth, "Pictures Can't Say Ain't," *Versus,* 12 (December 1975): 85–108; and Leonard Zusne, *Visual Perception of Form* (New York: Academic Press, Inc., 1976). For a discussion of research on media and learning, see Gavriel Salomon, *Interaction of Media, Cognition, and Learning* (San Fransisco: Jossey-Bass, 1979); E. Heidt, *Instructional Media and the Individual Learner* (New York: Nichols, 1976).

[3]For a more comprehensive examination of the elements of visual communication, see Donis A. Dondis, *A Primer of Visual Literacy* (Boston: MA: The MIT Press, 1974), pp. 39–66.

[4]The principle of perceptual completion is discussed in Hilgard (note 2).

[5]T.R. Donohue, "Viewer Perceptions of Color and Black-and-White Paid Political Advertising," *Journalism Quarterly,* 50 (1973): 660–65.

[6]Dan Nimmo, *Political Communication and Public Opinion in America* (Santa Monica, CA: Goodyear Publishing Co., 1978), p. 171. See Gary Yanker, *Prop Art* (New York: Darien House, 1972), p. 68.

[7]Alan G. Chute, "Effect of Color and Monochrome Versions of a Film on Incidental and Task-Relevant Learning," *Educational Communication and Technology Journal*, 28 (1980), 10–18.

[8]William J. Seiler, "The Effects of Visual Materials on Attitudes, Credibility, and Retention," *Speech Monographs*, 38 (November 1971): 331–34.

[9]Joel R. Levin and Alan M. Lesgold, "On Pictures in Prose," *Educational Communication and Technology Journal*, 26 (1978): 233–44. See Marilyn J. Haring and Maurine A. Fry, "Effect of Pictures on Children's Comprehension of Written Text," *Educational Communication and Technology Journal*, 27 (1979): 185–90.

[10]For more specific conclusions regarding the effects of various sorts of visual materials, see F.M. Dwyer, "Exploratory Studies in the Effectiveness of Visual Illustrations," *AV Communication Review*, 18 (1970): 235–40; G.D. Feliciano, R.D. Powers, and B.E. Kearle, "The Presentation of Statistical Information," *AV Communication Review*, 11 (1963): 32–39; William J. Seiler, "The Effects of Visual Materials on Attitudes, Credibility, and Retention," *Speech Monographs*, 38 (November 1971): 331–34; M.D. Vernon, "Presenting Information in Diagrams," *AV Communication Review*, 1 (1953): 147–58; and L.V. Peterson and Wilbur Schramm, "How Accurately are Different Kinds of Graphs Read?" *AV Communication Review*, 2 (1955): 178–89.

[11]For a clear exploration of the relationships between ideas and visuals, see Edgar B. Wycoff, "Why Visuals?" *AV Communications*, 11 (1977): 39, 59.

[12]See Feliciano et al., Vernon, and Peterson and Schramm (note 10).

 PROBLEMS AND PROBES

1.   Think of several courses you have taken in high school and/or college. How did the instructors use visual aids in presenting the subject matter of these courses? Were such materials effectively used? Was there a relationship between the subject matter of the course and the type of visual aid used? Give special consideration to proper and improper uses of the chalkboard by the instructors. What communicative functions are best served by the chalkboard? least served? Are there special problems with the use of visuals when audience members are taking notes while listening? Prepare a brief written analysis of these questions which includes several illustrations from the classes. How might your instructors have expanded or improved the visual presentation of information?

2.   Visual supporting materials capture appropriate moods, clarify potentially complex subjects, and sometimes even carry the thrust of a persuasive message. Examine magazine advertisements and "how-to-do-it" articles in periodicals; look at store windows and special displays in museums and libraries; and observe slide-projection lectures in some of your other college classes. Then *(a)* using the *types* considered in this chapter, classify the nonverbal supporting materials you have encountered; *(b)* assess the *purposes* these materials serve—clarification, persuasion, attention-focusing, mood-setting, and others you may wish to cite; *(c)* evaluate the *effectiveness* with which each of the materials you have examined is doing its job; and, finally *(d)*, prepare a report, a paper, or an entry in your journal on the results of your experiences and observations.

3.   Prepare an outline for a descriptive or a "how-to" speech (such as "What my paradise island looks like," or "How to use a typewriter") assuming you may use

visual aids. Now rewrite the outline assuming you may *not* use any visual aids. What new pressures are on you as a speaker? How can you handle them? Is it still possible to give an effective speech?

ORAL ACTIVITIES

1.   Present a short oral report in which you describe a speech you will give and the ways in which you plan to incorporate visual materials and coordinate them with the verbal materials. Specify the characteristics you might try to build into each visual aid to maximize clarity. If you can, bring in some rough-draft examples of the visuals for the purpose of illustrating your intentions.

2.   Prepare a short speech explaining or demonstrating a complex process. Use two different types of visual aids. Ask the class to evaluate which of these aids was most effective. Try this same speech without the use of any visual materials. What new pressures do you feel as a speaker? How can you deal with them? Can you still give an effective presentation?

3.   Repeat exercise #2 with a classmate. Working together, develop two different visual aids to enhance your joint presentation. Plan a performance in which the two of you share the delivery responsibilities. When one speaker talks, the other may be in charge of displaying visual aids. How effective are these duet performances? How does having a thoroughly initiated partner increase the speaking options?

SUGGESTIONS FOR FURTHER READING

Rudolph Arnheim, *Visual Thinking* (Berkeley: University of California Press, 1969).

Carolyn M. Bloomer, *Principles of Visual Perception* (New York: Van Nostrand Reinhold Co., 1976).

Donis A. Dondis, *A Primer of Visual Literacy* (Cambridge, MA: The MIT Press, 1973).

Vernon S. Gerlach and Donald P. Ely, *Teaching and Media: A Systematic Approach,* 2nd ed. (Englewood Cliffs, NJ: Prentice-Hall, Inc., 1980), esp. Chapters 11, 12, 13, 14.

W. Howard Levie, "A Prospectus for Instructional Research on Visual Literacy," *Educational Communication and Technology Journal,* 26 (1978): 25–36.

James Mangan, "Cultural Conventions of Pictorial Representation: Iconic Literacy and Education," *Educational Communication and Technology Journal,* 26 (1978): 245–68.

Les Satterthwaite, *Graphics: Skills, Media and Materials,* 4th ed. (Dubuque; IA: Kendall/Hunt, 1980).

Sol Worth, "Pictures Can't Say Ain't," *Versus,* 12 (1975): 85–108.

Leonard Zusne, *Visual Perception of Form* (New York: Academic Press, Inc., 1976).

PART FOUR

PUBLIC SPEAKING

Types
and Occasions

16

Speeches to Inform

Ours is a society which almost worships "the facts." Particularly because of such technological developments as electronic media, photostatic printing, computerized data storage and retrieval systems, and miniaturized circuits, most of us have available a staggering amount of information. Mere information, however, makes no decisions by itself; information is all but useless until it is shaped and interpreted by human beings, who then can employ it for the betterment of themselves and their society. As a speaker, you often will be called upon to assemble, package, and present information to others.

In this chapter we will discuss various types of informative speeches, outlining their essential features and reviewing some of their structural characteristics.

Types of Informative Speeches

Fundamentally, as we have noted previously, the main purpose of a speech to inform is to secure understanding among listeners. Creating understanding is not a matter of parading knowledge or discoursing before an audience on endless facts and figures. People, after all, seek information and understanding from speakers only in the face of perceived needs. Like all other oral transactions, informative speeches depend on the speaker's sensitivity to listeners' purposes, knowledge, and attitudes.

Because these needs, purposes, level of knowledge, and attitudes vary from situation to situation, informative speeches take many different forms. Some forms are no more complicated than the set of oral instructions you receive as you are about to begin a midterm examination, while others—such as those used in scientific reports offered at academic conventions—can be understood only by specialists in a field of endeavor. But, although the range of these forms is great, four types of informative speeches—*speeches of definition, demonstrations and instructions, oral reports,* and *explanations*—occur so frequently that they merit special attention.[1]

Speeches of Definition

Speeches of definition offer an audience a vocabulary for dealing with concepts it already knows, or present a vocabulary that identifies some aspect of the world about which the listeners know little. A definitional speech, therefore, tells people how to reexamine something familiar or how to think about something unfamiliar.

Almost everyone gives and listens to these sorts of speeches with great regularity. When you start college, someone tells you what an Associate of Arts degree or a core requirement is. When you take your first astronomy course, you are introduced to black holes in the universe. When you buy your first house, the realtor undoubtedly explains what earnest money is. These are definitional messages that give you words for dealing with concepts unfamiliar to you.

Or, in a junior high school science class, a teacher discusses weather changes by referring to the jet stream, high and low pressure domes, and humidity. A television talk show guest urges that you think of children, not as private possessions, but as pre-adults having the same basic human rights and responsibilities as older people. Politicians insist that we stop piecemeal attacks on the social services system in this country and find more fundamental ways to break the welfare syndrome. These are definitional messages delivered by speakers trying to get you to look at familiar objects, people, and processes in a new light.

Notice that most of these examples of speeches have two characteristics: (1) You are offered a *vocabulary*—"core requirements," "black holes," "earnest money"—for dealing with the objects, people, and processes under consideration, and (2) you are given an *orientation,* a way of thinking about some phenomenon. The idea of "core requirements," for example, forces you to think about intellectual breadth—the so-called "liberal arts"—as a goal for your college education; you may well have thought, previously, only about higher education as preparatory for a career. The notion of "the welfare syndrome" forces you to look beyond food stamps, unemployment compensation, and Social Security checks, in order to visualize what is essentially a separate subculture in this country—one with its own ways of thinking and acting. A good definitional speech, therefore, provides listeners with symbols to which they can attach ideas, and with conceptualizations that organize bits and pieces of information into coherent wholes.

Demonstrations and Instructions

These are the kinds of informative speeches with which you have been familiar since childhood. In a complex culture, classroom instructions, job instructions, and instructions for the performance of special tasks play a vital role. Teachers instruct students in ways of preparing assignments. Supervisors tell their subordinates how a task should be performed. Leaders explain to volunteer workers their duties in a fund-raising drive or a cleanup campaign. For convenience, such instructions usually are given to a group of persons rather than to individuals, and, even when written, often are accompanied by oral explanations that amplify and clarify the written material. The feedback mechanisms provided in public speaking are especially important and valuable when instructions are to be offered.

Frequently, though, we have to do more than "tell." We also have to "show" people how to carry out the desired actions. A demonstration speech is one in which a speaker describes to an audience the steps involved and the physical and mental skills required to carry out a certain task. A supervisor may need to walk through new office procedures even while telling employees about them. An instructor in an art class usually gives careful, step-by-step instructions in how to prepare a canvas while actually doing it.

Both speeches of demonstration and of instruction have two essential features: (1) Both involve the *serial presentation* of information, usually in clearly defined steps or phases. They normally are organized, therefore, in chronological and/or spatial patterns. (2) Both demand *utter clarity*, simply because your listeners are expected to be able to repeat or reproduce the steps through which you have instructed them.

Oral Reports

Academic reports, committee reports, and executive reports are typical of this kind of informative speech. Scientists and scholars announce their research findings at professional conventions or in radio and television interviews. Committees in business, industry, and government carry out special informational or advisory tasks, and then present oral reports to their parent organizations or work groups. Boards of directors report annually to stockholders on the past year's activities and accomplishments. The oral report is a staple kind of speech in a society such as ours which is organized into so many groups and subgroups, each with special concerns, tasks, and responsibilities.

An important aspect of the concept of "reporter" is the notion of *duty* or *charge*. Except for freelance journalistic reporters, most reporters operate within prescribed limits—limits set by the body of persons who hired, delegated authority to, or sanctioned the reporter in the first place. Each morning, a news correspondent is given events to cover by an editor or producer. The person preparing a monthly report on sales in Nevada has a very specific charge for the staff meeting. The club that sends a member to scout out the best restaurant for the spring banquet expects that person to make recommendations based on specific criteria (cost, aesthetic qualities, accessibility). Even the scientist reporting on a research project knows that the findings will be judged adequate or inadequate by the code of ethics and the scientific methods accepted by the scholarly community.

Oral reports, therefore, are speeches that assemble, arrange, and interpret information in response to an actual or perceived charge or expectation. They are born, essentially, of the need to delegate tasks when there is too much informational ground to be covered in too short a time, and when too many people need to share the information to demand practically that they all go out and get it.

Because oral reports are so important, we will deal with them in some detail in Chapter 20.

Explanations

An explanatory speech is one in which the speaker either (1) makes clear the nature of a concept, process, thing, or proposal, or (2) offers a supporting rationale for a contestable proposition or claim. The notion of "making clear" means that speeches of explanation have much in common with definitional messages, because one function of a definition is to clarify. Normally, though, an explanatory speech is less concerned with the word or vocabulary than it is with connecting one concept with a series of others. For example, a definitional speech on " political corruption" would concentrate on the term, telling us what sorts of acts committed by politicians are comprehended by the term. An explanatory speech on corruption, however, would go into more depth, indicating perhaps the social-political conditions likely to produce corruption or the methods that

This guide on a street tour is explaining some concepts of Victorian architecture. An important purpose in any informative speech is to help the audience grasp and remember important data about the subject.

are available for eliminating it. The "making clear" involved in an explanatory speech, therefore, is considerably broader and more complex than that demanded of a definitional speech.

The key, though, to most explanatory speeches lies in the second notion—"offering a rationale." Most explanations do their explaining from a particular point of view. Suppose, for example, you wanted to tell an audience how the American Revolution came to be. You could offer, potentially, a great number of explanations, depending on your point of view. One explanation might be economic, stressing the idea that the Revolution was the result of disagreements between Americans and Britons over trade and taxation policies. Another might be political, noting that the Americans felt a strong need for self-government. A third might be social or cultural, for surely the Revolution could not occur until the colonists had a strong sense of their own social identity as separate from the Mother Country. Similarly, you could offer several different explanations of how contagious diseases spread: You could talk about the biochemical processes of contagion, the physiological processes of debilitation, the environmental means by which diseases spread, or even the sociological relationships between subgroups of people which allow viruses to spread through some parts of a population but not others.

The point is, each of these explanations of the American Revolution and the spread of communicable diseases is "correct": each explains satisfactorily how war and pestilence spread through a country. There are probably as many different explanations of phenomena as there are vantage points. So, by now you have probably heard economic, sociological, and political explanations of urban decay; moral, educational, and sociological ramifications of the country's high divorce rate; and every explanation possible of the effects of excessive TV viewing.

Explanations, therefore, represent some of the most sophisticated and complicated kinds of informative speeches you will ever give. They are called for whenever an audience is in *confusion* or *ignorance*. An explanation is called for any time concepts are fuzzy, information is only partial, effects cannot easily be attributed to their causes, or competing claims are at loggerheads. Explanatory speeches arise whenever people ask the questions "What?", "How?", or "Why?" when trying to understand ideas and physical processes.[2]

Essential Features of Informative Speeches

Four qualities should characterize any speech to inform: (1) *clarity*, (2) *the association of new ideas with familiar ones*, (3) *coherence*, and (4) *the motivation of the audience*.

Clarity

This quality is largely the result of effective organization and the careful selection of words. Informative speeches achieve maximum clarity when your listeners can follow you and understand what you are saying.

Regarding your speech organization, observe the following rules: (*a*) Do not have too many points. Confine your speech to three or four principal ideas, grouping whatever facts or ideas you wish considered under these headings. Even if you know a tremendous amount about your subject matter, remember that you cannot make everyone an expert in a single speech. (*b*) Clarify the relationship between your main points by observing the principles of coordination.

Word your transitions carefully—"Second, you must prepare the chair for caning by cleaning out the groove and cane holes," "The Stamp Act Crisis was followed by an even more important event—The Townshend Duties," "To test these hypotheses, we set up the following experiment." Such transitions allow auditors to follow you from point to point. (*c*) Keep your speech moving forward according to a well-developed plan; do not jump back and forth between ideas, charging ahead and then backtracking. That creates more smoke than light.

Regarding your selection of words, follow the advice we offered in Chapter 12: (*a*) Use a precise, accurate vocabulary when you can do so without getting too technical. In telling someone how to finish off a basement room, you might say, "Next, take one of these long sticks and cut it off in this funny-looking gizmo with a saw in it, and try to make the corners match." An accurate vocabulary helps your listeners remember what supplies and tools to get when they approach the same project: "This is a ceiling molding; it goes around the room between the wall and the ceiling to cover the seams between the paneling and the ceiling tiles. You make the corners of the molding match by using a mitre box, which has grooves that allow you to cut 45 degree angles. Here's how you do it." (*b*) Simplify when possible, including only as much technical vocabulary as you need. Try not to make a speech on the operation of a two-cycle internal combustion engine sound as if it came out of a lawnmower mechanic's operational manual. An audience bogged down in unnecessary detail and vocabulary can become confused and bored. (*c*) Use reiteration when it clarifies complex ideas, but don't simply repeat the same words. Seek rephrasings that will help solidify ideas for those who had trouble getting them the first time, thusly: "Unlike a terrestrial telescope, a celestial telescope is used for looking at moons, planets, and stars; that is, its mirrors and its lens are ground and arranged in such a way that it focuses on objects thousands of miles, not hundreds of feet, away from the observer."

Association of New Ideas with Familiar Ones

Audiences grasp new facts and ideas more readily when they can associate them with what they already know; therefore, in a speech to inform, try to connect the new with the old. To connect the new with the old, of course, you need to have done enough solid audience analysis so that you know what experiences, images, analogies, and metaphors to call upon in your speech.

Sometimes, the associations you ought to make are obvious. A college dean talking to an audience of manufacturers on the problems of higher education presented his ideas under the headings of raw material, casting, machining, polishing, and assembling. He thus translated his central ideas into an analogy his audience, given their vocations, would be sure to understand and appreciate. At other times, if you cannot think of any obvious associations, you may have to rely upon commonplace experiences or images we all have had or can call up. For instance, the figure on page 293 shows how you might explain the operation of the human eye pupil by comparing it to the operation of a camera lens aperture. One can refer to everyday familial experiences, buildings, or topological features of the immediate vicinity, or metaphors of the type we discussed in Chapter 12.

Sometimes you may simply not be able to think of everyday assocations. In that case, you probably will have to rely upon *definitions*. Several different methods of definition may prove helpful:

Dictionary Definition. Put the term or concept to be defined into a general class or category and then carefully distinguish it from the other members of this class. ("An apple is a *fruit* that is *red* and *round* and *hard* and *juicy*." "Man is a *rational* animal.")

Etymology. Clarify meaning by telling the history of a word—tracing the source from which it derived. ("*Propel* comes from the Latin prefix *pro* meaning *forward* and the verb *pellere* meaning to *drive*. Therefore, a *propeller* is an instrument which drives something forward.")

Negation. Clarify the meaning of a term or concept by telling what *it is not*. ("By *socialism* I do not mean *communism*, which believes in the common ownership of all property. Instead, I mean . . .")

Example. Clarify by mentioning an actual example or instance of what you have in mind. ("You all have seen the Methodist church on Maple Street. That is what I mean by English Gothic architecture.")

Use in a Context. Clarify the meaning of a term or concept by actually using it in a sentence. "*Keyed* is a slang term for *excited* or *roused*. For instance, if I say, 'He was all *keyed up*,' I mean that he was excited indeed.")

Coherence

Coherence, as we have said, is in part a matter of organization—of finding a pattern which fits your subtopics together in a meaningful manner. Sometimes, it is relatively easy to create a sense of coherence, as for example when giving a speech on the executive, legislative, and judicial branches of government, for there are only these three branches. At other times, especially when you are not doing a complete enumeration of some subject, you have to manufacture coherence. When Benjamin Franklin designed a flag for the colonies, he tried to relate the thirteen units to each other by drawing a snake segmented into thirteen pieces, thus indicating that they were related to each other yet independent as well.

Occasionally, you may have to do a little forcing. Suppose you decided to give a speech on the Nielsen television program rating system. You might decide to talk about only three aspects of the system—what it is, how it works, and how it is used by network executives to determine what programs to continue and which shows to drop. To give this speech coherence, you could use a question-answer organizational pattern and move into the body of your speech in this

ASSOCIATION OF NEW IDEAS WITH FAMILIAR ONES

Human Eye / **pupil**   Camera Lens / **aperture**

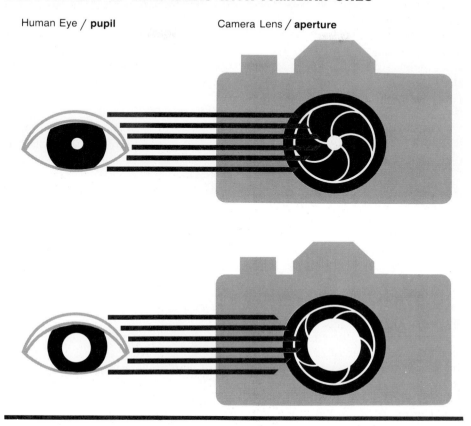

fashion: "People who worry about the effect of the Nielsen ratings on what they watch usually ask three questions: 'What *is* a Nielsen rating, anyhow?' 'How is the rating done?' 'Why do the networks rely on it for making decisions on shows?' To answer these common questions, and to explain the 'what,' 'how,' and 'why' of television ratings, today I first will . . .'" Notice that this speaker has taken a common trio of words—what/how/why—and used them as an organizing principle, to give a sense of coherence to this explanatory speech.

Motivation of the Audience

Finally, and perhaps most importantly, you must be able to motivate the audience to listen. This is an essential feature of good informative speeches that many people ignore. Many of us blithely assume that because *we* are interested in something, *they* also will want to hear about it. To you, stamp-collecting may be an

One of the essential qualities of an informative speech is to first capture and hold the listeners' interest and then to motivate them by pointing out why they need to know what the speaker is about to tell them. The information is supplied in the context of the speech.

interesting, relaxing, and profitable hobby, but until your listeners are likewise convinced that it is, they will yawn through your speech on American commemoratives.

Keep in mind, therefore, what we have said about attention (Chapter 8) and motivation (Chapter 6) even when preparing informative speeches: (*a*) Use the factors of attention to engage the members of your audience, to draw them into your speech. (*b*) Once you have captured them initially, be sure to build in motivational appeals, reasons why they should want to know what you are about to tell them. If you indicate that your talk will increase their interpersonal effectiveness, provide them with additional income, reduce their confusion about important matters, and the like, you will be going a long way toward making your speech relevant and compelling.

Remember, too, that the Motivated Sequence can be used often when building an informative speech. The Attention Step should pique their curiosity, the Need Step can effectively engage their motive drives, and then the Satisfaction Step can provide them with the information which alleviates those drives. (Review Chapter 8, "The Motivated Sequence and Speeches to Inform," pp. 161–163.)

Structuring Informative Speeches

Now that we have described the various types of informative speeches and treated their essential features, it is time to examine ways in which you can structure each of those types. Of course, potentially any of the organizational patterns we have described earlier can be used, but, traditionally, some of these patterns are better suited to particular types than others.

Speeches of Definition

Introduction • Because definitional speeches treat either unfamiliar concepts or familiar concepts in a new light, their introductions must create a sense of *curiosity* and *need* in listeners. Curiosity is a special problem in speeches on unfamiliar concepts, for we are all tempted to say, "Well, if I've made it this far through life without knowing anything about black holes or carcinogens or trap blocking, why should I bother with learning more about these ideas now?" The answer to that question, to a large extent, depends upon your ability to make people wonder about the unknown. You may well want to concentrate part of your introduction to a definitional speech, therefore, on making listeners desire to know more about unknown aspects of their everyday environment or even far-away segments of life.

Speeches on both unfamiliar and familiar concepts, however, must be attentive to the needs or wants of the listeners. This means that their introductions should include motivational materials—explicit statements which indicate how the information at least potentially can affect the audience members. In definitional speeches, thus, one often hears statements such as the following: "Understanding the dynamics of trap blocking will allow you to better appreciate line play in football, and therefore increase your enjoyment of the game every Saturday afternoon in our stadium." "Most students fill out the 'short form' of their U.S. income tax return each April without giving it much thought. If you understand some of the deductions and educational expenses you as a student are allowed to write off, however, and if you take the few extra minutes you'll need to use the 'long form,' you may discover you can save a significant amount of money each year."

Body • Most definitional speeches you will hear use a topical or one of the task-related patterns we discussed earlier in the book. This is because such speeches usually are describing various aspects or facets of some thing or idea. It often just seems natural, for example, to use a topical pattern when giving a speech on a career in computer programming and to organize the body of the speech around such topics as "the duties of a computer programmer," "skills needed by a computer programmer," and "training you will need to acquire to become a computer programmer."

There are occasions, too, when other patterns may serve your specific purpose well. You might use an effect-cause pattern, for example, when preparing an informative speech on "the laws of supply and demand." You could enumerate a series of effects with which people are already familiar—soaring prices coupled with seemingly fantastic sales, interest rates which apparently change every other week—and then discuss the laws of supply and demand which contain the causes for such confusing fiscal patterns in society.

Conclusion • Conclusions for definitional speeches frequently have two characteristics: (1) They usually include a summary, especially if a good many facts, figures, and ideas have been covered, and (2) they often stress the kinds of applications people can make of the ideas they have been given. So, for example, a speech on Transcendental Meditation could conclude with a review of the main features of TM and with a list of some of the situations in which a person might want to meditate. As with all good conclusions, the ending of even a definitional speech should not come abruptly, as a dictionary definition does; rather, be sure that you round it off for your listeners, tying it up in a useful way.

Demonstrations and Instructions

Introduction • In most situations where you will be called on to give instructions or offer a demonstration, you will need to spend little time piquing curiosity or motivating people to listen. After all, if you are instructing your listeners in a new office procedure or giving a workshop on how to build an ice boat, you already have the prerequisite interest and motivation—otherwise, they would not have come. If your listeners' attendance is not voluntary (as can be the case in speech communication classrooms!), then of course you will have to pay

One type of speech to inform is the speech that demonstrates how to carry out a certain process or procedure. In this case the speaker is demonstrating the steps in preparing a recipe. The recipe itself has already been copied and handed out to the audience.

attention to motivational matters, but normally you must concentrate your introduction on two other tasks: (1) *Preview* your speech. If, say, you are going to take the members of your audience through the seven steps involved in making a good tombstone rubbing, give them an overall picture of the process before you start describing each operation in detail. (2) *Encourage* them to follow along, even through some of the more difficult steps. A process like tombstone rubbing, for example, looks easier than it is; many are tempted to quit listening and trying along the way. If, however, they are forewarned and are promised special help with the difficult techniques, they are more likely to bear with you.

Body • As we suggested earlier, you will find that most speeches of demonstration and instruction are packaged in a chronological and/or spatial pattern, simply because you are teaching people a serial process you want them to be able to carry out on their own. A non-sequential organizational pattern would be very confusing. Even when the truncated motivated sequence is used, in this type of speech, one normally arranges the material for the Satisfaction Step with the aid of a sequential pattern.

In other words, speakers usually have little trouble organizing the body of this type of speech. Their problems are more likely to be technical ones: *(a) The problem of rate.* If the glue on some project needs to set before you can go on to the next step, what do you do? You cannot just stand there and wait for it to dry. You need to have preplanned some material for filling the time—perhaps additional background, perhaps a brief discussion of what problems one can run into at this stage. Preplan your remarks carefully for those junctures; otherwise, you are likely to lose your audience. *(b) The problem of scale.* How can you show various embroidery stitches to an audience of twenty-five? When dealing with minute operations, you often must increase the scale of operation. In this example, you might use a large piece of poster board or even a 3' by 4' piece of cloth stretched over a wood frame. By using an oversized needle and yarn instead of thread, and stitches measured in inches instead of millimeters, you could more easily make your techniques visible to all audience members. At the other extreme, as in the case of a speech on how to make a homemade solar heat collector, you probably would be well-advised to work with a scaled-down model. *(c) The coordination of verbal and visual materials.* Both instructions and demonstrations usually demand that speakers "show" while "telling." To keep yourself from becoming flustered or confused, be sure to practice talking while doing—offering demonstrations while explaining to others what you are doing. Decide where you are going to stand when showing a slide so that the audience can see both you and the image; practice talking about your aerobic exercise positions while you are actually doing them; work a dough press in practice sessions as you tell your mythical audience how to form professional-looking cookies. If you do not, you will inevitably get yourself into trouble before your real audience.

Conclusion • Conclusions for informative speeches usually are composed of three parts: (1) First, *summaries* are offered. Most audiences need this review, which reminds them to ask questions about procedures or ideas they do not understand fully. (2) Second, some *bolstering* has to take place. People trying their hands at new processes or procedures usually get into trouble the first few times, and need to be reassured that this is natural and can be overcome. (3) Finally, *future help* should be offered. What sounded so simple in your talk can be much more complicated in execution. So, if possible, make yourself available for later assistance: "As you fill out your registration form, just raise your hand if you're unsure of anything and I'll be happy to help you." Or, point to other sources of further information and assistance: "Here's the address of the U.S. Government Printing Office, whose pamphlet X1234 is available for only a dollar; it will give you more details"; "If you run into a filing problem I haven't covered in this short orientation to your job, just go over to Mary McFerson's desk, right over here. Mary's experienced in these matters and is always willing to help." These sorts of statements not only offer help, but assure your audience members that they won't be labeled as dull-witted if they actually have to ask for it.

Explanations

Introduction • Introductions to explanatory speeches may well have to rely on many of the techniques we have described thus far. You may have to raise curiosity in some instances (e.g., how many of your classmates wonder about the causes of the American Revolution at ten o'clock in the morning?). You might also have to generate a need or desire to listen, again, especially if your topic seems distant or irrelevant. And, too, if the explanation is going to be somewhat complex, a forecast of coming ideas is almost mandatory. Finally, you may well need to encourage your listeners to follow along, telling them you will go into greater detail especially in the sections of greatest difficulty.

Body • Most explanations fit well into causal and topical organizational patterns. If you are trying to explain how or why something operates the way it does, either cause-effect or effect-cause orders work very well. Or, if you are trying to explain how some problem can be or should be solved, you might find it advantageous to use a straightforward problem-solution format, especially if your listeners are unsure what the solution might be. These organizational patterns are well suited to explanatory speeches because, as we noted earlier, explanations seek to interrelate phenomena and/or ideas.

Conclusion • Typically, conclusions of good explanations develop additional implications or call for particular actions. If, for example, you have explained how contagious diseases spread through a geographical area, you probably will want to conclude that speech by discussing a series of actions which could be taken to halt the process of contagion. Or, in explaining what courts are starting to mean by the idea of "children's rights," you might close by asking your listeners to consider what the idea should mean to them—how they should change their thinking and their behaviors toward six-year-olds. As was the case with definitional speeches, do not simply sit down when you have completed the explanation; reinforce its importance to your listeners by treating its implications. In that way, it will gain considerably more meaning for them and will more likely be remembered.

A Sample Speech to Inform

The following text is Joyce Chapman's speech, "The Geisha," one she delivered when she was a freshman at Loop College, Chicago. It illustrates well most virtues of a good informative speech: (1) It provides enough detail and explanations to be clear. (2) It works from familiar images of geishas, adding new ideas and information in such a way as to enlarge audience members' conceptions. (3) Its organizational pattern—a topical pattern—makes it both easy to follow and coherent. (4) And, it includes the sorts of motivational appeals to make an audience want to listen.

● The Geisha³

Joyce Chapman

Introduction
Personal reference

As you may have already noticed from my facial features, I have Oriental blood in me and, as such, I am greatly interested in my Japanese heritage. One aspect of my heritage that fascinates me the most is the beautiful and adoring Geisha.   /1

I recently asked some of my friends what they thought a Geisha was, and the comments I received were quite astonishing. For example, one friend said, "She is a woman who walks around in a hut." A second friend was certain that a Geisha was, "A woman who massages men for money and it involves her in other physical activities." Finally, I received this response, "She gives baths to men and walks on their backs." Well, needless to say, I was rather surprised and offended by their comments. I soon discovered that the majority of my friends perceived the Geisha with similar attitudes. One of them argued, "It's not my fault, because that is the way I've seen them on TV." In many ways my friend was correct. His misconception of the Geisha was not his fault, for she is often portrayed by American film producers and directors as: a prostitute, as in the movie, *The Barbarian and the Geisha*, a streetwalker, as seen in the TV series, "Kung Fu," or as a showgirl with a gimmick, as performed in the play, *Flower Drum Song.* /2

Central idea

A Geisha is neither a prostitute, streetwalker, or showgirl with a gimmick. She is a lovely Japanese woman who is a professional entertainer and hostess. She is cultivated with exquisite manners, truly a bird of a very different plumage. /3

Orientation

I would like to provide you with some insight to the Geisha, and, in the process perhaps, correct any misconception you may have. I will do this by discussing her history, training, and development. /4

Body
First point: history

The Geisha has been in existence since 600 A.D., during the archaic time of the Yakamoto period. At that time the Japanese ruling class was very powerful and economically rich. The impoverished majority, however, had to struggle to survive. Starving fathers and their families had to sell their young daughters to the teahouses in order to get a few yen. The families hoped that the girls would have a better life in the teahouse than they would have had in their own miserable homes. /5

During ancient times only high society could utilize the Geisha's talents because she was regarded as a status symbol, exclusively for the elite. As the Geisha became more popular, the common people developed their own imitations. These imitations were often crude and base, lacking sophistication and taste. When American GIs came home from World War II, they related descriptive accounts of their wild escapades with the Japanese Geisha. In essence, the GIs were only soliciting with common prostitutes. These bizarre stories helped create the wrong image of the Geisha. /6

Second point: training

Today, it is extremely difficult to become a Geisha. A Japanese woman couldn't wake up one morning and decide, "I think I'll become a Geisha today." It's not that simple. It takes sixteen years to qualify. /7

At the age of six a young girl would enter the Geisha training school and become a Jo-chu, which means housekeeper. The Jo-chu does not have any specific type of clothing, hairstyle, or make-up. Her duties basically consist of keeping the teahouse immaculately clean (for cleanliness is like a religion to the Japanese). She would also be responsible for making certain that the more advanced women would have everything available at their fingertips. It is not until the girl is sixteen and enters the Maiko stage that she concentrates less on domestic duties and channels more of her energies on creative and artistic endeavors. /8

The Maiko girl, for example, is taught the classical Japanese dance, Kabuki. At first, the dance consists of tiny, timid steps to the left, to the right, backward and forward. As the years progress, she is taught the more difficult steps requiring syncopated movements to a fan. /9

The Maiko is also introduced to the highly regarded art of floral arrangement. The Japanese take full advantage of the simplicity and gracefulness that can be achieved with a few flowers in a vase, or with a single flowering twig. There are three main styles: Seika, Moribana, and Nagerie. It takes at least three years to master this beautiful art. /10

During the same three years, the Maiko is taught the ceremonious art of serving tea. The roots of these rituals go back to the thirteenth century, when Zen Buddhist monks in China drank tea during their devotions. These rituals were raised to a fine art by the Japanese tea masters, who set the standards for patterns of behavior throughout Japanese society. The tea ceremony is so intricate that it often takes four hours to perform and requires the use of over seventeen different utensils. The tea ceremony is far more than the social occasion it appears to be. To the Japanese, it serves as an island of serenity where one can refresh the senses and nourish the soul. /11

One of the most important arts taught to the Geisha is that of conversation. She must master an elegant circuitous vocabulary flavored in Karyuki, the world of flowers and willows, of which she will be a part. Consequently, she must be capable of stimulating her client's mind as well as his esthetic pleasures. /12

Third point:
development

Having completed her sixteen years of thorough training, at the age of twenty-two, she becomes a full-fledged Geisha. She can now serve her clients with duty, loyalty, and most important, a sense of dignity. /13

The Geisha would be dressed in the ceremonial kimono, made of brocade and silk thread. It would be fastened with an obi, which is a sash around the waist and hung down the back. The length of the obi would indicate the girl's degree of development. For instance, in the Maiko stage the obi is longer and is shortened when she becomes a Geisha. Unlike the Maiko, who wears a gay, bright, and cheerful kimono, the Geisha is dressed in more subdued colors. Her make-up is the traditional white base, which gives her the look of white porcelain. The hair is shortened and adorned with beautiful, delicate ornaments. /14

As a full-fledged Geisha, she would probably acquire a rich patron who would assume her sizable debt to the Okiya, or training residence. This patron would help pay for her wardrobe, for each kimona can cost up to $12,000. The patron would generally provide her with financial security. /15

The Geisha serves as a combination entertainer and companion. She may dance, sing, recite poetry, play musical instruments, or draw pictures for her guest. She might converse with them or listen sympathetically to their troubles. Amorous advances, however, are against the rules. /16

Conclusion

So, as you can see the Geisha is a far cry from the back-rubbing, streetwalking, slick entertainer that was described by my friends. She is a beautiful, cultivated, sensitive, and refined woman. /17

REFERENCE NOTES

[1]Should you wish for a good deal more detail on each of these types of informative speeches, read Bruce E. Gronbeck, *The Articulate Person; A Guide to Everyday Public Speaking* (Glenview, IL: Scott, Foresman and Company, 1979), Chapter 4, "Defining," Chapter 5, "Demonstrating," Chapter 6, "Reporting," and Chapter 7, "Explaining."

[2]For a difficult but highly interesting discussion of the what/how/why aspects of explanation, see W. V. Quine and J. S. Ullian, *The Web of Belief* (New York: Random House, Inc., 1970), Chapter 7, "Explanation."

[3]"The Geisha" by Joyce Chapman, *Communication Strategy: A Guide to Speech Preparation* by Roselyn L. Schiff et al. Copyright © 1981 by Scott, Foresman and Company.

PROBLEMS AND PROBES

CHAPTER REPORT   Presumably, attention-gaining and attention-holding devices work best when they are adapted carefully to both the subject matter and the audience's predispositions. To investigate this truism, do one of the following projects:

a. Examine ads for one product across several different kinds of magazines. E.g., compare ads for Volkswagen products in *Cosmopolitan* ("modern" women), *Car and Driver* (a "buff" magazine), *Newsweek* (a general circulation type audience), and *Fortune* (with an upper-income business readership); or, pick any other product likely to be advertised across a variety of magazines.

b. Scan two or three issues of *Vital Speeches of the Day,* noting the speakers, the subject matter, the audience present, and the occasion.

In either project, first identify by type the attention-getting strategies; next, think about the suitability of that strategy type to the subject matter and the main portion of the audience; and finally, write an essay on the topic, "The Relationship Between Attention Strategies and Audience Predispositions," using your case study as a source of examples.

1.   Attend an informative speech such as an expository sermon, oral report, guest lecture, or informative television or radio address. Write a short paper analyzing the content of the speech. Consider the following questions as you write: Did the speaker keep the leading ideas few in number? Were the terms used by the speaker concrete and unambiguous? Was the organization of the speech appropriate and effective?

2.   In a concise written report, indicate and defend the type of arrangement (chronological sequence, spatial sequence, etc.) you think would be most suitable for an informative speech on at least five of the subjects listed below. (See the types of speech structure discussed in Chapter 9.)

   The campus parking situation
   Recent developments in the women's rights movement
   Indian jewelry of the Southwest
   Saving our environment
   How the stock market works
   Censorship of the arts
   Wonder drugs of the 1980s
   The fraternity tradition
   Space stations: Living in a weightless world
   What life will be like in 2000

3.   Select a principle of physics, chemistry, biology, or a similar science and describe how you might explain this principle to: *(a)* a farmer, *(b)* an automobile mechanic, *(c)* a twelve-year-old newsboy, *(d)* a blind person, *(e)* a well-educated adult who is just learning to speak English. See how inventive you can be in making the principle clear without resorting to highly technical language.

4.   Listed below are possible subjects for a speech. Select three of these subjects for a speech to inform (general purpose), and list what you think would be appropriate specific purposes. Using the same subjects for a speech to persuade (gen-

eral purpose), list what you think would be appropriate specific purposes. What are the differences between the specific purposes for the two types of speeches? Are there any similarities?

The Electoral College

Coeducational housing on campus

Health food

Use and abuse of drugs

American cities

The political process in America

For each of the subjects you selected above, write an appropriate central idea and proposition statement. How do your central idea statements differ from your propositions? Compare your specific purposes and central ideas and propositions with those of members of a small task group. Do the central ideas seem strictly informative, or could there be some kind of ultimately persuasive goal hidden in the central ideas?

 ORAL ACTIVITIES

1. Select five terms or concepts that are likely to be strange to your classmates and, using one or more of the methods of definition described on page 292, orally make their meaning or significance clear to a classroom audience. Be prepared to explain why in each case you used the method or methods you did.

2. Plan a two- to four-minute speech in which you will give instructions. For instance, you might explain how to calculate your life-insurance needs, how to "door knock" for a political candidate, or how to make a charter or group flight reservation. This exercise is basically descriptive in nature, so limit yourself to use of a single visual aid.

3. Prepare a speech to inform for delivery in class. Using one of the topics suggested below or a similar one drawn from your personal speech journal and approved by your instructor, select and narrow the area of the subject to be covered, develop whatever visual aids may be appropriate, and settle on the order or pattern you will be following in setting forth the information. Take special pains to make clear why the audience needs to know the material you are presenting. Suggested topics:

Contemporary American writers (artists, musicians)

The physical effects of marijuana

How to become a better listener

The agencies of the United Nations

A first lesson in aircraft-recognition

Changing perspectives in American foreign policy

How to read lips

The romance of archaeology

Exercising to lose weight

How television programs are rated

4. Since history courses have a way of getting rushed at the ends of terms, you may not have spent much time studying events since World War II. To get a better idea of the historical factors that have influenced your parents' and your own lives, prepare a six- to eight-minute report on an important historical event since World War II.

5. Describe a unique place you have visited on a vacation, for example, a church in a foreign city, or an historical site. Deliver a four- to five-minute speech to the class in which you describe this place as accurately and vividly as possible. Then ask the class to take a moment to envision this place. If possible, show them a picture of what you've described. How accurately were they able to envision this place? How might you have insured a more accurate description? What restrictions did you feel without the use of visual aids?

 ## SUGGESTIONS FOR FURTHER READING

Lewis Donohew and Leonard Tipton, "A Conceptual Model of Information Seeking, Avoiding, and Processing," in *New Models for Communication Research,* ed. Peter Clarke, Sage Annual Reviews of Communication Research, Vol. 2 (Beverly Hills: Sage Publications, Inc., 1973), pp. 243–68.

Bruce E. Gronbeck, *The Articulate Person: A Guide to Everyday Public Speaking* (Glenview, IL: Scott, Foresman and Company, 1979), Chapters 4–7.

Werner J. Severin and James W. Tankard, Jr., *Communication Theories: Origins Methods Uses,* Humanistic Studies in The Communication Arts (New York: Hastings House, Publishers, 1979), Chapter 4, "Information Theory."

W. V. Quine and J. S. Ullian, *The Web of Belief* (New York: Random House, Inc., 1970), Chapter 7, "Explanation."

Magdalen D. Vernon, "Perception, Attention, and Consciousness," in *Foundations of Communication Theory,* ed. Kenneth K. Sereno and C. David Mortensen (New York: Harper & Row, Publishers, 1970), pp. 137–51.

17

Speeches to Persuade and Actuate

We live in a complex society. No longer can one person working alone accomplish a task of any magnitude. Others also must be convinced that the task is worthwhile and agree to lend their support and encouragement, even their time, money, and energy. To bring about such convictions, today's advocate must be able to persuade people to change their minds about ideas and problems, and to move them to action. Speeches to persuade and actuate, therefore, fill evening newscasts, political rallies and conventions, neighborhood meetings, public hearings, and church basements. Informative speeches assemble and package important data and ideas, and persuasive and actuative messages bring about subsequent alterations in thought and action.

Speeches to persuade and actuate represent your greatest challenges. They come in many specific forms, their essential features are numerous, and their structures usually are more complicated than other oral messages we have discussed so far. Yet, they, too, must be mastered by the person who wishes to take part in organizations and society at large. In this chapter we will examine various types of persuasive and actuative speeches in enough depth to improve your speaking skills in these areas.

Types of Persuasive and Actuative Speeches

There are many ways to classify persuasive and actuative speeches. Although everyone agrees, generally, that persuasive speeches are designed to alter people's beliefs about and attitudes toward phenomena, processes, or persons, and that actuative speeches advocate social-political change and urge individual action, many classification schemes are possible. We will discuss various types from the vantage of their *essential content,* for that will allow you to think systematically about both the logical and the psychological aspects of persuasion and actuation. From this point of view, we may say that there are two major types of speech which seek to affect audience judgment—*claims of fact* and *claims of value;* and, two types of messages which attempt to alter audience behavior—*claims of policy* and *claims of action.*

Initially, we will discuss each of these types of claims in terms of questions listeners are likely to ask about them, and, later, discuss their psychological dimensions more fully.

Claims of Fact

If you were attempting to persuade your listeners that "the routine of assembly-line work causes mental depression" or that "price controls on raw agricultural products result in food shortages," you would in each case be presenting a factual claim—asserting that a given state of affairs exists or that something is indeed true. When confronted with a claim of this sort, two questions are likely to arise in the mind of a thoughtful listener:

1. *By what criteria or standards of judgment should the truth or accuracy of this claim be measured?* If you were asked to determine a person's height, you would immediately look for a yardstick or other measuring instrument. Listeners likewise look for a standard when judging the appropriateness of a factual claim. In the first of the examples given above, before agreeing that assembly-line workers do experience "mental depression," the members of your audience would almost certainly want to know what you as a speaker mean by that term. In the second example, they would, no doubt, demand a definition of "shortages." Does it mean "the disappearance, for all practical purposes, of a given kind of food" or merely "less of that food than everyone might desire"? Against what standard, precisely, is the accuracy of the claim to be judged?

2. *Do the facts of the situation fit the criteria as thus set forth?* Is it a fact that all, or at least a reasonable majority of, assembly-line workers experience those feelings or symptoms which you have previously defined as constituting "mental depression"? Does the amount of produce and other raw agricultural products presently on supermarket shelves fall within the limits set by your definition of "shortages"? If you can first get your listeners to agree to certain standards or measurements for judgment and then present evidence to show that a given state of affairs meets these standards, you will, in most instances, be well on your way toward winning their belief.

Claims of Value

When, instead of asserting that something is or is not so, you assert that something is good or bad, desirable or undesirable, justified or unjustified, you are advancing a claim of value—a claim concerning the intrinsic *worth* of the belief or action in question. Here, as in the case of claims of fact, it is always appropriate to ask: (1) *By what standards or criteria is something of this nature to be judged?* (2) *How well does the item in question measure up to the standards specified?*

The goal of a persuasive speech is to influence the beliefs and actions of the listeners. In attaining this goal, the speaker should supply valid arguments and motivations for the listeners' thinking, behaving, or doing as the speaker recommends.

We may, for example, assert that the quality of a college is to be measured by the distinction of its faculty, the excellence of its physical plant, the success of its graduates in securing positions, and the reputation it enjoys among the general public; and then proceed to show that because the college we are concerned with meets each of these tests, it is indeed a good one.

Claims of Policy

A claim of policy recommends a course of action for which you seek the audience's approval. Typical examples are: "Federal expenditures for pollution control *should be* substantially increased"; "The student senate *should have* the authority to expel students who cheat"; "Fines for overtime parking in city lots *should be* increased from $2 to $5." In each instance, you are asking your audience to endorse a proposed "policy" or course of action. When analyzing a policy claim, four subsidiary questions are relevant:

1. *Is there a need for such a policy or course of action?* If your listeners do not believe that a change is called for, they are not likely to approve your proposal.

2. *Is the proposal practicable?* Can we afford the expense it would entail? Would it really solve the problem or remove the evil it is designed to correct? Does such a policy stand a reasonable chance of being adopted? If you cannot show that your proposal meets these and similar tests, you can hardly expect it to be endorsed.

3. *Are the benefits your proposal will bring greater than the disadvantages it will entail?* People are reluctant to approve a proposal that promises to create conditions worse than the ones it is designed to correct. Burning a barn to the ground may be a highly efficient way to get rid of rats, but it is hardly a desirable one. The benefits and disadvantages that will accrue from a plan of action always must be carefully weighed along with considerations of its basic workability.

4. *Is the offered proposal superior to any other plan or policy?* Listeners are hesitant to approve a policy if they have reason to believe that an alternative course of action is more practicable or more beneficial.

Claims of Action

A claim of action not only seeks the audience's approval of some course of action, but goes a step farther, specifying the actions they as individuals or as a group ought to take. Such claims include propositions such as the following: "Give generously to the United Way"; "Vote for Henry Johnston for the Board of Supervisors"; "Find Elizabeth Frank innocent of these charges"; "Attend next Monday's School Board meeting to protest the proposed school closing." To alter audience members' behavior in these sorts of ways, you must convince them, as in the cases of policy claims, that there is a need for a change, a practical plan, benefits to be accrued by taking the action, and no other course of action superior to this one. But, in addition to producing a state of *psychological conviction*, you also must offer them the *motivational inducement* to act personally—to do something rather than not do it, to act now rather than later, and to act in a particular way. After all, the determination and enthusiasm which your listeners feel as you conclude your speech may dissipate rapidly when they come out on the cold street corner where they have agreed to hand out literature and when they encounter the rebuffs of the first persons they ask to contribute money or buy tickets. Your motivational inducement, therefore, must be strong enough to bring about the requisite commitment-to-act even in the face of obstacles.

Essential Features of Persuasive and Actuative Speeches

Regardless of the specific sort of claim being advanced, persuasive and actuative speeches face a series of challenges that speakers must meet. These challenges comprise their essential features: (1) *Adaptation to psychological states;* (2) *change by degrees;* (3) *saliency and its effect upon strategies;* and (4) *credibility.*

Adaptation to Psychological States

By psychological states we refer to audience members' *general predisposition to respond* to certain messages even before they are delivered. The general psychological states of audiences, as we noted in Chapter 5, tend to vary a good deal from situation to situation, from group to group; you must try to assess that state, therefore, before you construct any persuasive or actuative speech. While the social-scientific communication research on psychological states of listeners increases with each new issue of journals such as *Human Communication Research* and *Communication Monographs,* there are some indisputable truisms which follow from research already done. We can discuss these conclusions conveniently under three headings—audiences' general predispositions toward the topic, their cognitive complexity or sophistication, and their dependence upon reference groups.

General predisposition toward topics • As we have said earlier, generally speaking an audience may have any one of five attitudes toward your topic and purpose. It may be (*a*) favorable but not aroused to act; (*b*) apathetic toward the situation; (*c*) interested in it but undecided what to do or think about it; (*d*) interested in the situation but hostile to the proposed attitude, belief, or action; or (*e*), hostile to any change from the present state of affairs. Furthermore, when talking about beliefs and attitudes in Chapter 5, we noted that, for all of us, our specific beliefs about some thing or our specific attitudes toward it may be well fixed or very infirm, depending upon their importance to us and our view of the world. All of this means that you must pre-gauge these dispositions toward your purpose and topic, and be able to adjust your communicative strategies accordingly.

More specifically: (1) When an audience is hostile toward your claim, be sure that you present a *two-sided message.* A one-sided speech offers only arguments for your claim, while a two-sided speech takes into account opposing ideas and proposals and then answers them. If you expect resistance, do not simply ignore it. (2) If the hostility is extreme, deal with it *early* in the speech; if it is moderate or if the audience is all but perfectly neutral, deal with opposing arguments *late* in the speech. In other words, the skilled persuasive or actuative speaker always tries to deal with the main thrust of the audience's predispositions toward the purpose and topic near the beginning.

Regarding specific beliefs and attitudes: (3) The more *fixed* and *important* the beliefs and attitudes you are trying to change, the more resistant individuals will be. Conversely, the more a person's beliefs and attitudes depend upon peripheral authorities and experiences, the easier they are to change. (4) The more *central* some set of beliefs, attitudes, and values are to a person, the more likely it is that you will run into a *network* of interconnected concepts. As a study by Prescott demonstrated clearly, for example, if people are against abortion they are likely to be in favor of physical punishment of children, capital punishment for criminals, and domineering fathers, and against prostitution, nudity, premarital sex, and drugs.[1] You as a persuader, therefore, must attempt to assess the degree to which you are invading cognitive or emotional networks when you advocate change. If you are, you should either attempt to deal with the whole complex (which is extremely difficult to do) or work hard at separating one issue from the interconnected ones.

Cognitive complexity • This term refers to the conceptual sophistication of people—not simply the number of things they know, but rather their abilities to deal mentally with a wide range of causes, implications, and associated notions when thinking about some idea or event. A person's cognitive complexity is in part intelligence, in part maturity, and in part experience. Although not all the evidence on the effects of cognitive complex is as yet in, this much we know: (1) Cognitively complex audiences demand and can follow relatively *sophisticated arguments*. (2) They respond better to *two-sided* rather than one-sided presentations. (3) And, they require a comparatively large amount of *evidence* before they will change beliefs and attitudes. We also know that (4) cognitively complex speakers generate more *strategically sound tactics* and hence are (and are perceived as) more *effective communicators*.[2]

Demagogues for years have assumed that they can hoodwink any audience, but as our population as a whole has gained experience in group dynamics and decision-making, and as our country's general educational level has risen markedly, we are undermining that assumption. Unless you are dealing with a group of fledgling five-year-olds, you had better be prepared to offer well-developed analyses of problems and their solutions, replete with authoritative supporting materials, with answers to counterarguments, and with logical structures. You may not need all of those materials once you are perceived as a true expert, but few of us have achieved or will attain that level.

All speeches to persuade and to actuate involve meeting the following challenges: Adapting to the psychological state of the audience; understanding that listeners may change their position only to a modified degree; reflecting the relevance and interest level of a topic; and maintaining a high level of personal credibility.

Reference groups • As you will recall (Chapter 5), reference groups are collections of people and organizations which affect individuals' beliefs, attitudes, and values. You may or may not hold an actual membership in such groups; you may belong, say, to the Young Republicans Club and not belong to a sorority, yet each group may well influence your beliefs. Some groups you may join voluntarily, as in the examples just noted, while others are involuntary, as for instance your membership in a male or female gender group or your cultural-ethnic heritage. Some groups may affect you positively, as do those which believe what you do, while others can produce negative reactions, as is the case with people who say, "If the communists are for it, I'm against it." So, we may think of reference groups as *membership* and *nonmembership groups, voluntary* and *involuntary groups,* and *positive* and *negative groups.*

Individuals vary, of course, in the degree to which they rely upon reference groups when they are making a decision on what to think or do; yet, all of us, to some extent, have beliefs, attitudes, and values rooted in our group experiences. As a speaker, you should use this aspect of people's general psychological state when constructing all persuasive and actuative messages: (1) Citing the opinions of voluntary, positive membership groups which *coincide* with positions you are taking is likely to increase your effectiveness. This is a matter, as the Greeks noted 2500 years ago, of "Praising Athens to the Athenians," of using the positive characteristics of the group to influence the individual member of that group. (2) Citing the opinions of voluntary, negative nonmembership groups which *oppose* positions you are taking is likely to increase your effectiveness. Such groups can be thought of as "devils" to which people react; if the claims you are defending go counter to the thinking and actions of devil-groups, your audience will tend to agree with your proposals. (3) The greater people's *roles* are in any group, the more that group's norms and beliefs will influence their thought and behavior. Corporate executives, for example, tend to have more important roles in business than do new, relatively powerless workers; hence, it is more difficult to produce radical business-oriented changes in executives than in front-line workers.[3]

In summary, audiences' predisposing psychological states—their attitudes toward the purpose and topic, their cognitive complexity, and their group memberships—can affect, even decisively, their reactions to your persuasive and actuative messages, and hence should help you determine your overall strategies.

Change by Degrees

A second essential feature of all persuasive and actuative speeches is that people will change only so much, for the most part, when they hear a speech. It is almost literally impossible, except in the rarest of circumstances (e.g., radical religious experiences), to make wholesale changes in people's beliefs, attitudes, and values. Ordinarily, you should attempt to make *incremental changes*—moving people toward some goal in a step-by-step fashion. The "distance" you can move an audience is determined by two principal psychological factors: *(a)* their *initial attitudinal predisposition,* and *(b)* the *latitude of change* they as individuals can tolerate.

Initial attitudinal predisposition • Imagine a line which represents someone's attitude toward, say, abortion; imagine, too, that it is divided into ten segments, with "1" representing "extremely favorable toward abortion laws"; "3," "moderately favorable"; "4," "mildly favorable"; "5," "neutral"; "6," "mildly unfavorable"; "8," "moderately unfavorable"; and "10," "strongly unfavorable toward abortion laws." If you attempted to convince someone who was strongly unfavorable ("10") that federal abortion laws should be fervently supported (a "1" position), you undoubtedly would fail miserably in most circumstances. Even in the face of credible speakers and well-thought out arguments, most radical "anti's" could be "moved" only a short way toward the "pro" position—say, to a "6" or a "5," maybe a "4" position. Trying to change them too much in a single speech can produce what we earlier termed a *boomerang effect;* such people in the face of the strong "1" speech will become even more committed to their "10" position.[4]

Obviously, it is impossible for a speaker to interview all audience members, writing down their attitudinal predispositions numerically. Good audience analysis, however, allows you at least to guess shrewdly, and adjust your appeals and plans of action accordingly.

Latitudes of change • A second question of degree can be phrased: How much change does an individual tolerate? The answer to this question tends to vary from individual to individual as well from topic to topic. Some people—often termed *authoritarian or dogmatic personalities* in the research literature—tolerate little change. These people have a narrow "latitude of acceptance"; in terms of our numerical scale, we can say that their attitudes are anchored firmly on, say, the "6" or the "5" and "6" positions. Other people, however, are more non-authoritarian or non-dogmatic; they may well accept proposals across the entire "3–6" range without trouble; in other words, they are what we normally call "open-minded" personalities, and hence more easy to persuade or to move to action.[5]

Again, it behooves the rhetorically sensitive speaker to attempt to assess the authoritarianism or dogmatism of listeners. Deeply committed groups—especially those on the "right" or "left" ends of the social-political spectrum—are extremely difficult to persuade in a single speech; they may well demand a sustained campaign in which you move them toward your desired end only by small steps at a time. You must try, in your audience analysis, to estimate the latitudes of acceptance operative in that group, and adjust your appeals and proposals accordingly, just as you did when you assessed its initial attitudinal predisposition.

Saliency and Its Effect on Strategies

Saliency refers to the relevance and interest level of some belief, attitude, or topic. For example, topics making front-page news are highly salient to people, as are beliefs and attitudes we think about regularly; so are experiences we often have, and people we are close to. Two important aspects of saliency, especially,

INCREMENTAL APPROACH TO ATTITUDE CHANGE

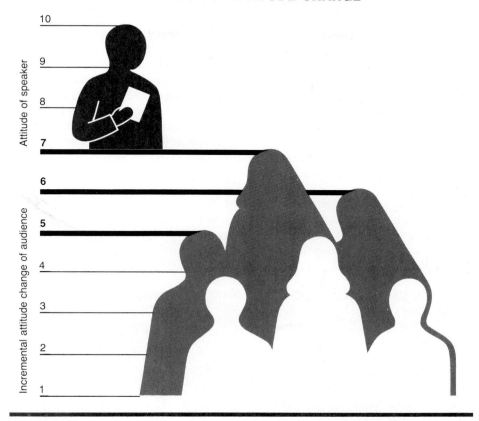

are important to you as you consider persuasive and actuative speeches: (1) The more salient a particular topic, the more likely members of your audience will have *preknowledge* of it and perhaps even specific beliefs about and attitudes toward it. (2) And, the more salient a particular topic, the more likely listeners will *resist changes* in their beliefs and attitudes. Topics in the news or those dealing with everyday occurrences probably need little in the way of development of their Attention Step, for example, while those with low saliency may well demand considerable background. And again, if you are attacking a highly salient belief or attitude, you can expect listeners to oppose your positions; as we suggested earlier, you probably ought to deal explicitly with their opposition early in the Need Step, and work hard in the Satisfaction Step to demonstrate that new beliefs and reformed attitudes are necessary if the problem is to be solved. Finally, a third facet of saliency should be noted: (3) Quote salient *authorities* in your persuasive and actuative speeches. George Washington, for example, was indeed President of the United States and hence an authority, but he perhaps is not nearly so salient an authority as a president from recent years.[6]

Credibility

This last point brings us to another essential feature of all persuasive and actuative speeches: A good deal of your potential effectiveness will depend upon your perceived credibility or *ethos*. In Chapter 1 we outlined several factors which can determine an audience's sense of your credibility—their sense of your expertise, truthworthiness, competency, sincerity or honesty, friendliness and concern for others, and personal dynamism. While you should work to maximize all these factors whenever you speak, some of these factors are especially important in persuasive and actuative speeches:

1. Try to maximize an audience's sense of your *competency* and *sincerity* when seeking to *persuade*. People are unlikely to change their beliefs and attitudes if they think you have incompetently reviewed alternatives and evaluated the current attitudes toward some proposal; and, if they find you

This speaker at a student rally has undoubtedly succeeded in persuading members of his audience to either agree with his position or to accept his credibility.

pig-headed and insincere, they will be convinced you have ulterior motives in mind as you talk to them. You can increase their confidence in your competency by: (a) carefully sorting through all of the competing positions, ideas, and proposals relevant to some topic before you come to your judgment; (b) reviewing various criteria for judgment (see above) to show that your recommendations or positions flow from accepted and generally held criteria; and (c) showing that recommendations you offer will actually solve problems you have identified in the Need Step. And, you can increase their sense of your sincerity by: (a) showing yourself to be open to correction and criticism should any listener wish to question you; (b) exuding personal warmth in your relations with them; (c) maintaining direct eye contact with listeners; and (d) recognizing anyone who has helped you understand and work on this problem. These simple-but-important pieces of advice, if followed, should bolster your credibility when persuading others.

2. Heighten the audience's sense of your *expertise, friendliness,* and *dynamism,* especially when seeking to move them to *action.* People are unlikely to change their routines and behaviors on your recommendation unless they feel you know what you are talking about, have their best interests in mind, and get excited by your commitment and enthusiasm. A perception of expertise can be created by: (a) documenting your sources of information; (b) using varied sources of information as cross-checks on each other; (c) carefully presenting your information and need analyses in well-organized ways; (d) building easy-to-understand visual aids when you use them; (e) providing enough background information on controversial issues so that your listeners can understand why you are proposing what you are; (f) separating causes from effects, short-term from long-term effects, hard facts from soft wishes or dreams, and one proposal from others in a competent manner; and (g) delivering your speeches in a forthright and calm manner. A sense of friendliness and concern for others can be generated by: (a) treating yourself and others as human beings no matter what the topic and no matter how much you disagree with others; and (b) depersonalizing issues, talking in terms of the "real world" and its problems rather than in terms of personalities and ideologies. And, an audience's perception of your dynamism can be fostered by (a) a use of vivid examples, sharp and fresh metaphors, active rather than passive verbs, and short, hard-hitting "oral" sentences rather than long, cumbersome "written" sentences; and (b) a use of varied, conversational vocal patterns, an animated body, direct eye contact with freedom from your notes, and a firm upright stance.[7]

In summary, remember that a public speaker's principal communicative virtue is the presence of a living, active human being behind the podium—a person *embodying* a message. People command more attention and interest than written words; and, people, unlike films and videotapes, can feel, can react to audience members, can create a sense of urgency and directness. Hence, personal presence and credibility are extremely valuable assets for the would-be persuader and actuator.

Overall, then, by adapting your message and appeals to the general psychological states of your listeners, by being sure you are not asking anyone to change too much at one time, by adapting your materials to the degree of topic saliency, and by showing yourself to be a credible individual, you will be meeting the central demands of all situations calling for persuasive and actuative public discourse.

Structuring Persuasive and Actuative Speeches

Presumably, any of the organizational patterns we discussed in Chapter 9 could be used for structuring persuasive and actuative speeches; the judicious speaker will consider each carefully when thinking about order for materials. For the sake of convenience and for comparative purposes, however, we will illustrate utilitarian structures for persuasive and actuative speeches here by employing the motivated sequence. It represents a time- and experienced-tested formula for meeting the demands of most speaking situations.

The Motivated Sequence and Claims of Fact

Generally, for claims of fact, the Need and Satisfaction Steps become the crucial segments. Basically, one must work through the Attention Step in a normal manner. Then, in the Need Step, state clearly the point to be established and show your listeners why it is important; do this by pointing out why the matter at hand concerns them personally and why it concerns the community, state, nation, or world of which they are a part. Then, in the Satisfaction Step, if they are not already obvious, set forth the criteria upon which a proper judgment rests, and advance the exact point to be proved, offering evidence and argument to support your factual claim. Visualizing the results of accepting your claim normally involves picturing the advantages of accepting it and the disadvantages of rejecting it. And, an Action Step may or may not be called for, depending upon the force or direction of your claim.

The five steps of the motivated sequence, adapted as just suggested, are illustrated in the outline entitled "Safe at Home" on page 317.

The Motivated Sequence and Claims of Value

When speaking on a claim of value with a view to persuading your listeners that they should agree with your judgment of a person, practice, institution, or theory, you may adapt the basic pattern as follows: (1) Capture the attention and interest of the audience. (2) Make clear that a judgment concerning the worth of the person, practice, or institution is needed. Do this by showing (a) why a judgment is important to your listeners personally, and (b) why it is important to the community, state, nation, or world of which they are a part. (3) To satisfy

A SAMPLE OUTLINE OF A SPEECH ON A CLAIM OF FACT

Safe At Home

Specific Purpose:
To convince listeners to take steps
to prevent home accidents.

**Attention
Step**

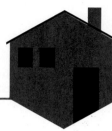

I. Everyone has heard the expression "safe at home."
II. But is your home really a safe place to live?

**Need
Step**

I. This is a question of importance to each of us.
  A. Our own well-being is at stake.
  B. The well-being of our families is at stake.

**Satisfaction
Step**

I. In answering the question of home safety, we must consider two *additional* questions.
  A. How many accidents occur in the home?
  B. How serious are these accidents?
II. In neither case are the facts encouraging.
  A. Statistics gathered by the National Safety Council show that, in the year 1979, accidents in the home were responsible for 4,200,000 disabling injuries.
  B. In the same year, home accidents were the cause of 27,500 deaths.

**Visualization
Step**

I. Unless we are aware of these dangers and guard against them, we, too, may be numbered among the victims of home accidents.
  A. We may be "laid up" for long periods of time.
  B. Our children and loved ones may be killed or permanently injured.

**Action
Step**

I. Take steps today to avoid such tragedies.
  A. Put firm railings and good lights on all staircases.
  B. Keep matches and combustible materials out of the reach of children.
  C. Dispose of all plastic bags as soon as they are emptied.
  D. Keep all poisonous substances under lock and key.
II. Remember, your home will be a safe place only if you yourself make it so.

the need, *(a)* set the criteria upon which an intelligent judgment may be based, and *(b)* advance what you believe to be the correct judgment, showing how it meets the criteria. (4) Picture the advantages that will accrue from agreeing with the judgment you advance or the evils that will result from failing to endorse it. (5) Finally, appeal for the acceptance of the proposed judgment, if appropriate.

Adapting the motivated sequence to the demands of a claim of value should produce a speech outline much like the following:

CONTRIBUTE TO CHARITIES WISELY[8]

Specific Purpose: To persuade listeners to evaluate carefully the efficiency and effectiveness of the charitable organizations to which they contribute.

Attention Step

   I. In 1975, Americans gave over 11.6 billion dollars to charitable organizations, not counting contributions to religious and educational institutions, but some experts have estimated that 116 million dollars was wasted because it went to fraudulent or poorly managed organizations.

Need Step

   I. There are differences in the ways charities distribute their funds.
     A. Example of a charity which uses 94 percent of its contributions for administration.
     B. Example of a charity—United Way—which distributes ninety cents out of every dollar collected.

 II. Unless we all simply decide to stop giving to charities, we must come up with criteria for evaluating organizations and procedures for investigating them.

Satisfaction Step

   I. How, then, can you evaluate charities?
     A. Fund-raising and administrative costs should total less than 50 percent of the total public contributions.
     B. An effective charity should be controlled by an active, unsalaried governing board, with no paid employees serving as voting members of that board.
     C. It should use reputable promotional and fund-raising methods.
     D. It should publicly disclose a complete and independently audited annual financial report. (Each of these criteria could be justified by appeals to authority and example.)

 II. These criteria can be applied by both governmental units and individuals.
     A. Both Florida and Pennsylvania have laws governing what percentage of their total contributions charities can spend on fund-raising.
     B. The federal government similarly regulates charities soliciting in more than one state.
     C. As an individual, you also can check into charities you might wish to support.
       1. Ask for an annual report before contributing.

2. The Council of Better Business Bureaus publishes a rating list.
3. The National Information Bureau discloses pertinent information.

Visualization Step

I. If both government and individuals do their investigative jobs properly, imagine the benefits which would accrue from the extra money spent on those who need it.
   A. The number of poor that could be fed and clothed would increase.
   B. Additional medical and health care facilities could be built.
   C. Research into killing and crippling diseases could proceed with more vigor.

Action Step

I. You have the power to direct your contributions to the most beneficial charities.
   A. Keep the evaluative criteria—efficiency, disinterestedness, fairness, and openness—in mind when you receive a call for help.
   B. And when you give, open your heart, your pocketbook, and, yes, your mind—give, but give wisely.

The Motivated Sequence and Claims of Policy

Because the motivated sequence has been designed primarily for use in actuative speeches, the format as a whole requires little or no adaptation when speakers are treating claims of policy—claims which urge listeners to consider generally the adoption of new ways of acting toward some problem area. Here, we will illustrate it in fuller detail than we did in Chapter 8.

The following outline is based upon a speech which then-United States Senator John Culver presented before the Chicago Council on Foreign Relations.[9] Observe that each of the steps in the motivated sequence appropriate to an actuative speech is fully represented. Note also the liberal use of examples and statistics, and the strong motivation present in the closing appeal for action.

WORLD TRADE IN WEAPONS MUST CEASE

Attention Step

I. Suppose a proposal were made that the United States go into the international heroin business.
   A. Such a proposal sounds outlandish.
   B. It would, however, "have some things going for it."
      1. It would stimulate industry and provide employment.
      2. It would be beneficial to our balance of payments.
      3. It would give us influence of sorts in some quarters.
      4. It could be argued that if we didn't produce and sell heroin, someone else would.

II. Today the United States and its allies are heavily involved in another deadly traffic, that of arms and military equipment.
   A. This traffic has produced more death and suffering than all of the drugs produced since the beginning of time.
   B. It is escalating rapidly.

C. It sometimes is justified by arguments similar to those I have cited for the heroin business.

Need Step

I. World trade in arms and military equipment has reached gigantic proportions.
   A. Trade in conventional weapons has soared to $18 billion annually.
      1. Developed and developing nations are laying in arsenals of the most sophisticated weapons they can obtain.
      2. United States arms sales to other countries amount to about one half of what we produce for our own use—$10 billion a year.
      3. The aerospace industry of the United Kingdom ships nearly one third of its annual production abroad.
      4. The Soviet Union accounts for nearly one fourth of the world's arms transfers.
         a. It sends to the less-developed countries twice as much in weapons as in economic assistance.
         b. It has helped to equip the pro-Soviet faction in Angola and elsewhere.

II. Arms exports from the United States are so large that they can no longer be monitored as the law directs.
   A. The executive branch has not always weighed the political, economic, and security factors involved in weapons sales.
      1. President Nixon decided on his own that Iran should get virtually any conventional weapons it desired.
      2. President Ford openly bypassed the normal decision-making process when he permitted the delivery of certain highly advanced weapons to Israel.
   B. Control by Congress is ineffective.
      1. Until 1974, Congress had practically no voice in arms sales.
      2. Recently, Congress faced the impossible task of reviewing forty-three separate sales proposals in the final hectic month before adjournment.

III. The benefits allegedly derived from foreign arms sales are by no means assured.
   A. In some countries the improved internal security resulting from arms purchases has led to increasingly repressive regimes.
   B. Savings from reduced unit costs of weapons produced in greater quantity, according to findings by the Congressional Budget Office, have been the exception rather than the rule.
   C. A "worst-case analysis" has shown that if we completely eliminated foreign military sales, by 1981 there would be only three-tenths of a percent difference in the unemployment rate.

IV. The problems arising from foreign arms sales are already seriously jeopardizing our national defense.
   A. The defense-readiness of our own forces has suffered.
      1. The Army claims an overall deficiency of 61 percent in tanks.
      2. We are transferring some of our most advanced technology to other countries.
      3. Many countries to which we are selling arms are unable to absorb, utilize, and maintain the new equipment.

      a.   Large quantities of uncrated weapons are stacked up on the docks of Persian Gulf countries.

      b.   United States technicians complain that they cannot train adequate numbers of local personnel to operate and maintain the sophisticated weapons.

B.   Our arms merchants have been thoughtlessly arming potential adversaries.

    1.   We have armed both Greece and Turkey.

    2.   We have sold weapons to both Pakistan and India.

    3.   We have given Israel $4.4 billion worth of military assistance since 1973, but have given the Persian Gulf states four times as much.

C.   The oil-rich states of the Middle East can afford weapons which the underdeveloped nations of Africa cannot.

V. One year ago, one hundred members of Congress joined me in urging Secretary of State Kissinger to sponsor an international conference on arms control.

    A.   The Secretary ordered a full-scale review of possible limitations on weapons sales.

    B.   The resulting report gave little hope that any initiative toward such a conference would come from our government.

Satisfaction Step

I. In the face of the foregoing situation, I have suggested that a step-by-step approach be taken to control international arms sales.

    A.   This approach could be limited to the Middle East and Africa.

    B.   It could be broadened to include other areas as well.

II. First, we should consult with our Canadian and Western European friends.

    A.   We should explore mutual needs and interests.

    B.   We should link discussion of arms sales to discussions on standardizing weapons among the NATO nations.

III. Second, we should seek to eliminate bribery and corruption in arms sales.

    A.   Tentative guidelines are now being worked out by the Organization for Economic Cooperation and Development.

    B.   Appropriate agencies of the United Nations also could attack the problem.

IV. Third, we should reduce the export of highly complex technology systems.

    A.   We have been successful in restricting the transfer of computer know-how to Eastern European nations.

    B.   We can be equally successful in devising feasible agreements on limiting arms sales to Third-World nations.

Visualization Step

I. Successful cooperation among our Canadian and Western allies would pave the way for future bargaining with the Soviet Union, China, and Eastern Europe.

Action Step

I. We must make the effort, difficult though it may be.

    A.   The world looks to the United States for moral leadership and deceleration of the arms race.

    B.   It is our responsibility to initiate action before it is too late and the momentum is irreversible.

The Motivated Sequence and Claims of Action

Claims of action can be defended and advocated very efficiently by using the motivated sequence in a straightforward fashion. Only take care that the Action Step contains a listing of the specific behaviors you wish your listeners to carry out; that, after all, is the primary goal of these kinds of speeches. Do you wish them to contribute money? Then, either pass the hat or give them pre-addressed envelopes. Do you want them to attend a rally or public hearing? Be sure to tell them the time and place. Would you like them to write their congressional representatives? Hand out a sheet containing the names and addresses of their Washington representatives. Remember that it is all too easy for people to nod in approval on one day, and then be diverted into other activities the next. Make the call to action specific, concrete, and compelling.

A Sample Speech to Persuade

Following is the text of a student speech advocating particular actions. It was prepared by Todd Ambs of Eastern Michigan University, and was presented in one of the annual contests sponsored by the Interstate Oratorical Association. Mr. Ambs faced particular problems in presenting this speech on hypertension and heart disease: (1) His audience generally was composed of college students, who undoubtedly felt they were too young to worry about heart disease; and (2) the setting was a speech contest, one where audience members probably were more concerned about their own speeches than about Mr. Ambs' call for action. As you read the speech, notice how he attempted to break down the attitudes of apathy and complacency through a combination of fear appeals, statistics, specific instances, and authoritative testimony; pay particular attention to his call for action both for governmental agencies and individuals "hardened" to persuasive speeches.

● The Silent Killer[10]

Todd Ambs

Attention Step
For many Americans, life can seem to be a maze of numbers. We use many numbers so often that to be without them seems almost impossible. How long could college students survive without their student numbers? How many businesses could operate without a phone number? How many of you have never had use for your social security number? The answers to these questions are easy. But there is one other set of numbers that could set us on the road to preventing an estimated 300,000 deaths and over two million serious illnesses each year, if we would only pay attention to them. For no student number, phone number, or social security number will ever be as vital to you as your blood pressure reading. /1

The human blood pressure is a veritable measuring stick of good health. Normal blood pressure, that is anything between 90/70 to 140/90, is generally a good indication of normal health. Unfortunately, over 25 million Americans do not have a blood pressure within this range. They suffer from high blood pressure, or hypertension. /2

Indeed, according to the Department of Health, Education, and Welfare, this year, 310,000 Americans will perish from illnesses whose major contributing factor is hypertension. Two million will suffer strokes, heart attacks, and kidney failure as a direct result of hypertension. Even more startling is the realization that of that 25 million, 11 million aren't even aware of their condition. According to Dr. Theodore Cooper, Director of the Heart and Lung Institute, "Hypertension can be brought under control through proven treatment which is neither unduly hazardous, complicated or expensive." /3

Need Step
Before we can fully understand the magnitude of the problem though, we need to know what high blood pressure does to the body. When the pressure of the blood becomes too great for the arterial walls, high blood pressure results. This is somewhat like giving your circulatory system a headache. Fatty tissues, salts and fluids build up and the heart must be made to work harder than it should to keep the blood flowing properly. In this case, however, one tiny time pill won't relieve the pressure, or the irreparable damage that follows. /4

That information may sound familiar to many of you. But then, why is hypertension still responsible for one out of every eight deaths in this country! /5

The National High Blood Pressure Council attempted to answer that question when they said: "Half of those who have high blood pressure don't even know that they do. Of those who do, only half are being treated, only half again of those have their blood pressure under control. Patients and physicians alike just don't seem to take this condition very seriously." /6

Such carefree attitudes leave many people's lives just hanging in the balance because high blood pressure has no symptoms. Contrary to popular belief, high blood pressure is not confined to trapeze artists, overactive children, or the Annie Hall's of the world. There is, in fact, no direct correlation between tension and nervousness and high blood pressure. The only way you can tell if you have high blood pressure is to get it checked. As Dr. Frank Finnerty, author of the book, *High Blood Pressure— The Silent Killer,* put it: "You can look great and feel healthy and have been living for years with the hidden time bomb of high blood pressure doing internal damage to your body." For Bill, a 49-year-old account executive, the time bomb was about to explode. One minute he was walking along seemingly in the best of health. The next he was on the ground clutching his chest. The heart attack would be the last event in Bill's life. He would never know the anguish that his family would suffer when they discovered that high blood pressure, a totally preventable condition, had caused his death. The silent killer had quietly destroyed life again. /7

A routine physical could have saved Bill's life. And it could save yours. But unfortunately, our hectic, fast-paced lifestyles often provide easy excuses for not getting that needed physical. Lack of time, money, and the ever-popular lack of awareness can all be easy rationalizations for our failure to diagnose and treat hypertension. And our health care systems have failed to adjust to this reality at home, or especially on the job. A recent major manufacturing study found that on the average, businesses spend over $300 per employee per year, for illnesses caused by hypertension. Dr. Andrea Foote and Dr. John Erfurt, the country's leading specialists in hypertensive care, painted the picture in this light: "The current inadequacy of treatment suggests that the problem is a matter of social organization and lies primarily in the inability of the health care delivery system to provide health care for this disease." /8

And here we reach the apex of the problem. Simple diagnosis must be followed by constant treatment if hypertension is to be controlled. Unfortunately, many people do not continue this vital treatment. Mike Gorman, Executive Director of the Citizens for the Treatment of High Blood Pressure, estimates that at least 50% of those diagnosed drop out of treatment after a few months. One man who had a severe attack of high blood pressure on his vacation came home, followed a steady treatment plan, and brought his pressure down. After a while, he foolishly decided to try foregoing the medication. Within a month, he had a stroke which left him with irreversible brain damage. This man should have known better. He was a doctor, who was about to be nominated to the A.M.A. presidency. Unbelievably, a man who had frequently prescribed treatment for hypertension, and ignored his own warnings! The precautions must be heeded; anyone can be a victim. /9

Satisfaction Step
Obviously then, the public needs to be made aware of the dangers of hypertension, health care systems should be improved to provide adequate health care for the disease, and finally, hypertensives must realize that constant treatment is essential to effective control. /10

Thankfully, the goals I have mentioned are not just mere ideals proposed by a few specialists in hypertensive care. In 1972, the National Heart, Lung and Blood Institute organized the National High Blood Pressure Education Program, a program that all of us can get involved in. Their goal is to alert people to the dangers of hypertension through location, diagnosis, and treatment. The results have been astounding. According to the National Center for Health Statistics, 290,000 people leading normal lives today would have died, were it not for the Hypertensive Education Program. Over eight million people now have their blood pressure under control, a 100% increase since 1972. /11

And it touches all sectors of society, for the Hypertensive Education Program is nationwide. Here in Michigan, for instance, you can contact Steve Renke at the University of Michigan's hypertensive care unit in Ann Arbor, if you want to help. /12

Visualization Step
But we cannot rest on the laurels of this program. A disease which claims the lives of over 300,000 people annually is hardly under control. Doctors Foote and Erfurt have found that blood pressure control, for employed people, can best be carried out in the work setting. Their Worker Health Program was tested at four different job sites. As a result, 92% of the hypertensives at these jobs have their blood pressure under control, and the cost to the businesses involved has been cut from $300 per employee to $6.21. The program has been so successful that Blue Cross/Blue Shield of Michigan and Connecticut are now undergoing pilot programs of their own, based on the Worker Health Program. /13

On the local level there are things you can do as well. In 1970, Savannah, Georgia, had the infamous title of Stroke Capital of the World. Today, Savannah has 14 permanent blood pressure reading stations and the stroke toll in that city has been cut in half. A program, like one of these, can work in your community. /14

Action Step
So often, those of us in forensics use persuasive ploys instead of getting right to the heart of the problem. As a result, we tend to perform, instead of persuade. And you in turn as an audience listen, but don't hear. *Please,* if you do nothing else today, hear what I'm saying. There are people in this country who are dying because they have high blood pressure and there is not enough being done about it. You could be one of the 11 million Americans who has high blood pressure and does not even know it. If you are lucky enough to not be inflicted with the malady of hypertension, certainly someone that you know is. Don't let yourself or someone you know become a number on a fatality sheet. Get your blood pressure checked and save a life, your own. /15

The arts of persuasion and actuation are fundamental to any democratic society. Unless enough citizens are skilled both in preparing and listening to appeals for changes of mind and action, a country is likely to fall victim to unscrupulous, self-serving advocates. As we have noted in this chapter, it is by no means easy to deliver or to react to effective persuasive communications. Yet, if you as a speaker systematically analyze your audiences, as a listener analyze the persuasive appeals aimed at you personally, and work your way through situations demanding such speeches a step at a time, you, too, can make a real contribution as an informed and enlightened citizen.

REFERENCE NOTES

[1]The classic research on audience predipositions and order of ideas in the face of those predispositions is summarized in Carl I. Hovland et al., *The Order of Presentation in Persuasion* (New Haven, CT: Yale University Press, 1961). Additional studies on one-sided vs. two-sided presentations are capsulized in Erwin P. Bettinghaus, *Persuasive Communication,* 3rd ed. (New York: Holt, Rinehart and Winston, 1980), esp. pp. 141–43. The main source of research on central and peripheral beliefs and attitudes is Milton Rokeach, *Beliefs, Attitudes, and Values* (San Francisco: Jossey-Bass, 1968); Rokeach's main findings are also summarized in Bettinghaus, pp. 23–26. A similar discussion in highly readable form can be found in Daryl Bem, *Beliefs, Attitudes and Human Affairs* (Belmont, CA: Brooks/Cole Publishing Co., 1970). The study of attitudinal networks referred to in this chapter is J. W. Prescott, "Body Pleasure and the Origins of Violence," *The Futurist,* 1975, pp. 64–74.

[2]The great research studies on intellectual sophistication and persuasion were done originally by the Yale group, and are summarized in Carl I. Hovland, Irving Janis, and H. H. Kelley, *Communication and Persuasion* (New Haven, CT: Yale University Press, 1953). More modern research, on the topic of cognitive complexity, currently is being done principally at the University of Illinois, under the leadership of Jesse Delia and Ruth Ann Clark. Those studies are too numerous to review here, although a good number of them (with useful footnotes to other pieces) can be found in the November 1979 issue of *Communication Monographs* (Vol. 46). And, as evidence of our fourth point here, see Claudia L. Hale, "Cognitive Complexity-Simplicity as a Determinant of Communication Effectiveness," *Communication Monographs,* 47 (November 1980), 304–311.

[3]The general notions standing behind reference group theory are developed in H. H. Kelley, "Two Functions of Reference Groups," in H. Prohansky and B. Seidenberg, eds., *Basic Studies in Social Psychology* (New York: Holt, Rinehart & Winston, 1965), pp. 210–14. The idea of positive and negative groups is developed in Theodore M. Newcomb's article, "Attitude Development as a Function of Reference Groups," in the same book, pp. 215–25. The conclusions about the effects of reference groups on beliefs and attitudes we offer here, as well as other propositions, are defended in Bettinghaus' fine chapter, "Successful Persuasion: Predicting Group Response," in his book (n. 1), pp. 70–88.

[4]The view that attitudes, in part, are cognitions which can be thought of as existing on a continuum is central to most so-called "balance theories" of attitudes. A must for starting any investigation of these theories is R. P. Abelson et al., *Theories of Cognitive Consistency: A Sourcebook* (Chicago: Rand McNally, 1968). And, periodically, new anthologies appear, summarizing the continuing research programs. Among the best are J. P. Robinson and P. R. Shaver, eds., *Measures of Social Psychological Attitudes* (Ann Arbor, MI: Institute for Social Research, 1973); H. Triandis, *Attitude and Attitude Change* (New York: John Wiley and Sons, 1971); and Martin Fishbein, ed., *Readings in Attitude Theory and Measurement* (New York: John Wiley and Sons, 1967). For a condensed treatment of balance theories, see Herbert W. Simons, *Persuasion; Understanding, Practice and Analysis* (Reading, MA: Addison-Wesley Pub. Co., 1976), esp. pp. 119–28.

[5]The basic research on latitudes of acceptance and rejection is covered in Muzafer Sherif, Carolyn Sherif, and Roger Nebergall, *Attitude and Attitude Change* (Philadelphia: Saunders, 1965).

[6]A more expanded discussion of saliency and its effects can be found in Kenneth E. Andersen, *Persuasion: Theory and Practice*, 2nd ed. (Boston, MA: Allyn and Bacon, Inc., 1978), esp. pp. 95–96, 110–11, 250–53.

[7]The latest complete summary of research on credibility supporting these and other conclusions is Stephen Littlejohn, "A Bibliography of Studies Related to Variables of Source Credibility," in *Bibliographical Annual in Speech Communication: 1971*, ed. Ned A. Shearer (New York: Speech Communication Association, 1972), pp. 1–40. New research on credibility, showing that it tends to vary from situation to situation and topic to topic is represented by such studies as Jo Liska, "Situational and Topical Variations in Credibility Criteria," *Communication Monographs*, 45 (March 1978), 85–92.

[8]This outline is based on a speech given by Steve Favitta, Central Missouri State University, in 1978. We have omitted the supporting materials, but most may be found in "New CT Ratings on 53 Charities," *Changing Times*, November 1976; and "United Way: Are the Criticisms Fair?" *Changing Times*, October 1977. This altered outline is used with the permission of Mr. Favitta. Text supplied courtesy of Professor Roger Conaway and Professor Dan Curtis.

[9]Outline from speech to the Chicago Council on Foreign Relations by Senator John C. Culver. Reprinted by permission.

[10]"The Silent Killer" by Todd Ambs. Reprinted from *Winning Orations* (1980) by special arrangement with the Interstate Oratorical Association, Larry Schnoor, Executive Secretary, Mankato State University, Mankato, Minnesota.

PROBLEMS AND PROBES

CHAPTER REPORT   Social-scientific research relative to persuasion abounds in scholarly journals; each new issue of such journals as the *Quarterly Journal of Speech, Communication Monographs, Journal of Communication, Communication Research,* and *Human Communication Research* contains studies extending and modifying our knowledge of persuasive processes. "State-of-the-art" essays, that is, essays which attempt to inventory what we think we know (or do not know) about persuasion, therefore, are often necessary. Pick a communication variable—say, "source credibility," "communicator style," "organizational patterns and persuasive effects," "self-disclosure and persuasive effects," "measurements of attitudes and attitude-change"—and write a "state-of-the-art" essay on it. To find scholarly articles dealing with your topic, consult the footnotes and "Suggestions For Further Reading" in this book, the bibliographies of persuasion textbooks we have cited earlier (e.g., Simons, Bettinghaus, Andersen, and Zimbardo/Ebbesen/Maslach), and current listings in the index to *Psychological Abstracts* or the *Social Science Index*. Read several of the articles you have found, and write an essay summarizing our current state of knowledge regarding your topic.

1. Make a list of ten of your personal beliefs or convictions. Which items in this list would you say constitute claims of fact? which claims of value? and which claims of policy? Explain your choices.

2. Assume you have been asked to deliver a lecture on the importance of a strong national defense (or another topic of interest to you). First, outline and analyze the speech as a claim of fact. How will the attitude of your audience affect the structure and appeal of the speech? Next, outline and analyze the same speech topic as a claim of value and as a claim of policy. What factors do you consider as you prepare each of these speeches? Do you see the importance of audience analysis as it relates to each of these speeches?

3. Analyze the differences between an appeal to persuade and an appeal to actuate in relation to the essential features of these appeals (i.e., adaptation to psychological states, change by degrees, saliency, credibility) for each of the following situations: *(a)* you want your parents to stop smoking; *(b)* you try to convince your best friend not to drop out of school; *(c)* you want a stranger to donate money to the American Cancer Society. Why do your appeals differ among the above situations? Which factors are the most difficult to analyze in each of the above situations and why?

4. Comment on this statement: "Most people act out of desire rather than reason; they only use reason to justify to themselves what they want to do anyway." Use the remark to formulate at least three useful principles for speeches to actuate.

 ## ORAL ACTIVITIES

1. Build and present to the class a five- to seven-minute persuasive speech designed to win acceptance for a claim of fact, value, or policy. Follow carefully the steps in the motivated sequence appropriate to the type of speech chosen. Make sure that you have an abundance of appropriate facts and data, that your reasoning is sound, and that your major ideas are cast in a form that will motivate your listeners. In developing your remarks, keep in mind the probable attitude of the audience toward your claim or proposal, and make such adaptations as may be necessary.

2. Present a five- to eight-minute speech, the purpose of which is to persuade members of your speech class to take a recommended action. Show that a problem or situation needing remedy *actually* exists. Show your listeners why *they* (and not someone else) should be concerned, and why you think a specific action

on their part will be a concrete, influential move toward a remedy. On a future "check-up" day, see how many members of the audience actually have taken the recommended action. For example, you may urge an audience to *sign a petition* proposing that graduating seniors should be excused from their final examinations or that the college should establish a cooperative bookstore. Or, you may ask members of your class to *write letters* or send mailgrams to *their congressional representatives* urging that all election campaigns should be financed publicly or that Bill X should be passed. (Be sure to tell them who their representatives are and where they can be reached.) Or, you can ask members to *attend a meeting* of a newly organized campus group to *participate* in an activity such as giving blood during the next visit of the Red Cross Bloodmobile.

3. As a small group, examine closely the texts of several political speeches, advertisements for goods and services, and brochures describing social organizations or clubs. You may also use your speech journal as a source. Category by category (speeches, advertisements, organizational brochures), list the motives appealed to in each type of persuasive discourse. Upon critical inspection, do you find any common patterns in these motive appeals? Do politics, business, and social services each appeal to certain motives more often than others? Do these three types of persuasion appeal principally to one or two levels in Maslow's prepotent hierarchy; and, if so, what do these facts lead you to conclude about each type of persuasion?

 ## SUGGESTIONS FOR FURTHER READING

Erwin P. Bettinghaus, *Persuasive Communication,* 3rd ed. (New York: Holt, Rinehart & Winston, 1980).

Ernest G. Bormann, *Communication Theory* (New York: Holt, Rinehart & Winston, 1980), Chapter 1, "The Development of Contemporary Communication Theory."

Stephen Littlejohn, "A Bibliography of Studies Related to Variables of Source Credibility," in *Bibliographical Annual in Speech Communication: 1971,* ed. Ned A. Shearer (New York: Speech Communication Association, 1972), pp. 1–40.

Werner J. Severin and James W. Tankard, Jr., *Communication Theories: Origins Methods Uses.* Humanistic Studies in The Communication Arts (New York: Hastings House, Publishers, 1979), Chapter 12, "Beginnings of Attitude Change Research," and Chapter 13, "Further Developments in Attitude Change."

Philip G. Zimbardo, Ebbe B. Ebbesen, and Christina Maslach, *Influencing Attitudes and Changing Beliefs,* 2nd ed. (Reading, MA: Addison-Wesley Publishing Company, 1977).

18

Speeches on Special Occasions

Sensitivity to audience expectations and situational demands is a requisite in any speech setting. In seeking to engender understanding or conviction, you will make decisions regarding the structure of your speeches, the selection of language, and the choice of illustrating or supporting materials. Your decisions should be guided by your knowledge of the implicit *communication rules* (see Chapter 1) that govern what specific circumstances require.

The impact of these underlying rules is most apparent in specialized speech situations. Our society has evolved rules that affect communication behavior in such settings as presenting or accepting awards, introducing speakers, and delivering eulogies. You know that the speaker at a funeral service should not violate implicit rules governing the situation by speaking ill of the dead or by conducting the ceremony in an insincere and indifferent manner (e.g., forgetting the name of the deceased). In addition to adhering to these implicit rules, the speaker must also recognize that funeral services, because of their recurring nature, suggest themes that all such events should address in order to satisfy audience expectations. In this instance, the funeral service should accomplish four tasks: acknowledge the fact of death, ease the audience's realization of its own mortality, move the audience's relationship with the deceased from the present to the past tense, and fashion a new relationship for the future based on memories of the person.[1] The speaker who fails to address these four themes (and the order suggests the structure for the funeral sermon) or violates one of the implicit rules provides far less than the audience expects as a "fitting" response to the occasion.[2]

Similarly, when you accept an award, you are expected to address the themes that are commonly expressed in such situations and to be sensitive to the rules governing your communication behavior. Thus, expressing humility ("this award was possible because of teamwork") and appreciativeness ("I am truly grateful for the recognition") addresses themes that audiences have come to expect in such circumstances. Violating expectations by appearing arrogant ("I always knew I was better than anybody else") would discredit you in the eyes of your audience. What you may *feel* about such an award and what you can *say* in accepting it may be quite different. Even if the audience agrees with your feelings, expressing sentiments in this fashion would be considered unbecoming; your status as a deserving individual would be damaged by your revealing an insensitivity to socially approved customs that apply to such events.

Although there are innumerable special occasions we could consider in this chapter, we shall limit ourselves to some representative, commonly recurring types: speeches of introduction, speeches of tribute, speeches of nomination, speeches of good will, and speeches to entertain. We shall consider each of these special types of speeches briefly, noting the *purpose* of the speech, the *manner* in which it usually is delivered, the kinds of *ideas* it contains, and the principles by which it is *organized*.

Types of Special Occasion Speeches

Speeches of Introduction

Speeches of introduction usually are given by the person who arranged the program or by the chairperson or president of the group to be addressed. Sometimes, however, they are presented by another person who, because of personal association or professional interests, is especially well acquainted with the featured speaker.

Purpose and manner of speaking • The *purpose* of a speech of introduction is, of course, to create in the audience a desire to hear the speaker you are introducing. Everything else must be subordinated to this aim. You are not being called upon to make a speech yourself or air your own views on the subject. You are only the speaker's *advance agent;* your job is to sell him or her to the audience. This task carries a two-fold responsibility: (1) You must arouse the listeners' curiosity about the speaker and/or subject, thus making it easier for the speaker to get the attention of the audience. (2) You must do all that you reasonably can to generate audience respect for the speaker, thereby increasing the likelihood that listeners will respond favorably to the message that is presented.

When giving a speech of introduction, your *manner of speaking* should be suited to the nature of the occasion, your familiarity with the speaker, and the speaker's prestige. If you were introducing a justice of the United States Supreme Court, for instance, it would hardly be appropriate to poke fun at him. Nor would this approach be tactful if the speaker were a stranger to you, or the occasion serious and dignified. On the other hand, if you are presenting an old friend to a group of associates on an informal occasion, a solemn and dignified manner would be equally out of place.

Formulating the content of the speech of introduction • The better known and more respected a speaker is, the shorter your introduction can be. The less well known he or she is, the more you will need to arouse interest in the subject or build up the speaker's prestige. In general, however, observe these principles:

Talk about the speaker • Who is he? What is her position in business, education, sports, or government? What experiences has he had that qualify him to speak on the announced subject? Build up the speaker's identity, tell what he knows or what she has done, but do not praise his or her ability as a speaker. Let speakers *demonstrate* their skills.

Emphasize the importance of the speaker's subject • For example, in introducing a speaker who is going to talk about the oil industry, you might say: "All of us drive automobiles in which we use the products made from petroleum. A knowledge of the way these products are manufactured and marketed is, therefore, certain to be valuable to our understanding and perhaps to our pocketbooks."

Stress the appropriateness of the subject or of the speaker • If your town is considering a program of renewal and revitalization, a speech by a city planner is likely to be timely and well received. If an organization is marking an anniversary, the founder may be one of the speakers. Reference to the positions these persons hold is obviously in order and serves to relate the speaker more closely to the audience.

Organizing the speech of introduction • The necessity of a carefully planned introduction depends on the amount of time available and the need to elaborate on the topic's importance or the speaker's qualifications. A simple introductory statement, "Ladies and Gentlemen, the President of the United States," obviously requires little in the way of organization. For longer, more involved introductions, consider how much attention should be devoted to the background and expertise of the speaker and to the interest, importance, or urgency of the topic. A good way to start is to make an observation or expression designed to capture the attention of the audience and proceed to develop one or both of the above topics as the circumstances warrant. Remember that your introduction should not be longer than the speech it introduces—keep biographical details, personal allusions to your involvement with the speaker or topic, and details of the topic itself to a minimum. In other words, be brief. The virtues of an excellent introduction, displaying tact, brevity, sincerity, and enthusiasm, are evident in the following introduction prepared by Barbara Miller.

● Introducing A Classmate[3]

Barbara Miller

We all have come to know Greg Latham in this class. When we introduced ourselves during the first week of class, you learned that Greg was raised on an Illinois farm, later moving to Chicago when farming became a losing proposition for the five members of his family. Greg's dual background—rural and urban—has obviously affected him strongly, as you can tell from various topics he's addressed in speeches to us. The farmer in him emerged when he delivered his first speech, the one classifying various types of pesticides. He changed into a city slicker, however, in his visual-aids speech—the clever battleplan for making your way through and around Chicago's expressway and tollway systems. Three weeks ago, in the group discussion on health care, he once again put on his straw hat and bib overalls, speaking out strongly for the need to increase health care facilities in rural areas. /1

Today, we will see Greg combine his double background. If you followed the state legislature's recent public hearings, if you read the front page of *The State Journal* last week, or if you saw ABC's special report on foreign investments in American land two nights ago, the term "agribusiness" became a part of your vocabulary. Agribusiness, which involves the consolidation of farming operations within corporate structures, may well profoundly affect each of us within a decade. Greg this morning will trace those direct effects upon your daily life in his speech, "Agribusiness: Panacea or Pandora's Box?" /2

Speeches of Tribute

As a speaker you may be called upon to pay tribute to another person's qualities or achievements. Such occasions range from the awarding of a trophy after an athletic contest to delivering a eulogy at a memorial service. Sometimes tributes are paid to an entire group or class of people—for example, teachers, soldiers, or mothers—rather than to an individual. Frequently, awards are presented to groups or to individuals for outstanding or meritorious service. In such cases, public tribute often is paid, and the presentation calls for appropriate remarks from a speaker. The following typically require a speech of tribute:

Farewells • In general, speeches of farewell fall into one of three subcategories: (1) When people retire or leave one organization to join another or when persons who are admired leave the community where they have lived, the enterprise in which they have worked, or the office they have held, public appreciation of their fellowship and accomplishments may be expressed by associates or colleagues in speeches befitting the circumstances. (2) Or the individual who is departing may use the occasion to present a farewell address in which she voices her gratitude for the opportunities, consideration, and warmth afforded her by co-workers and, perhaps, calls upon them to carry on the traditions and long-range goals which characterize the office or the enterprise. In both of these situations, of course, verbal tributes are being paid. What distinguishes them, basically, is whether the retiree or departing one is *speaking* or is being *spoken about*. (3) More rarely, when individuals—because of disagreements, policy-differences or organizational stresses, for example—decide to resign or sever important or long-standing associations with a business or governmental unit, they may elect to use their farewell messages to present publicly the basis of the disagreement and the factors prompting the resignation and departure.

Dedications • Buildings, monuments, or parks may be constructed or set aside to honor a worthy cause or to commemorate a person, a group, a significant movement, an historic event, or the like. At their dedication, the speaker

A fitting occasion for a speech of dedication was the unveiling of "Chicago," a 40-foot-high commemorative sculpture by the Spanish artist, Joan Miro.

says something appropriate about the purpose to be served by whatever it is that is being set aside and about the personage(s), event, or occasion thus commemorated.

The following remarks were made by Mr. Harold Haydon at the unveiling of "Nuclear Energy," a bronze sculpture created by Henry Moore and placed on the campus of the University of Chicago to commemorate the achievement of Enrico Fermi and his associates in releasing the first self-sustaining nuclear chain reaction at Stagg Field on December 2, 1942. The unveiling took place during the commemoration of the twenty-fifth anniversary of that event. Mr. Haydon was Associate Professor of Art at the University and is presently art critic for the *Chicago Sun-Times*. By combining specific references to the sculptor and his work with more general observations concerning the function of art and humankind's hopes and fears in a nuclear age, Mr. Haydon produced a dignified and thoughtful address, well suited to the demands of the occasion.

● ## The Testimony of Sculpture[4]

Harold Haydon

Since very ancient times men have set up a marker, or designated some stone or tree, to hold the memory of a deed or happening far longer than any man's lifetime. Some of these memorial objects have lived longer than man's collective memory, so that we now ponder the meaning of a monument, or wonder whether some great stone is a record of human action, or whether instead it is only a natural object.   /1

There is something that makes us want a solid presence, a substantial form, to be the tangible touchstone of the mind, designed and made to endure as witness or record, as if we mistrusted that seemingly frail yet amazingly tough skein of words and symbols that serves memory and which, despite being mere ink blots and punch-holes, nonetheless succeeds in preserving the long human tradition, firmer than any stone, tougher than any metal. /2

We still choose stone or metal to be our tangible reminders, and for these solid, enduring forms we turn to the men who are carvers of stone and moulders of metal, for it is they who have given lasting form to our myths through the centuries. /3

One of these men is here today, a great one, and he has given his skill and the sure touch of his mind and eye to create for this nation, this city, and this university a marker that may stand here for centuries, even for a millennium, as a mute yet eloquent testament to a turning point in time when man took charge of a new material world hitherto beyond his capability. /4

As this bronze monument remembers an event and commemorates an achievement, it has something unique to say about the spiritual meaning of the achievement, for it is the special power of art to convey feeling and stir profound emotion, to touch us in ways that are beyond the reach of reason. /5

Nuclear energy, for which the sculpture is named, is a magnet for conflicting emotions, some of which inevitably will attach to the bronze form; it will harbor or repel emotion according to the states of mind of those who view the sculpture. In its brooding presence some will feel the joy and sorrow of recollection, some may dread the uncertain future, and yet others will thrill to the thought of magnificent achievements that lie ahead. The test of the sculpture's greatness as a human document, the test of any work of art, will be its capacity to evoke a response and the quality of that response. /6

One thing most certain is that this sculpture by Henry Moore is not an inert object. It is a live thing, and somewhat strange like every excellent beauty, to be known to us only in time and never completely. Its whole meaning can be known only to the ever-receding future, as each succeeding generation reinterprets according to its own vision and experience. /7

By being here in a public place the sculpture "Nuclear Energy" becomes a part of Chicago, and the sculptor an honored citizen, known not just to artists and collectors of art, but to everyone who pauses here in the presence of the monument, because the artist is inextricably part of what he has created, immortal through his art. /8

With this happy conjunction today of art and science, of great artist and great occasion, we may hope to reach across the generations, across the centuries, speaking through enduring sculpture of our time, our hopes, and fears, perhaps more eloquently than we know. Some works of art have meaning for all mankind and so defy time, persisting through all hazards; the monument to the atomic age should be one of these. /9

Memorial services • Services to pay public honor to the dead usually include a speech of tribute or *eulogy*. Ceremonies of this kind may honor a famous person (or persons) and be held years after his or her death. Witness, for example, the many speeches paying tribute to Abraham Lincoln. More often, however, a eulogy honors someone personally known to the audience and only recently deceased.

At other times, a memorial—particularly to a famous person—honors certain of the qualities that person stands for. In that case, the speaker uses the memorial to renew and reinforce the audience's adherence to certain ideals, compelling it to think about problems facing humanity in general. The following brief, but vividly phrased, remarks eulogize Wernher von Braun, renowned scientist and space pioneer. The guiding genius behind Germany's "buzz bomb" and rocket weaponry in World War II, von Braun came to this country when hostilities ended, became an American citizen, and was a major directing force behind the U.S. space program, which ultimately landed the first men on the moon. Written and presented by Eric Sevareid on *CBS Evening News*, June 17, 1977, the commentary pays tribute to von Braun's dream while at the same time recognizing the country's pressing technological and social problems. In a number of respects, it is an excellent example of a eulogy.

● Eulogy for Wernher von Braun[5]

Eric Sevareid

A generation ago, the Allied military, using the old-fashioned airplane, did their best to kill the German, his associates, and their new-fashioned rockets, which were killing the people in London. Yesterday, Wernher von Braun, American citizen, died peacefully in George Washington's hometown of Alexandria, Virginia. /1

Without this man, Hitler would not have held out as long as he did; without him, Americans would not have got to the moon as soon as they did. /2

Counting up the moral balance sheet for this man's life would be a difficult exercise. The same could be said for the Wright brothers. Perhaps the exercise is meaningless. Airplanes would have come anyway from someone, somewhere, and so would modern rockets. And what was done with these instruments would have been equally beyond the control of the individuals who first made them work. /3

There's always a dream to begin with, and the dream is always benign. Charles Lindbergh, as a young man, saw the airplane, not only as an instrument to liberate man from the plodding earth, but as a force for peacefully uniting the human race through faster communication and the common adventure. Now its benefits are measured against its role in returning warfare to the savagery of the Middle Ages, burning whole cities with their occupants. /4

And rockets are now the easiest instrument for sending the ultimate atomic weapon against any spot on the globe. They've also put men into space; and von Braun, like Lindbergh with the upper atmosphere, saw goodness in that. He said once, when men manning an orbital station can view our planet as a planet among planets, on that day fratricidal war will be banished from the star on which we live. /5

Lindbergh was wrong about aircraft in the atmosphere; there's no reason to believe that von Braun was right about spacecraft in space. /6

Everything in space, von Braun said, obeys the laws of physics. If you know these laws and obey them, space will treat you kindly. The difficulty is that man brings the laws of his own nature into space. The issue is how man treats man. The problem does not lie in outer space, but where it's always been: on terra firma in inner man. /7

Purpose and manner of speaking for the tribute speech • The *purpose* of a speech of tribute is, of course, to create in those who hear it a sense of appreciation for the traits or accomplishments of the person or group to whom tribute is paid. If you cause your audience to realize the essential worth or importance of that person or group, you will have succeeded. But you may go further than this. You may, by honoring a person, arouse deeper devotion to the cause he or she represents. Did he give distinguished service to his community? Then strive to enhance the audience's civic pride and sense of service. Was she a friend to youth? Then try to arouse the feeling that working to provide opportunities for young people deserves the audience's support. Create a desire in your listeners to emulate the person or persons honored. Make them want to develop the same virtues, to demonstrate a like devotion.

When delivering a speech of tribute, suit the *manner* of speaking to the circumstances. A farewell banquet usually blends an atmosphere of merriment with a spirit of sincere regret. Dignity and formality are, on the whole, characteristic of memorial services, the unveiling of monuments, and similar dedicatory ceremonies. Regardless of the general tone of the occasion, however, in a speech of tribute avoid high-sounding phrases, bombastic oratory, and obvious "oiliness." These hollow elements will quickly dampen or destroy its effect. A simple, honest expression of admiration presented in clear and unadorned language is best.

Formulating the content of speeches of tribute • Frequently, in a speech of tribute a speaker attempts to itemize all the accomplishments of the honored person or group. This weakens the impact because, in trying to cover everything, it emphasizes nothing. Plan, instead, to focus your remarks, as follows:

Stress dominant traits. If you are paying tribute to a person, select a few aspects of her personality which are especially likeable or praiseworthy, and relate incidents from her life or work to illustrate these distinguishing qualities.

Mention only outstanding achievements. Pick out only a few of the person's or group's most notable accomplishments. Tell about them in detail to show how important they were. Let your speech say, "Here is what this person (or group) has done; see how such actions have contributed to the well-being of our business or community."

Give special emphasis to the influence of the person or group. Show the effect that the behavior of the person or group has had on others. Many times, the importance of people's lives can be demonstrated not so much by any traits or material accomplishments as by the influence they exerted on associates.

Organizing the speech of tribute • Ordinarily you will have little difficulty in getting people to listen to a speech of tribute. The audience probably already

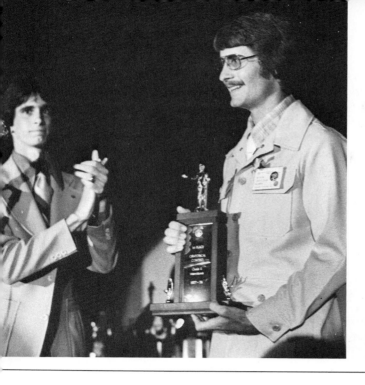

Both the presentation of and the acceptance of an award, such as this trophy, provide an appropriate opportunity for a speech of tribute and for an acceptance speech.

knows and admires the person or group about whom you are to speak, and listeners are curious to learn what you are going to say concerning the individual or individuals being honored. Consider the following steps in preparing your speech: First, direct the attention of the audience toward those characteristics or accomplishments which you consider most important. There are three commonly used ways to do this: (a) Make a straightforward, sincere statement of these commendable traits or achievements or of the influence they have had upon others. (b) Relate one or more instances which vividly illustrate your point. (c) Relate an incident which shows the problems faced by your subject.

Second, were there obstacles or difficulties that the person or group being honored had to overcome? If so, dramatize the impact of the accomplishment by noting these problems and their successful resolution. Or you might place the specific achievement in a broader context by focusing on organizational problems which the person or group had to meet, or—in a still larger sense—the problems of society that their accomplishments helped solve. Thus, you might describe the extent of the air pollution problem in a large city before paying tribute to the individuals who developed and enforced an effective pollution-control plan.

Third, develop the substance of the tribute itself—relate a few incidents to show how the personal or public problems you have outlined were met and surmounted. In doing this, be sure to demonstrate at least one of the following: (a) how certain admirable traits—vision, courage, and tenacity, for example—made it possible to deal successfully with these problems; (b) how remarkable the achievements were in the face of the obstacles encountered; (c) how great the influence of the achievement was on others.

Fourth, synthesize the attributes of the person or group in a vivid, composite picture which summarizes the accomplishment and its significance. It will help you to achieve this if you: *(a) Introduce an apt quotation.* Try to find a bit of poetry or a literary passage which fits the person or group to whom you are paying tribute, and introduce it here. *(b) Draw a word picture of a world (community, business, or profession) inhabited by such persons.* Suggest how much better things would be if more people had similar qualities. *(c) Suggest the loss which the absence of the individual or group will bring.* Show vividly how much he, she, or they will be missed. Be specific: "It's going to seem mighty strange to walk into Barbara's office and not find her there ready to listen, ready to advise, ready to help." In closing, connect the theme of the speech with the occasion on which it is presented. Thus, in a *eulogy,* suggest that the best tribute the audience can pay the person being honored is to live as that person did or to carry on what he or she has begun. In a *dedication* speech, suggest the appropriateness of dedicating this monument, building, or plaque, to such a person or group, and express the hope that it will inspire others to emulate their accomplishments. At the close of a *farewell* speech, extend to the departing person or persons the best wishes of those you represent, and express a determination to carry on what they have begun. Or, if you yourself are saying farewell, call upon those who remain to carry on what you and your associates have started.

By adapting the foregoing principles and procedures to the particular situation in which you find yourself, you should be able to devise a useful framework upon which to build a speech of tribute. To complete your speech, however, you will need to fill out this plan with vivid illustrative materials and appropriate motivational appeals.

Speeches of Nomination

The speech to nominate contains elements found in both speeches of introduction and speeches of tribute. Here, too, your main *purpose* is to review the accomplishments of some person whom you admire. This review, however, instead of standing as an end in itself (tribute) or of creating a desire to hear the person (introduction), is made to contribute to an actuative goal—obtaining the listeners' endorsement of the person as a nominee for an elective office.

In a speech of nomination, your *manner of speaking* generally will be less formal and dignified than when you are giving a speech of tribute. It should, however, be businesslike and energetic. In general, the content of the speech will follow the pattern of a speech of tribute; but the illustrations and supporting materials should be chosen with the intent of showing the nominee's qualifications for the office in question. Although the speech to nominate has certain special requirements, fundamentally it is a speech to actuate. Organize it, therefore, as follows: Begin with a statement of your intent—to rise to place a name in nomination. Second, describe the qualifications required by the job, the problems to be dealt with, and the personal qualities needed in the individual to be selected. Next, name your candidate and state this person's qualifications for the position—describe the individual's training, experience, success in similar positions and personal qualities. Your objective is to show why you believe your nominee will be an excellent choice for the position. Finally, urge audience endorsement as you formally place the person's name in nomination.

An alternative to this pattern is to begin with the name of the nominee. This is an acceptable practice if the audience is already favorably disposed toward the nominee. However, if your choice is likely to stir opposition, it may be wiser to establish first the qualities needed for the position and then, in naming your candidate, indicate how this nominee's qualifications will satisfy the requirements.

Not all nominations, of course, need to be supported by a long speech. Frequently, especially in small groups and clubs, the person nominated is well known to the audience, and his or her qualifications are already appreciated. Under such circumstances, all that is required is the simple statement: "Mr. Chairman, given her obvious and well-known services to our club in the past, I nominate Marilyn Cannell for the office of treasurer."

Speeches to Create Good Will

The fourth type of speech we will discuss is the speech to create good will. While *ostensibly* the purpose of this special type of speech is to inform an audience about a product, service, operation, or procedure, *actually* it is to enhance the listeners' appreciation of a particular institution, practice, or profession—to make the audience more favorably disposed toward it. Thus, the good-will speech is also a mixed or hybrid type. Basically, it is informative, but—at the same time—has a strong, underlying persuasive purpose.

Typical situations requiring speeches for good will • There are numerous situations in which good-will speeches are appropriate, but the three which follow may be considered typical:

Luncheon meetings of civic and service clubs • Gatherings of this kind, being semisocial in nature and having a built-in atmosphere of congeniality, offer excellent opportunities for presenting speeches of good will. Members of such groups—prominent men and women from many walks of life—are interested in civic affairs and in the workings of other people's businesses or professions.

Educational programs • School authorities, as well as leaders of clubs and religious organizations, often arrange educational programs for their patrons and members. At such meetings, speakers are asked to talk about the occupations in which they are engaged and to explain to the young people in the audience the opportunities offered and the training required in their respective fields. By use of illustrations and tactful references, a speaker may—while providing the desired information—also create good will for his or her company or profession.

Special demonstration programs • Special programs are frequently presented by government agencies, university extension departments, and business organizations. For example, a wholesale food company may send a representative to a meeting of nutritionists to explain the food values present in various kinds of canned meat or fish products, and to demonstrate new ways of preparing or

If the audience listening to an after-dinner speaker seems bored or distracted, the speaker is not accomplishing the purpose of creating good will for the subject of his or her message.

serving them. Although such a speech would be primarily informative, the speaker could win good will indirectly by showing that his or her company desires to increase customer satisfaction with its products and services.

Manner of speaking in the speech for good will • Three qualities—modesty, tolerance, and good humor—characterize the manner of speaking appropriate for good-will speeches. Although you will be talking about your business or vocation and trying to make it seem important to the audience, you should never boast or brag. In giving a speech of this type, let the facts speak for themselves. Moreover, show a tolerant attitude toward others, especially competitors. The airline representative, for instance, who violently attacks trucking companies and bus lines is likely to gain ill will rather than good. Finally, exercise good humor. The good-will speech is not for the zealot or the crusader. Take the task more genially. Don't try to force acceptance of your ideas; instead, show so much enthusiasm and good feeling that your listeners will respond spontaneously and favorably to the information you are providing.

Formulating the content of the speech for good will • In selecting materials for a good-will speech, keep these suggestions in mind: *Present novel and interesting facts about your subject.* Make your listeners feel that you are giving them an inside look into your company or organization. Avoid talking about what they already know; concentrate on new developments and on facts or services that are not generally known. *Show a relationship between your subject and the lives* *of the members of your audience.* Make your listeners see the importance of your organization or profession to their personal safety, success, or happiness. Finally, *offer a definite service.* This offer may take the form of an invitation to the audience to visit your office or shop, to help them with their problems, or to answer questions or send brochures.

Organizing the speech for good will • Because of its close relationship to speeches to inform and to persuade, the organization of the materials we have just described can be discussed in terms of the motivated sequence. Each step is fleshed out in the following discussion:

Attention step • The purpose of the beginning of your speech will be to establish a friendly feeling and to arouse the audience's curiosity about your profession or the institution you represent. You may gain the first of these objectives by a tactful compliment to the group or a reference to the occasion that has brought you together. Follow this with one or two unusual facts or illustrations concerning the enterprise you represent. For instance: "Before we began manufacturing television parts, the Lash Electric Company confined its business to the making of clock radios that would never wear out. We succeeded so well that we almost went bankrupt! That was only fifteen years ago. Today our export trade alone is over one hundred times as large as our total annual domestic business was in those earlier days. It may interest you to know how this change took place." In brief, you must find some way to arouse your listeners' curiosity about your organization.

Need step • Point out certain problems facing your audience—problems with which the institution, profession, or agency you represent is vitally concerned. For example, if you represent a radio or television station, show the relationship of good communications to the social and economic health of the community. By so doing, you will establish common ground with your audience. Ordinarily the need step will be brief and will consist largely of suggestions developed with only an occasional illustration. However, if you intend to propose that your listeners join in acting to meet a common problem, the need step will require fuller development.

Satisfaction step • The meat of a good-will speech will be in the satisfaction step. Here is the place to tell your audience about your institution, profession, or business and to explain what it is or what it does. You can do this in at least three ways: (1) *Relate interesting events in its history.* Pick events which will demonstrate its humanity, its reliability, and its importance to the community, to the country, or to the world of nations. (2) *Explain how your organization or profession operates.* Pick out those things that are unusual or that may contain beneficial suggestions for your audience. This method often helps impress upon your listeners the size and efficiency of your operation or enterprise. (3) *Describe the services your organization renders.* Explain its products; point out how widely they are used; discuss the policies by which management is guided—especially those which you think your audience will agree with or admire. Tell what your firm or profession has done for the community: people employed, purchases made locally, assistance with community projects, improvements in health, education, or public safety. Do not boast, but make sure that your listeners realize the value of your work *to them*.

Visualization step • Your object here is to crystalize the good will that the presentation of information in the satisfaction step initially has created. Do this by looking to the future. Make a rapid survey of the points you have covered or combine them in a single story or illustration. Or, to approach this step from the opposite direction, picture for your listeners the loss that would result if the organization or profession you represent should leave the community or cease to exist. Be careful, however, not to leave the impression that there is any real danger that this will occur.

Action step • Here, you make your offer of service to the audience—for example, invite the group to visit your office or plant, or point out the willingness of your organization to assist in some common enterprise. As is true of every type of speech, the content and organization of the speech for good will sometimes need to be especially adapted to meet the demands of the subject or occasion. You should, however, never lose sight of the central purpose for which you speak: to show your audience that the work which you do or the service which you perform is of value to them—that in some way it makes their lives happier, more productive, interesting, or secure.

Speeches to Entertain

To entertain, amuse, or divert is frequently the purpose of an after-dinner speech, but talks of other kinds also may have the enjoyment of the listener as their principal end. Often a travel lecture, although it also presents a great deal of factual material, has as its overall purpose entertaining an audience with exciting or amusing tales of adventures in a strange land. Club meetings, class reunions, and similar gatherings of friends and associates also provide occasions for the sharing of fond memories. In these situations, the speaker may depend chiefly on humor, interesting anecdotes, or curious bits of information.

Although humor—often in the form of exaggerated descriptions, puns, irony, unexpected turns of phrase, jokes, and the like—is usually a primary element in a speech to entertain, such a speech is more than a string of unrelated one-liners. One story or observation should lead naturally into the next, and all material should serve to bring out a central point around which the speech is built. Use stories and anecdotes to develop a common theme—some sentiment of loyalty or appreciation for the group addressed or even a serious thought concerning your subject. Thus, you need to choose illustrations and comparisons, carefully connecting them to your central idea.

When arranging speech materials mainly to entertain, develop a series of illustrations, short quotations or quips, and stories, each following the other in fairly rapid succession and each bearing upon the central theme. As a point of departure, at least, consider building a speech to entertain in the following steps:

1. Relate a story or anecdote, present an illustration, or quote an appropriate verse.

2. State the essential idea or point of view implied by your opening remarks.
3. Follow with a series of additional stories, anecdotes, or illustrations that amplify or illuminate your central idea. Arrange these supporting materials so that they are thematically or tonally coherent.
4. Close with a striking or novel restatement of the central point you have developed. As in Step 1, you may use a bit of poetry, a striking quotation, or even a brief anecdote to provide the necessary "clincher" and sum up your speech as a whole.

By organizing your materials in this way, you not only will provide your listeners with entertainment, but you will also help them to remember your central idea.

The following speech illustrates the four steps we have described. In addition, it demonstrates how light and humorous materials may be used to develop a potentially useful thought.

● A Case for Optimism[6]

Douglas Martin

I'm sure you have heard the verse that runs:

Poem embodying contrast used as opening

'Twixt optimist and pessimist
The difference is droll:
The optimist sees the doughnut,
The pessimist, the hole.   /1

Statement of central idea

The longer I live, the more convinced I am of the truth of this poem. Life, like a doughnut, may seem full, rich, and enjoyable, or it may seem as empty as the hole in the middle. To the pessimist, the optimist seems foolish. But who is foolish—the one who sees the doughnut or the one who sees the hole?   /2

Contrast

Somebody else pointed out the difference between an optimist and a pessimist this way: An optimist looks at an oyster and expects a pearl; a pessimist looks at an oyster and expects ptomaine poisoning. Even if the pessimist is right, which I doubt, he probably won't enjoy himself either before or after he proves it. But the optimist is happy because he always is expecting pearls.   /3

Illustration

Pessimists are easy to recognize. They are the ones who go around asking "What's good about it?" when someone says "Good morning." If they would look around, they would see *something* good, as did the optimistic merchant whose store was robbed. The day after the robbery a sympathetic friend asked about the loss. "Lose much?" he wanted to know. "Some," said the merchant, "but then it would have been worse if the robbers had got in the night before. You see, yesterday I just finished marking everything down 20 percent."   /4

Illustration	There is another story about the happy-go-lucky shoemaker who left the gas heater in his shop turned on overnight and upon arriving in the morning struck a match to light it. There was a terrific explosion, and the shoemaker was blown out through the door almost to the middle of the street. A passerby, who rushed up to help, inquired if he were injured. The shoemaker got up slowly and looked back at the shop, which by now was burning briskly. "No, I ain't hurt," he said, "but I sure got out just in time, didn't I?" /5
Testimony (pro and con)	Some writers have ridiculed that kind of outlook. You may recall the fun Voltaire made of optimism in *Candide:* "Optimism," he said, "is a mania for maintaining that all is well when things are going badly." A later writer, James Branch Cabell, quipped: "The optimist proclaims that we live in the best of all possible worlds; the pessimist fears this is true." These writers, I suppose, couldn't resist the urge to make light of optimists; but I, for one, refuse to take *them* seriously. I like the remark by Keith Preston, literary critic and journalist: "There's as much bunk among the busters as among the boosters." /6
Beginning the summary	Optimism, rather than the cynicism of Voltaire, is the philosophy I like to hear preached. There was a little old lady who complained about the weather. "But, Melissa," said her friend, "awful weather is better than no weather." So quit complaining, I say, and start cheering; there is always something to cheer about. And stop expecting the worst. An optimist cleans his glasses before he eats his grapefruit. /7
Restatement	Give in to optimism; don't fight it. Remember the doughnut. And, as Elbert Hubbard advised:

> As you travel on through life, brother,
> Whatever be your goal,
> Keep your eye upon the doughnut
> And not upon the hole. /8

Speeches of introduction, tribute, nomination, good will, and entertainment represent but five of the many *speeches for special occasions.* As we noted at the beginning of this chapter, the themes of each speech are often predetermined by the social customs and communication rules of the society or community. Hence, your sensitivity to the expectations of your audience toward the purpose of the speech, the manner of its delivery, and the organization of its themes will help ensure a fitting response—one that does justice to the communication rules implicit in the situation or occasion.

REFERENCE NOTES

[1]For a discussion of these themes and others unique to recurring situations, see Kathleen Jamieson, *Critical Anthology of Public Speeches* (Chicago: Science Research Associates, 1978).

[2]See Lloyd Bitzer, "The Rhetorical Situation," *Philosophy & Rhetoric,* 1 (Winter 1968): 1–14.

[3]A speech of introduction given at The University of Iowa, winter term, 1978. Reprinted with the permission of Ms. Miller.

[4]"The Testimony of Sculpture," by Harold Haydon. Copyright © 1968, *The University of Chicago Magazine*. Reprinted with permission from *The University of Chicago Magazine*.

[5]"Eulogy for Wernher von Braun" by Eric Sevareid. Copyright © 1977 by CBS, Inc. Reprinted by permission of the Harold Matson Company, Inc.

[6]Based in part on material taken from *Friendly Speeches* (Cleveland: National Reference Library).

PROBLEMS AND PROBES

CHAPTER REPORT In what way do occasions create special constraints on what a speaker can or must do to satisfy an audience? In developing a response to this question, read Kathleen Jamieson, *Critical Anthology of Public Speeches* (Chicago: SRA, 1978). Present your conclusion in a written essay or as part of a class discussion on the role of constraints in shaping the form and character of speeches.

1. Prepare for delivery in class a five-minute good-will speech on behalf of a campus organization (or some national organization, such as the Boy Scouts or YWCA) to which you belong. Be prepared to answer questions after your speech is completed.

2. Prepare a five-minute speech paying tribute to:
    a. A man or woman important in national or world history.
    b. A group of volunteers who participated in a successful (or unsuccessful) charity drive.
    c. Someone in your home community or college who, though never famous, contributed in a significant way to the success, well-being, or happiness of many others.
    d. A group of scientists who have just completed an important project.
    e. An outstanding athlete or team which has received state or national recognition.
    f. Founders of an organization for civic betterment.
    g. An especially talented student in your class.

3. Consider the one person you know whom you believe has had the greatest influence on your life. For example, perhaps a teacher, relative, or some public figure has significantly inspired you or helped you in some way. Construct a three- to four-minute speech of tribute to that person in which you try to make your listeners want to emulate him or her.

4. This chapter has argued that good-will speeches usually are informative speeches with underlying persuasive purposes. Describe various circumstances under which you think the informative elements should predominate in this type of speech, and then describe other circumstances in which the persuasive elements should be emphasized. In the second case at what point would you say that the speech becomes openly persuasive in purpose? Or, if you prefer to work with advertisements, scan magazines to find so-called public service ads—ones which emphasize what a company is doing to help society with its problems or to promote social-cultural-aesthetic values. Then ask yourself similar questions about these advertisements.

5. In this chapter we have discussed speeches of introduction and tribute, but we have ignored the *responses* which speakers make to them. After you have been introduced, given an award, and received a tribute, what should you say? Knowing what you do about speeches of introduction and tribute, what kinds of materials might you include as attention, satisfaction, and visualization steps? (Those wishing to read about speeches of this type should see Eugene E. White's book mentioned in "Suggestions for Further Reading.")

ORAL ACTIVITIES

1. Assume that you are to act as chairperson on one of the following occasions (or on some other similar occasion):
   a. A student-government awards banquet.
   b. A special program for a meeting of an organization to which you belong.
   c. A kickoff banquet for a schoolwide charity fund-raising program.
   d. A student-faculty mass meeting called to protest a regulation issued by the dean's office.

In your role as chairperson, *(a)* plan a suitable program of speeches or entertainment; *(b)* allocate the amount of time to be devoted to each item on the program; *(c)* outline a suitable speech of introduction for the featured speaker or speakers; *(d)* prepare publicity releases for the local media; *(e)* arrange for press coverage; etc. Work out a complete plan—one that you might show to a steering committee or a faculty adviser.

2. Giving speeches to entertain is quite difficult because humor is a delicate art that only few can master. However, many audiences, as well as speakers, have come to expect the inclusion of jokes and funny stories in even the most serious of presentations. Make a collection of jokes, anecdotes, and cartoons which fit a certain genre such as ethnic, religious, or sex-role related. Analyze your collection with audience adaptation in mind. How might these jokes be offensive to some groups? How might they be modified so they are no longer offensive? How useful is material which is offensive even though it may seem funny to you? Also collect jokes, anecdotes, and cartoons which are not offensive to anyone and suggest how they might be useful in speaking situations. Be prepared to share your observations with your classmates.

3. Your instructor will prepare a list of special-occasion, impromptu speech topics, such as:
   a. Student X is a visitor from a neighboring school; introduce him/her to the class.
   b. You are Student X; respond to this introduction.
   c. Dedicate your speech-critique forms to the state historical archives.
   d. You have just been named Outstanding Classroom Speaker for this term; accept the award.
   e. You are a representative for a Speechwriters-for-Hire firm; sell your services to other members of the class.

You will have between five and ten minutes in which to prepare, and then will give a speech on a topic assigned or drawn from the list. Be ready also to discuss the techniques you employed in putting the speech together.

4. As a group, plan a banquet for a real or fictitious organization. At minimum, develop a format which includes the presentation and acceptance of an award, a welcome and a response to a welcome, and a speech of introduction and a brief humorous speech. Design a program for the event, and actually present the banquet performance for the rest of the class.

 SUGGESTIONS FOR FURTHER READING

R. R. Allen and Ray E. McKerrow, *The Pragmatics of Public Communication,* 2nd ed. (Dubuque, IA: Kendall/Hunt, 1981), Chapter 7, "Ceremonial Speaking."

Karlyn Kohrs Campbell and Kathleen Hall Jamieson, *Form and Genre: Shaping Rhetorical Action* (Annandale, VA: Speech Communication Association, n.d.).

Guy R. Lyle and Keven Guinagh, *I Am Happy to Present: A Book of Introductions,* 2nd ed. (Bronx, NY: The H. W. Wilson Company, 1968).

Larry A. Samovar and Jack Mills, *Oral Communication: Message and Response,* 4th ed. (Dubuque, IA: William C. Brown Company, Publishers, 1980), Chapter 10, "Special Occasions—The Unique Communication Situation."

Rudolph F. Verderber, *The Challenge of Effective Speaking,* 4th ed. (Belmont, CA: Wadsworth Publishing Company, Inc., 1979), Chapter 18, "Speeches for Special Occasions."

Eugene E. White, *Practical Public Speaking,* 3rd ed. (New York: The Macmillan Company, 1978), Chapter 15, "Speeches of Special Types."

19

Argumentation: Reasoning with Audiences

Argument is a type of communication wherein a speaker—using reason-giving discourse—seeks acceptance of a particular claim in opposition to a claim or claims advanced by others. As a public activity, argument may be considered the lifeblood of democratic institutions. Decision making by means other than executive fiat requires the freedom to construct and appraise arguments for and against specific claims. Because there are seldom certain, absolute answers to the subjects under discussion, each argument brought forward to support a claim may be resisted by an equally reasonable counterargument. Thus, public disputes over such matters as nuclear waste disposal, wage and price controls, and military preparedness require careful attention to the sufficiency and accuracy of the evidence being cited and its relationship to the claim. In earlier chapters we have already examined some of the substance and strategies of argument. Arguments must be adapted to the audiences that we analyzed in Chapter 5, must utilize the motive appeals identified in Chapter 6, must employ the forms of support suggested in Chapter 7, must be structured as are most other speeches, and cannot be divorced totally from the psychological appeals described in Chapter 17. Argument, in fact, often is treated in public speaking textbooks merely as a kind of reasoned persuasion.

When you move beyond these concerns, however, and into the *forms* of discourse, you soon discover why arguments can be of special significance in the life of the oral communicator. You soon discover why some people are afraid of arguing ("I want to discuss this with you, not argue about it") and why others relish an argumentative encounter ("Now *that* was a good fight"). Arguments represent a special type of communicative transaction in all cultures; and in our culture, many of the most important decisions—in legislatures, in courtrooms, in club meetings, and in corporate board meetings—are made via argumentation.

In this chapter, we shall examine the communication principles that underlie sound argumentation, note the occasions that require argument, and examine the process by which arguments are constructed, tested, and rebuilt.

Argument as a Species of Communication

In the final analysis, what makes argument special is not that it is a *fight*, which it is; not that ordinarily you are *attacked*, which you are; and not even that it is perfectly *logical*, which frequently it is not. Rather, what distinguishes argument from other communicative forms is the fact that it is *rule-governed*. We have noted, in Chapter 18, the impact of communication rules on *occasions*. In this chapter we will focus on the specialized rules that govern *an act of arguing* with other persons. Instead of merely offering information or attempting to persuade others that you are right and they are wrong, *the act of arguing commits you to communicating according to certain rules*, especially *(a) social conventions* and *(b) technical regulations*.

Social Conventions

In this and most other societies, there are tacit yet potent *conventions* or habitual *expectations* which govern argument. That is, when you decide to argue with another person, you are making, generally, commitments to four standards of judgment or four of these conventions:

1. Convention of bilaterality • Argument is explicitly bilateral: it requires at least two persons or two competing messages. The arguer, implicitly or explicitly, is saying that he or she is presenting a message which can be examined and evaluated by others. Now, the seller of toothpaste seldom invites this kind of critical examination of the product; Procter and Gamble is in the business of persuasion, not argumentation. A U.S. senator, in contrast, assumes a party label and pits a proposed solution to some social problem against solutions proposed by others, thus specifically calling for counteranalysis or counterargument. The arguer invites reasoned inquiry in return.

2. Convention of self-risk • By at least implicitly calling for a critique of your ideas and propositions from others, you assume certain risks, of course. There is always the risk of failure, naturally; but you face that risk any time you open your mouth. More importantly, in argument there is the risk of being proven *wrong*. For example, when you argue that a federal system of welfare is preferable to a state- or local-based system of relief, you face the possibility that your opponent will convince *you* that local control creates fewer problems and more benefits than does federal control. The bright light of public scrutiny often can expose your own as well as your opponent's weaknesses and shortcomings. That risk is potent enough, indeed, to make many people afraid of arguing publicly.

3. The fairness doctrine • Arguers also commit themselves to some version of what the radio and television industry calls the "fairness" doctrine. The fairness doctrine of the Federal Communication Commission maintains that all competing voices ought to be given equal access to the airways to express their viewpoints. Similarly, arguers say, in effect, "You may use as much time as I have (or as much time as you need) to criticize my claims and reasons." This is why, for example, most legislative bodies are reluctant to cut off debate by invoking closure rules even in the face of political filibustering. Our legislative bodies are committed to the fairness doctrine: the idea that debate (argument) ought to be as extended and as complete as possible in order to guarantee that all considerations be aired, considered, and defended.

4. Commitment to rationality • Arguers commit themselves to rationality, to a willingness to proceed logically. That is, when you argue, you are at least implicitly saying, "Not only do I believe X, but I have *reasons* for doing so." When you argue, for instance, that nonreturnable bottles should be banned by state law, someone else has the right to say "No" (the convention of bilaterality) and the right to assert a contrary proposition (the fairness doctrine). But—in addition—all parties to the argument have a right to ask, "*Why* do you believe that?" (the convention of rationality). As an arguer, you are committed to *giving reasons*, reasons that you think support your claim and ought to be accepted by unsure or doubtful listeners. Argument, therefore, is a rational form of communication, not in the sense that speakers often use syllogisms or other strictly logical structures, but in the sense that all arguers believe they have good reasons for the acceptance of their claims. They are obligated to provide those reasons; they cannot get away with saying, "Oh, I don't know—I just feel that is true." When reasons are given, if they are relevant to the claim being advanced and if they are acceptable to the audience hearing the claim defended, then the arguer will have met the commitment to rationality.

Technical Rules

In some cases, arguers are committed not only to generalized conventions or accepted bases of argument, but also to arguing in accordance with particular formalized procedures or unusual technical strictures. At a monthly meeting of a hobby club, for example, you may well find that you are expected to offer motions and amendments according to *Robert's Rules of Order*.[1] In many formal meetings, Robert's or some other set of parliamentary procedures are used. Parliamentary procedures are technical rules. They limit *what* you can say (some motions are "out of order"), *how* you can say it (you may not be allowed to defend an idea unless your motion is seconded), and even *when* you can say it (everything you say must be germane to the motion under consideration). The essential details of parliamentary procedure for handling motions are shown in the chart on pages 386–387. Argumentation in legislatures and courtrooms is governed by such specifically defined rules, as it is in many clubs and other decision-making organizations.

In other settings and contexts, arguers are expected to follow somewhat different, but analogous, technical rules. The social scientist who has made a study, say, of the effect of source credibility upon the persuasiveness of messages must report the results in a specific way. The "scientific method" is, in effect, a set of rules—rules of procedure, statistical rules for proper measurement, and rules of inference: what we can infer about the whole society as the result of a limited experiment carried out on a small portion of that society. The social scientists who—in writing reports of their findings—do not carefully define, scrupulously measure, and statistically compare data, and who then draw broad conclusions about the universe from a limited study, will not be published. The argument, as social scientists view their work, would not be "proper," and the report would be rejected. Various academic and business disciplines thus lay out their own rules for arguing; rules which must be followed if you are going to engage in argument in a given profession or field.[2]

Occasions Requiring Argument

We have already alluded to a few of the occasions on which speakers argue; but because of the variety of rules which can apply in communicative contexts, we need to review these occasions more systematically. Typical public and non-public occasions for oral arguments include:

A business meeting in an organization provides a forum for the argumentative process. Other occasions may include formal meetings or informal group discussions.

Political assemblies—the House of Representatives and the Senate; student-government councils; student organizations devoted primarily to political action; county, regional, state, and national political party conventions; the social and political action caucuses of labor unions.

Business meetings of organizations and clubs—board meetings of corporations and businesses; the monthly meetings of book clubs, investors' clubs, etc.; quarterly or annual meetings of church or synagogue congregations.

Formal meetings of other organizations—parent-teacher organizations' action and finance sessions; decision-making sessions in YMCA and YWCA meetings; college and university faculty meetings devoted to policy-making.

Problem-solving discussions—nonparliamentary business and industrial meetings where ideas are openly explored before anyone is committed to particular plans: many congressional committee hearings; community forums; radio and television call-in programs.

Classrooms—in-class discussions of readings, lectures, and outside-of-class events deserving commentary; student-to-student discussion groups; student-teacher exchanges; and recitations.

Informal social gatherings—"bull sessions" in dormitory rooms; cocktail party chatter; conversations along the street; gatherings in restaurants, bars, and college food centers; employer-employee, husband-wife, and parent-child exchanges.

The Process of Argument

In Chapter 17 we gave careful attention to the kinds of situations in which speakers seek to defend claims of fact, value, policy, and action. Our stress here is the notion that arguing with others usually involves *two speeches*—yours and your opponent's. This type of transaction demands the *orchestration* of *materials:* appeals, speeches, and general analytical techniques. This is because as an arguer you often have an explicit opponent and occasionally a chance for a second speech in defense of your claim (or one which can be given by someone else defending your claim). You must, therefore, think in terms of *multiple* messages. More specifically, you may plan your argumentative approach in terms of five elements involved in the process of disputing a claim: (1) constructing your case; (2) framing your argument; (3) validating your argument; (4) responding to reservations; and (5) rebuilding your case.

Constructing Your Case

This is your first concern: finding suitable materials for the development of your argument. Assume, for example, that your community is considering the use of its present land-fill dump as a site for the disposal of hazardous wastes. In presenting an argument against this proposal at a city council hearing called to review the merits of the plan, you know that in attacking this policy claim you must (1) gain attention, (2) develop the specific criteria for allowing hazardous

Presenting a case in a court of law provides an opportunity for utilizing the steps in an argumentative approach: constructing the case; framing the argument; validating the argument; responding to reservations; and rebuilding the case.

waste disposal at the dump, (3) demonstrate the failure of the dump to meet the established criteria, (4) note the advantages to be gained by the acceptance of your analysis, and (5) appeal for a "no" vote on the proposal.[3] As you think about this skeletal outline in terms of your argument, notice that you have several prominent problems to overcome in constructing your case:

A. You must demonstrate that the *criteria* for allowing hazardous waste disposal provide a relevant, comprehensive, and significant set of standards for judging any proposed dump site. If you cannot do this, your opponents can argue that the criteria you propose are irrelevant or insignificant. In the event that your set of criteria is incomplete, your opponent can counter by arguing that you have unfairly "stacked the deck" by your selection of "convenient" standards.

B. Even if your criteria are acceptable, you must address the *relationship* between the criteria and the dump site in question. Does the site meet the standards considered acceptable? If this is not answered in direct, explicit fashion, you leave yourself open to the accusation of having failed to discharge your major burden. However, dealing with this issue does *not* mean that your opponents will quit the fight—they can still object to the relationship you seek to establish.

C. The *advantages* that would flow from acceptance of your position may appear obvious and important to you, but they often must be weighed against other advantages to be gained by your opponent's position. You may be faced with issues that have little to do with the case you are building: e.g., a chemical company employing 2,000 workers has threatened to close its plant if it cannot use the existing site; the town stands to profit from dump fees charged for disposal and claims a reduction in property tax as a side benefit.

Thus, your carefully constructed case may meet the problems cited in A and B, but will nonetheless be challenged by counterarguments that, in effect, do not even question the strength of your claim. Instead, they shift the focus of argument to the relative merits of safety versus economic health in the community: What level of risk is acceptable in order to sustain the economic life of the community? In so doing, your opponents will not directly refute your allegations, but instead will seek to minimize their significance in relationship to the economic benefits to be realized. The developmental outline above is, of course, only one of several that might be applied; even a cursory inspection of the topic and of the demands of this type of speech will indicate those points you must argue especially well.

Returning to problems associated with the hypothetical case considered above—establishing *criteria*, developing a *relationship* between criteria and dump site, and noting *advantages*—think about how you might proceed to solve them.

Where can you find supporting materials to establish criteria for determining a dump site's safety? Are there any governmental studies or agency standards that would be of value? Are there technical reports from scientists? Have respected persons within the community commented on the issue of criteria? What criteria have other communities used when faced with similar questions? In other words, the suitability of the criteria can be obtained by various kinds of *testimony*—from technical reports, government-approved standards, expert opinion—and from *parallel* cases (the experiences of other towns).

How can you demonstrate the reliability of your conclusion that the dump site fails to meet the standards? Have other dumps with similar features been used for disposal, and have they been judged successful? Have studies been done to determine the characteristics of the land-fill (e.g., proximity to underground water sources)? Have scientists or others already commented on the suitability of the site? Given specific information on the characteristics of the dump site, the relationship to criteria can be accomplished in a fairly straightforward manner, by citing the relevant features of the dump and drawing conclusions that the site will not meet the necessary conditions adequately. You also can argue from parallel cases, using past experiences at similar dump sites as a basis for comparison to the potential experience with this dump site. You also could develop, in more dramatic style, a *hypothetical illustration* of what would happen in a "worst case" scenario if the dump site were utilized.

How do you deal with issues that challenge the advantages you cite? To begin with, the advantages you might stress would center on the health of citizens in the area surrounding the dump site or those affected by its use. Although this general advantage may seem obvious, it may be useful to underline its significance with *testimony* from medical experts or from respected town leaders on the problems that dumping hazardous waste products would cause. Without anticipating, at this stage of the analysis, other issues that may be brought forward (e.g., unemployment, increased revenue), the best approach is to build the strongest case you can for the health issue. When, and if, the argument shifts to a comparison of advantages, you will have made it more difficult for the opposition to undermine the significance of your advantage. Leaving it as "obvious" may only serve to quicken its dismissal by the opponents.

With the preceding analysis as a guide, it does appear possible to construct a reasonable case for your position. The foregoing has, in a general fashion, identified the potential sources and kinds of information that may prove helpful and has revealed several possible points on which you can be attacked. Of course, you still have to assemble the actual *materials*—the technical data, expert opinion, relevant parallel cases—that will allow you to present your case. As you put this together, the next two elements of the process will assist you in *framing* and *validating* your argument.

Framing Your Argument

There are various approaches to outlining the argument that you will present. Writing in 1958, the British philosopher Stephen Toulmin proposed that arguments be diagrammed in a visually clear pattern in order to ensure that all elements—explicit and implicit—were recognized and their potential weaknesses noted. The following elements, and the visual model which illustrates the relationships between and among them, will aid in the analysis and criticism of your or others' arguments.

1. Claim • Put simply, what are you proposing for audience consideration? This can be, as we suggested in Chapter 17, a claim of fact, value, policy, or action.

2. Data • What materials, in the form of illustrative parallels, expert opinion, statistical data, agency studies, etc., can you advance to support the claim?

3. Warrant • What is the relationship between the opinion, statistical data, or parallel cases and the claim you are defending? On what kind of assumption or inferential pattern does its acceptance as support for the claim depend? Materials do not function as evidence or support for no reason; "facts" do not speak for themselves. What makes an audience believe in the strength of the reasons as support lies in the following kinds of assumptions that warrant acceptance of the link between Data and Claim: (a) an expert knows what he or she is talking about, (b) past economic, social, or political practices are reliable predictors of future occurrences, or (c) inferential patterns suggest the linkage is sound.

We know, for example, that the credibility of the "expert" is a major determinant in gaining acceptance of the opinions being offered. In the development of the argument, this factor operates as an implicit warrant connecting the opinion to the claim. In matters involving economics, we know that the regularity of certain marketplace functions such as supply and demand exert a powerful influence on events. Hence, when we claim that the prices of finished products will rise as a result of the increases in the cost of raw materials, we are tacitly assuming the normal operation of the marketplace. Likewise, the value of using parallel cases as support for your position rests on the regularity of an inferential pattern—when two cases are parallel, similar results can be expected.

4. Backing • Does the audience accept the relationship as given? If not, what further evidence would be necessary to establish the relationship between the material being adduced and the claim itself? Where these assumptions are held in common by you and your audience, explicit development of the expertise of the source is unnecessary. Thus, if the audience accepts the opinion of the local university scientist, an extended development of his or her credentials would be a waste of time. If an audience already understands the logical pattern of an analogy, time spent explaining why an analogous case is worthy of consideration *as an analogy* would be fruitless.

But, when the relationship is not automatically accepted by the audience, you will have to provide additional support focused on the assumption rather than on the claim itself. Thus, in supporting your argument against waste disposal with a study by university scientists from another community, you may need to establish their expertise to increase the likelihood of audience acceptance of their opinion. If the audience members are not familiar with economic patterns—and you can't always assume they are—then you may have to spend time showing the relationship between the data offered and the claim. In either case, the question reveals the necessity of another step in the development of your argument that you may ignore at your peril.

5. Reservations • Can significant counterarguments be raised? In most cases, arguments on the opposite side are not only readily available, but may even be as strong as your own reasons. *Reservations* that were anticipated in the example of hazardous waste disposal could easily become the stronger arguments if you were caught "stacking the deck" in order to support your position. Economic survival may outweigh safety considerations if the impact of a plant's closing is felt severely enough by the community. In general, think of reservations as "unless" clauses in your argument.

6. Qualifiers • How certain is the claim? Note that this does not ask how certain *you* are: you may be absolutely sure of something for which you cannot begin to offer concrete verifiable proof. The question refers to how much one can "bank" on the claim being acceptable as a basis for belief or action.[4]

Using our previous example, how qualified is the claim that the dump site is not suitable for the disposal of hazardous wastes? With only a "gut" feeling that the site is unacceptable, you would be ill-advised to come forward with an unguarded assertion that the site is definitely unsafe. If, on the other hand, you have as evidence a comprehensive study of the site by a recognized expert on disposal issues, you may wish to revise your claim to reflect the appropriate qualification: "We are virtually certain that this dump site does not meet the standards necessary for safe disposal of hazardous wastes."

These six elements operate as a general framework for the construction and analysis of your argument(s). The interrelationships between and among the elements can best be displayed through a visual diagram. The numbers in the diagram refer to the elements as discussed above.

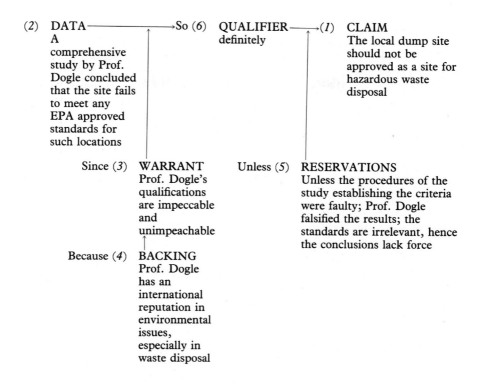

(2) DATA ──────────→So (6) QUALIFIER ──→(1) CLAIM
A definitely The local dump site
comprehensive should not be
study by Prof. approved as a site for
Dogle concluded hazardous waste
that the site fails disposal
to meet any
EPA approved
standards for
such locations

Since (3) WARRANT   Unless (5) RESERVATIONS
Prof. Dogle's Unless the procedures of the
qualifications study establishing the criteria
are impeccable were faulty; Prof. Dogle
and falsified the results; the
unimpeachable standards are irrelevant, hence
↑ the conclusions lack force
Because (4) BACKING
Prof. Dogle
has an
international
reputation in
environmental
issues,
especially in
waste disposal

The model, as developed from the questions and diagrammed above, has three principal uses. First, by setting forth the arguments components in the manner indicated, you will be able to visually capture the relationships between and among the components. How, for example, is the data you present linked to the claim: What sorts of warrants (assumptions, precedents, rules of inference) are you employing to ensure that the audience sees the connection between the evidence and the claim?

Second, given the brief description of evidence, and the identification of the assumption on which its relationship to the claim rests, you can more clearly and easily determine whether you wish to offer the claim as a definite one, or as only probable, likely, or possible. You also will be reminded to reflect on the audience's grasp of the assumption. Is it a generally accepted relationship? If it is, you need not even mention the relationship as it will be obvious and acceptable to the hearers. But if it is not, you will want to elaborate more on the linkage between the materials and the claim. Not following through the development of your case by diagramming the argument may mean overlooking possible points of contention or disagreement that can be remedied in the period before you present the case.

Finally, by thinking through the possible reservations, you will be in a better position to shore up weaknesses in your materials and, where necessary, to build a stronger base from which to respond to issues that tend to undermine rather than directly refute your case (e.g., arguing that economic considerations outweigh possible safety risks). As you react to possible reservations, avoid the temptation to build into your case answers to every possible counterargument. Your case will become cumbersome, and there is nothing to be gained by answering reservations your opponents haven't even thought of yet.

Validating Your Arguments: Tests for Data and Warrants

Once you have framed your arguments and noted potential sources of strength and weakness, your next task is to assess critically the *soundness* of the arguments you are developing. Data—facts, figures, authoritative sources—furnish an essential base, but seldom carry strong conviction unless you relate them to your claim by clear and cogent reasoning. The following brief review of common reasoning patterns will assist you in appraising the strength of your arguments. The application of the appropriate tests to each of the forms of reasoning will highlight errors and weaknesses in the soundness of your reasons. The relationship between these tests and the Data and Warrants employed in your arguments is further clarified in the examples on pp. 359–361.

Reasoning from sign • When we use an observable mark or symptom as proof for the existence of a given state of affairs, we are said to be reasoning from *sign*. A flag seen at half-mast is a sign that someone of importance has died; a rash and fever are signs that a child has measles; burnt fields with scrawny crops are a sign that a given region has experienced drought conditions.

Signs traditionally have been classified as either *infallible* or *fallible*. An infallible sign is a sure or certain indication of the existence of a given state or condition: a fallible sign signifies probability or likelihood rather than certainty. Ice on the pond, for example, is an infallible sign that the temperature is 32°F or below; a large diamond ring on a lady's finger is a fallible sign that she is wealthy. When testing the reliability of a judgment or conclusion based upon a sign, therefore, always ask: *Is the mark or symptom taken as a sign fallible or infallible?* As a sign approaches the level of infallibility, its power to influence belief in the existence of a given state of affairs increases; to the extent that it is fallible, its force is correspondingly diminished.

Reasoning from cause • When something happens, we assume that it had a cause; and when we see a force in operation, we realize that it will produce an effect. The rate of violent crime goes up, and we hasten to lay the blame on drugs, bad housing, public apathy, or inept public officials. We hear that the star on our football team is in the hospital with a broken ankle, and we immediately become apprehensive about the results of Saturday's game. We reason from known effects to inferred causes, and from known causes to inferred effects. There is perhaps no other form of reasoning so often used by speakers, nor is there any form of reasoning which is more likely to contain flaws. Always test causal reasoning for soundness by asking:

1. *Has a result been mistaken for a cause?* When two phenomena occur simultaneously, it sometimes is difficult to tell which is the cause and which the effect. Do higher wages cause higher prices, or is the reverse true?

2. *Is the cause strong enough to produce the result?* A small pebble on the track will not derail a passenger train, but a large boulder will. Be careful that you don't mistake a pebble for a boulder.

3. *Has anything prevented the cause from operating?* If a gun is not loaded, pulling the trigger will not make it shoot. Be certain that nothing has prevented the free operation of the cause which you assume has produced a given situation.

4. *Could any other cause have led to the same result?* Note that at the beginning of the section, four different, possible causes were listed to account for the increase in violent crime. Each one of these causes is cited—by some persons—as the sole cause. Be sure that you diagnose a situation correctly; don't put the blame on the wrong cause or all the blame on a single cause if the blame should be divided among several causes.

5. *Is there actually a connection between the assumed cause and the alleged effect?* Sometimes people assume that merely because one thing happens after another, the two are causally connected. Developing a pain in your back shortly after you have eaten strawberries does not mean, however, that the pain was caused by the strawberries. Do not mistake a coincidence for a true cause-effect relationship.

Reasoning from random instances • This form of reasoning consists of drawing a general conclusion about a given class of persons or objects after studying several members of that class selected at random. For instance, if you wished to determine whether the peaches in a basket are ripe, you might examine three or four of them or may even dig down to test those on the bottom. If the sample thus examined meets your approval, you reason that all of the peaches will be of the same nature, and, therefore, purchase them with confidence. Reasoning in

---

REASONING FROM SIGN

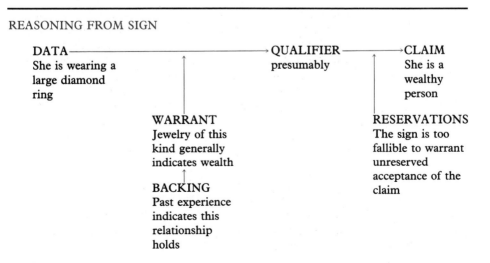

DATA ──────────────────→ QUALIFIER ──────→ CLAIM
She is wearing a   presumably   She is a
large diamond   wealthy
ring   person

WARRANT   RESERVATIONS
Jewelry of this   The sign is too
kind generally   fallible to warrant
indicates wealth   unreserved
                                             acceptance of the
BACKING   claim
Past experience
indicates this
relationship
holds

REASONING FROM CAUSE

DATA————————————————————→ QUALIFIER————————→ CLAIM
(effect) The   strong   Officials
crime rate has   probability   responsible
gone up   for law
                                                                        enforcement
                                                                        are inept

WARRANT   RESERVATIONS
There is a direct   Unless ineptness
relationship   in this instance is
between rate of   insignificant—too
crime and ineptness   little to produce
                                                        effect; there are
BACKING   other causes—
In case after   such as drugs,
case, high crime   bad housing; there
rates have been   is no connection
traced to ineptness   in this instance
of officials   between ineptness
                                                        and the crime rate

REASONING FROM RANDOM INSTANCES (GENERALIZATION)

DATA————————————————————→ QUALIFIER —————————→ CLAIM
Peaches selected   probably   The peaches
at random are   in the basket
ripe   are ripe

WARRANT   RESERVATIONS
When samples   Unless the sample
selected at random   size was too small,
are of a certain kind,   unfairly chosen, or
you can conclude that all   there are
are of the   exceptions that
same kind   have not been
                                                        taken into account
BACKING
The theory of
random choice
is based on
universal
mathematical
principles

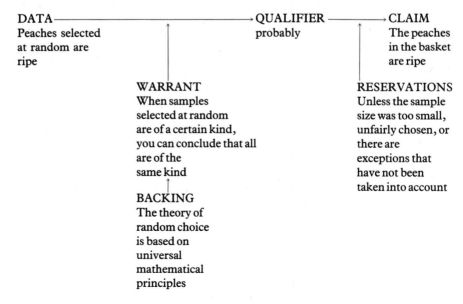

REASONING FROM PARALLEL CASE

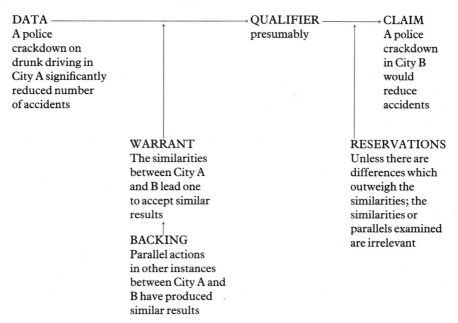

DATA ⟶ QUALIFIER ⟶ CLAIM

DATA
A police crackdown on drunk driving in City A significantly reduced number of accidents

QUALIFIER
presumably

CLAIM
A police crackdown in City B would reduce accidents

WARRANT
The similarities between City A and B lead one to accept similar results

BACKING
Parallel actions in other instances between City A and B have produced similar results

RESERVATIONS
Unless there are differences which outweigh the similarities; the similarities or parallels examined are irrelevant

REASONING FROM AXIOM

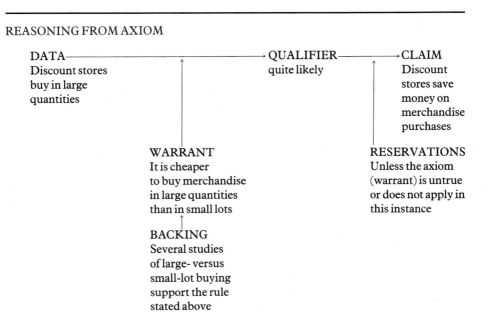

DATA ⟶ QUALIFIER ⟶ CLAIM

DATA
Discount stores buy in large quantities

QUALIFIER
quite likely

CLAIM
Discount stores save money on merchandise purchases

WARRANT
It is cheaper to buy merchandise in large quantities than in small lots

BACKING
Several studies of large- versus small-lot buying support the rule stated above

RESERVATIONS
Unless the axiom (warrant) is untrue or does not apply in this instance

this way from a random sample to a general conclusion plays an important role in much of our thinking, not only in daily life but also in conducting scientific experiments and polling public reactions to persons or events. In order to be sound, however, three tests must be successfully met:

1. *Is the sample large enough to support the conclusion arrived at?* One robin does not make a spring, nor can only two or three examples prove that a broad or general claim is true.

2. *Are the instances fairly chosen?* To show that something is true of such large cities as New York, Chicago, and Los Angeles does not prove that it also is true of all or most of the nation's cities and towns.

3. *Are there any outstanding exceptions to the generalizations offered?* One well-known instance which differs from the general conclusion you urge may cause doubt unless you can show that in this case unusual or atypical circumstances were at work.

Reasoning from parallel case • Whereas in reasoning from random instances we draw a general conclusion about most or all of the members of a given class, in reasoning from a parallel case we compare one object or item with another to which it is closely similar. Suppose, for instance, you wished to prove that a certain method of teaching French would enable students to learn the language more easily and quickly. You might take as the basis for your proof a method of teaching Spanish which already is recognized by your listeners to be highly effective in these respects, and then reason that because the two languages are very much alike in all essential regards, the method of instruction used for Spanish would also ease and hasten the learning of French. Or you might contend that because a police crackdown on drunk driving significantly reduced the number of traffic accidents in City A, it would have the same effect in neighboring City B.

As we pointed out when discussing comparison as a form of support in Chapter 7, since in reasoning of this kind the claim or conclusion rests on a single piece of evidence, it is crucial that the matters compared be closely analogous. In testing proof by parallel case, therefore, these two questions are relevant:

1. *Do the points of similarity between the objects or items being compared outweigh the points of difference?* No two things or situations are ever exactly alike in every possible detail; but unless the matter you employ as fact or evidence and the matter concerning which you advance your claim are more alike than different, clearly your reasoning will be deficient.

2. *Are the characteristics singled out for comparison relevant to the point to be proved?* Two things may be alike in many respects, but have little or no bearing on the claim you are trying to establish. The police in City A and City B, for instance, may both wear blue uniforms, drive Ford cars, and have a policemen's ball once a year. These similarities, however, are not relevant to your purpose. On the other hand, such matters as the level of morale, the type of training, the size of the forces, and the methods of patroling streets do bear on the question

of whether the sort of crackdown that was successful in City A also would succeed in City B. It is to such essential or crucial items of comparison that you must direct attention when reasoning from one case to another.

Reasoning from axiom • This form of reasoning consists of applying an accepted rule or principle to a specific situation. For example, it is generally conceded that by buying in large quantities you may get merchandise more cheaply than by buying in small lots. When you argue that discount stores save money because they purchase goods in large quantities, you are, therefore, merely applying this general rule to a specific instance. Reasoning from axiom may be tested as follows:

1. *Is the axiom, or rule, true?* For many years people believed the world was flat, or that prices responded automatically to changes in supply and demand. Before applying an axiom, make sure of its validity. Remember also that no matter how true a principle may be, you cannot base an argument upon it unless you can first convince your audience of its truth.

2. *Does the axiom apply to the situation in question?* A rule that is itself true or valid may be improperly applied. For instance, to argue, on the basis of the above-mentioned principle, that discount stores buy goods more cheaply than individual merchants is warranted; but to argue on this same basis that the customer can always buy goods from discount stores at lower prices is not valid. Additional proof would be required to establish this further contention.

Responding to Counterarguments

As you construct your case and outline your argument, you will be sensitized to potential attacks. We already have mentioned possible strategies for dealing with counterattacks; in this section we flesh them out in more detail. For instance, if you are opposing the use of the local community dump as a hazardous waste disposal site, your opponents may counter your arguments by maintaining that your parallel instances are insufficient or irrelevant as evidence of the unsuitability of the present site. They also may attack your evidence concerning the composition of the soil, its likelihood of leaching substances into the local water supply, and so on. Other opponents will no doubt bring up the threatened closure of the town's major employer if the site application is not approved, or will concentrate their responses on the projected revenue loss to the city. Thus, even before you actually present what might be called your "constructive case," you will need to be aware of some potential objections and vulnerabilities.

Do not, however, build defensive reactions into your initial argument. If you are a speaker who attempts to anticipate and answer all possible objections before they are lodged, you are in double danger: (1) You may appear paranoid and thereby cause listeners to say, "Boy, if she is this unsure, then maybe the proposal isn't any good." (2) Worse, you may actually suggest negative aspects of your proposal others had not thought of! You may, in other words, actually fuel discontent by proposing counterarguments.

As a rule, therefore, you should set forth your initial case directly and simply, and then sit back and await the counterarguments presented by others. You may even want to work from a so-called "flow-chart"—a sheet of paper which enumerates your principal arguments down the left-hand side, with space along the right-hand side for recording objections. In that way, you can identify where you are being questioned, note carefully how the attacks affect your overall analysis, and think specifically in terms of answers.

In sum, reacting critically to attacks on your arguments involves (a) a careful recording of counterarguments so as to be fair, and (b) a decision on how to answer germane objections. You have to be cool and dispassionate enough to do both.

Rebuilding Your Case

Having isolated and considered possible counterarguments, your next task is to answer those arguments so as to rebuild your initial case. This rebuilding requires *rebuttal* and *reestablishment*.

Rebuttal • Your first rebuilding task is to rebut counterarguments. In our example this would mean answering to the satisfaction of your audience objections based on revenue loss to the city or potential unemployment if the plant closes because the application fails. To refute the revenue loss argument, you might indicate that the loss is projected rather than actual; you also may be able to demonstrate insignificance if the amount of revenue collected would not appreciably affect local tax rates. The objection regarding projected unemployment is

The debate format allows the participants a chance to present their arguments, respond to counterarguments, and reestablish their initial case within a prescribed time limit.

much harder to meet as there will be members in the audience who are dependent on the plant for their own jobs. You might be able to argue that closure is likely on other grounds, hence negative action on the dump site is a moot point. This is, however, a weak counter, as your opponents may quickly point out that approving the application is precisely the gesture the company needs to be convinced that it should remain. You also may be able to rebut the argument by examining the potential impact of such unemployment and by noting the probability of new industry absorbing much of the loss without the same risk to the health and safety of the community. Finally, you may have no other choice but to rebut by facing the possibility straight on and arguing that the risk to health and safety outweighs any possible economic considerations.

Whatever tack you take, you should be careful to handle the rebuttal fairly and clearly. "Fairly" involves stating the objection in words closely approximating those of the objector, so that everyone feels you have understood and are answering the central thrust of the attack. "Clearly" demands that you carefully explain and make evident the nature of your reaction to the objection, that you assemble whatever evidence you need to provide the necessary answers, and that—once you have done these things—you indicate why you think you have answered the objection properly. A rebuttal, therefore, involves three steps: (1) counterassertion, (2) evidence, and (3) an indication of the argumentative significance of your answer.

Reestablishment • In most instances, however, you cannot be content merely to answer opponents' objections. You also should take the extra step of reestablishing your case as a whole. That is, you should first point out what portions of your argument have *not* been attacked and indicate their importance. Then you should introduce more evidence in support of your reconstructed case—further testimony, additional parallel cases—to bolster your argument as a whole. To return to our earlier example, you might indicate that no one has questioned your evidence on the site's unsuitability or the parallel cases you have presented. Underscoring these points once again with new material (perhaps held in reserve for just this eventuality) that paints a more dramatic picture of the safety risks may cause the audience to heed the issue, in spite of the counterarguments.

On Tuesday, October 28, 1980, the League of Women Voters sponsored the second in a series of debates between the candidates for the Presidency. The participants in this debate—then President Jimmy Carter, the Democratic candidate, and the former Governor of California, Ronald Reagan, the Republican candidate—used this opportunity to dramatize the differences between their respective political philosophies. The debate also dramatized the differences between their oral styles. Carter portrayed a calm, serious-minded individual accustomed to the pressures of the Presidency; Ronald Reagan relied on his own more relaxed, often humor-laden approach to the discussion of issues. The following exchange, which occurred in the second half of the debate, aptly illustrates the perspectives of the candidates on the nuclear arms control issue. Note that Carter continually refers to Reagan's position as an attempt to "scrap" the

Salt II treaty proposal, while Reagan counters with what he considers a responsible, reasonable approach to the treaty—one which falls short of "scrapping" the project. The panelist posing the question was Marvin Stone, Editor of *U.S. News and World Report*. The debate format allowed each participant the chance to comment on the question, with two follow-up opportunities to refute the opponent or extend his own analysis of the question.

● Presidential Debate, 1980[6]

MR. STONE: Governor Reagan—arms control: The President said it was the single most important issue. Both of you have expressed the desire to end the nuclear arms race with Russia, but by methods that are vastly different. You suggest that we scrap the Salt II treaty already negotiated, and intensify the build-up of American power to induce the Soviets to sign a new treaty—one more favorable to us. President Carter, on the other hand, says he will again try to convince a reluctant Congress to ratify the present treaty on the grounds it's the best we can hope to get.

Now, both of you cannot be right. Will you tell us why you think you are?

GOVERNOR REAGAN: Yes. I think I'm right because I believe that we must have a consistent foreign policy, a strong America, and a strong economy. And then, as we build up our national security, to restore our margin of safety, we at the same time try to restrain the Soviet build-up, which has been going forward at a rapid pace, and for quite some time.

The Salt II treaty was the result of negotiations that Mr. Carter's team entered into after he had asked the Soviet Union for a discussion of actual reduction of nuclear strategic weapons. And his emissary, I think, came home in 12 hours having heard a very definite *nyet*. But taking that one no from the Soviet Union, we then went back into negotiations on their terms, because Mr. Carter had cancelled the B-1 bomber, delayed the MX, delayed the Trident submarine, delayed the Cruise missile, shut down the Missile Man—the three—the Minute Man missile production line, and whatever other things that might have been done. The Soviet Union sat at the table knowing that we had gone forward with unilateral concessions without any reciprocation from them whatsoever.

Now, I have not blocked the Salt II treaty, as Mr. Carter and Mr. Mondale suggest that I have. It has been blocked by a Senate in which there is a Democratic majority. Indeed, the Senate Armed Services Committee voted 10 to 0, with seven abstentions, against the Salt II treaty, and declared that it was not in the national security interests of the United States. Besides which, it is illegal, because the law of the land, passed by Congress, says that we cannot accept a treaty in which we are not equal. And we are not equal in this treaty for one reason alone—our B-52 bombers are considered to be strategic weapons; their Backfire bombers are not.

MR. SMITH: Governor, I have to interrupt you at that point. The time is up for that. But the same question now to President Carter.

MR. STONE: Yes. President Carter, both of you have expressed the desire to end the nuclear arms race with Russia, but through vastly different methods. The Governor suggests we scrap the Salt II treaty which you negotiated in Vienna . . . or signed in Vienna, intensify the build-up of American power to induce the Soviets to sign a new treaty, one more favorable to us. You, on the other hand, say you will again try to convince a reluctant Congress to ratify the present treaty on the grounds it is the best we can hope to get from the Russians.

You cannot both be right. Will you tell us why you think you are?

PRESIDENT CARTER: Yes, I'd be glad to. Inflation, unemployment, the cities are all very important issues, but they pale into insignificance in the life and duties of a president when compared with the control of nuclear weapons. Every president who has served in the Oval Office since Harry Truman has been dedicated to the proposition of controlling nuclear weapons.

To negotiate with the Soviet Union a balanced, controlled, observable, and then reducing levels of atomic weaponry, there is a disturbing pattern in the attitude of Governor Reagan. He has never supported any of those arms control agreements—the limited test ban, Salt I, nor the Antiballistic Missile Treaty, nor the Vladivostok Treaty negotiated with the Soviet Union by President Ford—and now he wants to throw into the wastebasket a treaty to control nuclear weapons on a balanced and equal basis between ourselves and the Soviet Union, negotiated over a seven-year period, by myself and my two Republican predecessors.

The Senate has not voted yet on the Strategic Arms Limitation Treaty. There have been preliminary skirmishings in the committees of the Senate, but the Treaty has never come to the floor of the Senate for either a debate or a vote. It's understandable that a senator in the preliminary debates can make an irresponsible statement, or, maybe, an ill-advised statement. You've got 99 other senators to correct that mistake, if it is a mistake. But when a man who hopes to be president says, take this treaty, discard it, do not vote, do not debate, do not explore the issues, do not finally capitalize on this long negotiation—that is a very dangerous and disturbing thing.

MR. SMITH: Governor Reagan, you have an opportunity to rebut that.

GOVERNOR REAGAN: Yes, I'd like to respond very much. First of all, the Soviet Union . . . if I have been critical of some of the previous agreements, it's because we've been out-negotiated for quite a long time. And they have managed, in spite of all of our attempts at arms limitation, to go forward with the biggest military build-up in the history of man.

Now, to suggest that because two Republican presidents tried to pass the Salt treaty—that puts them on its side—I would like to say that President Ford, who was within 90 percent of a treaty that we could be in agreement with when he left office, is emphatically against this Salt treaty. I would like to point out also that senators like Henry Jackson and Hollings of South Carolina—they are taking the lead in the fight against this particular treaty.

I am not talking of scrapping. I am talking of taking the treaty back, and going back into negotiations. And I would say to the Soviet Union, we will sit and negotiate with you as long as it takes, to have not only legitimate arms limitation, but to have a reduction of these nuclear weapons to the point that neither one of us represents a threat to the other. That is hardly throwing away a treaty and being opposed to arms limitation.

MR. SMITH: President Carter?

PRESIDENT CARTER: Yes. Governor Reagan is making some very misleading and disturbing statements. He not only advocates the scrapping of this treaty—and I don't know that these men that he quotes are against the treaty in its final form—but he also advocates the possibility, he said it's been a missing element, of playing a trump card against the Soviet Union of a nuclear arms race, and is insisting upon nuclear superiority by our own nation, as a predication for negotiation in the future with the Soviet Union.

If President Brezhnev said, we will scrap this treaty, negotiated under three American presidents over a seven-year period of time, we insist upon nuclear superiority as a basis for future negotiations, and we believe that the launching of a nuclear arms race is a good basis for future negotiations, it's obvious that I, as president, and all Americans, would reject such a proposition. This would mean the resumption of a very dangerous nuclear arms race. It would be very disturbing to American people. It would change the basic tone and commitment that our nation has experienced ever since the Second World War, with all presidents, Democratic and Republican. And it would also be very disturbing to our allies, all of whom support this nuclear arms treaty. In addition to that, the adversarial relationship between ourselves and the Soviet Union would undoubtedly deteriorate very rapidly.

This attitude is extremely dangerous and belligerent in its tone, although it's said with a quiet voice.

MR. SMITH: Governor Reagan?

GOVERNOR REAGAN: I know the President's supposed to be replying to me, but sometimes, I have a hard time in connecting what he's saying with what I have said or what my positions are. I sometimes think he's like the witch doctor that gets mad when a good doctor comes along with a cure that'll work.

My point I have made already, Mr. President, with regard to negotiating: it does not call for nuclear superiority on the part of the United States. It calls for a mutual reduction of these weapons, as I say, that neither of us can represent a threat to the other. And to suggest that the Salt II treaty that your negotiators negotiated was just a continuation, and based on all of the preceding efforts by two previous presidents, is just not true. It was a new negotiation because, as I say, President Ford was within about 10 percent of having a solution that could be acceptable. And I think our allies would be very happy to go along with a fair and verifiable Salt agreement.

MR. SMITH: President Carter, you have the last word on this question.

PRESIDENT CARTER: I think, to close out this discussion, it would be better to put into perspective what we're talking about. I had a discussion with my daughter, Amy, the other day, before I came here, to ask her what the most important issue was. She said she thought nuclear weaponry—and the control of nuclear arms.

This is a formidable force. Some of these weapons have ten megatons of explosion. If you put 50 tons of TNT in each one of railroad cars, you would have a carload of TNT—a trainload of TNT stretching across this nation. That's one major war explosion in a warhead. We have thousands, equivalent of megaton, or million tons, of TNT warheads. The control of these weapons is the single major responsibility of a president, and to cast out this commitment of all presidents, because of some slight technicalities that can be corrected, is a very dangerous approach.

REFERENCE NOTES

[1]See Henry M. Robert, *Robert's Rules of Order Newly Revised*, ed. Sarah Corbin Robert, Henry M. Robert III, William J. Evans, and James W. Cleary (Glenview, IL: Scott, Foresman and Company, 1981).

[2]See Richard Rieke and Malcolm O. Sillars, *Argumentation and the Decision Making Process* (New York: John Wiley and Sons, 1975), Chapters 10–13; Stephen Toulmin, Richard Rieke, and Allan Janik, *An Introduction to Reasoning* (New York: Macmillan, 1979), Chapters 13–17.

[3]See Charles S. Mudd and Malcolm O. Sillars, *Speech: Content and Communication*, 4th ed. (New York: Harper and Row, 1979), Chapter 7, "Analysis of Issues." Also, see the discussion of a criteria case in George Ziegelmueller and Charles S. Dause, *Argumentation: Inquiry and Advocacy* (Englewood Cliffs, NJ: Prentice-Hall, 1975), pp. 168–70.

[4]From *An Introduction to Reasoning* by Stephen Toulmin, Richard Rieke, Allan Janik. Copyright © 1979, Stephen Toulmin, Richard Rieke, and Allan Janik. By permission of Macmillan Publishing Co., Inc.

[5]Adaptation from Chapter 3, The Layout of Arguments from *The Uses of Argument* by Stephen Edelston Toulmin. © Cambridge University Press 1958. Reprinted by permission.

[6]"An NBIC-Verified transcriptional record of the Second Debate of the Series of Presidential Debates sponsored by the League of Women Voters Education Fund" from *The Pursuit of the Presidency 1980,* David Broder et al.

PROBLEMS AND PROBES

CHAPTER REPORT   How influential are political debates in campaign years? In researching this question, consult such sources as S. Kraus, ed., *The Great Debates, 1976,* and L. Bitzer and T. Reuter, *Carter vs. Ford.* Present your critical summary in written form or as part of a class discussion on the role of argument in decision making.

1.   Select a well-known speech from *Vital Speeches* (such as Kennedy's Inaugural Address, Martin Luther King's "I Have A Dream" speech, or Richard Nixon's "Checkers Speech"). Dissect and analyze the speech using Toulmin's model of argument. What social factors do you think affected the speakers as they constructed and framed their arguments? How else could the same message have been expressed? Would it have been equally as effective?

2.   Think through two or three of the informal arguments you have engaged in during the last few days: in the student union; in classroom discussions; in exchanges with an instructor, a close friend, or your roommate. *(a)* In any of them, did you present a relatively sustained speech? *(b)* What kinds of arguments and reasons for accepting those arguments did you offer as the disagreement progressed? *(c)* Did you or any of the other arguers become angry? If so, who handled it—and how? *(d)* Looking back, recall whether you or any others invoked conventions of self-risk ("How can you stubbornly hold that view?"), the fairness doctrine ("Come on! Give me a chance to explain!"), or a commitment to rationality ("That's the dumbest reason I ever heard! Don't you have any better reasons than that?"). Prepare a short paper summarizing the foregoing analysis and, in addition, clearly distinguish informal arguments of this type from the more formal ones we have considered in this chapter. Hand your written analysis to the instructor, and be prepared to discuss your ideas if called upon to do so.

3. Assume you are going to give a speech favoring the draft to an audience of fellow students who are hostile to your proposal. Outline your speech by utilizing Toulmin's model of argument. What factors do you consider as you construct and frame your argument? Assume several counterarguments are made from audience members. Rebuild your case utilizing the Toulmin model. What new factors must you now consider?

ORAL ACTIVITIES

1. Prepare a ten-minute argumentative exchange on a topic involving you and one other member of the class. Dividing the available time equally, one of you will advocate a claim: the other will oppose it. Adopt any format you both feel comfortable with. You may choose: *(a)* a Lincoln/Douglas format—the first person speaks four minutes; the second, five, and then the first person returns for a one-minute rejoinder; *(b)* an issue format—you both agree on, say, two key issues, and then each one of you speaks for two and a half minutes on each issue; *(c)* a debate format—each speaker talks twice alternatively, three minutes in a constructive speech, two minutes in rebuttal; and *(d)* a heckling format—each of you has five minutes, but during the middle of each speech, the audience or your opponent may ask you questions.

2. Turn the class into a parliamentary assembly; decide on a motion or resolution to be argued; and then schedule a day or two for a full debate. This format should utilize particular argumentative roles: advocate, witness, direct examiner, cross-examiner, summarizer. It allows each speaker to be part of a team; what you do affects not only yourself but also other speakers on your side of the argument. [For guidance in the use of this format, see John D. May, ed., *American Problems: What Should Be Done? Debates from "The Advocates"* (Palo Alto, CA: National Press Books, 1973)].

SUGGESTIONS FOR FURTHER READING

Douglas Ehninger, *Influence, Belief, and Argument: An Introduction to Responsible Persuasion* (Glenview, IL: Scott, Foresman and Company, 1974).
Richard D. Rieke and Malcolm O. Sillars, *Argumentation and the Decision Making Process* (New York: John Wiley & Sons, Inc., 1975).
J. Michael Sproule, *Argument: Language and Its Influence* (New York: McGraw-Hill, 1980).
Stephen Toulmin, Richard Rieke, Allan Janik, *An Introduction to Reasoning* (New York: Macmillan, 1979).

20

Speaking Before Groups

The *meeting* is an ever present reality in modern societies. As the world becomes more complex and as people demand to participate in decisions which affect their lives, we tend to rely increasingly upon groups and meetings for information, for decisions, and for collective action.

The world of business literally runs on group discussions and conferences. Regularly, members of business teams exchange data on sales, production, and growth; analyze those data in small groups; and make recommendations for adjustment and change to better meet the organization's goals. Research and development teams constantly discuss new ideas to increase efficiency, to expand the business into new territories, and to evaluate experimental programs and procedures. Boards of directors prepare and often orally present annual reports to the stockholders and the public.

Group and conference presentations are also found in private and public realms. Your college or university undoubtedly has a great number of committees—on personnel, resource allocation, promotion, the library system, curriculum, and the like—which meet periodically to review such matters and to make recommendations. Similarly, private groups and clubs listen to updates on matters of interest, hear reports from members, or enter campaigns for community action. And, of course, government—particularly in the legislative and executive branches—depends upon committees, subcommittees, and public hearings to formulate legislation and to discuss methods for making administration more equitable and efficient.

In this chapter and the next, we shall review several types of oral communication which occur in such meetings and groups. In this chapter, we will concentrate upon speeches you will give in group settings. *Oral reports*, presentations before *panels and symposia*, short talks which *answer questions and respond to objections*, and speeches offered within the constraints of *parliamentary procedure* will be treated here. In each of these types of discourse, you are building relatively sustained and formal pieces of oral communication. In Chapter 21, we will examine two other kinds of oral communication—interviews and discussions. These likewise occur in meetings, but, because they represent "interrupted" or "alternating" sorts of communication, they have special features which demand separate examination.

Oral Reports

An *oral report* is a speech in which one assembles, arranges, and interprets information gathered in response to a request made by some group. Thus, as we noted in Chapter 16, a business firm may ask one of its members to assemble statistics relative to employment, sales, or cost overruns; a congressional committee may call in outside experts to offer testimony; a club may ask its treasurer to report on patterns or trends in its finances over a specified period; or a college might wish its registrar to report to the faculty on steps the school can take to recruit more students with particular backgrounds or interests. As these examples indicate, we may usefully think of two basic types of reportive speeches: the *factual report* concentrates upon assembling, arranging, and interpreting raw information; and the *advisory report* makes a set of recommendations relative to information which has been prepared.

Techniques for Making Oral Reports

Making reports to groups, large or small, does not differ substantially from delivering a successful informative speech. But, unlike the usual speech to inform, the report is normally made in response to a specific request from others who expect to use information they have called for. Therefore, as a reporter, you should be aware of certain restrictions. Above all, bear constantly in mind your role as an *expert*—the *source* of predigested information for an assemblage of people who, in turn, will act upon it. That role carries with it tremendous responsibilities. It demands that you prepare with special care and that you present your material with clarity and balance. The success of a business firm, the government's legislative program, or your club's future—all may depend upon your reporting abilities. Therefore, keep the following guidelines in mind as you prepare and deliver your report:

The information you present must be researched with great care. Although you may be asked only to present a series of statistical generalizations in a short, five-minute report, your research must be extensive and solid. You must assemble your material "cleanly," free of bias or major deficiency. The quarterly report for a business which relies upon material gathered from only one of the territories in which it operates may not only be partial, but also skewed. Furthermore, even though you may be asked only to report the bare facts or "bottom lines" of your information, in a question-and-answer session you could be asked to expand upon what you say—to supply the figures on which you based your statistical

TYPES OF GROUP PRESENTATIONS

Oral Report

Panel

Symposium

Response to Questions

conclusions. So, have all of your information available even if you have only a short time for your actual presentation.

When making recommendations rather than merely reporting information, be sure to include a complete rationale for the advice you present. Suppose, for example, that you have been called upon by your student-government council to recommend ways in which certain developmental monies should be spent. First, you will need to gather information on certain needs: Does this campus require additional buses (and should you, therefore, recommend further subsidy for public transportation)? Could it use more student-sponsored scholarships? Might it profit from a "careers week" in which recruiters from various businesses, industries, and other endeavors put on special seminars for interested students? To make recommendations on these needs, you must have financial information on the costs incurred in filling each demand. Second, you will need to assemble data on student interest, based upon interviews and patterns of usage observed in the past. Third, in order to make sound recommendations, you then will have to rank-order the options open to the group. Fourth, you will need to build a rationale for your rank-ordering, including answers to such questions as: What student needs will each course of action meet? Why do you consider one need more pressing than the other? Why should student government, and not some other college or university agency, act to meet that need? Were student government to act on a specific need, what other kinds of university, community, and/or governmental supports would be forthcoming over the short and long term?

Answers to such questions in each case provide the rationale for decision. This is important for two reasons: (1) Such a rationale enhances your *image* or *credibility* because it demonstrates your ability to think through and rationally solve problems. Unless your credibility is strong, your recommendations have little chance for action. (2) More importantly, if your rationale is a good one, it probably will be adopted by the audience as a whole; for the audience, in turn, has constituencies—the student body, specific organizations represented on the government council, etc.—to which it must answer when it takes action. In other words, by not only making recommendations but also offering reasons, you allow your auditors to meet objections, to urge the action, etc., in the important second step of persuasion—the appeal to secondary audiences.

Make full use of visual aids when making reports. Because reports often have to be short and to the point and yet contain a great amount of information, the reporter must decide how to present a maximum amount of useful material in the shortest period of time. The advice on the employment of visual aids presented in Chapter 15 (pages 275–281) is germane. Use each aid to its maximum advantage. Were you to give the speech to the student-government council mentioned earlier, for example, you might (1) offer statistical data on a mimeographed handout, with summaries in the form of bar or pie graphs; (2) audiotape and replay sample student interviews; (3) employ a brief slide show to help the audience visualize either the problems or the solutions (for example, slides of "career days" at other schools); (4) exhibit a flipchart with diagrams of proposed bus routes, a floor plan for a ballroom setup for a career-days fair, or an organizational chart delineating the sources of scholarship monies currently available on campus; or (5) hand out a dittoed sheet containing the wording of a motion you would introduce to make official your recommendations. Under these circumstances, you could limit your remarks to those aspects of the report best enhanced by your voice—the rationales or persuasive appeals. The employment of such visual aids, therefore, would help to keep you within the assigned time limit and would make full use of both the verbal and the visual communication channels.

Whatever you do, stay within the boundaries of your report-making charge. As a reporter, you are a conduit—a pipeline between the audience and some subject of interest. You therefore must be highly sensitive to the audience's expectations:

Were you charged with gathering information only? Or were you told what kind of information to bring in? Did your instructions say to assemble recommendations for action? Were you to include financial and impact analyses along with those recommendations? Most reporters are given a charge—a duty to perform. If you depart too far from that charge—if you make recommendations when you are expected only to gather information, *or* if you only gather information when you have been asked to make recommendations—you are likely to create ill will among your listeners. When this occurs, your work often will be for naught; you will have failed as a reporter. So, clarify the boundaries within which you are operating; when given a task, ask for relevant instructions. In that way, as you discharge your duties, you probably will satisfy the group and, consequently, will also increase (or at least not decrease) your own credibility and status.

Presentations in Teams: Panels and Symposia

When a group is too large to engage in effective roundtable discussion or when its members are not well enough informed to make such discussion profitable, a *panel* of individuals—from three to five, usually—may be selected to discuss the topic for the benefit of others, who then become an audience. Members of a panel are chosen either because they are particularly well informed on the subject, or because they represent divergent views on the matter at issue.

Another type of audience-oriented discussion is the *symposium*. In this format, several persons—again, from three to five, usually—present short speeches, each focusing on a different facet of the subject or offering a different solution to the problem under consideration. Especially valuable when recognized experts with well-defined points of view or areas of competence are available as speakers, the symposium is the discussion procedure commonly employed at large-scale conferences and conventions.

Various modifications of the panel and the symposium are possible, and sometimes the two formats may be successfully combined. Frequently, the set speeches of the symposium are followed by an informal exchange among the speakers. Then the meeting might be opened for audience questions, comments, and reactions. The essential characteristic of both the panel and the symposium is that a few persons discuss a subject or problem while many persons listen.

When you are asked to participate in a communication event with this type of format, remember that the techniques you employ do not vary substantially from those used for any other type of speech. Bear in mind, however, that you are participating as a member of a *group* who is centering its remarks, information, and opinions upon a specific topic or problem. You, therefore, have an obligation to function as *part of a team,* to do what you can to coordinate your communicative behaviors with the efforts of others in order to give your audience a full range of viewpoints and options. Thus, in an important sense you must sacrifice part of your individual freedom and latitude for the greater good of all. With this important caution in mind, we can proceed to discuss techniques useful in preparing for and participating in group and conference presentations.

Preparation for Panels and Conferences

Because in panels and conferences you are one of a team of communicators, it is important that you take others into account as you prepare your remarks. This taking-into-account involves considerations which you do not have to face in other speaking situations. First, *you have to fit your comments into a general theme.* If, say, the theme of your panel is "The State of American Culture at the Beginning of Its Third Century," not only will you be expected to mention "American," "culture," "two hundred years," and the like, but probably you will also be expected to say something about where society has been over those two hundred years, where you think it is today, and how you see it evolving. The theme, in other words, goes far toward dictating how you will treat your subject, and perhaps even forces you to approach it in a particular way.

Also, *remember that you may be responsible for covering only a portion of a topic or theme.* In most symposia and panels, the speakers divide the topic into parts, to avoid duplication and to provide an audience with a variety of viewpoints. For example, if you are discussing the state of American culture, you might be asked to discuss education, while others will examine social relations, the state of science and technology, leisure time, etc., thus dividing the theme *topically*. Or, alternatively, you might be asked to discuss *problems* (depersonalization, the "plastic" world, the limits of the work force) while other participants examine *solutions* (individual, corporate, ethical, political). Part of your preparation, therefore, involves coordinating your communicative efforts with those of others.

The more you know about the subject under discussion, the better. To be ready for any eventuality, you must have a flexibility born of broad knowledge. For each aspect of the subject or implication of the problem you think may possibly be discussed, make the following analysis:

First, review the facts you already know • Go over the information you have acquired through previous reading or personal experience and organize it in your mind. Prepare as if you were going to present a speech on every phase of the matter. You will then be better qualified to discuss any part of it.

Second, bring your knowledge up to date • Find out if recent changes have affected the situation. Fit the newly acquired information into what you already know.

Third, determine a tentative point of view on each of the important issues • Make up your mind what your attitude will be. Do you think that Hemingway was a greater writer than Faulkner? If so, exactly how and why? What three or four steps might be taken to attract new members into your club? On what medical or health-related grounds should cigarette-smoking be declared illegal? Stake out a tentative position on each question or issue that is likely to come before the group, and have clearly in mind the facts and reasons that support your view. Be ready to state and substantiate the opinion at whatever point in the discussion seems most appropriate, but also be willing to change your mind if information or points of view provided by others show you to be wrong.

Fourth—and finally—to the best of your ability anticipate the effect of your ideas or proposals on the other members of the group or the organization of which the group is a part • For instance, what you propose may possibly cause someone to lose money or to retract a promise that has been made. Forethought concerning such eventualities will enable you to understand opposition to your view if it arises and to make a valid and and intelligent adjustment. The more thoroughly you organize your facts and relate them to the subject and to the people involved, the more effective your contributions to the discussion will be.

Participating in Panels and Conferences

Your style and vocal tone will, of course, vary according to the nature and purpose of the discussion as a whole, the degree of formality that is being observed, and your frame of mind as you approach the task. In general, however, *speak in a direct, friendly, conversational style.* As the interaction proceeds, differences of opinion are likely to arise, tensions may increase, and some conflict may surface. You will need, therefore, to be sensitive to these changes and to make necessary adjustments in the way you voice your ideas and reactions.

Present your point of view clearly, succinctly, and fairly. Participation in a panel or conference should always be guided by one underlying aim: to help the group think objectively and creatively in analyzing the subject or solving the problem at hand. To this end, you should organize your contributions not in the way best calculated to win other people to your point of view, but rather in the

Participants in a conference or panel act as members of a communication "team." Yet each member must be knowledgeable about the general subject under discussion and should consider the effect of his or her proposals upon the others in the panel or group.

fashion that will *best stimulate them to think for themselves*. Therefore, instead of stating your conclusion first and then supplying the arguments in favor of it, let your contribution recount how and why you came to think as you do. Begin by stating the nature of the problem as you see it; outline the various hypotheses or solutions that occurred to you as you were thinking about it; tell why you rejected certain solutions; and only after all this, state your own opinion and explain the reasons that support it. In this way, you give other members of the group a chance to check the accuracy and completeness of your thinking on the matter and to point out any deficiencies or fallacies that may not have occurred to you. At the same time, you will also be making your contribution in the most objective and rational manner possible.

Maintain attitudes of sincerity, open-mindedness, and objectivity. Above all, remember that a serious discussion is not a showplace for prima donnas or an arena for verbal combatants. When you have something to say, say it modestly and sincerely, and always maintain an open, objective attitude. Accept criticism with dignity and treat disagreement with an open mind. Your primary purpose is not to get your own view accepted, but to work out with the other members of the group the best possible choice or decision that all of you together can devise, and as a team to present a variety of viewpoints to the audience.

A Sample Keynote Address

All of these virtues are visible in the following speech, delivered at a large public convention—the 1976 Democratic National Convention. The speaker was Barbara Jordan, then a member of the United States House of Representatives from Texas; the speech was the traditional keynote address. A keynote speech for a political convention is designed to emotionally charge the party faithful and to capture an important theme for the upcoming electoral contest. Ms. Jordan did all of that and more; she made use of her own credibility as a politically successful black woman to underscore the main theme of Carter's 1976 campaign—a rededication of public officials to the American dream, so much a part of the bicentennial celebrations across the country. Both personal and public appeals, therefore, were united in this electrifying speech.

● Democratic Convention Keynote Address[1]

Barbara Jordan

One hundred and forty-four years ago, members of the Democratic Party first met in convention to select a Presidential candidate. Since that time, Democrats have continued to convene once every four years and draft a party platform and nominate a Presidential candidate. And our meeting this week is a continuation of that tradition./1

But there is something different about tonight. There is something special about tonight. What is different? What is special? I, Barbara Jordan, am a keynote speaker./2

A lot of years passed since 1832, and during that time it would have been most unusual for any national political party to ask that a Barbara Jordan deliver a keynote address . . . but tonight here I am. And I feel that not withstanding the past that my presence here is one additional bit of evidence that the American Dream need not forever be deferred./3

Now that I have this grand distinction what in the world am I supposed to say?/4

I could easily spend this time praising the accomplishments of this party and attacking the Republicans but I don't choose to do that./5

I could list the many problems which Americans have. I could list the problems which cause people to feel cynical, angry, frustrated: problems which include lack of integrity in government; the feeling that the individual no longer counts; the reality of material and spiritual poverty; the feeling that the grand American experiment is failing or has failed. I could recite these problems and then I could sit down and offer no solutions. But I don't choose to do that either./6

The citizens of America expect more. They deserve and they want more than a recital of problems./7

We are a people in a quandary about the present. We are a people in search of our future. We are a people in search of a national community./8

We are a people trying not only to solve the problems of the present: unemployment, inflation . . . but we are attempting on a larger scale to fulfill the promise of America. We are attempting to fulfill our national purpose; to create and sustain a society in which all of us are equal./9

Throughout our history, when people have looked for new ways to solve their problems and to uphold the principles of this nation, many times they have turned to political parties. They have often turned to the Democratic Party./10

What is it, what is it about the Democratic Party that makes it the instrument that people use when they search for ways to shape their future? Well I believe the answer to that question lies in our concept of governing. Our concept of governing is derived from our view of people. It is a concept deeply rooted in a set of beliefs firmly etched in the national conscience, of all of us./11

Now what are these beliefs?/12

First, we believe in equality for all and privileges for none. This is a belief that each American regardless of background has equal standing in the public forum, all of us. Because we believe this idea so firmly, we are an inclusive rather than an exclusive party. Let everybody come./13

I think it no accident that most of those emigrating to America in the 19th century identified with the Democratic Party. We are a heterogeneous party made up of Americans of diverse backgrounds./14

We believe that the people are the source of all governmental power; that the authority of the people is to be extended, not restricted. This can be accomplished only by providing each citizen with every opportunity to participate in the management of the government. They must have that./15

We believe that the government which represents the authority of all the people, not just one interest group, but all the people, has an obligation to actively underscore, actively seek to remove those obstacles which would block individual achievement . . . obstacles emanating from race, sex, economic condition. The government must seek to remove them./16

We are a party of innovation. We do not reject our traditions, but we are willing to adapt to changing circumstances, when change we must. We are willing to suffer the discomfort of change in order to achieve a better future./17

We have a positive vision of the future founded on the belief that the gap between the promise and reality of America can one day be finally closed. We believe that./18

This, my friends, is the bedrock of our concept of governing. This is a part of the reason why Americans have turned to the Democratic Party. These are the foundations upon which a national community can be built./19

Let's all understand that these guiding principles cannot be discarded for short-term political gains. They represent what this country is all about. They are indigenous to the American idea. And these are principles which are not negotiable./20

In other times, I could stand here and give this kind of exposition on the beliefs of the Democratic Party and that would be enough. But today that is not enough. People want more. That is not sufficient reason for the majority of the people of this country to vote Democratic. We have made mistakes. In our haste to do all things for all people, we did not foresee the full consequences of our actions. And when the people raised their voices, we didn't hear. But our deafness was only a temporary condition, and not an irreversible condition./21

Even as I stand here and admit that we have made mistakes I still believe that as the people of America sit in judgment on each party, they will recognize that our mistakes were mistakes of the heart. They'll recognize that./22

And now we must look to the future. Let us heed the voice of the people and recognize their common sense. If we do not, we not only blaspheme our political heritage, we ignore the common ties that bind all Americans./23

Many fear the future. Many are distrustful of their leaders, and believe that their voices are never heard. Many seek only to satisfy their private work wants. To satisfy private interests./24

But this is the great danger America faces. That we will cease to be one nation and become instead a collection of interest groups: city against suburb, region against region, individual against individual. Each seeking to satisfy private wants./25

If that happens, who then will speak for America?/26

Who then will speak for the common good?/27

This is the question which must be answered in 1976./28

Are we to be one people bound together by common spirit sharing in a common endeavor or will we become a divided nation?/29

For all of its uncertainty, we cannot flee the future. We must not become the new puritans and reject our society. We must address and master the future together. It can be done if we restore the belief that we share a sense of national community, that we share a common national endeavor. It can be done./30

There is no executive order; there is no law that can require the American people to form a national Community. This we must do as individuals and if we do it as individuals, there is no President of the United States who can veto that decision./31

As a first step, we must restore our belief in ourselves. We are a generous people so why can't we be generous with each other? We need to take to heart the words spoken by Thomas Jefferson:/32

Let us restore to social intercourse that harmony and that affection without which liberty and even life are but dreary things./33

A nation is formed by the willingness of each of us to share in the responsibility for upholding the common good./34

A government is invigorated when each of us is willing to participate in shaping the future of this nation./35

In this election year we must define the common good and begin again to shape a common good and begin again to shape a common future. Let each person do his or her part. If one citizen is unwilling to participate, all of us are going to suffer. For the American idea, though it is shared by all of us, is realized in each one of us./36

And now, what are those of us who are elected public officials supposed to do? We call ourselves public servants but I'll tell you this: we as public servants must set an example for the rest of the nation. It is hypocritical for the public official to admonish and exhort the people to uphold the common good if we are derelict in upholding the common good. More is required of public officials than slogans and handshakes and press releases. More is required. We must hold ourselves strictly accountable. We must provide the people with a vision of the future./37

If we promise as public officials, we must deliver. If we as public officials propose, we must produce. If we say to the American people it is time for you to be sacrificial; sacrifice. If the public official says that we (public officials) must be the first to give. We must be. And again, if we make mistakes, we must be willing to admit them. We have to do that. What we have to do is strike a balance between the idea that government should do everything and the idea, the belief, that government ought to do nothing. Strike a balance./38

Let there be no illusions about the difficulty of forming this kind of a national community. It's tough, difficult, not easy. But a spirit of harmony will survive in America only if each of us remembers that we share a common destiny. If each of us remembers when self-interest and bitterness seem to prevail, that we share a common destiny./39

I have confidence that we can form this kind of national community./40

I have confidence that the Democratic Party can lead the way. I have that confidence. We cannot improve on the system of government handed down to us by the founders of the Republic, there is no way to improve upon that. But what we can do is to find new ways to implement that system and realize our destiny./41

Now, I began this speech by commenting to you on the uniqueness of a Barbara

Jordan making the keynote address. Well I am going to close my speech by quoting a Republican President and I ask you that as you listen to these words of Abraham Lincoln, relate them to the concept of a national community in which every last one of us participates: As I would not be a slave, so I would not be a master. This expresses my idea of Democracy. Whatever differs from this, to the extent of the difference is no Democracy./42

Responses to Questions and Objections

In most meetings (and at other times as well), listeners are given a chance to ask questions of speakers. Panelists frequently direct questions to each other; professors ask students to clarify points made in classroom reports; clubs' treasurers often are asked to justify particular expenditures; political candidates normally must field objections to positions they have taken.

Sometimes, questions require only a short response—a bit of factual material, a "yes" or "no," a reference to an authoritative source. These sorts of questions need not concern us. But at other times, questions from listeners can require a good deal more, specifically: (1) Some questions call for *elaboration and explanation.* So, after an oral report, you might be asked to elaborate on some statistical information you presented, or called upon to explain how some financial situation arose. (2) Other questions call for *justification and defense.* Politicians often must defend stands they have taken. In open hearings, school boards seeking to cut expenditures justify their selection of school buildings to be closed. At

The speaker at a meeting must be prepared to respond to questions or objections from members of the audience. The response given should be brief and impersonal but should seek to answer objections in an orderly and systematic manner.

city council meetings, the city manager often has to defend ways council policies are being implemented. In these two situations, a "speech" is called for in response to questions and objections.

Techniques for Responding to Questions

Questions calling for elaboration and explanation are, in many ways, equivalent to requests for an informative speech. That is, think about them as you would any situation wherein you are offering listeners ideas and information in response to their needs and interests. This means:

Give a "whole" speech • Your response should include an introduction, a body, and a conclusion. Even though you may be offering an impromptu speech (see Chapter 3), you nonetheless are expected to structure ideas and information clearly and rationally. A typical pattern for an elaborative remark might look like this:

1. Introduction: a rephrasing of the question, to clarify it for the other audience members; an indication of why the question is a good one; a forecast of the steps you will take in answering it.
2. Body: first point, often a brief historical review; second point, the information or explanation called for.
3. Conclusions: a very brief summary (unless the answer was extraordinarily long); a direct reference to the person asking the question, to see if further elaboration or explanation is called for.

Directly address the question as it has been asked • Nothing is more frustrating to a questioner than an answer which misses the point or which drifts off into territory irrelevant to the query. Suppose, after you have advocated a "pass-fail" grading system for all colleges, you are questioned about how graduate schools can evaluate potential candidates for advanced degrees. The questioner is calling for information and an explanation. If, in response, you launch a tirade against the unfairness of letter grades or the cowardice of professors who refuse to give failing grades, you probably will not satisfy the questioner. Better would be an explanation of all the other factors—letters of recommendation, standardized tests, number of advanced courses taken, etc.—in addition to grade point averages that graduate schools can employ when evaluating candidates. If you are unsure what the point of the question is, do not hesitate to ask before you attempt an answer.

Be succinct • While you certainly do not want to give a terse "yes" or "no" in response to a question calling for detail, neither should you talk for eight minutes when two minutes will suffice. If you really think a long, complex answer is called for, you can say, "To understand why we should institute a summer orientation program at this school, you should know more about recruitment, student fears, problems with placement testing, and so on. I can go into these topics if you would like, but for now, in response to the particular question

I was asked, I would say that . . ." In this way, you are able to offer a short answer, yet are leaving the door open for additional questions from auditors wishing more information.

Be courteous • During question periods, you may well be amazed that one person asks a question you know you answered in your oral report, and another person asks for information so basic you realize your whole presentation probably went over his or her head. In such situations, it is easy to become flippant or overly patronizing. Avoid these temptations. Do not embarrass a questioner by pointing out you have already answered that query, and do not treat listeners like children. If you really think it would be a waste of the audience's time for you to review fundamental details, simply say that the group does not have time to discuss them, but that you are willing to talk with individuals after the meeting to go over that ground.

Techniques for Responding to Objections

A full, potentially satisfying response to an objection is composed of two sorts of verbal-intellectual activities. *Rebuttal* is an answer to an objection or counterargument, and *reestablishment* is a process of rebuilding the ideas originally attacked.

Suppose, for example, that at an office meeting you propose your division institute a "management-by-objectives" system of employee evaluation. With this approach the supervisor and employee together plan goals for a specified period of time; so, you argue, it tends to increase productivity, it makes employees feel they are in part determining their own future, and it makes company expectations more concrete. During a question period, another person might object to management-by-objectives, saying that such systems are mere busywork, that supervisors are not really interested in involving underlings in work decisions, and that job frustration rather than job satisfaction is the more likely result.

You then return to the podium, *rebutting* those objections with the results of studies at other companies much like your own (reasoning from parallel case); those studies indicate that paperwork is not drastically increased, that supervisors like to have concrete commitments on paper from employees, and that employee satisfaction must increase because job turnover rates usually go down (reasoning from sign). Furthermore, you *reestablish* your original arguments by reporting on the results of interviews with selected employees in your own company, almost all of whom think the system would be a good one.

In this extended illustration, we see most of the principal communicative techniques used by successful respondents:

Be both constructive and destructive when responding to objections • Do not simply tear down the other person's counterarguments. Constructively bolster your original statements as well. Reestablishment not only rationally shores up your position, but it psychologically demonstrates your control of the ideas and materials, thereby increasing your credibility.

Answer objections in an orderly fashion • If two or three objections are raised by a single questioner, sort them out carefully and answer them one at a time. Such a procedure helps guarantee that you respond to each objection, and aids listeners in sorting out the issues being raised.

Attack each objection in a systematic fashion • A speech which rebuts the counterarguments of another ought to be shaped into a series of steps, to maximize its clarity and acceptability. A so-called "unit of rebuttal" proceeds in four steps:

1. State the opponent's claim which you seek to rebut. ("Joe has said that a management-by-objectives system won't work because supervisors don't want input from their underlings.")
2. State your objection to it. ("I'm not sure what evidence Joe has for that statement, but I do know of three studies done at businesses much like ours, and these studies indicate that . . .")
3. Offer evidence for your objection. ("The first study was done at the XYZ Insurance Company in 1976; the researchers discovered that . . . The second . . . And the third . . .")
4. Indicate the significance of your rebuttal. ("If our company is pretty much like the three I've mentioned—and I think it is—then I believe our supervisors will likewise appreciate specific commitments from their subordinates, quarter by quarter. Until Joe can provide us with more hard data to support his objection, I think we will have to agree . . .")

Keep the exchange on an impersonal (intellectual) level • All too often counterarguments and rebuttals degenerate into name-calling exchanges. We all are tempted to strike out at objectors. When you become overly sensitive to attacks upon your pet notions and other people feel similarly threatened, a communicative free-for-all can ensue. Little is settled in such verbal fights. Reasoned decision-making can occur only when the integrity of ideas is paramount. And, the calm voice of reasonableness is more likely to be listened to than emotionally charged ranting.

In sum, answering questions and responding to objections can be a frightening experience. Many of us feel threatened when we are made accountable for what we say by questioners and counterarguers. Yet, we must overcome our natural reticence in such situations, if we are to weed out illogic, insufficient evidence, prejudices, and infeasible plans of action from our group deliberations.

Parliamentary Procedure

In many groups, parliamentary procedure is used to control the communication processes. At a monthly meeting of a consumer organization, for example, you may well find that you are expected to introduce ideas (motions) according to *Robert's Rules of Order* or some other system.[2]

In a book such as this one, we certainly do not have room to describe fully all of the motions you may confront, and to review communicative tactics—when

PARLIAMENTARY PROCEDURE FOR HANDLING MOTIONS

Classification of motions	Types of motions and their purposes	Order of handling	Must be seconded	Can be discussed	Can be amended	Vote required [1]	Can be reconsidered
Main motion	(To present a proposal to the assembly)	Cannot be made while any other motion is pending	Yes	Yes	Yes	Majority	Yes
Subsidiary motions [2]	To postpone indefinitely (to kill a motion)	Has precedence over above motion	Yes	Yes	No	Majority	Affirmative vote only
	To amend (to modify a motion)	Has precedence over above motions	Yes	When motion is debatable	Yes	Majority	Yes
	To refer (a motion) to committee	Has precedence over above motions	Yes	Yes	Yes	Majority	Until committee takes up subject
	To postpone (discussion of a motion) to a certain time	Has precedence over above motions	Yes	Yes	Yes	Majority	Yes
	To limit discussion (of a motion)	Has precedence over above motions	Yes	No	Yes	Two-thirds	Yes
	Previous question (to take a vote on the pending motion)	Has precedence over above motions	Yes	No	No	Two-thirds	No
	To table (to lay a motion aside until later)	Has precedence over above motions	Yes	No	No	Majority	No
Incidental motions [3]	To suspend the rules (to change the order of business temporarily)	Has precedence over a pending motion when its purpose relates to the motion	Yes	No	No	Two-thirds	No
	To close nominations [4]	[4]	Yes	No	Yes	Two-thirds	No
	To request leave to withdraw or modify a motion [5]	Has precedence over motion to which it pertains and other motions applied to it	No	No	No	Majority [5]	Negative vote only
	To rise to a point of order (to enforce the rules) [6]	Has precedence over pending motion out of which it arises	No	No	No	Chair decides [7]	No
	To appeal from the decision of the chair (to reverse chair's ruling) [6]	Is in order only when made immediately after chair announces ruling	Yes	When ruling was on debatable motion	No	Majority [1]	Yes
	To divide the question (to consider a motion by parts)	Has precedence over motion to which it pertains and motion to postpone indefinitely	[8]	No	Yes	Majority [8]	No

	In order only when a main motion is first introduced					Two-thirds	Negative vote only
Privileged motions	To object to consideration of a question	No	No	No	No	Chair decides	No
	To divide the assembly (to take a standing vote) — Has precedence after question has been put	No	No	No	No	No vote required	No
	To call for the orders of the day (to keep meeting to order of business) [6, 9] — Has precedence over above motions	Yes	No	No	No	No vote required	No
	To raise a question of privilege (to point out noise, etc.) [6] — Has precedence over above motions	Yes	No	No	No	Chair decides [7]	No
	To recess [10] — Has precedence over above motions	No	Yes	No [10]	Yes	Majority	No
	To adjourn [11] — Has precedence over above motions	No	Yes	No [11]	No [11]	Majority	No
	To fix the time to which to adjourn (to set next meeting time) [12] — Has precedence over above motions	No	Yes	No [12]	Yes	Majority	Yes
Unclassified motions	To take from the table (to bring up tabled motion for consideration) — Cannot be made while another motion is pending	No	Yes	No	No	Majority	No
	To reconsider (to reverse vote on previously decided motion) [13] — Can be made while another motion is pending [13]	No	Yes	When motion to be reconsidered is debatable	No	Majority	No
	To rescind (to repeal decision on a motion) [14] — Cannot be made while another motion is pending	No	Yes	Yes	Yes	Majority or two-thirds [14]	Negative vote only

1. A tied vote is always lost except on an appeal from the decision of the chair. The vote is taken on the ruling, not the appeal, and a tie sustains the ruling.
2. Subsidiary motions are applied to a motion before the assembly for the purpose of disposing of it properly.
3. Incidental motions are incidental to the conduct of business. Most of them arise out of a pending motion and must be decided before the pending motion is decided.
4. The chair opens nominations with "Nominations are now in order." A member may move to close nominations, or the chair may declare nominations closed if there is no response to his/her inquiry, "Are there any further nominations?"
5. When the motion is before the assembly, the mover requests permission to withdraw or modify it, and if there is no objection from anyone, the chair announces that the motion is withdrawn or modified. If anyone objects, the chair puts the request to a vote.
6. A member may interrupt a speaker to rise to a point of order or of appeal, to call for orders of the day, or to raise a question of privilege.
7. Chair's ruling stands unless appealed and reversed.
8. If propositions or resolutions relate to independent subjects, they must be divided on the request of a single member. The request to divide the question may be made when another member has the floor. If they relate to the same subject but each part can stand alone, they may be divided only on a regular motion and vote.

9. The regular order of business may be changed by a motion to suspend the rules.
10. The motion to recess is not privileged if made at a time when no other motion is pending. When not privileged, it can be discussed. When privileged, it cannot be discussed, but can be amended as to length of recess.
11. The motion to adjourn is not privileged if qualified or if adoption would dissolve the assembly. When not privileged, it can be discussed and amended.
12. The motion to fix the time to which to adjourn is not privileged if no other motion is pending or if the assembly has scheduled another meeting on the same or following day. When not privileged, it can be discussed.
13. A motion to reconsider may be made only by one who voted on the prevailing side. It must be made during the meeting at which the vote to be reconsidered was taken, or on the succeeding day of the same session. If reconsideration is moved while another motion is pending, discussion on it is delayed until discussion is completed on the pending motion; then it has precedence over all new motions of equal rank.
14. It is impossible to rescind any action that has been taken as a result of a motion, but the unexecuted part may be rescinded. Adoption of the motion to rescind requires only a majority vote when notice is given at a previous meeting; it requires a two-thirds vote when no notice is given and the motion to rescind is voted on immediately.

to move to "table," to "refer to committee," to "rescind," etc.—you must learn to employ in parliamentary meetings. But, we can give you some general guidelines for speaking in a meeting governed by technical rules:

Listen carefully • A good chairperson will clarify what ideas (motions) are "on the floor," what sorts of comments are germane to a particular motion, and the like. You often are guided through parliamentary underbrush by informed conscientious leaders.

Ask questions • You can always "raise a question of privilege" (see the chart on pp. 386–387), to ask either the chairperson or the parliamentarian what is happening, what sort of motion is relevant to the discussion, when you can speak, or how you can properly accomplish a goal you wish to pursue.

Speak to the point • Always tailor your remarks to the specific motion on the floor. Do not discuss the entire main motion if a particular amendment has been offered, but rather speak only about the amendment; if there is a motion to table some matter, do not introduce another main motion until that one is taken care of. (See the chart.) If you listen carefully, to understand what sort of motion is before the group, and if you adapt your remarks precisely to that motion, you will not encounter technical trouble.

Avoid unnecessary parliamentary gymnastics • If the members of a group yield to the temptation to play with the rules, parliamentary procedure becomes counterproductive and rational decision making is seriously undermined. Refrain from piling one motion upon another, cluttering the floor with amendments to amendments, or raising petty points of order. Remember that parliamentary procedure is instituted to ensure equal, fair, controlled participation and the systematic introduction and consideration of complex ideas. Be sure its use aids rather than impedes orderly group progress.

Speaking before meetings, in summary, takes many forms. Oral reports save the time and energy of others if reporters are sensitive to their charges. Panels and symposia allow experts to share ideas and perspectives with others. Responses to questions and objections ensure maximum comprehension and interaction. And, speeches offered in assemblies governed by parliamentary procedure should produce reasoned and systematic decisions. With meetings and other kinds of group deliberations so important in this society, you are well advised to acquire and practice the skills necessary for productive communicative contributions.

REFERENCE NOTES

[1]"Democratic Convention Keynote Address" by Barbara Jordan, from *Vital Speeches of the Day*, August 15, 1976. Reprinted by permission of Vital Speeches of the Day.

[2]Henry M. Robert, *Robert's Rules of Order Newly Revised*, ed. Sarah Corbin Robert, Henry M. Robert III, William J. Evans, James W. Cleary (Glenview, IL: Scott, Foresman and Company, 1981).

PROBLEMS AND PROBES

CHAPTER REPORT   The talk show is an ever-present form of television communication, helping important or interesting people speak before the largest group possible in this country. Examine the "news" talk shows currently running. In your sample, look at news "round-up" shows such as *Washington Week in Review, Wall Street Week in Review,* or *Agronsky and Company* on PBS; the Sunday press shows such as *Face the Nation, Issues and Answers,* and *Meet the Press;* the morning shows, *The Today Show* and *Good Morning America;* the evening interview shows, including *The Tonight Show, The Tomorrow Show, ABC Nightline,* or a local version of one of these; or, a syndicated interview show such as *Kup's Show* or William F. Buckley's *Firing Line.* As you compare various sorts of talk shows and their formats, ask such questions as:

   a. What is the format of the show? (question-answer? group discussion? informal conversation? audience participation?)
   b. What is the communicative relationship between the host/questioners and the guest/interviews? (antagonistic? probing? interactive?)
   c. Does the show concentrate primarily upon information, opinions, self-disclosure, audience persuasion?

1.   With another member of the class, attend a meeting which includes a panel or symposium or watch a television program which utilizes a panel or symposium format. One of you should concentrate upon the exchange of ideas—propositions advanced, kinds of evidence marshaled in support of positions, interdependent suggestions for conclusions and/or solutions. The other observer should concentrate upon the socio-emotional climate created in the discussion—the extent and intensity of feelings expressed, the methods by which emotional support for others was evidenced, the extent and kind of interpersonal conflict that became apparent, ways in which personalized conflict was handled, etc. Then, together, prepare a short oral report on your findings—and their implications—for the rest of the class.

2.   Listen to or view on television the next speech given by our President, or review a recent text of a presidential speech. (Remember that *The New York Times* prints a presidential speech the day after it is delivered.) Pretend you are a member of the immediate audience and construct an appropriate question. This is a bit more difficult than it seems at first. Structuring an appropriate question means listening well and organizing thoughts quickly and clearly.

3.   Assume that, as part of a mythical National Student Week, you have been asked to arrange on your campus a panel, symposium, open forum, or workshop to which all students and faculty members will be invited. Select a subject that you think would be of interest to such an audience. Indicate whom you would ask to participate, and how you might instruct them for their preparations. Where and when would you hold the meeting? How long would it last? What would be the audience's role? In carrying out your charge and in answering the additional questions, be prepared to defend your choices and answers.

4.   Select and watch one of the weekly television discussion shows on which persons from government, business, or the professions are questioned by a person or a panel ("Meet the Press," "Face the Nation," "Issues and Answers," "Firing Line," etc.). To what extent do the formats and procedures used on these shows adhere to principles of communication outlined in this chapter? Do you think

any of the departures you see make the sessions more or less effective means for capturing and maintaining public interest? Also note the extent to which a moderator (if there was one) controlled the direction and emphases of questioning.

5. Interview an executive of a local business or industry of some size, and explore with that person the extent to which oral reports are used in the business. Attempt to find out *(a)* the kinds of reports made orally, *(b)* the frequency of such reports and report sessions of various kinds, and *(c)* the executive's perceptions of what the qualities of good reports are. You may also wish to discover what kinds of materials and problems are treated in written media, and what kinds in oral media.

 ## ORAL ACTIVITIES

1. Choose a question for a panel discussion or symposium. Carefully research the question, and choose five references which you consider to be the best. Plan a brief report in which you justify your choice of these materials, explain the general nature of the materials, and indicate how they will be useful in a discussion on this question. Be prepared to answer questions relating to your materials.

2. Pick a topic that is very important to you. The class will ask questions about the topic. After you have answered questions for a few minutes, the class will discuss the effectiveness of your responses. Also, consider how effective the questions were and whether there were questioners who made you feel especially comfortable, either in the way they asked the question or in the feedback they provided you.

3. Prepare a four-to-five minute persuasive speech which you will deliver extemporaneously. After your presentation, a classmate (who has been designated just prior to your performance) will spend one minute asking questions. Quickly record the classmate's questions, and then after about a minute stand to speak to them. You should spend only three minutes in this endeavor; therefore, you should spend your preparation time organizing your thoughts. Answer the most significant questions first; group related responses in order to save time.

4. During the next meeting, your class will pretend that it is the student senate of your university. Each class member should write a main motion suitable for presentation to the student assembly. The instructor will designate a person to chair the meeting. Conduct a business meeting in which you attempt to dispose of these main motions. You may introduce subsidiary motions only. Every five minutes rotate the chair—even if you are still discussing a main motion and related subsidiary motions. The next chair will resume the handling of any motions still before the assembly.

SUGGESTIONS FOR FURTHER READING

Cal Downs, David M. Berg, and Wil Linkugel, *The Organizational Communicator* (New York: Harper & Row, Publishers, 1977).

Bruce E. Gronbeck, *The Articulate Person: A Guide to Everyday Public Speaking* (Glenview, IL: Scott, Foresman and Company, 1979), Chapter 9, "Refuting."

Jean H. Michulka, *Let's Talk Business* (Cincinnati: South-Western Publishing Company, 1978), Chapter 10, "Business Presentations—Communicating One-to-Many."

General Henry M. Robert, with Sarah Corbin Robert, Henry M. Robert III, William J. Evans, and James W. Cleary, *The Scott, Foresman Robert's Rules of Order Newly Revised* (Glenview, IL: Scott, Foresman and Company, 1981).

Roger P. Wilcox, "Characteristics and Organization of the Oral Technical Report," in *Communicating Through Behavior,* ed. William E. Arnold and Robert O. Hirsch (St. Paul: West Publishing Company, 1977), pp. 201–6.

21

Participating in Interviews and Group Discussions

Our focus throughout the course of this book has been public speaking. However, as we pointed out earlier, there are other forms of oral communication which play an important part in your life. We will conclude this textbook, then, with a brief examination of two other types of oral communication—the *interview* and the *group discussion*. Both forms are found throughout the world of work, and even one's social life often functions through the medium of group discussions. Furthermore, both interviews and group discussions can be preparatory to public speaking. Thus, the interview, as we noted in Chapter 7, is one of the public speaker's primary means of gathering information. And, group decisions often are followed by oral reports and other speeches from leaders of those groups. We think, therefore, that this chapter will be a useful complement to our examination of public oral communication.

Interviews

While there are many specific kinds of interviews, generally all interviews fall into one of three categories. An *informational interview* is one wherein the parties are exchanging concepts and ideas. For example, polling agencies send around interviewers to find out how people assess the performance of the President or what they think about an upcoming campaign or a new line of products. A common example of this type of interview is the so-called employment interview, wherein a company's personnel department meets with prospective employees, finding out about their qualifications and personalities, and, in turn, telling them about the company.

An *evaluative interview* occurs whenever one party seeks to interpret and judge the performance of another or of some object. You may have had an "oral test" in school, for example. And in most businesses, employees are called in periodically for an evaluative session—called an appraisal interview—relative to their job performance, or to some new office procedure needing examination.

A *persuasive interview* takes place whenever one person is trying to convince another, in an interview format, to use a certain product, to accept a particular idea, to vote for a candidate, etc. Thus, a faculty member might try to convince you to major in some discipline. You may find someone at your door attempting to get you to attend a religious meeting, to buy a vacuum cleaner, or to vote for candidate Jones in the upcoming election.

All interviews, regardless of type, have certain features in common:

1. *Interviews are purposive* • People engaged in an interview are seeking to gather or express particular ideas, opinions, evaluations, or proposed courses of action. As we will see, the specific purpose of the interview controls what is said and how it is said during the time available for the exchange.

2. *Interviews usually are structured* • Any interview has a beginning, a middle, and an end, whether or not these divisions are formally fixed. The beginning of an interview normally sets its purposes and limits, allows the participants to establish mutual rapport, and lets both parties know what to expect in the course of the interaction. In the middle of an interview, there is an exchange of information, opinions, values, feelings, arguments. And, at the end, there usually is some sort of summary, mutual exchange of perspectives, final appeals, perhaps a projection for a future meeting, and an exchange of parting courtesies.

Interviews are structured substantively as well. That is, one or both of the parties usually come with prepared questions. So, in the informational interview we described in Chapter 7 (pages 130–131), the interviewer had prepared a list of questions in order to acquire the desired information from the interviewee. Employment and appraisal interviews are instances where both parties may have preplanned questions which are used to structure the transaction.

3. *Interviews are interactive processes* • There is a definite pattern of "turn-taking" in interviews, which allows the parties to concentrate upon one item at a time and which helps guarantee that the exchange proceeds for the benefit of both participants. The interactive pattern of interviews means that both parties must be extraordinarily careful listeners, for one person's comments should affect the next comment of the other. The pattern also demands that one be able to look ahead strategically, planning when to bring up a particular idea or opinion.

Formats for Interviews

The structure of interviews varies with the purposes to be achieved in them. An informational interview has a simple, straightforward structure.

INFORMATIONAL INTERVIEW

Opening:
1. Mutual greeting
2. Discussion of purposes
   a. Reason information is needed
   b. Kind of information wanted

Informational Portion:
1. Question #1, with clarifying questions if needed
2. Question #2, with clarifying questions if needed
3. [etc.]

Closing:
1. Summary by one or both parties
2. Final courtesies (promise to show interviewee any use made of the information, thanks and good wishes)

In some situations, this structure may need to be more complicated. In an employment interview, for example, where the exchange of information is two-way, the main portion of the interview may be subdivided. So, the first segment may involve a review of the applicant's background, the second might concentrate upon the job and its requirements, and the third could be devoted to negotiations. Also, in an employment interview, the closing could include reactions of both parties to each other and the job, and plans for a follow-up interview and/or later contact between them.

Evaluative interviews, because they call for interpretive criteria and commentary, tend to have a more complicated structure.

EVALUATIVE INTERVIEW

Opening:
1. Mutual greeting
2. Discussion of purposes
   a. Reason for evaluation
   b. Use to which the evaluation will be put
   c. Kinds of evaluative criteria to be used

Evaluative Portion:
1. Evaluative criterion #1, along with data upon which the evaluation is based
2. Evaluative criterion #2, along with data upon which the evaluation is based
3. [etc.]

Interpretive Portion:
1. Overall judgment of the person, process, or product being evaluated
2. Effect that judgment may have on the person's, process's, or product's future

Closing:
1. Summary, to verify accuracy
2. Final courtesies (promise to show interviewee any use or record made of the evaluation, perhaps plan for future evaluations on a preset schedule, final thanks)

Evaluative interviews are especially sensitive exchanges. The interviewee often feels threatened by the evaluative process, especially if it is being carried on by a superior at work. The interviewer, too, has to take care to keep an open mind and a sympathetic demeanor, to be sure the exchange is productive and not destructive. Above all, the purpose and possible future consequences of the interview at all times must be clear and explicit, to reduce hedging and fear.

A persuasive interview has a structure which is similar in many respects to the informational interview.

PERSUASIVE INTERVIEW

Opening:
1. Mutual greeting
2. Discussion of purposes
   a. Reason it is being conducted
   b. Gains the interviewee can make by participating

Informational Portion:
1. Information about the interviewee
2. Probing of needs and interests of interviewee

Persuasive Portion:
1. Ways in which the product or course of action can meet the needs and interests of the interviewee
2. Discussion of doubts or questions the interviewee has after the presentation of the product or action

Closing:
1. Summary, with probe of the probability that the interviewee will buy the product or take the desired action
2. Final courtesies

Notice that the middle portion of the interview is split into informational and persuasive segments. This occurs because interviewers attempting to sell a product (insurance, a used car, a new brand of coffee) or course of action (a trip to Europe, a political party, a religious meeting) first need to assess the personality and needs of the interviewee before attempting to show the person that the product or action will be satisfying. Thus, an insurance agent gathers as much information as possible about the family before offering a particular policy to meet its needs; a travel agent inquires about your financial situation, preferences in transportation, and personal interests before offering you a package deal.

Communicative Skills for Successful Interviewers

From this discussion of interviewing and structures for communicating, it becomes apparent that certain communicative skills are requisite for adept interviewers:

A good interviewer is a good listener • Unless you take care to understand what someone is saying and to interpret the significance of those comments, you may well misunderstand the person. Because questioning and answering are alternated in an interview, there is plenty of opportunity to clarify remarks and opinions. You can achieve clarification only if you are a good listener. (See Chapter 2, "Listening for Comprehension," pages 32–34.)

A good interviewer is open • Many of us may have become extremely wary of interviewers. We are cynical enough to believe that many interviewers have *hidden agenda*—unstated motives or purposes—which they are attempting to pursue. Too often interviewers have told interviewees they "only want a little information," when actually they are selling magazine subscriptions or a religious ideal. If, as an interviewer, you are "caught" being less than honest, your chances for success are vastly diminished. If you are engaging in a persuasive interview, or if the evaluative interview you are conducting could influence someone's future, it is better to state that honestly than to attempt to misrepresent yourself. Frankness and openness should govern all aspects of your interview communication.

A good interviewer builds a sense of mutual respect and trust • Feelings of trust and respect are created by revealing your own motivation, by probing the other party and getting the person to talk, and by expressing sympathy and understanding. Sometimes, of course, your assumptions of integrity and good

Conducting a successful interview to gather information may be done informally. An effective interviewer will ask a variety of types of questions, build a sense of mutual respect, be sincere as to the real purpose of the interview, and listen attentively to the respondents' comments.

will can be proved wrong. To start with suspicion and distrust, however, is to condemn the relationship without giving it a fair chance.

A good interviewer asks a variety of types of questions • A skilled interviewer asks both *primary questions* introducing some topic, as well as *follow-up questions* which probe more deeply or call for elaboration. Only in that way will answers be full and clear. One also has to be able to frame *direct questions* ("How long did you work at your last company?") and *indirect questions* ("What do you want to be doing in five years?"). Direct questions allow you to gather information quickly, while indirect questions let you see interviewees "think on their feet," structure material, and freely explore their own minds. And, careful interviewers use both *open* and *closed questions*. A closed question—"Have you had experience as a keypunch operator, a file clerk, or a typist?"—specifies the range of responses, while an open question—"What are you looking for in a job?"—allows the interviewee to provide the categories for response. Closed questions require little effort from the interviewee and are easy to "code" or record; open questions allow interviewers to observe the interviewees' habits, to let them feel in control of the interaction. Thus, primary, direct, and closed questions tend to produce a lot of information quickly; follow-up, indirect, and open questions produce more thought, more interpretation, and more grounds for understanding and analyzing interviewees and their motivations, capacities, and expectations. As you plan interviews, strategically blend questions of all these types.

Interviewing is a dimension of communication which is both challenging and fascinating. Those wishing to explore the communicative dynamics of interview communication are encouraged to read more about it elsewhere.[1]

Discussions

In Chapter 20, we reviewed group presentations, especially the oral report, panels and symposia, and answers to questions and objections within group settings. We noted that in all of these communicative efforts, you are engaged in relatively formal and sustained oral communication. Such presentations are the products of individuals, or individuals functioning as parts of a team communicating to or for an audience. There are times, in addition, when everyone in the group or meeting participates. These exchanges we term "group discussions." *A group discussion is a shared, purposive communication transaction in which a small group of persons exchange and evaluate ideas and information in order to understand a subject or solve a problem.*

As this definition suggests, there are two major sorts of discussions: In a *learning or study discussion,* participants seek to educate each other, to come to a fuller understanding of some subject or problem. A number of persons interested in art or literature or coin-collecting, for example, may gather monthly to share thoughts and expertise; book clubs, transcendental meditation groups, and Sunday School classes are learning groups,

In an *action or decision-making group,* participants are attempting to reach an agreement on what the group as a whole should believe or do, or are seeking ways of implementing a decision already made. In discussions of this kind, conflicting facts and values are examined, differences of opinion are evaluated, and proposed courses of action are explored for their feasibility and practicality, in an effort to arrive at a common judgment or consensus. So, a neighborhood block association may gather periodically to decide on projects to undertake. A city council must decide what to do with its federal revenue-sharing funds. A subcommittee in a business may be asked to arrive at useful ways for expanding markets. Once such decisions are made, these groups may meet later as action teams, discussing ways to implement their plans.

Essentials for Effective Communication in Groups

Group communication, to be productive, places certain demands upon (1) *the group as a whole*, (2) *the individual participant or discussant*, and (3) *the leader of the group*. Each of these components should bring to the discussion process a number of essential qualities and should assume particular responsibilities for its success.

Essentials for the Group as a Whole

The first essential for profitable group communication is *order*. This does not imply great formality; indeed, formality is often undesirable. It does imply, however, that only one person talk at a time, that members be courteous, and that they keep their remarks relevant. A second essential is *cooperation*. If one person monopolizes the discussion, it usually will get nowhere. Participants must be willing to share the speaking time and to listen to views at variance with their own. A third essential, in group decision-making particularly, is a *willingness to compromise*. There are times, of course, when compromise is not desirable; but reasonable concessions hurt no one and sometimes are the only way of reaching an agreement. Finally, the group should have a *feeling of accomplishment*. Unless the members believe they are getting somewhere, their interest and enthusiasm will soon diminish. For this reason, a commonly understood objective should be set and the field for discussion appropriately limited. Moreover, the topic should be phrased as a question and made as specific and impartial as possible. "What of our youth?" for example, is too vague and would probably result in a rambling exchange of generalities; but "Why do teenagers often rebel against parental authority?" is more specific and would give the group a definite problem to consider.

Essentials for the Participant

For the participant in group communication the most important requirement is a *knowledge of the subject* being considered. If you know what you are talking about, you will be forgiven many faults. Of equal importance and usefulness is an *acquaintance with the other members of the group*. It may not always be possible for you to know a great deal about the members of a particular group. However, to the extent that you can acquaint yourself with their values and interests, you will be able to judge more accurately the importance of their remarks and to determine more fairly the role you must play in order to make the group process profitable. Equally important is *close attention to the discussion* as it progresses. Unless you listen to what is going on, you will forget what already has been said or lose track of the direction in which the thinking of the group seems to be moving. As a result, you may make foolish or irrelevant comments, require the restatement of points already settled, or misunderstand the positions taken by other participants.

Essentials for the Leader

If a discussion is to prove fruitful, the leader of the group must be alert, quick-witted, and clear-thinking—able to perceive basic issues, to recognize significant ideas, to sense the direction an interchange is taking, to note common elements in diverse points of view, and to strip controversial matters of unnecessary complexity. Moreover, a good discussion leader must be capable of the *effective expression* needed to state the results of the group's analyses clearly and briefly, or to make an essential point stand out from the others.[2]

Another important quality of a discussion leader is *impartiality*. The leader must make sure that minority views are allowed expression and must phrase questions and comments fairly. In this way, a spirit of cooperation and conciliation will be promoted among participants who may differ from one another vigorously. Discussion groups are no different from other groups in preferring leaders who are fair. There is no place for a leader who takes sides in a personal argument or who openly favors some of the members at the expense of others. To help ensure that all may participate in a democratic, representative way— especially if the discussion is a formal, decision-making one—the leader should have a working knowledge of parliamentary procedure and the commonly employed motions. For a brief discussion of parliamentary procedure and a table of such motions, review pages 385–388.

Finally, a discussion leader should have an *encouraging or permissive attitude* toward the participants. There are times, especially at the beginning of a discussion, when people are hesitant to speak out. Provocative questions may stimulate them to participate, but even more helpful is a leader whose manner conveys confidence that the members of the group have important things to say about an important subject.

Developing the Discussion Plan

When people are communicating in groups, there is a possibility that much time may be lost by needless repetition or by aimless wandering from point to point. A carefully developed discussion plan will guard against this danger.

In a business environment, informal discussion groups are held for a variety of reasons. Among these are: gathering or exchanging information, employee orientation, problem-solving, and goal setting.

Ideally, the entire group should cooperate in framing the plan the discussion is to follow; but if this is impossible, the leader must take the responsibility for formulating it. In the pages immediately following, we shall consider separate plans for learning discussions and decision-making discussions. Although the plans outlined can be used in most situations, at times modifications may be required because of peculiarities in the composition of the group or because in a decision-making discussion the problem already has received considerable attention, either by individuals or by the group in earlier meetings.

A Plan for Learning Discussions

Sometimes a learning discussion concerns a book or parts of it, or is based upon a study outline or syllabus prepared by an authority in a given field. In such cases, the discussion generally should follow the organizational pattern used in this resource. The ideas in the book or outline, however, should be related to the experience of the individuals in the group; and an effort should be made to give proper emphasis to the more important facts and principles. When the group finds that previously prepared outlines are out of date or incomplete, the leader and/or the other participants should modify them so as to bring the missing information or points of view into the group's considerations.

When learning discussions are not based upon a book or outline, the leader and/or the group must formulate their own plan. The first step in this process is to *phrase the subject for discussion as a question.* Usually the question is framed before the actual discussion begins. If not, the leader and the members of the group must work it out together. Ordinarily, it is phrased as a question of fact or of value. (See pages 306–307.) Questions of fact, such as "What are the essentials for effective discussion?" or "What is our community doing to combat the increasing crime rate?" seek an addition to or a clarification of knowledge within the group; questions of value, such as "Is civil disobedience ever justified as a form of social protest?" or "Is our Middle Eastern policy effective?" seek judgments, appraisals, or preferences. The following suggestions should help you develop a satisfactory discussion plan for both types of questions.

Introduction • The introduction consists of a statement of the discussion question by the leader, together with one or two examples showing its importance or its relation to individuals in the group.

Analysis • In this step the group explores the nature and meaning of the question and narrows the scope of the discussion to those phases which seem most important. These considerations are pertinent:

1. Into what major topical divisions may this question conveniently be divided?
2. To which of these phases should the discussion be confined?
    a. Which phases are of the greatest interest and importance to the group?
    b. On which phases are the members of the group already so well informed that detailed discussion would be pointless?

At this point the leader summarizes for the group, listing in a logical sequence the particular aspects of the questions that have been chosen for discussion.

Investigation • In the investigative phase of the discussion, the members focus on the topics they have chosen in the preceding step. Under *each topic,* they may consider the following questions:

1. What terms need definition? How should these terms be defined?
2. What factual material needs to be introduced as background for the discussion (historical, social, geographic, etc.)?
3. What personal experiences of members of the group might illuminate and clarify the discussion?
4. What basic principles or causal relationships can be inferred from consideration of this information and these experiences?
5. Upon which facts or principles is there general agreement and upon which points is information still lacking or conflicting?

Final summary • At the close of the discussion, the leader briefly restates (1) the reasons which have been given for considering the question important and (2) the essential points which have been brought out under each of the main topics.

A summary need not be exhaustive; its purpose is merely to review the more important points in a way that will cause them to be remembered and that will make clear their relationship to each other and to the general subject.

A Plan for Decision-Making Discussions

Decision-making discussions characteristically raise questions of policy or of action. (See pages 307–308.) Examples of such questions are "What can be done to give students a more effective voice in the affairs of our college?" and "How can our company meet the competition from foreign imports?"[3] As you will see in the following suggested procedure, answering such questions also requires answering subsidiary questions of fact and of value.

The steps in the ensuing plan for decision-making discussions are adapted from John Dewey's analysis of how we think when we are confronted with a problem.[4] Although presented here in some detail, this plan is only one of several possible ways of deciding upon a course of action and, therefore, is intended to be suggestive rather than prescriptive. Any plan that is developed, however, probably should follow—in general—a problem-solution order. Moreover, steps in the plan always should be stated as a series of questions.

Defining the problem • After introductory remarks by the leader touching on the general purpose of the discussion and its importance, the group should consider:

1. How can the problem for discussion be phrased as a question? *(Note:* Usually the question has been phrased before the discussion begins. If not, it should be phrased at this time.)
2. What terms need defining?
   a. What do the terms in the question mean?
   b. What other terms or concepts should be defined?

Analyzing the problem • This step involves evaluating the problem's scope and importance, discovering its causes, singling out the specific conditions that need correction, and setting up the basic requirements of an effective solution. The following sequence of questions is suggested for this step:

1. What evidence is there that an unsatisfactory situation exists?
   a. In what ways have members of the group been aware of the problem, how have they been affected by it, or how are they likely to be affected?
   b. What other persons or groups does the situation affect, and in what ways are they affected?
   c. Is the situation likely to improve itself, or will it become worse if nothing is done about it?
   d. Is the problem sufficiently serious to warrant discussion and action at this time? (If not, further discussion is pointless.)

2. What are the causes of this unsatisfactory situation?
   a. Are they primarily financial, political, social, or what?
   b. To what extent is the situation the result of misunderstandings or emotional conflicts between individuals or groups?
3. What specific aspects of the present situation must be corrected? What demands must be met, what desires satisfied?
   a. What evils does everyone in the group wish corrected?
   b. What additional evils does a majority in the group wish corrected?
   c. What desirable elements in the present situation must be retained?
4. In light of the answers to Questions 1, 2, and 3 above, by what criteria should any proposed plan or remedy be judged?
   a. What must the plan do?
   b. What must the plan avoid?
   c. What restrictions of time, money, etc., must be considered?
5. In addition to the above criteria, what supplementary qualities of a plan are desirable, though not essential?

At this stage the leader summarizes the points agreed upon thus far. Particularly important is a clear statement of the agreements reached on Questions 4 and 5, since the requirements there set forth provide the standards against which proposed remedies are judged. Moreover, agreement regarding criteria tends to make further discussion more objective and to minimize disagreements based upon personal prejudices.

Suggesting solutions • In this step, every possible solution is presented. The group asks:

1. What are the various ways in which the difficulty could be solved? (If the group is meeting to discuss the merits of a previously proposed plan, it asks: What are the alternatives to the proposed plan?)
   a. What is the exact nature of each proposed solution? What cost, actions, or changes does it entail or imply?
   b. How may the various solutions best be grouped for initial consideration? It is helpful to list all solutions, preferably on a blackboard.

Evaluating the proposed solutions • When the discussants have presented all possible solutions which have occurred to them, they examine and compare these solutions in an attempt to agree on a mutually satisfactory plan. The following questions may be asked:

1. What elements are common to all the proposed solutions and are therefore probably desirable?
2. How do the solutions differ?
3. How do the various solutions meet the criteria set up in Questions 4 and 5 of the analysis step? (This question may be answered either by considering each plan or type of plan separately in the light of the criteria agreed

upon, or by considering each criterion separately to determine which solution best satisfies it.)

4. Which solutions should be eliminated and which ones retained for further consideration?
5. Which solution or combination of solutions should finally be approved?
   a. Which objectionable features of the approved solution or solutions should be eliminated or modified?
   b. If a number of solutions are approved, how may the best features of all the approved solutions be combined in a single superior plan?

As soon as agreement is reached on these matters, the leader sums up the principal features of the accepted plan. In groups which have no authority to act, this statement normally concludes the discussion.

Deciding how to put the approved solution into operation • When a group has the power to put its solution into operation, the following additional questions are pertinent:

1. What persons or committees should be responsible for taking action?
2. When and where should the solution go into effect?
3. What official action, what appropriation of money, etc., is necessary? (*Note:* If several divergent methods of putting the solution into effect are suggested, the group may need to evaluate these methods briefly in order to decide on the most satisfactory one.)

When these matters have been determined, the leader briefly restates the action agreed upon to be sure it is clear and fully acceptable to the group.

Participating in Discussions

As we noted earlier, one of the principal differences between a public speech and a discussion is that in discussions everyone contributes, alternating their comments with those of others. Furthermore, any final product must be constructed *interdependently*, with and through the ideas of others. All of this means that a successful discussant must have an array of communication skills.

A successful discussant is a good listener • In this respect, a good discussant is similar to an adept interviewer.

A successful discussant is ready to contribute • Some people in groups are willing to let everyone else do the talking. While you certainly are not encouraged to monopolize the discussion time or stifle the contributions of others, neither should you put the entire burden on others. Usually, you should speak out when you are asked a direct question, when you have a worthwhile idea to offer, or when you can correct or clarify the remarks of others. Take special care, then, to prepare adequately for the meeting, engaging in research and formulating your own ideas.

A successful discussant seeks to resolve conflict • If a group is operating in a free-wheeling and open atmosphere, conflict is inevitable. While you may think that the resolution of conflict is the duty of a "leader," that is only partially true. Everyone in a discussion should help a group work its way through disagreements. That may mean, for example, that you ought to be a *summarizer* ("There seem to be two positions being expressed on this issue"), a *stroker* ("Now, Joe, I don't think that remark was meant personally"), and/or a *facilitator* ("If we can solve this impasse, then we will be able to proceed to our primary task"). Whenever possible, help the leader to resolve conflict and the group will surely benefit.

If you do your share of listening, contributing, and facilitating, you will help the group achieve the state of interdependency and cooperation which is the hallmark of productive meetings.

Leading Meetings

If you are designated leader of a discussion, you must of course possess the skills we have just reviewed, and have the sensitivities and habits of mind we noted earlier. In addition, you often have certain formal responsibilties:

Building agenda • Leaders often are responsible for building and circulating the *agenda*—a list of topics or questions—for the meeting. Be sure you have input from group members before you construct one. Also check on the agenda's suitability at the beginning of the meeting.

The leader of a discussion group develops and executes procedures that encourage participation of all the group members. In addition, the leader should clarify the issues and encourage the group to work together toward a common goal.

Opening the meeting • You may also be called upon to offer introductory remarks. This may involve merely stating the question to be discussed and stressing its importance. Or, you might have to deliver a full-blown "speech," especially in cases where group members need a relatively complete orientation to a problem or question. In either case, offer your introduction with purpose and point, taking up no more of the group's time than is necessary and prudent, and maintaining your own impartiality. You probably will finish your introduction with an open call to others to start the actual discussion. You may need to prod them—calling upon a person you know has something to say about the first item, offering a provocative comment sure to stimulate discussion, or simply waiting until someone starts. Opening a discussion is occasionally difficult, but if you persist, it will begin.

Directing the discussion • The tendency of a group to stray from central issues or to stay upon one point too long can be greatly diminished if a leader is alert to the nature and direction of the discussion. Never be afraid to (*a*) refer back to the agenda, reminding participants where they are going; (*b*) summarize periodically, letting them know what they have decided; (*c*) search out the points of conflict, and be sure the group resolves them before proceeding; (*d*) note areas where more information or opinions are needed; and (*e*) repeat what must be accomplished at the meeting, spurring the group to be more efficient. Directing a discussion involves a series of balancing acts: On the one hand, everyone should be encouraged to talk, but not to the point of boredom or excessive repetition. Conflicts should be aired, but not to the extent that they kill group progress. A great variety of opinions should be expressed, but those opinions always should be ordered and compared with each other to aid the group in making decisions. "Directing" the discussion demands tact, sincerity, and even some direct pressure upon discussants.

Concluding the discussion • Finally, the leader is in charge of wrapping up the sum and substance of the discussion. This can involve a *final summary*—getting everyone to agree (with or without a vote) on what has been said and decided. Take careful notes to ensure that your summary is sound and equitable. You may also have to plan for *future meetings*, especially if the question is not exhausted. And, the leader is expected to create an atmosphere of *mutual satisfaction*, thanking everyone for their participation, reminding them of what was accomplished through hard work and open exchange. In that way, discussants will be more willing to come back and work in future meetings.

We have now come full circle. We have reviewed in *Principles and Types of Speech Communication* most of the forms of everyday public oral communication. We have concentrated upon the steps through which a public speaker proceeds when constructing and delivering informative, persuasive, and more specialized sorts of speeches. And, we have examined in less detail the kinds of public discourses which comprise the world of work and social interaction.

While you cannot learn everything there is to know about public oral communication in a single course or in one book, you now are ready to take up the challenges of public oral expression. As you strategically think through the rhetorical decisions you must make each time you rise to speak, we hope you will find a wealth of personal fulfillment and public service. You then will be putting the principles of speech communication to work in your life. If you do, we will have accomplished our purposes.

REFERENCE NOTES

[1]See, for example, Charles J. Stewart and William B. Cash, *Interviewing: Principles and Practices*, 2nd ed. (Dubuque, IA: William C. Brown Company, Publishers, 1978). For a treatment of interviewing with a strong business orientation, see Norman B. Sigband, *Communication for Management and Business*, 3rd ed. (Glenview, IL: Scott, Foresman and Company, 1982), especially Chapters 15 and 17.

[2]The distinction is sometimes drawn between the "appointed" or "nominal" group leader and the so-called "real" or "emergent" leader—the person who, because of superior knowledge, prestige, or insight, is most influential in moving the discussion forward and determining the direction it will take. However, for our purposes we prefer the term *leader* rather than *chairperson* to describe the individual who presides, because it seems to reflect more accurately the duties he or she is expected to perform.

[3]Not all discussions of this kind deal with problems or policies over which the group has immediate control. For example, a decision-making group may discuss "Should we deemphasize intercollegiate athletics?" or "What can the government do to ensure a stable food supply at reasonable prices?" The systematic investigation of these subjects, however, requires substantially the same steps as for matters over which the group has direct control. The only difference is that instead of asking, "What shall we *do?*" the group, in effect, asks "What shall we *recommend* to those in authority?" or "What *would* we do if we ourselves were in positions of authority?"

[4]See Chapter 7, "Analysis of Reflective Thinking," in *How We Think* by John Dewey (Boston: D. C. Heath & Company, 1933). Cf. pp. 145–147 of this textbook, where these steps are discussed in connection with the development of the motivated sequence.

PROBLEMS AND PROBES

CHAPTER REPORT   Communication researchers, thanks in large measure to the writings of sociologist Erving Goffman, are often concerned with understanding the ways in which your "self" and my "self" interact to produce a "performance" or a "social drama." To Goffman—and to others—communication is a matter of "actors" playing out a "script" in which each has particular motives, roles, and desired outcomes; the script is determined in part by what society expects of individuals in particular situations, in part by individuals' motives. Write an essay on the topic, "interpersonal communication as drama." As background, read Goffman's book, *The Presentation of Self in Everyday Life;* additional resources can be found in Bruce E. Gronbeck's article, "Dramaturgical Theory and Criticism: The State of the Art (or Science?)," *Western Journal of Speech Communication,* (Fall 1980), 315–30.

1. Good interviews generally contain a variety of question types. In your speech journal construct three examples of each of the question types discussed in this chapter (see page 397). The questions should be designed for an employment selection (i.e., an evaluative) interview. What sort of information is elicited by each type of question? Why is that information important to an interviewer? What are the strengths and weaknesses of each question type?

2. In your speech journal prepare a set of questions for each of three types of interviews—informational, persuasive, and evaluative. Specify the nature of each interview and the roles of each participant, for example, a persuasive interview between a salesperson and the manager of purchasing for a large corporation. Consider the purposes of each of the participants. How does the type of interview and the relationship between the parties affect the questions that each must ask? What might be adequate responses to each of the questions?

3. Find a published interview in a current periodical, such as *Rolling Stone, U.S. News and World Report,* or *Time.* Analyze the types of questions asked. Consider what type of interview it is, the purposes of each party, and who the intended audience for the interview is. Do you think that the purposes of each party were met? How was the interview opened and terminated? Do you think that the interview was a success? Why or why not?

4. In your speech journal discuss and evaluate the leadership of a discussion group in which you have participated. What criteria can you use in evaluating leadership? In what ways did the leader or leaders satisfy those criteria? Consider how the discussion progressed. Was there a clear agenda or discussion plan? Did the leader follow the discussion plan? If not, were digressions from the plan productive or distracting? How knowledgeable and prepared were the discussants? Overall, did you think that the discussion was successful?

 ORAL ACTIVITIES

1. Arrange and conduct an informational interview with an individual in the community (not an acquaintance or friend) who holds a job that you find interesting. Tape the interview if possible, or take notes unobtrusively. (In either case, be certain to obtain the interviewee's permission.) Report on the interview to the class, explaining the questions asked, the intentions behind each question, as well as the interviewee's responses. The class will then evaluate the success or failure of the interview, providing specific reasons for their evaluation.

2. Your instructor will divide the class into dyads. Meet briefly with your partner to decide on the type of interview and the specific situation that you will simulate, as well as who will be the interviewer and who the interviewee. Develop a series of questions to use in a ten-minute interview.

3. Along with several members of your class, consider the following situations, and then formulate specific questions which an interviewer might use to get information, to evaluate performance, or to persuade. What types of questions—direct, indirect, open, closed—did you choose and why?
    a. The interviewee worked only six months at the last job listed on his or her resumé.

b. The interviewer wants to know how many employees are using manual rather than electric typewriters with a correcting feature.

c. How does an interviewer ascertain whether Jane realizes that her work has become progressively poorer?

d. The interviewer seeks to account for a switch in a major from predentistry to accounting.

e. How does an interviewer determine what problems an employee has encountered in learning the new systems for billing?

4. The class will be divided into groups of three to five persons, and each group will be asked to build an agenda on a topic suggested by the instructor. Take ten or fifteen mintues to build the agenda, and then reassemble as a whole class. Each group will then present its agenda so that all class members can compare and contrast the various approaches to agenda building. Formulate answers to the following questions: How were the agenda different? Why were they different? Does the exercise indicate to you ways in which the agenda reflects a group's biases or concerns? Can you see why agenda building is more than a formality?

5. Your instructor will provide you with a list of twelve to fourteen statements of fact/opinion and belief/value. You and your classmates first will examine each statement and check it with an "agree" or "disagree." Then you will gather in small groups of four or five persons and compare your checkmarks. If all of you agree or all of you disagree with the statement, pass over it; but, if some of you agree and some of you disagree, talk about it; try to resolve your differences so that all of you either agree or disagree. Do this for all of the statements. After a specified period of discussion, gather again as a class and report on your attempts at res-olution-of-differences. What kinds of pressure did each of you experience? Did you (or others) yield? Did some of you yield more often than others? Why? What disagreements were resolved semantically (i.e., by checking how each member of your group was using a particular word)? Which ones were resolved by forcing other persons to question their attitudes and values? In general does the exercise reveal anything important about group processes and decision-making?

 ## SUGGESTIONS FOR FURTHER READING

Larry L. Barker, *Communication* (Englewood Cliffs, NJ: Prentice-Hall, Inc., 1978), Chapter 7, "Small Group Communication."

Roy M. Berko, Andrew D. Wolvin, and Darlyn R. Wolvin, *Communicating: A Social and Career Focus* (Boston: Houghton Mifflin Company, 1977), Chapter 9, "Small-Group Communication."

Patricia Hayes Bradley and John E. Baird, Jr., *Communication for Business and the Professions* (Dubuque, IA: William C. Brown Company Publishers, 1980), Chapter 6, "Dyadic Communication: Interviewing," Chapter 8, "Small Group Communication: The Process of Decision-Making," and Chapter 9, "Small Group Communication: Leadership."

William I. Gorden, *Communication: Personal & Public* (Sherman Oaks, CA: Alfred Publishing Co., Inc., 1978), Chapter 7, "Problem Solving and Decision Mak-ing."

Charles J. Stewart and William B. Cash, *Interviewing: Principles and Practices,* 2nd ed. (Dubuque, IA: William C. Brown Company Publishers, 1980).

APPENDIX

A Making Your Speaking Voice More Effective

B Analyzing and Criticizing the Speeches of Others

Appendix A

Making Your Speaking Voice More Effective

In Chapter 14, as you will recall, our emphasis was primarily on the psychological aspects and implications of vocal communication. Here, our concerns center on the *physiological* nature of the human voice as an instrument of communication and on some of the practical means by which you may improve its effectiveness.

Good vocal behavior is *habitual*. Any vocal skill, before it can seem natural and effective with listeners, must become so much a habit that it will work for you without conscious effort when you begin to speak, and will continue to do so throughout the course of your message. Second, however, effective vocal behavior is *responsive*. There are times, for example, when you will want to stretch your voice—to shout, to reach listeners with almost a whisper, to put purposively a sense of irony or disbelief into your vocal tones. In these instances, you need to have confidence in yourself and your vocal mechanism as you reach for non-ordinary vocal effects.

To improve your normal, habitual vocal patterns, and to provide yourself with a vocal instrument capable of reaching for special effects, you may well need to *practice* using it; simple vocal exercises, especially when monitored by a speech teacher with some training in voice and articulation, can be employed in practice sessions. (Comparatively severe voice problems, of course, should be taken to your school's speech correction clinic, where certified clinicians will work patiently and personally with you. Most of us, however, do not need the services of a clinic; we need, rather, to reform a few of our vocal habits.)

Below you will find nineteen exercises which you can do individually or in a group. You may feel a bit silly, at first, crying "hep, hop, hope, hoop," but remember, you are reciting these seemingly nonsense words and phrases for a purpose—for the improvement of your oral communicative abilities.

 **EXERCISES FOR VOICE PRACTICE**[1]

BREATH CONTROL

Before you can learn to control the voice, you must control the breathing processes. Before you can control the breath, you must develop a sensitivity to the physical processes involved in breathing. Try these exercises.

1. Get down on hands and knees. Breathe through your mouth. Take three or four deep breaths. You will notice that when you inhale, the diaphragm (or stomach, it will seem) drops down. When you exhale, the diaphragm rises as it contracts to expel the air from the lungs. Keeping your arms and shoulders stiff, breathe as rapidly as you can without becoming dizzy. This will help you develop a sensitivity to the respiratory mechanism while developing control over the basic muscles of respiration.

2. Humans don't usually breathe while on "all fours," however. Standing upright, take ten deep breaths, very slowly. Feel how the rib cage expands on inhalation and contracts when you exhale. Notice that if you slump forward (relax the shoulders) and drop your chin onto your chest, you can feel the interaction of the lungs and rib cage. Take five deep breaths while in that posture. Now stand as straight as you can, shoulders back, chin up. Take five deep breaths. You should notice that the air enters the lungs more quickly, with less effort.

3. Say "hep, hop, hope, hoop." Now repeat, putting a one-second pause between each word. Repeat the exercise using only one breath for all four words. Now try it again, saying each word as loudly as you can: remember, all in one breath. You are developing control of all the muscles of respiration as you do this repeatedly.

4. Say the entire alphabet, using only one breath. Can you do it? Many people can do it but they slur the pronunciation of the letters. Using distinct pronunciation, try it again. When you have mastered one "run-through" of the alphabet, try to get through all twenty-six letters again on one breath. The more you practice, the better you will control the flow of air. It is possible to articulate the alphabet clearly in five, six, or even seven repetitions in one breath.

5. A slightly more difficult exercise, similar to the one above, is to pronounce, with pause and feeling, using one breath, this classic piece of poetry:

    Mary had a little lamb,
    Its fleece was white as snow.
    And, everywhere that Mary went,
    The lamb was sure to go.

    How many times can you repeat that stanza on a single breath?

CONTROL OF PHONATION

Phonation is the process by which the sound which we call "voice" is produced. Since the voice is actually a vibration of the muscles of the larynx called the "vocal folds," these muscles must be cared for and control of them developed by practice.

6. Try to relax the throat; give a deep sigh, then a low, broken whisper, then count to ten as softly as you can without whispering.

7. Sing "low, low, low, low," dropping one note of the musical scale each time you sing the word until you reach the lowest tone you can possibly produce. Then sing your way back up the scale until you reach the tone you find most comfortable. Now sing "high, high, high," going up the scale until you reach the highest tone you can produce. Now, come back down to the tone you feel most comfortable with. This tone will be your optimum pitch—the one from which and around which most of your speech should be executed.

8. From your optimum pitch, drop two or three notes and then—very softly—sing "do-re-mi-fa-sol-la-ti-do." Repeat this process, increasing your volume each time until your voice is so loud that it is uncomfortable. This done, you will have examined your volume range. You should try to speak comfortably, but loud enough so that you are audible to all.

CONTROL OF RESONANCE

Resonance gives the voice the desirable quality that we seek. Always try to keep the throat relaxed, the mouth as open as possible, and nasal resonance restricted to nasal sounds (n, m, and ng) alone.

9. Sing "ah" with the mouth open; gradually bring the teeth together; notice the different quality of resonance as you reduce the resonating cavity.

10. Say "hung-ah-ng-eh-ng-ah-ng-eh-ng" and feel the resonance move from mouth to nose and vice versa.

11. Say "Hack goes to school." Hold your nose closed and repeat. You should hear no difference between the two pronunciations since the sentence contains no nasal sounds. Now say, "Nine new nannies nodding nearing noon." Hold the nose again and repeat the sentence. You should hear a marked difference in resonance since this sentence is filled with nasal sounds.

12. Speak clearly the following paragraph. There are no nasal sounds, but your speech mechanisms are not used to speaking for so long without nasal sounds so you might find this difficult. Check yourself for improper nasal resonance.

> He was a rare fellow. At first sight, people quickly perceived that he was hardly of the average sort. His hearty laugh, his quick, catlike posture shifts, his clear, careful gaze—all helped folks to appreciate his special qualities. Yet, he was always quiet. He saw beauty where others failed to detect it. He loved art as well as every object, every creature that had life. He was a rare fellow.

ARTICULATORY CONTROL

13. Each word in each of the following groups is to be pronounced differently, but careless speakers often blur the articulatory differences. Pronounce each word group, making sure that each word can be distinguished from the others. Get a friend or classmate to check your accuracy.

jest—gist—just
thin—think—thing
roost—roosts—ghost—ghosts
hold—hole—holder—holer—holler
allusion—illusion—elude
began—begun—begin
pan—pin—pen—pun—peen
wish—which—witch
character—caricature
conquerer—horror—mirror
affect—effect
twin—twain—twine

14. Control of articulation can best be gained by becoming proficient in the articulation of "tongue-twisters." You may have your favorites. Practice these, for
starters.

- Barry, the baby bunny's born by the blue box bearing rubber baby
buggy bumpers.
- The little lowland lubber was a lively lad, lucky, liberal, and likeable.
- He mangled his ankle as he bungled a shot out of the bunker.
- The sixth sheik's sixth sheep's sick.
- Oil from the cod's liver annoys the boy.
- While we waited for the whistle on the wharf, we whittled the white
weatherboards on a whim.
- Sid said to tell him that Benny hid the penny many years ago.
- Three gray geese in the green grass grazing; gray were the geese and
green was the grazing.
- The seething sea ceaseth and thus the seething sea sufficeth us.
- Polly played prettily on the Peterson's piano preparing for Plato Peter-
son's pleasant party.
- Charles Cherry Mitchell, the rich bachelor merchant, had wretched
speech as a child.
- Zeb, the boys zinged the zithers and zonged the xylophones busily and
brazenly on the plains of Zion.
- How, now, do brown cows and browner sows take their bows while they
carouse around their houses in their blouses?
- Clear around the rugged rocks the cunning ragged rascal climbed and
ran, raging and ranting, cursing and cajoling.

CONTROL OF RATE, PAUSE, AND INFLECTION

The way in which words are spoken influences meaning as much as the words
themselves. Practice using the voice as a tool for creating meaning.

15. Speak the following paragraph so that the meaning is clear to a listener who
has not heard it before.

Bill Bell builds bells. The bells Bill
Bell builds bang and bong on Beele
Boulevard. Bill builds bells with brass

bell balls. Bell's bell balls build big
bells. Bill Bell built brass ball-built
bells for the Beal's bull, Buell. Buell's
Bell-built brass bell banged when Buell
bellowed on Beele and bore Bell's bells
bong abroad. Bill Bell's bells, brass-
ball-built for Beal's Beele-based bull
Buell biased brass bell builders toward
Bell brass ball-built bells. Boy!

16. Vary the *rate* with which you say the following sentences in the manner indicated:

    a. "There goes the last one."
        (1) Use long quantity, expressing regret.
        (2) Use short quantity, expressing excitement.
        (3) Use moderate quantity, merely stating a fact.
    b. "The winners are John, Henry, and Bill."
        (1) Insert a long pause after *are* for suspense; then give the names rapidly.
        (2) Insert pauses before each name as if picking it out.
        (3) Say the whole sentence rapidly in a matter-of-fact way.

17. In the manner suggested, vary the *force* for the following:

    a. "I hate you! I hate you! I hate you!"
        (1) Increase the degree of force with each repetition, making the last almost a shout.
        (2) Say the second *"hate"* louder than the first, and the last one *sotto voce.*
        (3) Shout the first statement; then let the force diminish as if echoing the mood.
    b. "What kind of thing is this?"
        Repeat the question, stressing a different word each time. Try not to raise the pitch, but to emphasize by force alone.
    c. "I have told you a hundred times, and the answer is still the same."
        (1) Make the statement a straightforward assertion, using sustained force.
        (2) Speak the sentence with a sudden explosion of force, as though you were uncontrollably angry.
        (3) Speak the sentence with deep but controlled emotion, applying force gradually and firmly.

18. Practice reading aloud sentences from prose and poetry that require emphasis and contrast to make the meaning clear. Vary the pitch, rate, and force in different ways until you feel you have the best possible interpretation of the meaning. Here are some examples for practice:

    a. One of the most striking differences between a cat and a lie is that a cat has only nine lives.   *Mark Twain*
    b. So, Naturalists observe, a flea
        Has smaller fleas that on him prey:

And these have smaller still to bite 'em:
And so proceed ad infinitum.   *Jonathan Swift*

    c.   I have waited with patience to hear what arguments might be urged
against the bill; but I have waited in vain: The truth is, there is no argument that can weigh against it.   *Lord Mansfield*

    d.   Gentlemen may cry, peace, peace!—but there is no peace. The war has
actually begun! I know not what course others may take; but, as for me,
give me liberty, or give me death!   *Patrick Henry*

19. Read the following passages so as to give the effect of climax: first practice
the climax of increasing force, and then that of increasing intensity of feeling
with diminishing force.

    a.   There is no mistake; there has been no mistake; and there shall be no
mistake.   *Duke of Wellington*

    b.   Let us cultivate a true spirit of union and harmony . . . let us act under
a settled conviction, and an habitual feeling, that these twenty-four States
are one country. . . . Let our object be, OUR COUNTRY, OUR WHOLE
COUNTRY, AND NOTHING BUT OUR COUNTRY.   *Daniel Webster*

In closing, should you or your instructor wish to pursue further vocal training in a
good deal more depth, we would suggest the following textbooks:

Joseph A. DeVito, Jill Gianttino, and T. D. Schon, *Articulation and Voice: Effective Commu-
nication* (Indianapolis: The Bobbs-Merrill Company, Inc., 1975).
Donald H. Ecroyd, Murray M. Halfond, and Carol C. Towne, *Voice and Articulation: A Hand-
book* (Glenview, IL: Scott, Foresman and Company, 1966), esp. Chapters 3–7 and 9.
Robert G. King and Eleanor M. DiMichael, *Improving Articulation and Voice* (New York: The
Macmillan Company, 1966), esp. Chapters 2, 5, 6, and 8

REFERENCE NOTES

[1]Exercises for Voice Practice were prepared by Professors James L. Booth, Vernon Gantt,
Jerry Mayes, and Robert Valentine, of Murray State University.

Appendix B

Analyzing and Criticizing the Speeches of Others

The bulk of this book has been concerned with making you a more skillful producer of oral messages. Except for some comments on listening for evaluation in Chapter 2, however, we have not explicitly treated the problem of analyzing and evaluating the messages of others.

Because during your lifetime you will spend more hours listening than talking, it seems appropriate to conclude this book with a look at *communication analysis and criticism*. Since it would take a whole course to treat this subject in the large, here we will review only a few of the fundamentals of criticism. The advice given, however, in conjunction with further reading in suggested sources, should suffice at least to make more effective your evaluation of the speeches you hear and read.

Communication Analysis

The behaviors you adopt in analyzing classroom speeches are the same as those you engage in when you hear speakers outside of the classroom environment. Whether the speaker is a professor expounding on the merits of a new grading scheme, a scientist explaining her latest research, or an irate landlord exhorting the city Housing and Fair Rent Board to allow him to charge higher rents to college students, you will find yourself employing the same critical questions in analyzing the presentation. Some dimensions may be more important than others, but all of the elements suggested in the Evaluation Checklist in Chapter 2 are potentially useful in critiquing the presentations of others.

Your critical evaluation—if it is to be more substantial than "how boring!" or "Egad, his ideas are absurd"—requires close attention to *what* was said as well as to *who* is doing the "saying." *Criticism*, as we use the term, refers to a *descriptive-evaluative process of analysis*, one which (a) starts from clearly defined purposes or designs, (b) systematically describes an event from a particular point of view, and (c) only then makes a judgment (good/bad, beautiful/ugly, effective/ineffective, useful/useless, ethical/unethical, etc.). Even casual journalistic reports of important oral messages often reveal such purposes, methodical description, and judgment. These elemental aspects of criticism were apparent, for example, in television and press reporting of President Reagan's Inaugural and his February 1981 address to the nation on the state of the economy. As you react to such speeches, with the experience you are gaining in critiquing in-class speeches as a guide, you reveal your own purpose, method, and judgment. In defending your critical evaluation, you will undoubtedly go beyond the limited time available during class speeches and examine the impact of speaking in more detail. The basic elements will take on more elaborate form as you discover answers to such questions as: "Why was Supreme Court Justice Berger's address on the nation's crime problem received with elation by some and with unrelenting abuse by others?" "Why have journalists indicated that President Reagan's 'Bully Pulpit' style of leadership is a welcome change?" "To what does Senator Ted Kennedy owe his continuing popularity?" Answers will invariably take one of several forms. They may concentrate on *accounting for the effects* of particular speeches, determining the *cultural influence* or *pedagogic value* that a speech possesses, exploring the *symbolic import* of a speech, or assessing the speech's ability to *fulfill expectations* accompanying an occasion. In addition, critical evaluations may focus on the speech as an *ethically proper presentation*.

To Account for the Effects of Communication

Perhaps the most common end of rhetorical analysis is to account for the effects of a message or speaker on an audience. Almost anyone, with sense and a bit of energy, can *describe many of these effects*. When assessing the effects of a Presidential discourse, for example, you can:

- note the amount of applause and its timing;
- read newspaper accounts and commentary on it the next day;
- check public-opinion polls, especially those assessing "how the President is doing" and those dealing with the particular subject matter of the speech;
- notice how much it is quoted and referred to weeks, months, or even years after it was delivered;
- examine votes in Congress and election results potentially affected by the speech;
- read memoirs, diaries, and books treating the event, the speech, and the speaker;
- read the President's own accounts of the discourse.[1]

But mere description of effects is not criticism. You can do that, after all, without even looking at the speech. The important phrase, therefore, is *accounting for*. Rhetorical analysts discussing the effects of a discourse take that extra step—delving into the speaking process to see if they can find out what produced those effects. That is no easy task, yet it is the central one. The following are examples of where you might look in the communication process to find elements which can account for a message's reception by the audience:

1. *The Situation.* Did the situation make certain demands which the speaker had to meet? A series of events, the traditions of discourse surrounding the occasion (that is, the expectations we have about inaugurals or sermons), or even the date of the speech (it is one thing for a Presidential aspirant to make promises every four years in October, but quite another for the elected person to make them in January)— all can provide the critics with clues to situational demands.

2. *The Speaker.* Did the speaker have the authority or credibility to affect the audience, almost regardless of what he or she said? Some speakers have such reputations or carry so much charisma that they can influence an audience with the sheer power and dynamism of their words and presence. The rhetorical critic is interested in such phenomena and seeks to find specific word-patterns and speech behaviors which account for listeners' reactions to these factors.[2]

3. *The Arguments.* Did the speaker's message strike responsive chords in the audience? Were the motive appeals those to which this audience was susceptible? Why? Were the beliefs, attitudes, values, and ideological orientations advanced by the speaker likely to have made impressions on this audience? Why? Were the supporting materials—and specific combinations of the various types—useful in helping an audience comprehend and accept the overall message? Why? (These "whys" usually have to be answered by assessing the temperament of the times, the dominant ideologies in the culture, and the facts of the situation, as well as the internal and external characteristics of audiences discussed in Chapter 5.)

4. *Uses of Modes of Communication.* Were the linguistic, paralinguistic, bodily, and visual codes of communication used effectively? In other words, as a critic you must look at more than the words on a printed page. Oral communication always needs to be explained as completely as possible, either from videotapes or films, or—if necessary—newspaper descriptions of the speaker and the occasion.

5. *Audience Susceptibility.* In general, why was *this* audience susceptible to *this* message delivered by *this* speaker in *this* setting at *this* time? The critic seeking to explain the effects of a speech ultimately has to answer that single, all-important question.

A solid analysis of communication effects, therefore, demands a careful integration of "who did what to whom, when, and to what effect."[3] It demands thoughtful assessment—the hard work of deciding which among all of the elements of the speaking process were responsible for particular aspects of audience reaction. Ultimately, your quest for "why" will lead you to look at more than the speech itself. For example, determining why the audience was particularly receptive to President Johnson's call for a "blank check" during the 1964 "Gulf of Tonkin" crisis will require a historical examination of public attitudes at the time. To determine the effect of President Carter's "debates" on his 1976 victory and 1980 defeat will require more than an analysis of his arguments or his use of the media in both campaigns.

At times, it may be necessary to combine scientific research with historical explanation.[4] An example to illustrate this point is in order. Two teams of rhetorical analysts—Andrew A. King and Floyd D. Anderson, and Richard D. Raum and James S. Measell—were interested in techniques presumably used by Richard Nixon, Spiro Agnew, and George Wallace to *polarize* public opinion and divide voting groups in order to win elections in the '60s. King and Anderson examined with considerable care the speeches of Nixon and Agnew between 1968 and 1970, while Raum and Measell looked at Wallace's speeches between 1964 and 1972. Neither team felt that a mere listing of argumentative and linguistic techniques was enough, for the listing did not provide them with answers to the question, "Why did these techniques work?" Both teams, therefore, read the social-psychological literature on the concept of *polarization.* King and Anderson then used this research to shed light on ways words can be used to affirm a group's identity (in this case, that of the silent majority), and on methods for isolating or negating the voting power of an opponent. The concept of polarization seemed to them to explain why those tactics supposedly created two different political power blocs or "societies" in the late 1960s.

Raum and Measell, however, went further. They not only examined tactics and psychological dimensions of polarization, but also looked at the concept as they deemed it to occur in specific situations. George Wallace's effectiveness, they concluded, lay in the kinds of people he appealed to, in his vocabulary which charged his audiences emotionally, and in the ways in which Wallace made himself a social redeemer who could save the country from the "enemy."[5] You may not find it necessary to resort to such sophisticated strategies to explicate a message's effects. Nevertheless, your analysis of a contemporary speech may be based on information you possess about how people behave in crowds, what their attitudes are, or what a particular psychological theory would predict given certain speech strategies. This information becomes a central part of your critical evaluation. The difference is one of degree, not of kind, as you proceed to offer your interpretation of why a speaker succeeded or failed. The rigor of analysis may separate you from the professional rhetorical analyst, but the process is the same. The critical judgment in both cases is not based just on a "gut reaction" to the speech or on an uninformed response of liking or disliking.

To Explore the Critical Dimensions of Communication

So far, we have been discussing a focus on criticism which examines the effects of speeches—changes in attitudes or behavior, voting shifts, and acknowledgment of a speaker's rhetorical expertise are potential items mentioned or examined in the process of arriving at a critical judgment. This is not, however, the only way of looking at a speech. A speech, after all, is many things on many different levels; hence it is possible to talk about a number of different *critical perspectives*. A critical perspective is, in language we already have used, a human design or purpose. It is the reason-for-being of a piece of criticism, the particular viewpoint a critic is interested in bringing to bear on a discourse. Just as *you* can be looked at in a number of different ways—as a student, as a son or daughter, as an employee, as a lover—so, too, can a speech be examined from different vantages, depending upon the observer's purposes or designs. For example, speeches have been viewed critically in the following ways:

1. *Pedagogically.* You can use the speech as a model, as a way of examining public communicators who have made judicious rhetorical choices. You can learn how to speak well, in part, by looking at and listening to other speakers.

2. *Culturally.* Or you can examine a discourse to acquire a better understanding of "the times." For example, you may look at speeches from the Revolutionary War period or from the nineteenth century to better understand *how* our ancestors thought, *how* the great American values were spread through the society, and *how* we as a nation came to be what we are.

3. *Linguistically.* Because human beings are symbol-using animals—because we are distinguished from other animals by the complexity of our symbol systems—it makes sense to be particularly interested in the *language* used in public discourses. Some critics look at oral language to better comprehend the communicative *force* of words—how some words plead, others persuade, still others threaten, etc. Some critics are concerned with *condensation symbols*—the process by which certain words (for example, "communist" in the '50s, "hippie" in the '60s, "polluter" in the '70s) acquire a broad range of ideologically positive or negative connotations. Other critics are especially interested in *metaphors*—in ways we describe experi-

ences vicariously with words ("He's an absolute *pig*") or, in the case of *archetypal metaphors,* ways by which we can capture the essence of humanity by appealing figuratively to the great common human experiences (light and dark metaphors, birth and death metaphors, sexual metaphors, etc.). Whatever approach linguistic critics take, however, they ultimately pursue notions which illuminate what it means to communicate as a symbol-using human being.

4. *Generically.* In this decade especially, we have seen a great number of critics addressing the problem of classifying speeches into types or genres. For example, in this book we generally have classified speeches into three basic types—speeches to inform, to persuade, and to actuate—and we have done this because we think you are most interested in grouping communicative techniques by the ways in which they help you accomplish certain *purposes.* Other critics classify speeches by *situation* or *location*—for instance, the rhetoric of international conflict, the rhetoric of the used-car lot, the political-convention keynote address—in order to illumine the ways in which the location or expectations created by the occasion determine what must be said. Others argue that speeches are best categorized by *topic* because certain recurrent themes congregate around recurrent human problems. Hence, they write about the rhetoric of war and peace, the rhetoric of women's liberation, of reform or revolution. Whatever approach critics employ in the process of classification, however, they all generally have a singular goal: To categorize speeches in order to find *families of discourses* which have enough in common to help us understand dominant modes of thought or modes of expression typical of an age, a problem, or a set of speakers.[6]

Pedagogical, cultural, linguistic, and generic critics, therefore, all examine specific aspects of discourses, features they think deserve special attention. They make this examination in order to learn what these aspects tell us about communication practice (*pedagogy*), the condition of humanity (*culture*), the potentials of language codes (*linguistics*), or the dominant species of discourse (*genres*).

To Evaluate the Ethics of Communication

In an age of governmental credibility gaps, charges of corporate irresponsibility, situational ethics, and the rise of minorities who challenge the prevailing social and ethical systems of the United States, a host of ethical questions have come to concern speech analysts: Can we still speak of the democratic ideal as *the* ethical standard for speakers in this country? What are the communicative responsibilities which attend the exercise of corporate, governmental, and personal power? For example, President Nixon's speech on November 3, 1969, in which he talked about the "silent majority," his quest for peace, and three alternatives for ending the war in Vietnam—escalation, withdrawal, or gradual deescalation—naturally aroused considerable controversy. One critic, Forbes Hill, found no special ethical problems in the speech because the President's appeals to the majority of Americans were consistent with the country's values at that time. Another, Robert P. Newman, assuming the "democratic ideal" as his standard, decried the speech because he claimed that it violated the individual's right to know fully all that a government plans and does. A third critic, Karlyn K. Campbell, argued that the standards initially set for evaluating the alternatives were violated later in the speech. And Philip Wander and Steven Jenkins accused the President of lying.[7] Thus, each critic assumed a particular ethical posture, and from that posture proceeded to evaluate the speech in accordance with his or her own views and biases.

The Basic Requisites for Critical Analysis and Evaluation

Critical analysis, even at the most rudimentary level, requires a way of talking about the speech event and a method for observing what takes place. To produce justifiable evaluations of speeches, critics need a coherent vocabulary with which to talk and think analytically about speeches and a sense of what is required in obtaining the necessary information to assess the speech adequately.

A Coherent Vocabulary for Rhetorical Evaluation

Perhaps the most difficult task a beginning critic faces is that of settling on a rhetorical vocabulary. The "Who? What? When? Where? Why? and How?" questions of the journalist may provide a starting point for analysis, but they won't get the critic very far in examining the speech. Unlike the journalist, the critic is engaged in a systematic, coherent pursuit of specialized knowledge *about* communication. The description of the event itself is only a part of that process. While there are almost as many critical vocabularies as there are individual critics, we will isolate only three which have been used often enough to make them fairly familiar to readers and teachers. Each of these vocabularies also is different enough from the others to illustrate the variety of potentially useful concepts.

Textbook Vocabulary. The terms employed in this and other similar textbooks provide a common vocabulary for talking about and analyzing communication events. This vocabulary, as you are well aware by now, is based on a basic communication model which sees certain *speakers* sending particular *messages* to *target audiences* in some *situation*. It is especially useful when you (1) want to describe the entire speech or communication process, or (2) you are seeking fact-based generalizations about the communication process (e.g., what happens when this set of variables is mixed in a specific fashion).

Burkean Vocabulary. One popular alternative to textbook concepts is the critical vocabulary developed by the literary and social critic Kenneth Burke. Burke has written so profusely and creatively over a fifty-year period that he can no longer be thought of as limiting himself to one single, unified set of concepts. Nevertheless, it is possible to isolate from various portions of his writings a few key words or terms of particular utility in rhetorical criticism.[8] Basically, he has been interested in describing communicative transactions by examining *situations*, analyzing *rhetorical strategies* used by speakers in situations, and commenting symbolically on the *dramas* of human communication. *Situations* are taken apart by an appraisal of the *scene, agent, agency, act*, and *purpose*. In this "pentadic" structure of the situation, any given element may be dominant and thereby impart to the situation a specific character. Senator Ted Kennedy's Chappaquidick Address, for example, can be interpreted as a "scene" dominant speech. By noting how the circumstances forced him to commit acts which otherwise rational persons would not be likely to engage in, Kennedy sought to place the responsibility for his acts in the aftermath of the accident in the "scene" and not in the "agent."[9]

Various rhetorical *strategies* may be examined in relating the speech to an audience, or in determining how the principles of rhetoric were employed. *Identification*, for example, is a strategy whereby a speaker seeks to establish common ground with the audience. During her 1970 trial on charges of conspiring to free her alleged lover, Angela Davis employed several identification strategies to reduce the distance between herself—an avowed communist—and her jury. At the same time, she sought to maintain her identity as a self-styled radical.[10]

Rhetorical *dramas* are explored largely through an analysis of metaphoric language, prevailing myths, and powerful "dialectical" terms such as "democracy" or "liberty." These cultural symbols are the salient terms by which the community guarantees its continuance and its ability to deal with conflict and with offenders.[11] We "Save the World for Democracy" far more quickly than we would save it for a particular person or group. These are the essential terms and key concepts of Burke's critical vocabulary, as laid out in more detail below.

BURKE'S CRITICAL VOCABULARY

Situational Analysis: the Pentad

Agent—who performed an act

Agency—how it was performed (words, behaviors)

Act—what was done or said

Scene—where and for whom the act was done

Purpose—the end sought by the agent and other actors

Rhetorical Strategies

The Strategies of Ideas—scapegoating, victimage, purification, and other ritualistic procedures for uniting societies around enemies and ideas

The Strategies of Identification—methods for finding common ground on which you and I can "fit together" consubstantially

The Strategies of Form—the arousal and satisfaction of audience's expectations through the use of traditional organizational patterns (logical, progressive, etc.)

The Strategies of Language—the discovery of common symbols which evoke proper responses in audiences

The Strategies of Mimesis or Imitation—the use of bodily, paralinguistic, and visual modes which evoke desired responses in audiences

Dramatistic Analysis: Cultural Symbols

Metaphors—terms which embody attitudes or motives

Dialectical Terms—words which evoke visions of opposites, such as "democracy" and "totalitarianism," "belief" and "faith," "good" and "evil"

Myths—idealized patterns of acting together

Burke, you will note, thus calls for a *dramaturgical* approach to the study of communication. To him, we are all actors acting out certain roles or social routines because, if we do, others will act or respond appropriately through complementary roles in our divisive society. We can then achieve *consubstantiality*, or a feeling of oneness with others.

Space does not permit a longer explication of Burke's vocabulary, but even this brief look should be enough to suggest its potential usefulness. It is especially valuable for critics wanting to explore certain linguistic or symbolic dimensions of communicating, in that it urges us to recognize that individuals are inherently separated from each other and to come to grips with the idea that only through communicative transactions—ritualistic transactions—can we achieve the common identity necessary for social survival and cultural cohesion.

Bitzer's Vocabulary. Instead of examining the communication process as a whole, you may find it useful to examine a specific element or facet. Thus, in the Burkean scheme referred to above, you might concentrate on defining the situation in terms of the dominance of a particular element, or examining the relationship between the cultural symbols invoked by the speaker and the impact those symbols have on the people. Lloyd Bitzer offers a different approach, but one potentially just as selective, in his discussion of the "rhetorical situation."[12] In his view, the *situation* almost literally dictates what kinds of things must be said, to whom they must be said, and in what forms the messages must come. More specifically, he maintained that situations are marked by *exigencies* (events, peoples, or happenings which call forth discourse from someone), by *audience expectations* (thoughts of who should say what to whom, when, and where), and by *constraints* (the limits of choices speakers can make—for instance, the rules governing Congressional debate, the boundaries of social propriety, the availability or unavailability of certain audiences). If a speaker in a situation removes the exigencies, meets the expectations, and abides by the constraints, the speech will be a *fitting response*.[13] Thus the critical emphasis is upon *the primacy of situation.*

Bitzer's approach to rhetorical analysis and the vocabulary he uses are especially useful when—as a critic—you are studying the speeches of persons who act as representative spokespersons for a particular group: heads of government, Congressional politicians, leaders of churches, labor unions, and the like. Such speakers, because they are representatives, face many pressures—more, certainly, than most of us do. They sometimes must speak when they would rather be silent (for instance, the President who must talk about an embarrassing international incident or the labor leader who must condemn governmental actions and programs when unemployment rises). The pressures upon such persons are intensified by the fact that they are not speaking for themselves as individuals, but rather for groups or institutions. Hence, no matter where they stand personally, their public utterances must always be consistent with the organization's goals, reinforce its viewpoints, and voice its concerns. They may even be pressured by the forces inherent in certain occasions—by what custom dictates *must* be said in inaugurals, in Labor Day speeches, in Easter sermons, and the like. In short, when speakers are constrained by situationally imposed roles, Bitzer's approach helps us examine how these constraints affect the way such people talk publicly. To guide and help you to formulate an analysis of this kind, the essential terms and key concepts of Bitzer's critical vocabulary are provided on page 426.

These critical vocabularies—those of the textbooks, Burke, and Bitzer—are but three of the many available. The textbook vocabulary, as we have said, views the communicative transaction as a whole and, therefore, is able to "work on" a complete communicative event. The Burkean vocabulary shows what a critic with narrower concerns for particular dimensions of communication may look for. And the Bitzer vocabulary demonstrates what happens when the critic uses one element of the communication model—situation, in this case—to examine the whole process. Some of the readings cited in the "Checklist" on pages 428–430 suggest additional alternatives. Whatever the approach and vocabulary you choose, however, you should attempt to solve the problem of description by adopting some relatively coherent system of concepts.

Careful Observation

The second task you must grapple with as a critic is that of deciding *what* to look at and *how*. In part, of course, this problem is solved by your selection of a vocabulary. If, for example, you employ a textbook vocabulary, you know you will have to isolate motive appeals, look for an arrangement pattern, and see if you can find out how the speaker delivered the message. Yet, the vocabulary does not, as a rule, exhaust your task of looking. You may need to expand it to include searches for information both *inside* and *outside* the speech text itself.

Outside Observation. Often you have to look for relevant information about the speech, the speaker, the audience, and the situation *outside* the actual text of what was said. As we have already suggested, if you are interested in the effects of the speech, for example, you probably will want to check public-opinion polls, memoirs, diaries, the results of subsequent voting on the issue or issues, and newspaper and magazine reactions. If you are working from the textbook vocabulary, you probably will need to see what the audience knew about the speaker beforehand (prior reputation), what kind of people made up the audience present, and what kind of ratings were given to radio or television broadcasts of the speech. Or, if you are doing a cultural analysis of the speech, you will have to read whatever you can find on the cultural values and mores of the era in which the speech was delivered. You cannot, for example, do a study of Daniel Webster as a typical ceremonial orator of the 1830s or 1840s without having a solid grasp of what Americans were doing and thinking about during that so-called early national period. Webster's political generalizations, metaphors, and sweeping vision of the Republic make little sense unless you are acquainted with political-economic expansion, the settling of the Midwest and West, the growing fight between states' righters and nationalists, the problem of slavery, and other key cultural battles which characterized the period. To do many kinds of critical studies of speeches, therefore, you must spend time in the library—with newspapers, magazines, history books, and biographies.

Inside Observation. As a critic, you also will have to live with the speech for a while. Often, an initial reading of it produces either a "So what?" or a "What can I say?" reaction. You should read it time and again, each time subjectively projecting yourself into the situation, into the frame of mind of the speaker and the audience. You probably should even read the speech aloud (if you do not have a recording or videotape of it), trying to capture emphases, rhythms, and sounds. Part of *inside* observation, then, is a process of "getting the feel" of the speech.

The other part is discovering the key points on which it turns. Certain statements or phrases in great speeches became memorable because they were *pivotal.* They summarized or encapsulated an important idea, attitude, or sentiment. As you read over, say, Cicero's "First Oration Against Cataline," you are impressed by the initial series of eight rhetorical questions, which immediately put the Roman audience into an abusive frame of mind. You may be similarly impressed by the way Queen Elizabeth I used *I* and *we* in her speeches in order to make her dominance over Parliament eminently clear; by British Prime Minister David Lloyd George's preoccupation with light-dark archetypal metaphors, which elevate his discourse. Contemporary speeches, too—those published in *Vital Speeches of the Day,* for example—have certain elements in common: a heavy reliance upon particular forms of support, especially statistics; quotations from authorities; and explanations.

In other words, looking *inside* speeches intently forces your critical apparatus to operate. Your mind begins to catch points of dominance and memorability—aspects of discourse which *you* find noteworthy and even fascinating. When those insights are coupled with research you have done on the *outside*—in newspapers, magazines, books, etc.—you soon find that *you have something critical to say* about a particular speech or group of speeches.

Composing Your Critical Evaluation

Acts of criticism are arguments: your critical evaluation functions as a *claim* that must be supported with specific reasons that justify its soundness. Your process of observation and the vocabulary you employ comes together into a cogent explanation of why the speech was effective, how certain identification strategies functioned, or why cultural symbols in a speech were ignored by the audience. The "plan" for writing your critical evaluation outlined below is not the only way in which your argument may be organized. Nevertheless, it may be helpful as a general guide to the organization of your critical response. The plan also may be useful for other "term papers" or research papers you undoubtedly will be asked to write.

A PLAN FOR WRITING SPEECH CRITICISM

I. INTRODUCTION   A. As a "starter" for your paper, introduce a quotation, a description of events, a statement of communication principles, or whatever will indicate your approach to the speech or your point of view about it.

B. Make *a statement of questions or propositions*—the point or points you wish to develop or establish in the paper.

C. Make *a statement of procedures*—how you propose to go about answering the questions or proving the propositions.

II.	BODY	A.	After you have thus described the basic speech material or the situation with which you are dealing, take each step of your critical analysis one point at a time, looking, for example:

—at *agent/agency/act/scene/purpose* if you are using Burke's critical approach, or

—at *exigencies/audience expectations/constraints/fittingness* if you are using Bitzer's critical techniques, making sure in this latter approach that you have carefully described the situation around which you are building your analysis.

B.   As you offer the subpoints or propositions, liberally illustrate them with quotations from the speech or speeches you are analyzing—quotations which serve as evidence for your point of view or argument. Also quote from other critical observers to further support your position if you wish.

III.   CONCLUSIONS   A.   In your *summary*, pull the argument of your paper together by indicating how the subpoints fit together to present a valid and interesting picture of public communication.

B.   Draw *implications*, commenting briefly upon what can be learned from your analysis and this speech (or set of speeches) about communication generally. That is, you say—in effect—that this is a case study of something having larger implications.

With a coherent vocabulary for thinking about public communication, with patient and thoughtful observation, and with a plan for reporting your reactions, you should be able to produce useful and stimulating evaluations and analyses of speeches. Systematically getting inside rhetorical transactions and objectively and expertly critiquing the speeches of others are tasks you should now be equipped to execute. Ultimately, your practice in communication criticism will help you better understand the ways by which public discourse affects the beliefs, attitudes, values, and behaviors of yourself and your society.

In this short appendix, we have been able to describe only *briefly* a few critical frameworks or approaches and to allude to a limited number of actual speeches and speaking events. In the following pages, with the hope that you will want to read further and to find public speeches amenable to particular types of analyses, we are including a checklist of critical articles and speeches.

A CHECKLIST OF CRITICAL ARTICLES
AND SPEECHES FOR ANALYSIS

GENERAL READINGS ON RHETORICAL CRITICISM

Carroll C. Arnold, *Criticism of Oral Rhetoric* (Columbus, OH: Charles E. Merrill Publishing Company, 1974), especially Chapter 1.

Bernard L. Brock and Robert L. Scott, eds., *Methods of Rhetorical Criticism: A Twentieth-Century Perspective,* 2nd ed. (Detroit: Wayne State University Press, 1980).

Robert Cathcart, "The Nature of Criticism," *Post Communication: Rhetorical Analysis,* 2nd ed. (Indianapolis, IN: The Bobbs-Merrill Company, Inc., 1981).

Thomas B. Farrell, "Critical Models in the Analysis of Discourse," *Western Journal of Speech Communication,* 44 (Fall 1980), 300–314.

Marie Hochmuth, "The Criticism of Rhetoric," in *History and Criticism of American Public Address,* ed. Marie Hochmuth (New York: Longman, Green and Co., 1955), Vol. III.

EFFECTS ANALYSIS

Specific Readings on Effects Analysis

Paul Arntson and Craig R. Smith, "The Seventh of March Address: A Mediating Influence," *Southern Speech Communication Journal,* 40 (Spring 1975), 288–301.

Richard A. Cherwitz, "Lyndon Johnson and the 'Crisis' of Tonkin Gulf: A President's Justification of War," *Western Journal of Speech Communication,* 41 (Spring 1978), 93–104.

Donald M. Dedmon, "The Functions of Discourse in the Hawaiian Statehood Debates," *Speech* [Communication] *Monographs,* 33 (March 1966), 30–39.

John W. Rathbun, "The Problem of Judgment and Effect in Historical Criticism: A Proposed Solution," *Western Speech* [Western Journal of Speech Communication], 33 (Summer 1969), 149–59.

Sample Speeches to Study for Effects Analysis

Henry W. Grady's "The New South" of 1886 (use of humor to soften a doubting audience).

Billy James Hargis' "Christ Was a Reactionary" speech, 1967 (the principles of demogoguery).

Edmund Muskie's "Election Eve Address," 1970 (principles of political affirmation and refutation).

CRITICAL PERSPECTIVES

Readings on Specific Critical Perspectives

Burkean: Barry Brummett, "Symbolic Form, Burkean Scapegoating, and Rhetorical Exigency in Alioto's Response to the 'Zebra' Murders, *"Western Journal of Speech Communication,* 44 (Winter 1980), 64–73.

Linguistic: Robert L. Ivie, "Images of Savagery in American Justifications for War," *Communication Monographs,* 47 (November 1980), 279–94.

Generic: Kathleen Jamieson, "Antecedent Genre as Rhetorical Constraint," *Quarterly Journal of Speech,* 61 (December 1975), 406–15.

Burkean: David Ling, "A Pentadic Analysis of Senator Edward Kennedy's Address to the People of Massachusetts, July 25, 1969," *Central States Speech Journal,* 21 (Summer 1970), 81–86.

Linguistic: Michael Osborn, "Archetypal Metaphor in Rhetoric: The Light-Dark Family," *Quarterly Journal of Speech,* 53 (April 1967), 115–26.

Cultural: Robert L. Schrag, Richard A. Hudson, and Lawrence M. Bernabo, "Television's New Humane Collectivity," *Western Journal of Speech Communication,* 45 (Winter 1981), 1–12.

Generic: B. L. Ware and Wil A. Linkugel, "They Spoke in Defense of Themselves: On the Generic Criticism of Apologia," *Quarterly Journal of Speech,* 59 (October 1973), 273–83.

Cultural: Ernest J. Wrage, "Public Address: A Study in Social and Intellectual History," *Quarterly Journal of Speech,* 33 (December 1947), 451–57.

Sample Speeches to Study for Specific Critical Perspectives

For Burkean Perspectives:
Speeches presented in the Women's Rights Convention in Seneca Falls, New York, in 1848—especially the speeches of Elizabeth Cady Stanton and Lucretia Mott addressing women's roles in society.
Richard Nixon's 1960 campaign speeches—illustrating a variety of identification strategies.

For Generic Perspectives:
Political convention speeches—for instance, Barbara Jordan's keynote address at the 1976 Democratic Convention.
Inaugural addresses of the Presidents.
Presidential declarations of war.

For Cultural Perspectives:
The United Nations' Debate over the Arab-Israeli War of 1967—to see a wide variety of culture-based arguments.
Speeches of American Indians—to note differences in speech forms and cultural values.

For Linguistic Perspectives:
Martin Luther King, Jr.'s "I Have a Dream" speech of 1963—for an analysis of metaphors.
Abraham Lincoln's "Gettysburg Address" of 1863—for an analysis of archetypal metaphors.

ETHICAL EVALUATION

Specific Readings on Aspects of Ethical Evaluation

Anthony Hillbruner, "The Moral Imperative of Criticism," *Southern Speech Communication Journal,* 40 (Spring 1975), 228–47.

Edward Rogge, "Evaluating the Ethics of a Speaker in a Democracy," *Quarterly Journal of Speech,* 45 (December 1959), 419–25.

Sample Speeches to Study for Ethical Evaluation

Winston Churchill's speeches on the progress of World War II, 1940–1944—for manipulation of wartime information.

Senator Joseph McCarthy's speeches attacking communists in America, 1951–1954—for strategies of innuendo.

REFERENCE NOTES

[1] For an example of how skilled critics search out the effects of a controversial speech of this kind, see Paul Arntson and Craig R. Smith, "The Seventh of March Address [Daniel Webster]: A Mediating Influence," *Southern Speech Communication*, 40 (Spring 1975):288–301.

[2] For a discussion of ways to talk critically about *charisma*, see George P. Boss, "Essential Attributes of the Concept of Charisma," *Southern Speech Communication Journal*, 41 (Spring 1976):300–313.

[3] For a detailed discussion of the kinds of information which can be produced by "effects studies" (also called historical studies), see Bruce E. Gronbeck, "Rhetorical History and Rhetorical Criticism: A Distinction," *The Speech Teacher*, 24 (November 1975):309–320.

[4] On the relationships between rhetorical criticism and the social sciences, see John W. Bowers, "The Pre-Scientific Function of Rhetorical Criticism," in *Essays on Rhetorical Criticism*, ed. Thomas R. Nilsen (New York: Random House, Inc., 1968), pp. 126–145.

[5] Andrew A. King and Floyd D. Anderson, "Nixon, Agnew, and the 'Silent Majority': A Case Study in the Rhetoric of Polarization," *Western Speech*, 35 (Fall 1971):243–255; Richard D. Raum and James S. Measell, "Wallace and His Ways: A Study of the Rhetorical Genre of Polarization," *Central States Speech Journal*, 25 (Spring 1974):28–35.

[6] Literature for these "families of discourse" abounds. For samples of cultural studies, for instance, see Ernest Wrage, "The Little World of Barry Goldwater," *Western Speech*, 27 (Fall 1963):207–215; and Theodore Balgooyen, "A Study of Conflicting Values: American Plains Indian Orators vs. the U.S. Commissioners of Indian Affairs," *Western Speech*, 24 (Spring 1962):76–83. For an example of linguistic analysis—especially as it involves condensation symbols—look at Doris Graber, *Verbal Behavior and Politics* (Urbana: University of Illinois Press, 1976), especially Chapter 7. Additional examples of families of discourse are included in the "Checklist" at the close of this appendix.

[7] Forbes I. Hill, "Conventional Wisdom—Traditional Form: The President's Message of November 3, 1969," *Quarterly Journal of Speech*, 58 (December 1972):373–386; Robert P. Newman, "Under the Veneer: Nixon's Vietnam Speech of November 3, 1969," *Quarterly Journal of Speech*, 56 (December 1970):432–434; Karlyn Kohrs Campbell, "Richard M. Nixon," *Critiques of Contemporary Rhetoric* (Belmont, CA: Wadsworth Publishing Co., 1972), pp. 50–57; and Philip Wander and Steven Jenkins, "Rhetoric, Society, and the Critical Response," *Quarterly Journal of Speech*, 58 (December 1972):373–386.

[8] The key notions from Kenneth Burke explained here are taken primarily from *A Grammar of Motives* and *A Rhetoric of Motives* (orig. pub. 1945, 1950, separately; New York: The World Publishing Company, 1962). A fuller overview can be found in Marie H. Nichols, "Kenneth Burke: Rhetorical and Critical Theory," *Rhetoric and Criticism* (Baton Rouge: Louisiana State University Press, 1963), pp. 79–92; another is in Bernard L. Brock, "Rhetorical Criticism: A Burkean Approach," in *Methods of Rhetorical Criticism: A Twentieth-Century Perspective*, 2nd ed., eds. Bernard L. Brock and Robert L. Scott (Detroit: Wayne State Univ. Press, 1980), pp. 348–359.

[9] David A. Ling, "A Pentadic Analysis of Senator Edward Kennedy's Address to the People of Massachusetts, July 25, 1969," *Central States Speech Journal*, 21 (1970), 81-86.

[10] Virginia A. Kennedy, "Militancy in the Guise of Moderate Rhetoric: Angela Davis' Opening Defense Statement," paper presented at the Eastern Communication Association Convention, Ocean City, MD, 1980.

[11] See Ernest G. Bormann, "Fantasy and Rhetorical Vision: The Rhetorical Criticism of Social Reality," *Quarterly Journal of Speech*, 58 (December 1972), 396–407; Michael Calvin McGee, "The 'Ideograph': A Link Between Rhetoric and Ideology," *Quarterly Journal of Speech*, 66 (February 1980), 1-16.

[12] From "The Rhetorical Situation," by Lloyd F. Bitzer, *Philosophy and Rhetoric*, 1 (Winter 1968), 1–14.

[13] For a study clearly illustrating Bitzer's method of analysis, see Allen M. Rubin and Rebecca R. Rubin, "An Examination of the Constituent Elements in Presenting an Occurring Rhetorical Situation," *Central States Speech Journal*, 26 (Summer 1975):133–141.

Index

E

F

G

Problem, defining in groups, 402
Professional journals, source of support, 133
Pronunciation, 255
Proposition, in sample speech, 55
Proxemics, 238–40
Proximity, factor of attention, 152
Psychological bases of organization, 144–46
Public distance, 239–40
Purpose
  determining, 48–49, 65–71
  of listeners, 11
  of outline, 202
  speaker's, 7
  of speech occasion, 93

Q

Questionnaires, source of support, 131
Quotation, to end speech, 192

R

Radio broadcasts, as source of support, 134
Random instances, reasoning from, 359, 362
  figure, 360
Rate, 253
Rathbun, John W., 429
Rationality, and argument, 350
Raum, Richard D., 420
Reagan, Ronald, 366
Reality, factor of attention, 152
Reasoning, 358–68
  axiom, 363
    figure, 361
  from cause, 358–59
    figure, 360

parallel case, 362–63
  figure, 361
random instances, 359, 362
  figure, 360
from sign, 358
  figure, 359
Rebuttal, and argument, 364–65
Recording information, 134–36
Reestablishment, and argument, 365–66
Reexamination, and language, 217
Reference to occasion, to begin speech, 182
Reference to subject, to begin speech, 182
Regulation, and feedback, 38
Rein, Irving J., 168
Reiteration, and language, 216–17
Rephrasing, and language, 217
Reservations, and argument, 356, 357
Responses to objections, 384–85
Responses to questions, 382–84
Restatement, as support, 129–30
Reverence appeals, 108
Revulsion appeals, 108
Rhetorical criticism, bibliography, 428–29
Rhetorical drama, 424
Rhetorical question, to begin speech, 184–85
Rhetorical situation, 425
Rhetorical strategies, 424
  Burkean, 423–25
Rogers, Donald, 191
Rogge, Edward, 430
Roosevelt, Franklin Delano, 112–15
Rough draft, sample outline, 202–03
Ruch, Floyd, 152

S

Safety needs, 102
Saliency, and persuasive speeches,

Visual symbols, 270–71
  color, 271
  complexity, 271
  shape, 270
  size, 270
Visualization step, 147, 159–60, 165
  in sample speech, 150
Vital, factor of attention, 155–56
Vocabulary for critical analysis, 423–25
Vocal control, 260–61
Vocal style, 261–65
Voice, characteristics of effective,
    252–60
  articulation, 254
  intelligibility, 252–55, 262, 264
  loudness, 252–53
  pronunciation, 255
  rate, 253
  stress, 257–60, 265
  variety, 255–59, 265
Voice exercises, 412–17
Voice quality, 262

W

Walker, Russell, 54
Wander, Philip, 422
Warrant, and argument, 355–56, 357
  tests of, 358–63
Webster, Daniel, 226
Wells, H. G., 223
White, Noel D., 79
Wolvin, Andrew D., 409
Wolvin, Darlyn R., 409

Y

Yearbooks, source of support, 133

Z

Zimbardo, Philip G., 152
Zimmerman, Gordon I., 27

Checklist and Index for Evaluation and Improvement of Student Speeches

which appears on the Endsheet following this page

This chart indentifies many of the factors contributing to effective public speech communication. It may be used by both instructors and students in evaluating speech plans and manuscripts and also when reacting to speeches as they are being delivered. By using a plus (+) or minus (−) sign together with symbols keyed to specific items in the Checklist, the instructor may readily indicate point-by-point reactions to a speech or a speech outline. For example, a *plus* sign before SUBJ./8 indicates that the speaker has narrowed the speech subject satisfactorily; a *minus* sign placed before the code ADAPT./26 suggests that further attention should be given to using the factors of attention, etc. Students will find the Checklist especially helpful when preparing oral and written assignments or reviewing for examinations. The parenthetical reference to specific pages in the textbook makes it possible to find relevant textual explanations quickly and easily.